Climate Change Scepticism

Environmental Cultures Series

Bloomsbury's *Environmental Cultures* series makes available to students and scholars at all levels the latest cutting-edge research on the diverse ways in which culture has responded to the age of environmental crisis. Publishing ambitious and innovative literary ecocriticism that crosses disciplines, national boundaries, and media, books in the series explore and test the challenges of ecocriticism to conventional forms of cultural study.

Titles available:
Bodies of Water, Astrida Neimanis
Cities and Wetlands, Rod Giblett
Civil Rights and the Environment in African-American Literature, 1895–1941, John Claborn
Climate Change Scepticism, Greg Garrard, Axel Goodbody, George B. Handley and Stephanie Posthumus
Climate Crisis and the 21st-Century British Novel, Astrid Bracke
Colonialism, Culture, Whales, Graham Huggan
Ecocriticism and Italy, Serenella Iovino
Fuel, Heidi C. M. Scott
Literature as Cultural Ecology, Hubert Zapf
Nerd Ecology, Anthony Lioi
The New Nature Writing, Jos Smith
The New Poetics of Climate Change, Matthew Griffiths
This Contentious Storm, Jennifer Mae Hamilton

Forthcoming Titles:
Anthropocene Romanticism, Kate Rigby
Cognitive Ecopoetics, Sharon Lattig
Eco-Digital Art, Lisa FitzGerald
Teaching Environmental Writing, Isabel Galleymore

Climate Change Scepticism

A Transnational Ecocritical Analysis

Greg Garrard, Axel Goodbody, George Handley
and Stephanie Posthumus

BLOOMSBURY ACADEMIC
LONDON • NEW YORK • OXFORD • NEW DELHI • SYDNEY

BLOOMSBURY ACADEMIC
Bloomsbury Publishing Plc
50 Bedford Square, London, WC1B 3DP, UK
1385 Broadway, New York, NY 10018, USA

BLOOMSBURY, BLOOMSBURY ACADEMIC and the Diana logo are trademarks of Bloomsbury Publishing Plc

First published in Great Britain 2019

Cover design: Paul Burgess/Burge Agency
Cover image © Shutterstock

A catalogue record for this book is available from the British Library.

A catalogue record for this book is available from the Library of Congress.

ISBN: HB: 978-1-3500-5702-9
ePDF: 978-1-3500-5703-6
eBook: 978-1-3500-5704-3

Series: Environmental Cultures

Typeset by Integra Software Services Pvt. Ltd.
Printed and bound in Great Britain

To find out more about our authors and books visit www.bloomsbury.com and sign up for our newsletters.

Contents

Acknowledgements vi

1 Introduction 1
2 Climate Scepticism in the UK 41
3 *Klimaskepsis* in Germany 91
4 Climate Scepticism and Christian Conservatism in the United States 133
5 *Climato-scepticisme* in France 175
6 Science and Technology Studies, Ecocriticism and Climate Change 207
7 What We've Learned from Climate Sceptics 225

Notes 245
Bibliography 254
Index 280

Acknowledgements

The authors wish to thank the peer reviewers for their forthright and constructive comments, and also Richard Kerridge, who provided thoughtful, attentive editorial feedback that greatly improved the manuscript.

Greg Garrard acknowledges the research support provided by the University of British Columbia Humanities and Social Sciences fund, which allowed him to pursue research in the UK. He is especially grateful to colleagues in the Faculty of Creative and Critical Studies and the Dean's office who helped him take time out of his role as Associate Dean of Research to complete this project. Some text from the sections authored by Greg has appeared in his 'Michael Crichton: State of Fear', an entry in *Cli-Fi: A Reader*, eds. Axel Goodbody and Adeline Johns-Putra (Peter Lang 2018). Quotations from The Heretic © Richard Bean, 2011 by kind permission of Oberon Books Ltd. This project was originally inspired by reflection on the life of Dennis Burningham, Greg's stepfather. Born in rural Alberta, he had a career in the military and then the oil industry. He became a radical environmentalist, converted to Islam, and worked in the fossil fuel sector until he died. 'The deepest fault lines are within.' His son, Ben Burningham, is a decidedly interested, interesting 'disinterested' physicist who has taught Greg much. Above all, Greg wants to thank his wife Verity for her love, understanding and practical support throughout. As lead author, he dedicates this book to her.

Axel Goodbody is grateful to the Rachel Carson Center in Munich for the award of a three-month Visiting Research Fellowship, during which much of the work on Chapter 3 was completed.

George Handley is grateful to the Environmental Humanities Research Group at Brigham Young University and to Mark Weiner who all provided valuable feedback on drafts.

Stephanie Posthumus would like to acknowledge the additional research time awarded to her to work on this book project during her sabbatical year as well as the constant support of her family, Stéfan, Naomie and Élodie Sinclair.

1

Introduction

When we started writing this book in the year 2016, it seemed the worst possible time to write about climate scepticism. From a scientific perspective, the argument was basically over: the Summary for Policymakers of the Fifth Assessment Report (AR5) of the Intergovernmental Panel on Climate Change (IPCC) had stated:

> Anthropogenic greenhouse gas emissions have increased since the pre-industrial era, driven largely by economic and population growth, and are now higher than ever. This has led to atmospheric concentrations of carbon dioxide, methane and nitrous oxide that are unprecedented in at least the last 800,000 years. Their effects, together with those of other anthropogenic drivers, have been detected throughout the climate system and are *extremely likely* [95–100% probability] to have been the dominant cause of the observed warming since the mid-20th century.
>
> ('Synthesis Report Summary for Policymakers')

Moreover, an unprecedented array of international scientific organizations had offered the IPCC their support. Dozens of national and international academies of science, including the British Royal Society and the American Academy for the Advancement of Science, published statements confirming that the IPCC process is sound, and its conclusions commensurately robust. The only organizations maintaining non-committal positions represented scientists who mainly work in fossil fuel industries: the American Association of Petroleum Geologists and the American Institute of Professional Geologists ('Scientific Opinion on Climate Change'). While acknowledged areas of scientific uncertainty remain, the IPCC position is, as they say, 'settled science'.

In terms of global politics, too, the game seemed to be up. The much-hyped 2009 Copenhagen climate conference (COP 15 in United Nations parlance) turned out not to be, as one cringe-worthy marketing phrase had it, 'Hopenhagen'; it turned into an unseemly squabble between China and the

United States instead. However, the UN process got decisively back on track in Paris six years later, when COP 21 resulted in a global agreement to reduce greenhouse gas emissions so as to prevent more than 2°C rise in global mean surface temperature over pre-industrial averages. Once bilateral agreement was reached between the United States and China, it appeared that the international political consensus at last matched the scientific one.

Warm words and global agreements such as the Kyoto Protocol have had minimal impact in the past, but now there seems to be real change in the air. After a decade when the annual rate of increase of global CO_2 emissions was around 4 per cent, the rate of increase fell to 1 per cent in 2012 and 2013, and then just 0.5 per cent globally in 2014 (Olivier). The growth of renewable energy worldwide is astonishing, as David Boyd reports in *The Optimistic Environmentalist*:

> In 2000, the [International Energy Agency] predicted that global wind power would reach a total of 30 gigawatts by 2010. … Oops! Their forecast was exceeded in 2003, seven years early, and more than 30 gigawatts of wind power has been installed *every year* since 2009.
>
> (27)

While conservatives and climate sceptics object to wind farms blighting the uplands of the British Isles, the global energy revolution is getting under way. The Chinese spent more on installing renewable energy than fossil-fuelled power stations in 2013, and in 2014 their total demand for coal declined for the first time. Of course, a couple of good years do not a trend make. Nevertheless, when we embarked on writing this book in 2016, there were sound scientific, technical, cultural and economic reasons for thinking that the long, difficult transition from fossil fuels had begun.

What a difference a year makes. The assumption that climate sceptics have been left on the 'wrong side of history', as the complacent phrase has it, has proven premature. There were many reasons why 51.9 per cent of voters in the British referendum wanted to leave the European Union, but the incessant agitation of the right-wing press – as sceptical about climate science as it was antagonistic to the European project – played a significant role. Conservative and neo-fascist populism has hit a high tide mark across Europe and the United States, as embodied at the time of writing in the figure of President Donald Trump. All the other Republican contenders for his job expressed some degree of scepticism about climate science, both reflecting and further entrenching the partisan divide on the subject in the United States. Trump's electoral advantage derived, in large part, from his supporters' intense sense of grievance, who were told that 'Trump digs coal' and that the mining industry might yet be saved from destruction by vindictive environmentalists. His lie-littered speech on 1 June 2017 (Schipani), announcing the promised withdrawal of the United States from the Paris (COP 21) Agreement, included the observation: 'I was elected to represent the citizens of Pittsburgh, not Paris.' One year into the Trump Presidency (we can scarcely refrain from shivering to write those words, even now), there may be only 1,000 more Americans employed in coal mines than in 2016 (Thompson), but Obama's Clean Power Plan has been slated for repeal by Trump's Environmental Protection Agency administrator Scott Pruitt (Carter). The political battle, in the United States at least, is far from over.

The anxiety, bafflement and deep antipathy the authors share towards the resurgence of right-wing populism exemplifies the problem of political polarization but does nothing to solve it. While deriding Trump and the 'Brexiteers', and by extension their ostensibly gullible supporters, is emotionally satisfying for liberal environmentalists, it is also symptomatic of a widening gulf of comprehension, trust and empathy that is, we argue, profoundly dangerous. So, we set out deliberately to *understand* climate scepticism, not to vilify or even overcome it. Without surrendering our difference of opinion, we want to try to see the world from the perspective of climate sceptics by analysing a range of texts from four different countries. Righteous environmentalists that we are in real life, we are inclined to ask: 'Who do they think are, challenging the overwhelming scientific consensus on climate change?' In this book, though, we accept the task of asking, in all seriousness, 'Who do *they* think they are?'

Why study climate scepticism ecocritically?

You get interesting responses when people hear you are researching climate scepticism. Fellow environmentalist academics tend to think it is a worthwhile topic, but only if you are planning to develop still more persuasive means of challenging 'denialist' positions. A mixed group of scientists and humanists responded to a presentation of this research by suggesting that, while it was fine to discuss it in a scholarly context, we ought not to make it public in case it further undermined the scientific argument. A Cultural Studies professor who criticized our approach at a public discussion forum implied that we were allowing ourselves to be duped by the conspiracy of fossil fuel companies outlined in such books as Naomi Oreskes and Erick M. Conway's *Merchants of Doubt*. People outside academia respond differently: one of the present authors discussed the project on a local radio station, and immediately started getting anonymous emails extolling questionable theories about global warming. One memorable correspondent insisted he knew the warming trend was natural because the sun was more yellow when he was a child, thereby proving that solar irradiance had increased. A symposium relating to this book project was even attacked on a leading sceptical website, which might be a badge of honour.[1] The defensiveness of liberal academics reflect a concern that climate scepticism symbolizes a wider challenge to expert knowledge, including, potentially, their own. The cranky aggressiveness of initial communications from sceptics, both within and without academia, shows they do not expect a sympathetic hearing. Both reactions exemplify the growing polarization of the climate debate, the subject of the next section of this chapter.

Our first response, to both sides, is that we are not in a position to contest or defend the IPCC position. We are scholars of literature and culture, and so although we consider that, to the best of our knowledge, the IPCC's methods and conclusions are sound, we also acknowledge that we are simply unqualified to render a scientifically informed judgement. Given this respect for the IPCC consensus, we describe more catastrophic predictions as 'alarmist,' although we acknowledge arguments that, far from exaggerating the risks, the IPCC reports are too conservative. We have sought to understand the science of climate change, not least so we can grasp the technical objections to it, but we cannot reasonably participate in the debate as if we were climatologists or atmospheric chemists. Our situation is akin to that of scholars who read the Bible as literature: they know that, to Richard Dawkins or the Pope, the literal truth of the Bible matters very much indeed, but they adopt a position of *methodological agnosticism* (regardless of their personal beliefs) because their objective is comprehension, not endorsement or rejection. We propose to read climate scepticism 'as literature' for three good reasons: one is that it's what we are qualified to do and we wish to make a virtue of adversity. Another is that a few sceptical texts are unequivocally literary, and the others have at least some interest as texts, if not a lot of merit. The third, most ambitious, reason is that approaching climate sceptics through their texts, rather than examining them as a population or a conspiratorial foe, may help to undermine the stereotypical view environmentalists tend to hold of those with whom they disagree. And that, we claim, has inherent moral and cognitive value.

These provisos ought not to suggest that our approach to climate sceptics' texts will be uncritical. Rather, they clarify what kind of criticism matches our expertise to the texts we've chosen to read. Our approach is, in part, informed by the idea of 'frames', which we draw from the study of environmental communication. According to George Lakoff, co-author of the influential *Metaphors We Live By*, frame analysis responds to a shift in the scientific understanding of thinking:

> Most of us were brought up with a commonplace view of how we think that derives from the Enlightenment. Over the past 30 years, the cognitive and brain sciences have shown that this view is false. The old view claimed that reason is conscious, unemotional, logical, abstract, universal, and imagined concepts and language as able to fit the world directly. All of that is false. Real reason is: mostly unconscious (98%); requires emotion; uses the 'logic' of frames, metaphors, and narratives; is physical (in brain circuitry); and varies considerably, as frames vary. And since the brain is set up to run a body, ideas and language can't directly fit the world but rather must go through the body.
>
> (72)

Humans, according to Lakoff, understand words and sentences in relation to larger-scale subconscious frames of reference, or schemata, without which nothing could make sense. Climate sceptics and their opponents – let's call them 'warmists' for now, as the sceptics do – interpret statements relating to climate in relation to enculturated frames. The problem is that, as Lakoff shows, their respective frames are radically different. He lists six framing differences between the 'conservative' and the 'progressive', including the former's belief in human superiority (anthropocentrism) and the capacity of free markets to yield maximized human benefit (market fundamentalism). Less obvious is the conservative's preference for direct causation over systemic explanations, and his acceptance of Cost–Benefit Analysis and the 'Equivalent Value Metaphor', which together view environmental goods as interchangeable, or at least replaceable. Harms done to nature can be calculated in advance, weighed against other benefits, and if necessary offset by restoration or preservation elsewhere. Lastly, Lakoff identifies the pejorative stereotype of the 'Liberal Elite' that is prevalent among conservatives:

> The tax-and-spend, sushi-eating, latte-drinking, Birkenstock-wearing, do-gooder, know-it-all liberals! This [stereotype] tends to make conservative populists doubt and reject the science behind reports that establish the existence of and impact of global warming.

Lakoff's sympathetic characterization of the progressive moral system, though, does not acknowledge the stereotypes that also validate *the progressive's rejection* of the conservative's frames. If you need evidence, ask a progressive American to describe a typical Donald Trump supporter. It wouldn't be complimentary, would it? Further examples of unwitting liberal myopia will be introduced below.

Matthew Nesbit, an environmental communications scholar, agrees with Lakoff that conservatives have dominated the framing of climate change in the United States, and that reframing the debate will be crucial to building public support for determined political action. His definition of a frame is more narrative-oriented than Lakoff's:

> Frames are interpretive storylines that set a specific train of thought in motion, communicating why an issue might be a problem, who or what might be responsible for it, and what should be done about it.
>
> (Nisbet 15)

Nevertheless, the implications in terms of analysis are similar: to identify latent 'storylines' behind extant texts or other artefacts and evaluate their effectiveness. So, for example, Nesbit criticizes environmentalists' efforts to challenge conservatives' preferred framing with climate 'alarmism':

> Former U.S. Vice President Al Gore, many environmentalists, and even some scientists have attempted to counter the [conservatives'] *scientific uncertainty* and *economic consequences* frames by emphasizing a *Pandora's box* of looming 'climate crisis.' To instantly translate their preferred interpretation, these advocates have relied on depictions of specific climate impacts, including hurricane devastation, polar bears perched precariously on shrinking ice floes, scorched, drought-stricken earth, blazing wild fires, or famous cities or landmarks under water due to future sea-level rise.
>
> (19)

Nesbit warns that such framing may paradoxically reinforce the 'scientific uncertainty' storyline, because 'the error bars of uncertainty for each of the climate impacts are much wider than the general link between human activities and global warming'. Indeed, the limitations of climate models' projections are a constant – and not unjustified – refrain in the literature we survey. Moreover, sceptics' ridicule of the polar bear icon as a megafauna stand-in for all non-human life and as the presumptive preferred species, over humans, to preserve supports Nesbit's contention that the 'Pandora's box' framing may only exacerbate polarization. Instead, he identifies 'economic opportunity' and 'morality and ethics' framing as potentially more likely to circumvent polarization.

In the chapters that follow, each one focused on a national literature,[2] the co-authors adopt their own voice and critical approach; our collaboration implies dialogue, not homogeneity. Where appropriate we draw on the idea of frames to help link our analysis to the wider currents of research into the cultures of climate change. Our own analyses are framed by our individual concerns and interests: Handley, for example, critiques environmentalists' lack of attention to American sceptics' ideo-theological framing of the climate issue, whereas Garrard situates British scepticism in relation to party politicization of the environment in the 1980s and 1990s. At the same time, though, all our chapters reflect our concern that previous readings of scepticism have tended to understate the diversity concealed by binary categorization. For example, Martin Lack's study of British climate scepticism, *The Denial of Science*, classifies a wide range of texts and their authors according to a typology that includes 'Contrarianism', 'Cornucopianism', 'Economic Rationalism' and 'Prometheanism'. Although these are useful categories, they have the unintended effect of eroding the distinctiveness of individual texts. To a literary scholar, such differences make a difference, and so we extend typological or framing analysis with close reading, with the specific objective of eliciting the singularity of each text. We don't deny the accuracy or the value of population-level analyses; we merely maintain that traditional literary criticism has a distinct function and significance in relation to climate scepticism. We present both critical and admiring assessments of sceptical texts, but these are, as far as possible, literary judgements rather than political or scientific ones. By meeting sceptics on the terms they have proposed – by choosing to write a novel or a play or a popular scientific text – we seek to avoid reinforcing confrontational stereotypes. Instead, we take them more seriously *as writers* than anyone might expect, the authors themselves included.

In doing so we run the risk of implying that sceptical perspectives on climate change are equivalent to those of scientific experts. While our position on the latter point is discussed in Chapter 6, our general approach adopts the second and third of David Bloor's tenets for the 'Strong Programme' in the sociology of scientific knowledge ('SSK'):

2. It would be impartial with respect to truth and falsity, rationality or irrationality, success or failure. Both sides of these dichotomies will require explanation.
3. It would be symmetrical in its style of explanation. The same types of cause would explain, say, true or false beliefs.

(5)

Bloor's SSK seeks 'causal' sociological explanations for both scientific knowledge and its supposed opposites – ignorance, superstition, scepticism and so on – whereas our approach is interpretive. When we apply techniques of rhetorical critique 'symmetrically' to warmism and scepticism, we find that both positions represent themselves as 'David' to the opposition's 'Goliath', for example. At the same time, we 'impartially' bracket out scientific 'styles of explanation' of beliefs about climate change, even though we consider one set – embodied in the IPCC reports – true and the other false.

It seems unlikely that many people will notice our fragile neutrality; a popular academic text might sell a few thousand copies and be read, at least in part, a few thousand times more in university libraries. Defensiveness aside, though, we have two positive reasons for reading climate scepticism agnostically: one, addressed below, is that it is inherently valuable to challenge stereotypes, even of socially dominant groups, and the other is simply that there are no existing analyses of sceptical texts in the field of environmentally orientated literary and cultural criticism, also known as 'ecocriticism'. In fact, to our knowledge, ecocriticism has yielded no detailed studies of anti-environmentalist culture at all. Until now, approximately half of the political spectrum has been completely ignored – a pointed irony for a school of criticism that has always called itself 'political'. And yet identifying anti-environmentalist culture only to expose its obvious limitations from a liberal or radical left perspective would be facile – like shooting fish in a barrel while preaching to the choir. Better to approach scepticism with something like Frederick Buell's grudging admiration for anti-environmentalist rhetoric:

> Sometimes memorable because of its sheer panache, it is always carefully scripted, intentionally partisan rhetoric. It is also virtuosically polyphonic. Though its linguistic range is not perhaps as large as St. Paul's – it doesn't speak simultaneously in the tongues of men and angels – it does encompass a considerable range of voices nonetheless. It reaches across the gulf between the media-savvy, expertise-rich talking head on a highbrow television show to the hectoring vulgarity of Rush Limbaugh-style talk-back radio-show hosts.
>
> (10)

Our research broadly confirms Buell's assessment. We note, though, that having praised it for being 'virtuosically polyphonic', he goes on, like Lack, to characterize it in terms of five typical 'rhetorical shapes'. Indeed, scholars frequently acknowledge the diversity of climate scepticism while offering analyses that tend to minimize or eliminate it. Even so, Buell pays reluctant tribute to the rhetorical effectiveness of anti-environmentalism, and we believe that, like him, we have to open ourselves to the power of sceptical texts if we are to account for their influence.

How did ecocritics fail to address the enormous influence of anti-environmentalist rhetorics in our cultures? It was not that they went unnoticed, of course; the guile and sway of the opposition are a constant in ecocritics' conversations and on social media. The problem is that anti-environmentalism manifests overwhelmingly in forms ecocritics do not consider 'literary': in Heartland Institute press releases; in virulent, anonymous comments left on newspaper websites; obliquely in advertisements for meat products or petroleum companies. Despite cultural materialism, digital humanities and other movements that tempted literary scholars to abandon Literature, the discipline remains indebted to what Michel Foucault calls 'the author-function', that historically labile ascription of a particular type of 'authority' to texts that come with a person's name attached.

The choice of texts in this book reflects this assumption: it overwhelmingly considers substantial, coherent, authored texts, either printed or on film, not blogs or media briefings, important though they are. The book therefore embodies an overt, reflexive selection bias: we will be reading texts in a way that emphasizes their uniqueness, and to facilitate this, we have chosen texts to read that are likely to be distinctive. Blog posts and press releases, often anonymous and seldom artfully constructed, can usefully be 'read' using text-mining technologies to understand sceptical discourse at a broad population level (Boussalis and Coan). Such analysis provides persuasive evidence of variations in topic prevalence over time, but it relies on *prior* identification of 'conservative CTTs' (Conservative Think Tanks) as, in effect, authors and disregards the kind of generic and stylistic features that only close reading can uncover. Furthermore, the absence of coherent subjectivity – let alone emotional complexity or ambivalence – from such material reduces its usefulness to readers interested, as we are, in understanding the perspectives of individual climate sceptics.

At the same time, some of the texts we have chosen fall between genre lines, challenging the above characterization of 'substantial, coherent, authored texts'. For example, Claude Allègre's *L'Imposture climatique* (The Climate Imposture) is largely a collection of interview transcripts with comics and literary quotes added here and there. Co-written with journalist Dominique Montvalon, the text recreates the oral quality of the conversations between the two men, with nonverbal communication such as laughter indicated in parentheses. The usual careful attention to narrative strategies no longer serves the literary critic; instead, elements of rhetoric and argumentation become the main focus. Rather than examining the complexity of the individual fictional text, it is the varying tones and timbers of climate scepticism as a discourse in the process of constructing itself that become the object of literary analysis.

Literary critics typically remain wedded, as much personally as intellectually, to notions of aesthetics and the quality of writing. Although few take up the challenge of defending their evaluations systematically, they generally want to read, teach and analyse good books, not terrible ones. We will have to decide, in the course of the detailed analyses presented in this book, whether sceptical texts justify respectful treatment (spoiler alert: sometimes they do), but it is worth saying that good books are, to some degree, made by the quality of attention we bring to them. At this stage, we can reveal that British, German and French sceptical texts were better than we expected, and they became, on the whole, more interesting the more we thought and talked about them. The Americans ... well, we shall see.

Is Western politics increasingly polarized?

During the 2015 Canadian general election campaign, the photogenic Liberal leader Justin Trudeau insisted that 'Conservatives are not our enemies. They are our neighbours. They are our cousins and uncles and parents. They are our friends' (Payton). The contrast with the intensely partisan politics to the south and, increasingly, across the Atlantic was pointed: Hillary Clinton was unafraid to characterize her Republican opponents as 'enemies', although the prospect of luring away anti-Trump conservatives elicited more emollient language during the election campaign. Trudeau's comment could be interpreted as a mere political platitude, or an opportunistic bid to attract floating voters, but it also corresponds to the promise of 'sunny ways' that helped win his party the election. Canada did not suffer a financial crisis and rarely has to decide what to do about migrants at its borders. If Canada manifests less political polarization, though, it would seem to be the exception in North America and Europe.

Across the EU, national parliaments and the European Parliament have seen swings away from centrist parties towards the left and right: Syriza, a coalition of the Radical Left, holds power in Greece, and the British Labour Party, led by the socialist Jeremy Corbyn, performed surprisingly well in snap elections in the UK in 2017. In France, the growing popularity of Marine Le Pen, leader of the far-right National Front, prompted the emergence of new, pro-EU centrist party, 'La République en Marche!', that kept her from the presidency in the 2017 elections. The election of Emmanuel Macron notwithstanding, research shows the steep decline in support for centrist parties across Europe since the 2008–2009 financial crisis (Groskopf). The most striking evidence is a graph of the changing standard deviation, which 'evaluates the distribution, or spread, of the ideological scores [of political parties]. A larger standard deviation indicates greater polarization. By this measure, the EU is by far the most polarized it has ever been.' Commentators frequently have recourse to Yeats's words in 'The Second Coming': 'Things fall apart; the centre cannot hold; … /The best lack all conviction, while the worst/Are full of passionate intensity.' Divisive issues such as migration and terrorism are driving the polarization in European politics. By contrast, it is not yet clear to what extent public opinion on climate change in Europe affects, or is affected by, this shift.

On the face of it, the United States too is becoming more polarized, although the two-party plurality voting system makes it harder to track than in European countries with multiple parties elected by proportional representation. Until the 2016 election redrew the map, the partisan divide between the 'red' (Republican) and 'blue' (Democratic) Americas was a journalistic staple, for which the electoral map was a visual icon: blue states around the Great Lakes and down both coastlines, and red states throughout the 'flyover territory' of the Midwest and across the south. After the 2000 Gore–Bush election, Terry Mattingly wrote in *The Knoxville News-Sentinel*:

> The Year of Our Lord 2000 was the year of the map. … This election was Hollywood vs. Nashville, 'Sex and the City' vs. 'Touched by an Angel', National Public Radio vs. talk radio, 'Doonesbury' vs. 'B.C.', 'Hotel California' vs. 'Okie from Muskogee.' It was *The New York Times* vs. National Review Online, Dan Rather vs. Rush Limbaugh, Rosie O'Donnell vs. Dr. Laura, Barbra Streisand vs. Dr. James Dobson, the Supreme Court vs. – well, the Supreme Court.
>
> (cited in Fiorina, Abrams and Pope 4–5)

This simplistic distinction prevails throughout the American media, as Morris Fiorina and Samuel J. Abrams observe:

> We are told that red-state residents are more likely to be Evangelicals, gun owners, country music devotees, beer drinkers, and NASCAR fans, whereas blue-state residents are more likely to be agnostics or atheists, Volvo drivers, supporters of the fine arts, chardonnay sippers, and people who sail. Scores of such contrasts have been noted in one media outlet or another.
>
> (567)

And yet, they warn that surveys repeated over decadal timespans do not show that the distribution of public opinion in the American population has decisively shifted: 'In the aggregate, there is virtually no change in the distribution of American ideological identification' (570) from 1972 to 2004, before the financial crisis. On most issues, a normal distribution around a centrist position, rather than a bimodal distribution clustered at the extremes, is typical. On a few issues, such as gay marriage, opinion does appear to be polarized, but this could be a transient artefact of a longer-term trend from one consensus (hostile to homosexuality) to another (accepting of homosexuality). Overall, they conclude, 'we see a largely centrist public drifting slightly rightward on some issues, slightly leftward on others, but with only very small declines (of 2–5 percentage points) in the number of moderates' (574). If the US electorate is only slightly more polarized than in the past, why does 'the country now seems polarized and embattled to the point of dysfunction'? (Haidt 319).

Fiorina and Abrams agree with Haidt that the two main political parties have become more polarized: there are fewer moderate Republicans and fewer right-leaning 'Blue Dog' Democrats from the South. Moreover, the party's platforms have separated out and consolidated into opposing manifestoes with little common ground. American voters may not be more divided than before, but they are invited to choose between parties whose hard-fought partisan differences are highlighted daily by media organizations that are themselves perceived as partisan. Elite polarization manifests in vituperative political debates, as well as legislative gridlock and the recurrent threat of government shutdown and federal debt default.

Once the differences between the parties emerge with greater clarity, voters are then likely to align themselves more decisively – even if the overall distribution of opinion remains unchanged. Such 'party sorting' contributes to perceived polarization, in spite of the lack of evidence of a collapsing centre or significant growth of more radical viewpoints.[3] As divisive a figure as President Donald Trump is, his election-winning appeal clearly spanned the racism of the extreme right with the hostility to free trade and globalization more often associated with the left. His political hybridity (or incoherent opportunism) may mean that his presidency will counteract, not reinforce, party and ideological sorting.

One way to reconcile the fact that, in America, public opinion has scarcely budged since the 1970s while public discourse seems far more polarized is to examine voters' feelings towards one another, rather than their opinions. Shanto Iyengar and Sean D. Westwood undertook research to establish Americans' hostility to political opponents and propensity to discriminate against them, which they call 'affective and behavioural polarization'. Using cleverly designed implicit association tests to minimize our natural bias towards expressing socially acceptable views, they discovered that 'hostile feelings for the opposing party are ingrained and automatic in voters' minds' (Iyengar and Westwood 691). More remarkably, benchmarking their findings against racial bias, which many Americans consider the most profound cleavage in their society, they found that 'the level of partisan animus in the American public exceeds racial hostility'. Unlike racism, which is prevalent in spite of social norms opposing it, open hostility has been wholly normalized in political discourse. Not only were Iyengar and Westwood's subjects emotionally antagonistic towards political opponents, they were willing to discriminate against them in a simulated job search and a money-based trust game called 'Dictator'. By contrast, participants in the research betrayed relatively little subconscious racial hostility and avoided overt racial bias in their decisions.

Other developments may be exacerbating the polarization described by Westwood and Iyengar. Advanced demographic mapping has enabled parties to draw electoral boundaries that concentrate the opposition's voters and multiply the seats they might capture – a process called 'gerrymandering'. Gerrymandered seats, such as the absurdly shaped districts in North Carolina (Republican-controlled) and Maryland (Democrat-controlled) (Ingraham), are thought to encourage representatives to express polarized views at odds with their broadly centrist electorate. However, analysis by John Sides shows that safer seats are only modestly correlated with right-wing votes for Republicans, and that Democrats in safe seats are no more or less liberal than those representing marginal districts (Sides). More likely, he says, is that local party organizations have been captured by uncompromising activists, leading to primary selection processes biased towards more extreme candidates.

At the same time, internet news sites and social media have undermined the former dominance of the TV news organizations, with their commitment to balance and fact-based reporting. Although newspapers and, to a lesser degree, TV networks have always been seen as biased, openly partisan coverage – Fox News and Breitbart on the right and the *Huffington Post* on the left – is a twenty-first-century development. Increasingly, it is possible to exist in an informational 'echo chamber', encountering only versions of already strongly held opinions. Furthermore, vital modern sources of information, such as Google searches and Facebook news feeds, employ personalization algorithms that, in effect, reinforce prejudices by preferentially showing users things they will probably 'Like'. Eli Pariser terms the effect of all these algorithms the 'filter bubble':

> Your filter bubble is your own personal, unique universe of information that you live in online. And what's in your filter bubble depends on who you are, and it depends on what you do. But the thing is that you don't decide what gets in. And more importantly, you don't actually see what gets edited out.

So although the US electorate as a whole is not (yet) dramatically more polarized than in the 1970s, the relationship between the parties, voters' feelings about partisan opponents and public political discourse have entered an exceptionally confrontational phase. Trump's election has had ambiguous effects: his own interventions continue to coarsen and degrade political discourse, but there is also increased attention to filter bubbles and the risks of polarization (Bruni). The *New York Times* publishes links to articles from both right- and left-wing publications on its news site, to help readers gain a broader perspective (Dubenko). The right-leaning *Wall Street Journal* presented 'Blue Feed Red Feed': imaginary conservative and liberal Facebook feeds side by side (Keegon). *Strangers in Their Own Land*, a remarkable book by Berkeley sociologist Arlie Russell Hochschild, is the result of five years of research in Louisiana to understand why the very Americans who suffer the most from pollution also vote for politicians who oppose environmental regulation. Hochschild writes:

> Everyone I talked to wanted a clean environment. But in Louisiana, the Great Paradox was staring me in the face – great pollution and great resistance to regulating polluters. If I could truly enter the minds and hearts of people on the far right on the issue of the water they drink, the animals they hunt, the lakes they swim in, the streams they fish in, the air they breathe, I could get to know them up close.
>
> (21)

Hochschild's ethnographic methodology is very different from that of the present authors, but we share her objective: to challenge political polarization by scaling the 'empathy wall' between environmentalists and sceptics.

Polarization may be startlingly conspicuous in the United States, but it extends well beyond it. Westwood and Iyengar went on to collaborate with a group of researchers in the UK, Belgium and the Basque region of Spain so that they could test their affective polarization thesis cross-nationally. They expected to find that the deep social cleavages between Flemish and Walloon Belgians and Basques and Spaniards would outweigh party loyalties, whereas British and American participants would be more partisan. In Belgium and the Basque country, social cleavage is manifested in a plethora of political parties covering the full left-right spectrum *and* the ethnic divide, so it's possible to parse out allegiances more precisely than in two- or three-party states. What they discovered surprised them:

> Contrary to expectations, we find that in divided [Belgium, Basque country] and integrated [UK, USA] societies alike, animus based on party affiliation easily exceeds animus based on social group ties. Partisanship exerts a stronger psychological bond than affiliation with racial, religious, linguistic or ethnic groups, even when those cleavages are highly conflictual and the principal basis for the parties' ideological positions and electoral appeals.
>
> (Westwood et al.)

While the multiparty states exhibited less affective polarization overall than the UK and United States, the partisan effect was dominant in all four of them – even in a part of Europe scarred by violence between Basque separatists and the Spanish state that lasted over half a century. The authors conclude:

> Defined in terms of affect, voters' sense of partisanship represents the dominant divide in modern democracies and the strongest basis for group polarization.

This is an extraordinary finding. It implies that the holy trinity of literary and cultural studies – race, gender and class – no longer captures the most important sources of hostility, mistrust and discrimination in Western democracies. The corollary must be that counteracting political polarization is the most urgent task for the liberal academy, albeit that – outside political science – it is hardly yet recognized as such.[4]

Finally, it has become clear that cultural identity, not scientific knowledge, determines the stated beliefs of Americans, at least, when it comes to climate change. Challenging the meaning of results of opinion polls carried out on Americans, Dan Kahan observes that 'whether people "believe in" climate change, like whether they "believe in" evolution, *expresses who they are*' (11). Using a survey that deliberately seeks to measure knowledge of climate science *as opposed to* identity, Kahan found that the ostensibly large differences between Democrats and Republicans disappeared. He concludes:

> Unless one engages citizens in a manner that avoids identity threat, no amount of knowledge about climate science will forestall divisive cultural conflict on global warming. Not only did the item-response profile for 'belief in' human-caused climate change fail to display the characteristics of a valid indicator of climate-science comprehension. Those respondents [with the] *highest* level of such comprehension were also the *most* polarized in their 'beliefs in' human-caused global warming.
>
> (26)

In other words, climate sceptics cannot be dismissed as dummies who reject science, and they are unlikely to be persuaded by more, and more brilliantly communicated, science. Indeed, warmists surveyed by Kahan were just as likely to have scientifically *unsupported* views about climatic risks, such as that global warming would increase skin cancer or reduce photosynthesis (20). If Americans' lack of relationship, across the spectrum of opinion, between climate science comprehension and 'belief in human-caused global warming' can be generalized elsewhere, the IPCC/COP approach – overcoming resistance with scientific knowledge – is doomed. In this book, we explore an alternative pathway.

Why not stereotype climate sceptics?

When ecocritics think of themselves as political, they rarely mean *party* political, even though that is the predominant mode of political activity, progressive or reactionary, in Western society. The kind of political science analysis offered here will therefore seem incongruous in a book of literary criticism. To conservatives, though, the party affiliations of ecocriticism are pretty obvious: implicit positions range from 'soft left' ecological modernizers to more radical eco-socialism, eco-feminism and environmental justice, with few, if any, scholars explicitly to the right of centre. In that regard, ecocritics are at least as politically homogenous as climate sceptics, possibly more so. Moreover, Westwood and Iyengar's findings of affective polarization, in the United States and beyond, imply it is increasingly dangerous to ignore either the divide itself or the people and perspectives on the other side of it. The harm to institutional processes and to the quality of political discourse are obvious, and worrying enough, but growing alienation between ideological factions also has a cognitive cost in the form of intellectually and morally limiting stereotypes.

The social psychology literature on stereotyping is too vast to survey. However, there are two consistent findings that are relevant here: the perception of outgroup homogeneity and the countervailing value of perspective-taking. Stereotypes are, by definition, homogenous. Political scientists have found, over decades of research, that even trivial social differences can become the basis for ingroup/outgroup distinctions, and that outgroup members tend to be lumped together in consequence:

> Members of an outgroup are seen as more homogeneous or similar to one another than are members of an ingroup … , even when the basis for categorization is minimal in nature …. Evaluations of outgroup members are more polarized than those for ingroup members.
>
> (Park and Judd 110)

Moreover, one group usually thinks that it behaves well because they're good people ('dispositional attribution'), and behave badly only because of adverse circumstances ('situational attribution'), whereas the opposite is true of the other group. In psychology labs, social divisions based on insignificant or fictitious differences, such as wearing different shirts, can be created with distressing ease – so-called minimal group experiments – although they don't always lead to homogenizing outgroups. Prejudices about 'natural' outgroups, like political opponents, can be pernicious and obdurate by contrast.

Stereotypes have been shown to have a range of damaging consequences:

> Lack of differentiated thinking about a group facilitates more extreme evaluations of individual group members … , stronger inferences from the behavior of one member to the group as a whole … , and out-group discrimination.
>
> (Linville, Fischer and Salovey)

Climate sceptics are not a historically oppressed group, of course, and so the risk of discrimination may seem insignificant. Nevertheless, stereotyping, even of socially dominant groups, is harmful to clear thinking and damages the prospects for democratic negotiation over responses to climate change. 'Scientification', which puts environmental issues out of reach of democratic discussion by denominating them matters for scientific experts (Yearley) – the IPCC process, in other words – has been somewhat successful in terms of global inter-governmental politics but has energized the sceptical counter-movement at the national level where agreements have, in fact, to be implemented. Environmentalists cannot get around democracy, and so the polarized politics of climate must, at some point, be addressed.

Political stereotyping has come to attention only quite recently, even in social psychology, and almost all the extant Anglophone research examines American politics. One study of moral stereotyping found that Democrats and Republicans exaggerated the difference between their own values and those of the opposition, predictably enough, but they also stereotyped their *own* side. The authors conclude:

> The ideological 'culture war' in the U.S. is, in part, an honest disagreement about ends (moral values that each side wants to advance), as well as an honest disagreement about means (laws and policies) to advance those ends. But our findings suggest that there is an additional process at work: partisans on each side exaggerate the degree to which the other side pursues moral ends that are different from their own. Much of this exaggeration comes from each side underestimating the degree to which the other side shares its own values. But some of it comes, unexpectedly, from overestimating the degree to which 'typical' members of one's own side endorse its values.
>
> (Graham, Nosek and Haidt 12)

There are two salient points for our analysis here: one is that questioning stereotypes about climate sceptics will not, in any sense, eliminate the 'honest disagreement' that we have with them. We simply want to shift from poorly informed hostility to grounded dispute. The other is that ecocritics might be provoked to ask how their arguments with each other are conditioned by assumptions about what 'all' are thought to believe, and how the real diversity of opinion in the field articulates with the broad spectrum of environmental politics – clustered, still, around moderate values – outside the academy.

Graham, Nosek and Haidt's study showed that Democrats were more likely to stereotype Republicans than vice versa, but scholars too are susceptible. A 2015 article that confirmed their finding measured traits that were described in biased terms: 'Need for Cognitive Closure', 'Belief in a Dangerous World', 'Social Dominance Orientation' and 'System Justification' rather accurately represent liberal stereotypes of conservatives, and so it was not surprising that Democrats saw them as characteristic of the opposition, as the authors concede (Scherer, Windschitl and Graham 206). Even when the authors imagine future experiments to measure 'traits that are more strongly associated with liberals', they come up with positive ones such as 'openness to new experience'. Perhaps if a study measured 'Obedience to Political Correctness', 'Addiction to Government Spending' or 'Propensity to Sexual Deviance', Republicans would be equally likely to stereotype their opponents.

We discuss another striking example of the 'liberal bias' conservatives identify in social science research below. For now, we consider how ecocriticism might challenge political polarization by enabling what social psychologists call 'perspective-taking', or the 'ability to entertain the perspective of another' (Galinsky and Moskowitz 708). In a series of experiments involving both a natural grouping (young/elderly) and a minimal group (under-/over-estimators of the number of dots on a screen), exercises that encouraged subjects to see things from the outgroup's point of view counteracted the propensity to stereotype. The alternative strategy, of suppressing stereotypical assumptions, has been found to have paradoxical effects, presumably because trying *not* to think about something risks making it 'hyperaccessible'. In the exercises used by the experimenters, the most effective debiasing technique involved writing narrative essays from the outgroup's point of view.

This result will come as no surprise to English teachers. If there is one thing students everywhere learn from studying English Literature, it is not whether to be or not to be; it is to question stereotypes by seeing the world from the narrated perspectives of marginalized Others. Reflecting on the 9/11 attacks, the novelist Ian McEwan commented that the hijackers' crimes represented, among other things, a 'failure of imagination':

> If the hijackers had been able to imagine themselves into the thoughts and feelings of the passengers, they would have been unable to proceed. It is hard to be cruel once you permit yourself to enter the mind of your victim. Imagining what it is like to be someone other than yourself is at the core of our humanity. It is the essence of compassion, and it is the beginning of morality.

Despite a quite different philosophical heritage, Derek Attridge's account of the 'singularity of literature' similarly emphasizes perspective-taking:

> It is in the acknowledgement of the other person's uniqueness, and therefore the impossibility of finding general rules or schemata to account fully for him or her, that one can be said to encounter the other as other – in the same moment that those rules and schemata shift, however momentarily, to take account of the now no longer other.
>
> (loc. 796)

For Attridge, the encounter with alterity is far more disruptive than it appears in McEwan's humanistic account. *The Singularity of Literature* is also attentive to the formal uniqueness – the estranging 'how' of an other's viewpoint, not only its idiosyncratic 'what' – that contributes to the reader's dislocation when they take an other's perspective through writing. Notwithstanding such differences, Attridge and McEwan agree that it is the peculiar power and responsibility of literature to question stereotypes by showing us the world as others see it. When Attridge describes the other as 'that which the existing cultural order has to occlude in order to maintain its capacities and configurations, its value-systems and hierarchies of importance' (30), it is clear that he has in mind socially marginalized others, not angry white conservative males. So, we need to examine the evidence that climate sceptics, too, are subject to stereotyping.

Deniers, 'Flat Earthers' or sceptics?

It is a truism of modern literary studies that words – especially those used to label social groups – matter. While conservatives lament the tangled thicket of linguistic prohibitions they call 'political correctness', there are norms of speech that are observed across the political spectrum (norms that President Trump takes pleasure in transgressing). The most direct route to understanding stereotypes of climate sceptics is therefore the range of terms applied to them by their opponents.

The most familiar is the phrase 'climate sceptic', in which the second word conforms to one of its *OED* definitions by describing 'doubt or incredulity as to the truth of some assertion or supposed fact'. Many scientists, however, resist using this term because, they say, science is inherently 'sceptical', in the sense of questioning assumptions and reserving judgement until the evidence is compelling. A leading warmist website called 'Skeptical Science' says as much at the top of its home page:

> Scientific skepticism is healthy. Scientists should always challenge themselves to improve their understanding. Yet this isn't what happens with climate change denial. Skeptics vigorously criticise any evidence that supports man-made global warming and yet embrace any argument, op-ed, blog or study that purports to refute global warming. This website gets skeptical about global warming skepticism. Do their arguments have any scientific basis? What does the peer reviewed scientific literature say?
>
> ('Climate Science Glossary')

In other words, the people commonly called 'sceptics' actually engage in what psychologists call 'motivated reasoning' and 'confirmation bias', whereas peer-reviewed science aims systematically to counteract those aspects of human cognition. Highlighting the 'Most Used Climate Myths (and what the science really says)', the site provides 193 rebuttals of arguments used by 'deniers', from banal reactions like 'It's freakin' cold' (myth #23) to more abstruse objections like CO_2 saturation (#72) and Richard Lindzen's infrared iris hypothesis (#104). With immense patience, and without noticeable rancour, the site provides users with the choice of Basic, Intermediate and Advanced responses to common misconceptions. John Cook, who set up the site, argues that climate scientists are already sceptics, and so a different term should be used for opponents. 'Contrarian', a term that is in occasional use, accurately conveys anti-environmentalists' relationship to mainstream science, but unfortunately brings with it connotations of 'personal pettiness' (Van Rensburg 9). There are few acceptable alternatives.

'Denier', the most widely used alternative to sceptic, is inflammatory because it recalls 'Holocaust denial'. The analogy is frequently explicit, as when George Monbiot noted that climate change had been accepted by the tabloid newspaper *The Sun* as well as *The Economist*: 'Almost everywhere, climate change denial now looks as stupid and as unacceptable as Holocaust denial' ('How Much Reality?'). While Monbiot's comment attracted criticism, it was not unprecedented: Al Gore quoted Winston Churchill in *An Inconvenient Truth* to compare climate change to the Nazi threat and denialism to appeasement. *Popular Technology*'s website (for some reason) has collected a whole webpage of journalists and environmentalists drawing on the analogy in different ways and asks why the Jewish Anti-Defamation League has not objected (Andrew). James Delingpole, a vocal British sceptic, resents the way such stigmatizing language seeks to 'close down the debate':

> Suspect all the fuss about AGW [Anthropogenic Global Warming] might be a little overdone? You're just the kind of scummy Nazi-sympathising revisionist who thinks Hitler didn't murder six million Jews.
>
> (loc. 1118)

Monbiot rejects such protestations as disingenuous:

> Whether we're talking about people who are paid to deny that climate change is happening, or those who use the materials these flacks produce, denial is a precise and concise description of what they do. Their attempt to wriggle out of it by insisting that – by calling them what they are – we are somehow debasing the Holocaust is as contrived as all the other positions they take. We shouldn't fall for it.
>
> ('The Semantics of Denial')

Yet the Holocaust denial analogy has been deployed repeatedly by warmists, and always with stigmatizing intention. It is not necessarily a trivializing analogy – that depends on how much harm ultimately comes of climate change and the scale of social mobilization required to respond to it – but it is still utterly inappropriate: the Nazi genocide is an historical fact, whereas anthropogenic climate change is a hypothesis about current and future geophysical trends. However confident climate scientists are about their projections, they would presumably never claim that documented history and models of the future are epistemically equivalent.

Another denigrating term, favoured perhaps by those who find the Holocaust analogy discomforting or impolitic, is 'Flat Earther'. In a speech at Georgetown University, Barack Obama conveyed his impatience with climate sceptics, saying 'We don't have time for a meeting of the Flat Earth Society' ('Obama: No Time'). Secretary of State John Kerry later repeated the metaphor at the COP 21 talks in China: 'We need to make clear that those members of the Flat Earth Society are on the wrong side of history' (U.S. Department of State). However, given that the President of the Flat Earth Society does accept the science of climate change, the term 'Flat Earther' is, according to Chris Fleming, a vacuous slur:[5]

> For most people, being described as a 'flat Earther' is an insult. The idea of the Earth being flat is considered not only wrong, but a *model* of wrongness, the gold standard of being incorrect about something.

Not only is 'Flat Earther' less morally objectionable than the Holocaust analogy, its rhetorical implications are somewhat different. While both imply the existence of a large-scale conspiracy to cover up a counter-consensual 'truth', 'Flat Earther' consigns sceptics to the imagined past – the 'wrong side of history', in Kerry's phrase. Those on the extreme right who deny the Nazi genocide reject the expertise of historians, the testimony of survivors and the tangible evidence of the death camps – they deny historical facts, in other words – whereas those who question the spherical Earth fly in the face of common sense, with no obvious political motivation. Obama and Kerry's choice of metaphor seems to conform to the climate change communication advice of a report by the Institute for Public Policy Research (IPPR), a British liberal think tank, which recommends a rhetorical counter-measure to the sceptics' tactical emphasis on scientific doubt and uncertainty:

> Much of the noise in the climate change discourse comes from argument and counter-argument, and it is our recommendation that, at least for popular communications, interested agencies now need to treat the argument as having been won. This means simply behaving as if climate change exists and is real, and that individual actions are effective. … Where science is invoked, it now needs to be as 'lay science' – offering lay explanations for what is being treated as a simple established scientific fact, just as the earth's rotation or the water cycle are considered.
>
> (Segnit and Ereaut 25)

'Flat Earther' links climate science to the lay scientific understanding of the spherical Earth just as Segnit and Ereaut suggest. It lacks the deeply offensive connotations of Holocaust denial, and so is at least a less divisive insult.

In the case of a prominent psychologist who has studied climate scepticism, it appears that academic research, too, can function in a pejorative and stigmatizing fashion. It is impossible to know whether Stephan Lewandowsky intended his study of conspiracist ideation among climate sceptics as a taunt, but the title of the paper suggests it is: 'NASA Faked the Moon Landing – Therefore, (Climate) Science Is a Hoax.' The title, and the many news articles that followed the gist of it, reflects the fact that a very small number of respondents to an online survey of climate-related weblogs (3 out of a sample of 1145) claimed to be climate sceptics who also thought the moon landing was a hoax. The much more robust finding that free-market ideology correlated strongly with climate scepticism was already well known and scarcely warranted reporting. Lewandowsky's ethics clearance, research method and statistical analysis were attacked vociferously by sceptics, who considered that they had been slandered – some identifiably as individuals – by the article. Lewandowsky then published a co-authored article that accused his accusers of confirming his diagnosis of conspiracist ideation. It is beyond our scope and purpose to trace the controversy over 'Recursive Fury: Conspiracist Ideation in the Blogosphere in Response to Research on Conspiracist Ideation'[6] – interested readers can follow the posted links and draw their own conclusions – but it is worth noting that the effect, if not the intention, of the published papers was to portray climate sceptics as a bunch of 'nutters'. In Lewandowsky's work, peer review has a function beyond its practical advantage as the least-worst way to validate research findings by intersubjective means; it also constitutes the ingroup's badge of pride and honour, displayed to antagonize the stigmatized and stereotyped outgroup. Not, for the most part, being academics, the sceptics have no intellectually reputable recourse, and so they resort to complaints and threats of legal action to express their feelings of injustice. The 'conspiracist ideation' Lewandowsky and colleagues diagnosed in their papers might equally be interpreted as the frustration of intelligent, enquiring people who feel they are being insulted from behind the impenetrable wall of an ivory tower. Their rage recalls the Louisianans of Hochman's study, who were all too aware of being patronized, satirized and dishonoured by what she dubs 'blue-state catcalls taunting red-state residents' (23). As obvious as it might seem, conservatives and climate sceptics *know what is said about them*; they, too, are reflexive beings, responding to labels such as Hillary Clinton's notorious denunciation of 'half' of Trump's supporters as a 'basket of deplorables' with predictable resentment, defiance and perverse identification (Charles).

Of course, insult and condemnation may simply be justified; an historian or psychologist who 'stigmatized' the Nazis themselves would scarcely attract censure. But again, the analogy is dangerously imprecise, not only because of the unequivocal evil of German fascism, but because Nazis constitute – as NSDAP party members at least – an historically distinct, self-identified group. We accept political scientists' claim that Western citizens are less polarized in their beliefs than their party affiliations; hence our contribution to debiasing will include refusal of simple dualistic constructs of warmists and sceptics. Homogenizing the latter as deniers, Flat Earthers or even just uniformly 'bonkers' (Monbiot, 'The Semantics of Denial') is as factually inaccurate as it is counter-productive.

Scientists, too, employ stereotypes and pejorative terminology. Stefan Rahmstorf, a leading German climatologist, wrote in a briefing paper:

> The three archetypes of climate sceptics are the Paid Lobbyist (the coal industry, among others, is fighting emission reductions), the Don Quixote (emotionally committed laypeople, frequently pensioners, but also including a few journalists – many of them literally fighting windmills), and the Eccentric Scientist (they are few and far between and are hardly ever climatologists, often coming from related fields like geology).
>
> (79)

Rahmstorf's typology of climate scepticism – of the beliefs sceptics may hold – is discussed below; it is a constructive contribution that enables important discriminations to be made. His 'archetypes', though, are dismissive stereotypes that neither advance the discussion nor permit more sophisticated analysis.

Perhaps we should be more sympathetic to working scientists. Rahmstorf admits to understandable frustration born of long experience of giving reasoned replies to sceptical challenges:

> Many colleagues have responded to e-mail campaigns launched by the sceptics and got involved in extensive technical discussions with them. Most of us have found that factual arguments, even in unequivocal cases, were unable to convince one single climate sceptic. Nevertheless, the sceptics' arguments should be taken seriously and answered. (82)

The present authors have experienced, in a small way, the kind of futile discussions Rahmstorf describes. Major figures in the field, especially those such as Michael Mann and Phil Jones who are vilified by name, report an unceasing torrent of abusive and sometimes threatening emails. In that context, it is not surprising that scientists should not feel indulgent towards the opposition.

There is, though, increasing acceptance of the principled case for closer attention to terminology. For example, an influential paper by William Anderegg et al. demonstrates that the most highly qualified scientists with the strongest publication record are also the most likely to support the conclusions of the IPCC. Although they list 'climate denier' in their keywords and discuss 'climate change skeptics, contrarians, or deniers' (Anderegg et al. 12107) in their introduction, the language used throughout the essay is non-stigmatizing, if dualistic:

> We provide a broad assessment of the relative credibility of researchers convinced by the evidence (CE) of [Anthropogenic Climate Change] and those unconvinced by the evidence (UE) of ACC.

It is not exactly catchy, but 'unconvinced by the evidence' is, as they point out in a later defence of their paper, 'a categorization that is accurate, objective, inherently more neutral in tone, and makes no assumptions about individuals' funding, ideology, or motives' (Anderegg, Prall and Harold E152). In these respects, their terminology is different from almost all other publications in the field.

It is puzzling, therefore, that Saffron O'Neill and Max Boykoff criticize the Anderegg et al. article in a letter to PNAS, when its authors are actually *more careful* than most other social scientists. Even if their target is not the worst offender, we support their overall conclusion:

> The use of the terms skeptic, denier, or contrarian is necessarily subject-, issue-, context-, and intervention-dependent. Blanket labeling of heterogeneous views under one of these headings has been shown to do little to further considerations of climate science and policy. Continued indiscriminate use of the terms will further polarize views on climate change, reduce media coverage to tit-for-tat finger-pointing, and do little to advance the unsteady relationship among climate science, society, and policy.
>
> (O'Neill and Boykoff E151)

Unfortunately, 'UE' is awkward and unfamiliar, and wrongly suggests that, outwith the scientific community itself, acceptance or rejection of evidence is the key to individual beliefs about climate change, so although we acknowledge the objections to the term 'sceptic,' it is the one we use throughout this book because it is non-pejorative and widely recognized. There is, on the other hand, no social science terminology at all for those who consider themselves 'convinced by the evidence', presumably because this reasonable default position is shared by the scholars themselves. Our symmetrical approach rejects the notion of a neutral or invisible position, and so, in the absence of alternatives, we borrow the term 'warmist' from the sceptical community, while recalling that they (we) too are a diverse bunch.[7] Clearly *any* terminology could be regarded as reinforcing the very duality we set out to challenge, but given that we will need to make generalizations, we chose to use friendly and accepted terms.

What do we know about climate scepticism?

To a first approximation, you can probably predict the portrait of climate sceptics that emerges from the academic literature: they are angry conservative white men, middle-aged or older, whose ideas are derived from a small number of conservative think tanks funded by fossil fuel interests. As Aaron McCright and Riley Dunlap, the leading social science researchers in the field, observe:

> Even casual observers of denialist activities likely notice an obvious pattern; with rare exceptions (e.g., Sallie Baliunas), the most prominent denialists are conservative white males.
>
> ('Cool Dudes' 1163)

A large-scale analysis by Min Zhou of a 2010 data set of 45,119 individuals from thirty-two countries (in relation to 'environmental scepticism' rather than climate scepticism *per se*) uses statistical modelling to test relationships between a wide range of variables. In particular, Zhou asks whether broad country- or 'macro-level' characteristics, such as overall affluence or tangible environmental problems, correlate with environmental scepticism, or whether the characteristics of individuals matter more:

> The knowledge deficit perspective argues that environmental skepticism stems from ignorance and lack of scientific knowledge. The cultural orientation perspective emphasizes the role of individuals' fundamental cultural orientations (such as religiosity and political ideology) in shaping their levels of environmental skepticism. The social trust perspective views environmental skepticism as a result of people's general distrust of social institutions. The competing priority perspective suggests that when facing more salient risks other than environmental threats, people tend to employ skepticism as a mechanism to justify the lower priority assigned to the environment.
>
> (62)

Zhou's analysis is impressively complex – he tests a total of thirteen hypotheses – but the short answer is that macro-level country characteristics do not have a statistically significant relationship to environmental scepticism, whereas demographic differences do: men are consistently more likely to be sceptical than women; old people are more sceptical than young; rural residents are more sceptical than city-dwellers. Moreover, individual-level characteristics are also significant: people are more likely to be sceptical if they are religious, conservative, poorly educated, mistrustful of science and society, and lacking in self-assessed knowledge of environmental issues. Income level alone is not significant.

Thus far, the stereotype is confirmed, as one might expect – stereotypes are exaggerated and reified versions of observable differences; otherwise, they would be completely dysfunctional in social cognition – but Zhou adds a crucial qualification:

> While none of the specified country-level variables have statistically significant effects, there is indeed cross-country variation in environmental skepticism .... This cross-country variation may be due to unique historical and cultural contexts of individual countries, and cannot be simply attributed to national differences in affluence, world society connections, ecological conditions, and levels of democracy. (73)

Why does Canada have the lowest overall level of environmental scepticism in its study, and the Philippines the highest? Since broad variables do not account for it, scholarship ought to elucidate the 'unique historical and cultural contexts of individual countries'. Until the present study, research into climate scepticism has not done so.

The findings of another cross-national study, this time examining climate scepticism specifically and drawing on an International Social Survey of fourteen countries, are somewhat at variance with Zhou. Bruce Tranter and Kate Booth are surprised to find that 'climate sceptics are not merely those who care little about the environment' (Tranter and Booth 159), which perhaps accounts for the difference – Zhou's paper studies the latter. They find that 'age is not a particularly consistent predictor of climate scepticism, nor it appears is education, city location, religious orientation or postmaterial values' (161). Like Zhou, they conclude:

> The association between political parties on the left of the political spectrum is a far more consistent indicator of environmental concern, while in all countries with the exception of Australia, self-assessed knowledge of the

> solutions to environmental problems is associated with increased concern over environmental issues. (160)

So although political orientation, gender and indifference to environmental issues are 'relatively consistent predictors of climate scepticism on a country by country basis' (162), Tranter and Booth too acknowledge the limitations of population-level analysis:

> The factors that correlate with climate scepticism appear to vary according to the political and cultural context of each country. Contrary to expectations, climate sceptics are not merely the mirror image of environmentalists. (162)

While it is not a statistical analysis, our transnational research elaborates the 'political and cultural context' of four countries and re-affirms that anti-environmentalism in each of them has a history and cultural logic that is not merely the inverse of the history of environmentalism. Moreover, a few of the sceptics in our study, like Peter Taylor in the UK and Claude Allègre in France, even have impressive pro-environmental credentials.

Climate scepticism is, however, a minority viewpoint everywhere. Tranter and Booth find climate scepticism ranges from 2 per cent of their Spanish sample and 4 per cent of their Swiss sample to 12 per cent in the United States, 15 per cent in Norway and 17 per cent in Australia. One might observe that the latter three are all major fossil fuel producers, but then so is Canada with a prevalence of just 8 per cent. Anthony Leiserowitz's review of global opinion surveys finds that:

> Large majorities worldwide believe that human activities are a significant cause of climate change, yet many continue to confuse and conflate global warming with depletion of the ozone layer, which in turn leads many to support ineffectual solutions, such as the banning of aerosol spray cans. However, respondents from Europe, India, China and many developing countries are significantly more convinced that human activities are causing climate change than respondents from the United States. In turn, large majorities worldwide appear to prefer a precautionary approach, agreeing that action is needed now, even if there are major economic costs involved.
>
> (35)

Climate change is, on the whole, a poorly understood source of moderate concern for the majority of people surveyed, but there are substantial cross-national differences about which very little is known. There are, after all, plenty of conservative white men in Canada and Germany, but they are less often climate sceptics. It should also be noted that Leiserowitz finds that global warming is 'a relatively low priority compared to other pressing world, national, or even other environmental issues'.

The United States consistently ranks high in international surveys of climate scepticism. The most frequent explanation for this American exceptionalism is that the US conservative movement identified the threat from climate science and politics to free-market, fossil-fuelled capitalism in the early 1990s, and mobilized against it rapidly and successfully, as Boussalis and Coan argue:

> Specifically, extant literature suggests the following process: (1) conservative foundations and corporate groups provide the material base for pressing contrarian interests ...; (2) CTTs [Conservative Think Tanks] transform this material base into information, generating the narrative of climate denial ...; (3) the conservative 'echo chamber' – conservative media, sceptical blogs, and sympathetic policy makers – mediate and amplify key counterclaims ...; and (4) conservative politicians susceptible to the anti-climate messages seek to stymie policy changes in Congress.
>
> (90)

Various elements of this sequence can be traced in many scholarly articles and books on climate scepticism (McCright and Dunlap 'Challenging Global Warming'; McCright and Dunlap 'Anti-Reflexivity'; Dunlap and McCright; Washington and Cook). For example, a predecessor to the present analysis that surveys 108 books on climate scepticism refrains from engaging with any one of them *as a text* (Dunlap and Jacques). Instead, the article investigates links, on the part of either the author or the publisher, with such organizations as the Cato Institute, the Heartland Institute, the Marshall Institute and the British Institute of Economic Affairs, finding that '72% [of 108 books in total] have a verifiable link with a CTT' (705). Dunlap and Jacques note, moreover, two significant forms of diffusion from the original concentration of books published by American CTTs: climate scepticism is now published in 'nations that have a recent history of staunch conservative governments, influential CTTs, and a strong fossil fuels sector [such as] Canada, Australia, and the United Kingdom', and there are increasing numbers of 'citizen scientists' as well as industry-funded spokespersons involved:

> As denial evolved over time and spread throughout a larger segment of American society ..., as well as to other nations, the seeds sown by the contrarians have germinated and a wide range of individuals without backgrounds in natural science and thus relevant credentials for evaluating climate science feel free to write books denying AGW – and often publish them on their own!
>
> (712)

According to their analysis of the terminal degrees of authors, 'only 39% of ... volumes are authored or edited by individuals with scientific credentials as normally defined in academic circles' (i.e. PhD in a natural science) while '19% of the books are produced by individuals with other doctorates, primarily in economics, politics, and law, and the remaining 42% by individuals without a doctorate' (711). Perish the thought! A little later, Dunlap and Jacques sniff that 'not a single denial book is published by a university press' (712) – although some sceptics would consider that *prima facie* evidence that the liberal academy has already made up its mind about climate change, which is largely true.

We need to go carefully here, as there are complex issues at stake. For one thing, peer review is not perfect. Indeed, it may be compared to democracy, which Winston Churchill called 'the worst form of Government except for all those other forms that have been tried from time to time' ('Democracy'). Peer review (or 'mates review', as it is known among British sceptics) is subject to numerous potential distortions, but Dunlap and Jacques are correct to point out that it is reasonably effective at preventing egregious errors from circulating. In the sceptical literature, as they observe, 'denial claims are continually recycled, no matter how many times they are refuted by empirical test or shown to be logically untenable' (712). Moreover, the present authors know too well that university positions are competitive and academic expertise hard-won, so it can be galling when the views of CTT spokespersons, auto-didacts and ill-informed non-specialists are taken as seriously as those of fellow scholars. In the United States, in particular, CTTs have largely accomplished their core purpose, as Jacques, Dunlap and Freeman acknowledge:

> A key to the success of CTTs has been their ability to establish themselves as a true 'counter-intelligentsia' that has achieved equal legitimacy with mainstream science and academia – both of which have been effectively labelled as 'leftist' in order to legitimise CTT's as providing 'balance'.
>
> (356)

At the same time, sceptical objections to peer review are not without grounds and conservatives are correct to perceive 'liberal bias' in universities. To take just one striking example, there are numerous studies of climate scepticism in social science, but no studies at all of 'alarmists' who arguably exaggerate the risks of climate change – sometimes to an absurd degree (e.g. Oreskes and Conway *The Collapse of Western Civilization*). In this respect, the situation resembles the field of political psychology, which tends to pathologize conservativism, as Haidt points out:

> The goal of so much research was to explain what was wrong with conservatives. (Why don't conservatives embrace equality, diversity, and change, like normal people?)
>
> (185)

Furthermore, scepticism represents a challenge to the 'scientification' of climate change that is, in some respects at least, quite welcome. We return to these thorny issues of expertise and the democratization of knowledge in the penultimate chapter and conclusion.

The most influential research on climate scepticism locates its origins in a conspiracy of industrial interests and CTTs (Washington and Cook; Jacques, Dunlap and Freeman; McCright and Dunlap 'Anti-Reflexivity'; Boussalis and Coan; Hoggan and Littlemore). Historians Naomi Oreskes and Erick M. Conway had particular success with their book and documentary film, both entitled *Merchants of Doubt*, which identify the strategies and the specific personnel involved in decades of conservative activism against environmentalist and public health movements. According to their well-argued narrative, marketing methods were developed from the 1960s onwards to help the tobacco industry stave off regulation, increased taxation and legal liability once medical evidence began to accumulate that cigarettes caused cancer and heart disease. The tobacco companies learned, with the help of their 'Mad Men', to sow doubt in the mind of the public about the link between smoking and early death:

> This was the tobacco industry's key insight: that you could use normal scientific uncertainty to undermine the status of actual scientific knowledge. As in jujitsu, you could use science against itself. 'Doubt is our product,' ran the infamous memo written by one tobacco company executive in 1969, 'since it is the best means of competing with the "body of fact" that exists in the minds of the general public'.
>
> (*Merchants of Doubt* 34)

The strategy was extraordinarily successful: not only did smokers have a vested interest in ignoring inconvenient truths, but the conventional news media felt obliged to present 'both sides' of any story, regardless of the real balance of scientific evidence. TV viewers saw scientists arguing with other (industry-funded) scientists, and thought the medical case remained controversial. It was only when whistle-blowers from within the industry started leaking documents proving deliberate mendacity that the defence was finally destroyed.

A very similar strategy was used to attack climate science, but with two significant updates: the counter-arguments now came from CTT 'experts', not from talking heads in white coats who could easily be seen as industry stooges, and the CTTs also fomented vicious campaigns against individual climate scientists. The most remarkable sequence in the documentary of *Merchants of Doubt* is an interview with journalist Marc Morano, currently Communications Director for the conservative lobby group Committee for a Constructive Tomorrow (CFACT) but previously a producer for the right-wing talk radio host Rush Limbaugh. He acknowledges with pride that the sceptical team working for James Inhofe, a Republican senator from Oklahoma, decided to attack the scientists personally, rather than entering the scientific debate:

> We went after James Hansen and Michael Oppenheimer and had a lot of fun with it. We mocked and ridiculed James Hansen. I was authorized – I couldn't believe they let me do this – I did a two-part, probably 10,000 word, unbelievably scathing critique on James Hansen. I'm not going to question his scientific work, but in terms of his influencing the public.

Eventually Morano set up ClimateDepot.com so that he could be even *less* constrained in his personal attacks on climate scientists.

Morano relishes his reputation as the climate sceptics' 'attack dog' and is unrepentant about publishing scientists' email addresses so that right-wing trolls can send them obscene and threatening emails. And he is just one, particularly prolific and articulate, operative. Oreskes, Conway, Washington, Cook and other academics and journalists have gathered plentiful evidence of deliberate attacks on scientists: not only *ad hominem* articles and email campaigns, but spurious Freedom of Information requests, attempts to have academics sacked or defunded and of course the email hacking attack that gave rise to 'Climategate'. By sponsoring such tactics, CTTs threaten academic freedom and poison public political discourse. Our analysis is not naïve about this reality, and our efforts to understand climate scepticism don't imply that we condone it.

However, the deepest objection to *ad hominem* arguments is not that they are cruel or unfair or even, potentially, incitements to physical violence; it is that they are redundant. All human beings have interests, material and otherwise, that potentially affect their selection and acceptance of relevant evidence; no one is exempt from motivated reasoning. Just as Oreskes and Conway cast doubt on Fred Singer's statements by showing he was funded by Big Oil, climate sceptics claim that climate scientists' arguments are shaped by the interests of 'Big Eco' and the priorities of liberal-biased funding agencies. While the present authors do not accept that these are precisely symmetrical situations, we resist invoking *ad hominem* arguments against the sceptics in this book because they are, finally, irrelevant.

Much academic research on climate scepticism unveils the conservative conspiracy to undermine the scientific consensus or pathologizes and stigmatizes sceptics. There are, though, a number of useful typologies that apply to the beliefs sceptics hold, rather than their political affiliations. The first comes from Stefan Rahmstorf:

> We can distinguish trend sceptics (who deny there is global warming), the attribution sceptics (who accept the global warming trend but see natural causes for this), and the impact sceptics (who think global warming is harmless or even beneficial). Representatives of the various sceptics' camps quarrel, sometimes ferociously, in internet forums.
>
> (77)

Opinion surveys that have sought to distinguish between these different brands of climate scepticism have found that 'impact scepticism appears far more common than both trend and attribution scepticism' (Poortinga et al. 1019), which suggests a basic rationality to public opinions – the long-term impacts of climate change are indeed much less certain than the existence of the warming trend and its attribution to predominantly human influences. However, contrary to Rahmstorf's view, Poortinga et al. found that these were not wholly independent views, and that 'people who are sceptical about one aspect of climate change also tend to be sceptical about other aspects' (1019). For Bob Henson, the three beliefs are part of a series of fall-back positions he outlines in a satirical summary of 'the classic sceptical view':

> *The atmosphere isn't warming; and if it is, then it's due to natural variations; and even if it's not due to natural variation, then the amount of warming will be insignificant; and if it becomes significant, then the benefits will outweigh the problems; and even if they don't, technology will come to the rescue; and even if it doesn't, we shouldn't wreck the economy to fix the problem when many parts of the science are uncertain.*
>
> (272, italics in original)

While this probably does epitomize the strategy of a CTT such as the Heartland Institute, it does not capture the diversity of sceptical viewpoints we have found. The texts we analyse incorporate a wide array of claims, some admittedly consistent across several sources, but many quite idiosyncratic. Moreover, we find that scepticism means somewhat different things in the four countries we study. In the United States, climate science attracts the conspiracist language of 'hoax,' whereas in the UK, where there is cross-party support for the IPCC process, sceptics see themselves as 'heretics' resisting an overweening orthodoxy.

German climate sceptics frequently adopt a similar rhetoric, albeit with a Lutheran spin, while in France, the term 'imposture' is used by critics who claim to be following in the great tradition of French philosophical rationalism by revealing the 'untruths' of climate change science.

As population-level research on climate scepticism has accumulated, there has been a proliferation of scholarly terminology. Indeed, James Painter wryly suggests, 'Discussion about the typology of scepticism has generated such a large amount of analysis by climate scientists, sociologists, and media academics that a cynic would say we need a new typology of typologies' (*Poles Apart* 20). Painter himself added 'policy sceptics', such as Nigel Lawson and Bjørn Lomborg (Painter 'Communicating Uncertainties'), who claim not to challenge the scientific consensus itself, but question environmentalists' policy prescriptions. *Living in Denial*, Kari Norgaard's ethnography of a Norwegian town (fictionalized as 'Bygdaby'), derives a related category of 'implicatory denial' from the sociologist Stanley Cohen, in which what is denied is not the literal truth of climate change, but a minimization of the potential implications for most Western lifestyles. Norgaard mournfully acknowledges:

> What I observed in Bygdaby – indeed, what we all can observe in the public silence on climate change in the United States and around the world – is not in most cases a rejection of information per se, but the failure to integrate this knowledge into everyday life or to transform it into social action.
>
> (loc. 277)

Some scholars seek to categorize discourses, rather than beliefs or opinions, such as Nat Segnit and Gill Ereault, whose study of British sceptical discourses is discussed in the UK chapter. Kersty Hobson and Simon Niemeyer derive a five-way typology from their analysis of respondents' scripts during an extended process of deliberative democracy in Australia, including emphatic negation, unperturbed pragmatism, earnest acclimatization, noncommittal consent and the nigh-oxymoronic proactive uncertainty (402). Stuart Capstick and Nicholas Pidgeon's mixed methods study of the UK public subsumes Rahmstorf's trend-attribution-impact typology under the heading of 'epistemic scepticism', along with doubts about scientific propriety and the workings of the IPCC. It goes on to define 'response scepticism', which combines Painter and Norgaard's observations with 'doubts around human nature and the human condition' (Capstick and Pidgeon 391) that have long been recognized in cultural theory of risk as the signature of the fatalist (Adams 167–68). They also take note of scepticism about the way climate change is communicated in the media, and 'climate change fatigue' ('you know: "oh god, not another polar bear"' [394]), which is no doubt salient in popular response scepticism if not likely to feature in sceptical publications. Finally, Willem van Rensburg suggests reorganization of the phenomena into three categories: evidence, process and response. The first type of scepticism is '*core* and *definitional*' – anyone who refuses to accept the scientific evidence is a sceptic by definition – whereas the latter two are 'the concomitant class of critiques that are highly congruent with and supportive of evidence scepticism' (Van Rensburg 6). As he points out, neither Mike Hulme nor Naomi Klein are evidence sceptics, but they have expressed scepticism about the IPCC process and the neoliberal political response to climate change, respectively.

The development and refinement of such typologies is obviously helpful for understanding climate scepticism at the level of national populations and media ecosystems. At the same time, it contrasts strikingly with the paucity of academic taxonomizing of the other side (warmists? catastrophists? Elon Musk-eteers?), despite the diversity of discourse and belief that lies there too. More importantly, the typological approach itself risks masking the complex reality admitted by Hobson and Niemeyer, whose five discourses were derived from close interaction with thirty-five individuals: with a few exceptions, 'mapping specific individuals onto each category proved infeasible, as many had a mix of viewpoints and were thus spread across several categories' (Hobson and Niemeyer 402). They go on to question whether the five sceptical discourses they identify are applicable beyond Australia, where there is a Climate Sceptics Party and sceptical conservative newspapers, and where leading politicians frequently question climate science. While our literary critical methodology renders us unable to answer that particular question – most of our authors are Emphatic Negators who betray little vacillation or ambivalence – it is important to recall that, for climate change as for other political differences, the sound and fury of polarization drown out enormous inner turmoil as well as effacing individual diversity. We therefore return, in the final subsection of the Introduction, to the rationale for a consciously individualizing approach to climate sceptical texts.

Counteracting cultural polarization

We have already encountered social science scholarship that acknowledges the heterogeneity of climate scepticism and the importance of cultural differences, but then adopts a statistical, population-level methodology that suppresses the first and gives no account of the second. This is not a criticism; it is simply the way social science research is usually conducted. Moreover, scholars frequently admit the limitation: in addition to the examples already given, Boussalis and Coan accept that 'aggregating across diverse science and political themes [using a text-mining methodology] masks important heterogeneity in sceptical discourse' (97). It does, though, suggest there is a need for qualitative analysis that is at once *rougher and finer-grained* than quantitative research: transnational, so that broad cultural differences can be assessed at that level, and at the same time open to the diversity and singularity of individual sceptical texts.

Such an approach is far from usual in ecocriticism, not only because it considers anti-environmentalist artefacts, but because it seeks to compare cultural differences in environmental risk perception between four different countries. In that sense, we engage self-consciously with what Timothy Clark calls the 'methodological nationalism' of ecocriticism: 'Methodological nationalism names the assumption, usually implicit but all-pervading in many critical readings, that the nation-state and its boundaries form a natural or at least self-evidently justified context for discussion of the literary and cultural artefacts that arise within its borders' (Clark 54–5). While ecocritics frequently work across a range of 'national' literatures, especially those with postcolonial interests, many are constrained by linguistic ability and the professional demands of academia to effective nationalism (or Anglophonia, at best). Besides two of the present authors, critics such as Clark, Hannes Bergthaller, Kate Rigby and Ursula Heise who are able to undertake genuinely bilingual ecocriticism – all of it Anglo-Germanic, in the instances given – are few and far between. In some ways, then, the organization of our analysis reflects the outmoded assumption that Britain, France, Germany and the United States form, jointly and severally, a 'justified context' for discussion of the texts we have chosen; we suspect that French rationalist and eco-sceptical traditions, the 'paranoid style in American politics' (Hofstadter), British irreverence and hyperbolic comedy, and the centrality of environmentalism to contemporary German identity are vital to comprehending the distinctive forms that scepticism takes in those countries. At the same time, though, we opted to co-author this book because national boundaries are not 'self-evidently' justified. As Sheila Jasanoff acknowledges, 'Some will charge that cross-*national* comparison, in particular, is full of intellectual dangers: it reifies national boundaries, overlooks heterogeneity and change, and perhaps even reinforces parochial stereotypes of national identity' (11). Our treatments of each national culture of climate scepticism are designed, like Jasanoff's transnational analysis in *Designs on Nature*, 'to bring into sharper relief its … heterogeneity, especially as displayed in its multifaceted, culturally differentiated encounters with science and technology.' Moreover, we will identify global commonalities and cultural differences in light of the variable extent to which organized scepticism has served as a transnational counter-movement to global environmentalism.

It remains only to recall how and why our 'methodological transnationalism' seeks to use close reading and perspective-taking to counteract polarizing stereotypes. The trend away from bipartisan consensus on climate change is clear. Indeed, it is arguable that *politicizing climate change* – representing it consistently *as* a partisan issue – has been at least as important to CTTs in the United States and the UK as casting doubt on the science. Their efforts, lately reinforced by leftists' adoption of the issue precisely *as* a challenge to capitalism (Klein), have been remarkably successful. In the United States, McCright and Dunlap report:

> The 18-point difference between the percent of liberals (67.1 percent) and the percent of conservatives (49.4 percent) who believe global warming has already begun in 2001 becomes a 44-point difference in 2010–74.8 percent for liberals and 30.2 percent for conservatives. A similar trend exists for party identification, as the gap between Democrats and Republicans grows from 11 percent to 41 percent over the decade.
>
> ('The Politicization of Climate Change' 175)

Dunlap and McCright's finding is replicated in research on the UK (Poortinga et al.), whereas polarization is less pronounced in non-Anglophone populations. Still, scholars such as Guillemot and Aykut betray an awareness of the risk when they seek to use Science and Technology Studies to pre-empt a 'bipolar climate' in France. Andrew Hoffman argues that, in the United States at least, climate change is approaching what he calls 'logic schism':

> A contest … in which opposing sides are debating different issues, seeking only information that supports their position and disconfirms their opponents' arguments. Each side views the other with suspicion, even demonizing the other, leading to a strong resistance to any form of engagement, much less negotiation and concession.
>
> (9)

He suggests that 'the debate is reaching a level of polarization where one might begin to question whether meaningful dialogue and problem solving has become unavailable to participants' (3). If he is correct, our attempt at a depolarizing analysis may be too late.

Admittedly, our correspondent who discerned a change in the colour of the sun was uninterested in any counter-evidence, and Hobson and Niemeyer's experiment showed that some Emphatic Negators were not open to reasoned discussion – but they were 2 participants out of a study group of 103. McCright and Dunlap's study evidences a growing gap between liberals and conservatives (ideological polarization) and Democrats and Republicans (partisan polarization), accelerating strikingly after 2008, but around one-third of Republicans accepted the science of climate change all along and they found no discernible trend in moderate opinion on climate change. McCright and Dunlap acknowledge that polarization over time might be evidence of party and ideological sorting, rather than change in fundamental beliefs about climate science. In other words, accepting or rejecting the scientific consensus, especially on an issue seen as a low priority by many citizens, becomes simply 'the kind of thing people like us do'.

Perhaps contemporary anxieties – about Donald Trump, about so-called 'social' media – are motivating nostalgia for a lost golden age of consensus and mutual respect that careful historical perspective would dismiss. America, Germany and France in the late 1960s, or 1970s Britain, were very far from polite or harmonious: the Red Army Faction's seven-year campaign of terror took 47 lives in Germany, while the Provisional IRA's war with Ulster Unionists and the British state killed at least 3,600 from 1970 to 1997. There is evidence of growing polarization of opinion on climate change in the twenty-first century, but differing views seem to have no relationship to individuals' carbon emissions at the population level; instead, higher emissions are closely associated with greater wealth and the country, province or state of one's residence. The appearance of a 'culture war', when diverse, largely moderate, opinions remain the norm, is sustained by the political stereotypes that prevail within the ideological filter bubble each of us inhabits.

Climate change already poses an inherent challenge for what psychologist Dylan Evans calls our 'risk intelligence', because of the substantial scientific uncertainty and dizzying temporal and spatial scale of its possible impacts. As he points out:

> It is hard to occupy the middle ground, treating global warming as a serious threat but without freaking out about it. Once we allow ourselves to start contemplating it at all, our minds quickly become overwhelmed.
>
> (57)

Warmists have, as sceptics never fail to observe, a penchant for worst-case thinking, which tends, Evans says, to 'substitute imagination for thinking, speculation for risk analysis, and fear for reason'. The ability to estimate climatic risks is further debilitated by the filter bubble that most internet users increasingly inhabit, which sustains our stereotypes of the enemy without. Evans relates how, in the aftermath of the Iraq War, he realized that he inhabited a liberal filter bubble, and so decided to seek out contrary views deliberately. Reading Donald Rumsfeld's autobiography and listening to conservative talk radio (extensively, not just the 'embarrassing sound bites' played by the liberal media), he was forced to question his simplistic assumptions. 'It is essential to retain a healthy degree of skepticism', Evans admits, 'but such skepticism should be applied impartially to those from all sections of the political spectrum and not reserved exclusively for those we disagree with' (91).

Ecocriticism itself is a filter bubble. If you research 'climate fiction', you will read dozens of novels that endorse or (more usually) exaggerate the IPCC consensus; you *might* read one – Michael Crichton's *State of Fear* – that contradicts it, and you will probably not think highly of it. Students occasionally venture sceptical opinions, but most keep silent out of rational self-preservation. Why challenge the deeply held beliefs of the person who is grading you, after all? If your social circles are largely liberal and educated, it is easy to underestimate how widespread climate scepticism actually is, and hard to understand why anyone would endorse it.

In that context, it is all the more urgent to ask: 'Who do climate sceptics think they are?' Not only can questioning climate sceptic stereotypes contribute to depolarizing the debate in the interests of democratic progress; it can help recalibrate climatic risk intelligence, it can diversify the voices heard at environmental debates, and it can promote the art of perspective-taking.

We are more various than we know.

2

Climate Scepticism in the UK

Greg Garrard

Before embarking on a detailed analysis of sceptical British texts, I will provide some historical and scholarly context. There have been many studies of anti-environmentalism in the United States (Helvarg; Brick; Ehrlich and Ehrlich; Switzer) and one on the global 'backlash' (Rowell), but none focuses exclusively on the UK. The sole treatment of anti-environmentalism within ecocriticism comes from the United States (Buell), just like the various exposés of climate scepticism discussed in the Introduction. As this chapter will show, British climate scepticism is possessed of a prehistory and some distinctive local features that reward closer inspection.

Nevertheless, the Anglo-American axis of organized anti-environmentalism is obvious: British climate sceptics such as Christopher Monckton, James Delingpole and Nigel Lawson are darlings of the American conservative think tanks (CTTs) that promulgate sceptical perspectives, while Martin Durkin's *The Great Global Warming Swindle* (2007), a British documentary shown on Channel 4, includes interviews with Richard Lindzen, Patrick Michaels and Fred Singer, all prominent American sceptics. *Energy and Climate Wars* (2010) (Glover and Economides) exemplifies this axis: it is a laboured, derivative defence of the fossil fuel industry co-authored by a British journalist and an American petroleum engineer. It wears its Heartland Institute affiliations on its sleeve, with three back cover blurbs from international oil men. Apart from a few embarrassing attempts at satire and some disconcerting evidence of radical Catholic conservatism, it conforms point for point to the environmentalist stereotype of the Anglo-American industry shill.

Glover and Economides are conservative white men, in keeping with the existing research on climate scepticism; if I qualify the stereotype further with 'anglophone', it will encompass almost all of the authors addressed in this chapter. Within that superficial homogeneity, though, we will encounter a globally popular motoring journalist who baits environmentalist 'carborexics', a Kuhnian philosopher of science who laments the effect of climate activism on conservation, a leading comic playwright whose satire of climate orthodoxy brilliantly skewers British university culture and a theologian-biologist who claims God causes climate change (and evolution) by triggering supernovas. Climate scepticism in the UK might seem all too familiar to interested observers, but is, in reality, considerably richer and stranger than might be assumed.

The prehistory of anti-environmentalism in the UK

Noting that there is no extant history of opposition to environmentalism in the UK, the next thing to say is that it would, if it existed, be more than just the inverse of the history of environmentalist thought and activism; just as 'environmentalism' in the UK is a complex, shifting, internally conflicted phenomenon, so is resistance to it, with strands that have their own internal logics, rather than being exclusively reactive. Farming and industrial interests have always featured in debates about conservation and pollution control measures in Britain, but they have seldom spoken with one voice. The situation is akin to that in the United States, as described by Jacqueline Vaughn Switzer:

> Despite the attempts by journalists and environmental group leaders to portray the environmental opposition [in the United States] in the most negative of possible lights, the 'enemy' is not nearly as powerful or monolithic a foe as they would like the public to believe. The environmental opposition suffers from a lack of cohesiveness among its myriad groups, a lack of resources with which to mobilize its members or influence policy, the absence of an articulated policy program, and the countervailing forces of public opinion.
>
> (275)

At the time of writing, with President Donald Trump in the White House and fossil fuel money ($889 million in 2016 from the Koch brothers alone (Mayer)) continuing to cascade through the American political system, I would want to qualify or reject at least one of those conclusions. Even so, Switzer's ethnographic approach, like that of Arlie Russell Hochschild's *Strangers in Their Own Land* (2016), effectively demonstrates her contention that 'the environmental opposition is made up of a much broader constituency than has generally been identified' (14).

In British history, too, 'businesses' demands are highly individualized and fragmented. While some coalitions have been forged, disputes over clean air or water legislation often pit one industry against another, with little agreement on the appropriate path of redress' (Switzer 284). The British experience is different from the American because the political system, lacking checks and balances on executive power, typically seeks compromise between competing interest groups, and because, until the advent of Tony Blair's 'New Labour' in the mid-1990s, environmentalism was attacked by both the pro-business right and the pro-union left. Environmental charities had many members but little sustained political clout through most of the twentieth century. It was the growing influence of the European Union that transformed environmental politics in the UK, greatly strengthening the green movement but also eliciting new forms of resistance.

This chapter surveys the development of anti-environmentalism at three key moments in British political history: the origins of the 'Back to Nature' movement in the 1880s; the Clean Air Act of 1956; and the apparent 'greening' of Margaret Thatcher's government between the 1981 Wildlife and Countryside Act and the First Assessment Report of the Intergovernmental Panel on Climate Change (IPCC) in 1990. The backstory contextualizes the most consistent feature of British climate sceptics' identities: as 'heretics' contesting an oppressive politico-scientific orthodoxy. First, though, it is worth asking how British climate scepticism came by its unmistakable tone of sneering ridicule, which, despite much variation in sophistication and effectiveness, is arguably its other characteristic feature. French, German and American sceptics employ comic modes too, of course, but for British writers, scorn and satire are the keynotes.

Love of nature has seemed widely admirable in Britain since the advent of Romanticism in the second half of the eighteenth century; it has seemed laughable for almost as long. Jonathan Bate argues that 'the origins of the conservation movement may be traced back to the principles of picturesque tourism' (*The Song of the Earth* 132). Thomas Gilpin's essays, in particular, provided an aesthetic framework that gave shape to Romantic-period poetry, painting and tourism guidebooks. William Wordsworth opposed mass tourism in the Lake District, but he also profited from it with healthy sales of his *Guide to the Lakes*, which was, according to Bate, 'without question the most widely read work of the most admired English poet of the first half of the nineteenth century' (*Romantic Ecology* 41). Much later, the picturesque informed the creation of the first national parks, with their physical infrastructure of paths leading to vistas, and even, in the United States, the construction of scenic highways, or 'Parkways' (Wilson 32–37). As soon as the picturesque was codified its strictures were mocked by satirical poets, novelists and illustrators.

Wordsworth was the perfect butt for such jokes, despite his attempts to complicate the picturesque and extend its moral range, because his poetry is short on humour and long on elevated reflections. George Gordon, Lord Byron, found fame with *Childe Harold's Pilgrimage*, which inspired its own bout of picturesque tourism. Nevertheless, Byron brilliantly satirizes Romantic 'self-communion' in stanzas 90–96 of the first canto of *Don Juan*, where Juan wanders 'by the glassy brooks/Thinking unutterable things' (Ferguson, Salter and Stallworthy 856) in a desperate – and ultimately futile – attempt to sublimate his desire for the married Donna Julia. For Byron's sardonic narrator, nature functions as a temporary distraction for a lovesick teenager, as well as a handy source of imagery for writers:

> There poets find materials for their books,
> And every now and then we read them through,
> So that their plan and prosody are eligible,
> Unless, like Wordsworth, they prove unintelligible.

Every time Juan's reflections threaten to soar away into 'Longings sublime, and aspirations high' in the sestet of Byron's *ottava rima*, they are brought crashing down to earth in the concluding couplet: 'If you think 'twas Philosophy that this did,/I can't help thinking puberty assisted.' Byron, having invented for his own use and benefit the Romantic persona of the brilliant, brooding, damaged hero, conjured another perennial figure in his caricature of Wordsworth as the idealistic, abstruse, humourless, self-denying nature lover who is, above all, in need of a good shag.

Wordsworthian Romanticism is targeted again in Oscar Wilde's 1891 diatribe against literary realism in 'The Decay of Lying'. Wilde's spokesman Vivian comments:

> Wordsworth went to the lakes, but he was never a lake poet. He found in stones the sermons he had already hidden there. He went moralizing about the district, but his good work was produced when he returned, not to Nature but to poetry.

Wilde repeats Byron's claim of unacknowledged egotism and adds a further complaint against Wordsworth's habit of conjoining extensive 'moralizing' with tediously quotidian subject matter – such as 'the address to Mr Wilkinson's spade', says Vivian. Wilde's residual respect for Wordsworth as a poet is outweighed by his campy scorn for the bad Wordsworth, the green Wordsworth, who exemplifies foolish idealization of Nature and maintains a lamentable attachment to mere facts.

Vivian, by contrast, proclaims his emancipation from enjoyment of Nature, which he castigates for her 'lack of design, her curious crudities, her extraordinary monotony, her absolutely unfinished condition.' In this respect, if no other, Wilde's character was echoed by Ronald Reagan, who asked, in response to a proposal to create a Redwood National Park in California: 'A tree is a tree. How many more do you have to look at?' ('FACT CHECK: Ronald Reagan "If You've Seen One Tree … "'). According to Vivian, only Art can redeem Nature by rounding off its rough edges and, more importantly, restoring our proper sense of egotism. While only a few climate sceptics would extol Art for its capacity to liberate us from Nature – their protestations about 'truth' and 'evidence' would only prove to Vivian their lack of style and imagination – James Delingpole and Christopher Booker deny that climate 'alarmism' is founded in science in the first place. In their view, examined in more detail below, prior commitment to a certain kind of *story* about Nature distorts environmentalists' sense of reality. Or as Vivian puts it,

> Where, if not from the Impressionists, do we get those wonderful brown fogs that come creeping down our streets, blurring the gas-lamps and changing the houses into monstrous shadows? … Nature is no great mother who has borne us. She is our creation. It is in our brain that she quickens to life. Things are because we see them, and what we see, and how we see it, depends on the Arts that have influenced us.
>
> (12)

'The Decay of Lying' was published not long after the first manifestations of what we now call 'green politics' in the UK. The most enduring legacy of the period, *News from Nowhere* (1890) by the writer, designer and socialist William Morris, epitomizes a moment in the history of the British left when the misery of the working class was clearly articulated in environmental, as well as economic, terms. Morris's pastoral utopia was written in the aftermath of the 1888 'matchgirls strike' at Bryant and May in the East End of London, which might reasonably be considered the first gesture of environmental justice activism in British political history. Morris was more directly provoked, however, by the publication of *Looking Backward* (1887) by the American socialist Edward Bellamy.

Bellamy's utopian novel had an enormous impact in socialist circles. Set in the year 2000, it depicts a technological New Jerusalem, an empire of machinery in the service of Reason, with a planned economy implemented by a united industrial army. Morris shared Bellamy's concern for working-class living conditions and admired his vision of communal ownership, but quailed before its total rationalization of both humanity and nature: a 'machine-life … on all sides' (Morris 357) in which neither the quality of labour nor its relation to the natural world would change, but only the quantity of work, which machines will reduce. Morris believed that 'the multiplication of machinery will just – multiply machinery', and that only an anarcho-communist society could liberate both humanity and nature from the tyranny of industrial capitalism. In *News from Nowhere*, he set out to depict such a society, using Bellamy's 'dreamer wakes' device to put his own protagonist, William Guest, in the pastoralized English 'Nowhere' of 2102.

Despite the general holiday atmosphere and unfeasibly good weather, Morris's utopia remains a trenchant critique of the oppression of both humans and nature under industrial capitalism. The utopian Ellen, for example, with whom Guest falls in love, is mystified by our masochism:

> Don't you find it difficult to imagine the times when this little pretty country was treated by its folk as if it had been an ugly characterless waste, with no delicate beauty to be guarded, with no heed taken of the ever fresh pleasure of the recurring seasons, and changeful weather, and diverse quality of the soil, and so forth? How could people be so cruel *to themselves*?
>
> (208, my italics)

The suppression of the instinct for natural beauty was linked in Morris's mind to the annihilation of healthy human instincts for pleasure in work, as the capitalist mode of production replaced useful work with useless toil, use value with exchange value. Over the century of labour activism that followed, though, Bellamy's vision largely won out over Morris's.

This schism notwithstanding, the most pronounced opposition to 'back to nature' socialism came from corporate interests and conservative politicians, as the Bryant and May strike of 1888 demonstrated. The plight of 'matchgirls', whose occupational exposure to white phosphorus could cause an excruciating, disgusting form of necrosis known as 'phossy jaw', had been a progressive cause for decades. There had been sporadic campaigns to reduce the risk, and yet Louise Raw recounts that 'the grandchildren of East Enders who lived near the factory recall tales of the glowing piles of fluorescent vomit which marked the Bryant and May workers' homeward routes at the end of each shift' (Raw 90). The matchgirls' strike, and the support it attracted from writers such as Annie Besant, drew an 'aggressively confident and choleric' (97) from the company. While the details were dictated by the local context, the outline of Bryant and May's argument remains familiar today: the workers' suffering was exaggerated;

they had been stirred up by socialist agitators; and in any case the continuing manufacture of white phosphorus 'Lucifers' was necessitated by the market. Successive Conservative governments backed the company, including Lord Salisbury's administration which vetoed a European treaty to ban the production of Lucifers. The lord was not for turning.

The matchwomen's strike sought environmental as well as social justice. It therefore attracted support from liberals, Romantic and industrial socialists, and sympathetic conservatives, albeit on somewhat different grounds. William Morris's supportive article 'The Commonweal' attacks the cruelty of 'the manufacturing capitalists' and their supporters in the 'capitalist press', which ensures only that 'certain persons are able to live a luxurious and useless life without working, and matches are made so cheap that the public buy twice as many as they want of them and waste half' ("Sweaters and Sweaters"). While the first complaint is common-or-garden socialism, the second epitomizes Morris's nascent environmentalism, which was not shared by most of his comrades. His opposition to the 'manufacturers' ideal, to wit, human machinery which will give not more, but less, trouble than the machinery of mere dead matter' might also be levelled against *Looking Backward*, despite Bellamy's good intentions.

The contest of Romantic and industrial visions of socialism was to have reverberations well beyond the febrile atmosphere of the resurgent socialist movement of the late 1880s. At that moment there was, as Peter C. Gould explains, 'a relatively high level of tolerance offered to different progressive ideas' (29) thanks to the small number of people involved and the 'negligible' socialist literature available. Quite soon, though, Morris and his fellow advocates of going 'back to nature' were sidelined by 'scientific socialism' and the 'new unionism' of the 1890s, which prevailed in the British left throughout most of the following century. Thereafter, overt environmental politics tended to be squeezed out by the contest of capital and labour, allowing organizations such as the National Trust and the RSPB to maintain broad-based support across the ideological spectrum. Contemporary British climate scepticism, I suggest, emerges out of the re-politicization of environmentalism in the late twentieth century, first in a 1970s groundswell, and then at the nexus of Margaret Thatcher's ideological Conservatism and an increasingly influential European regulatory regime.

Smoke abatement had long been one of the most important causes for British environmentalism. Since the eighteenth century, rapid industrialization had been fuelled overwhelmingly by coal, primarily the bituminous kind that spewed sooty, sulphurous smoke. Despite the seemingly obvious effects on buildings, plants, air quality and human lungs, smoke came to be considered 'pollution' only in the 1870s and 1880s, having been previously labelled as 'benign or even beneficial' (Thorsheim 195). Doctors and scientists, as well as writers such as Charles Dickens, John Ruskin and William Morris, were instrumental in reconceptualizing nature as inherently 'pure and fragile' (195), and threatened by technology. Indeed, Peter Thorsheim records that painters celebrated or decried smoke and fog according to whether such phenomena aligned with their aesthetic theories: pre-Raphaelites such as William Holman Hunt supported smoke abatement, whereas J.M.W. Turner and Claude Monet enjoyed the visual effects of multi-coloured fogs (55). Vivian's argument in 'The Decay of Lying' that London fogs 'did not exist till Art had invented them' is merely a Wildean exaggeration of this difference of opinion.[1]

If Wilde is to be believed, it was the waning of nebulophiliac Impressionism, not the development of 'smokeless' fuels, the reports of Parliamentary committees or the activism of the National Smoke Abatement Society (NSAS), that made effective legislation against air pollution possible in 1956. In J.B Sanderson's appraisal, the NSAS did struggle with the Byronic stereotype of the environmentalist: 'Above all, the Society had to avoid the crippling accusation of crankiness. In its early days it was often dismissed as an organisation of eccentrics' (239). The membership of the NSAS typified the British 'consensus' approach to policymaking, including local authorities, philanthropic organizations, proto-environmentalists and industry interest groups such as the Coal Utilization Council and the mighty National Coal Board. Sanderson commented in 1961 that 'the Society has the advantage that its cause is difficult to oppose openly, though indirect opposition is far from difficult because of the still strong romantic tradition surrounding the open fire' (242). Nevertheless, previous initiatives had been gutted at the Parliamentary committee stage by industry lobbying: a 1909 Bill to enable London County Council to regulate industrial pollution in the capital ended up 'in a deplorably emaciated condition' – a 'veritable mouse of legislation' – thanks to the concerted efforts of 'the London Underground Railways, the Central London Railway, the London Chamber of Commerce, the Electricity Supply Companies of London, the Gas Light and Coke Company, and the South Metropolitan Gas Company' (Ashby and Anderson 195). As a result, smoke abatement made modest progress at the municipal level before the 'great London fog' of December 1952 altered the political and discursive landscape.

Londoners were initially fatalistic about the 'pea-souper' that blanketed the city for four days. Newspapers focused on the increases in 'housebreaking and street crime'. In the aftermath, though, nearly 5,000 deaths were attributed to it (including several prize animals at the Smithfield Agricultural Show), and the term 'smog' began to be used increasingly in the press. Sanderson comments, 'For smoke abaters, this word was a valuable addition to the political vocabulary; "fog" is almost a natural phenomenon, "smog" is an evil to be eliminated' (246). Under growing public and backbench pressure, the Conservative government set up the Beaver Committee to review pollution control measures. Its report in November 1954, which aligned with the views of the NSAS, ultimately led to the Clean Air Act (CAA) of 1956.

The political history of the CAA has been addressed in summary (Brimblecombe) and in detail (Kenny; Thorsheim) elsewhere. Here it is necessary only to stress how industrial and union opposition affected the passage and implementation of the CAA. Crucially, the Beaver Committee refocused attention from industrial pollution to domestic hearths from the outset, pointing out that 'although houses and commercial buildings together used less than 20 percent of the coal consumed each year in Britain, they produced 45 percent of the country's smoke' (Thorsheim 175). Still, overt opposition to the CAA was muted because in 1956 the alternatives were also derivatives of coal: domestic gas was extracted from it; electricity was generated by burning it; and smokeless cokes with cheerful names like Sunbrite, Cleanglow and Coalite were made by baking it in giant kilns, causing severe local pollution (Thorsheim 136). Moreover, the coal industry was protected with taxes and import bans on foreign competitors, including fines levied from the mid-1960s into the 1970s on the nationalized Central Electricity Generating Board for using coal from overseas (Chick 9–10). Nonetheless, Scarrow claims that resistance to environmental improvement ran deep: 'In coal mining areas the clean air movement was ... perceived, not incorrectly, as being a direct threat to the entire coal industry' (268). A 'Blue Card Information' leaflet on the CAA distributed by the National Union of Mineworkers in 1963 exemplifies this left-wing resistance: it seeks to shift the stigma of coal onto oil-fired boilers, claiming that 'oil firing gives rise to more frequent complaints and more serious pollution of the atmosphere by acidic oil smuts which attack and rapidly destroy cellulosic materials and fabrics on which they fall' (Hesler 5–6). The strongest message, conveyed in bold in an opening message, is more direct:

> In the interests of the membership generally, it is of the utmost importance that members of Local Authorities, Welfare and Club Committees and similar bodies should at all times advocate and press for the use of coal or coal derivatives in any undertaking coming under their jurisdictions.
>
> (1)

Alongside wider concerns about the future of the industry, most coal miners were paid partly with 'concessionary coal', which was often sold illegally on the side. They understandably resisted pressure to accept smaller (albeit legal) cash payments instead and sought to dissuade local councils from declaring smokeless zones. Only when Margaret Thatcher's government orchestrated widespread pit closures in the 1980s did the skies begin to clear over Britain's coal mining regions.

The unintended benefits of Thatcher's politically motivated destruction of the coal mining industry were not the only ironic outcome of her premiership from an environmental perspective. In the early 1980s, the Conservatives' pandering to the Countryside Landowner's Association (CLA) and the National Union of Farmers (NFU) in the Wildlife and Countryside Act prompted Britain's large, well-funded environmental organizations to get clever in (relative) defeat. Later, water privatization inadvertently undermined the Conservatives' allies in the nuclear industry and jolted the government into introducing effective regulation of aquatic pollution (McCormick 102–3). Finally, Margaret Thatcher herself dismissed the environment brief she held in opposition as 'humdrum' and led, according to John McCormick, the opposition to environmental regulation more openly and effectively than any previous prime minister (McCormick 58–59). Then suddenly, in a speech to the Royal Society on 27 September 1988, Thatcher announced that the Conservatives supported sustainable development, and suggested that 'with all these enormous changes (population, agricultural, use of fossil fuels) concentrated into such a short period of time, we have unwittingly begun a massive experiment with the system of the planet itself' ('Speech to the Royal Society'). Regardless of how credible it turned out to be, Thatcher's apparent conversion was a turning point in British environmental politics. Its impact demonstrated, Mike Robinson claims, 'that as Prime Minister, Mrs Thatcher had been the most significant impediment to the "greening" of British politics until this time' (179).

At first, the 1980s seemed little different to previous decades: Britain still had 'no such thing as a coherent and recognizable environmental policy' (McCormick 10), in large part because none of the three main political parties accorded the issue any sustained attention. As with the great London fog, British governments reacted to events and to public pressure where necessary, but not otherwise. Just as before, trade unions energetically embraced some environmental issues, notably around workplace health and safety (Robinson 99–100), but considerable reciprocal suspicion and hostility remained between environmentalists and trade unionists (42). Moreover, as the drafting of the

Wildlife and Countryside Bill demonstrated, an influential 'policy community' of ministries and interest groups (the CLA, the NFU and the Ministry of Agriculture and Fisheries (MAFF) in this case) made government policy, in effect, well before it was subjected to Parliamentary scrutiny (76–87). With the exception of the RSPB, the conservation organizations, including organs of the state such as the Countryside Commission, were barely involved at all.

So far, so predictable. Two factors of long-term significance, though, distinguished the Wildlife and Countryside Act: first, it was made necessary by 'EEC [European Economic Community, predecessor to the European Union] Directive 79/429 on the Conservation of Wild Birds which the government was obliged to enact by April 1981' (Cox and Lowe 51), and second, the Bill was introduced into the Lords, not the Commons, due to a lack of Parliamentary time in the lower house. Ironically, this decision slowed the Bill's passage almost to a standstill by subjecting it to unprecedented scrutiny by well-informed peers, some of them board members of conservation organizations: 'In all, it took several hundred hours of debate carried out over eleven months and resulting in a record 2300 amendments before the Act was passed' (McCormick 78). Although it seemed the anti-environmentalist farming lobby eventually won its campaign against 'coercive restrictions' and 'official interference' in favour of 'sensible ground rules' (Cox and Lowe 64), the WCA catalysed new relationships between the European Commission, which was keen to extend its environmental mandate, and a range of newly energized, professionalized and (within the constraints of charitable status) politicized environmental organizations. As a result, Britons experienced a shift in what Sheila Jasanoff calls their 'civic epistemology':

> Science … achieves its standing by meeting entrenched expectations about what authoritative claims should look like and how they ought to be articulated, represented, and defended. … I use the term civic epistemology to refer to these historically and politically situated, culturally specific, public knowledge-ways.

Thatcher's neoliberalism helped spawn a competing environmental knowledge-base, anchored in Brussels, which was later complemented by the global United Nations IPCC/COP process. The shift from a mainly national civic epistemology to a transnational one elicited the self-identified climate 'heretics' encountered in the third section of this chapter.

Margaret Thatcher may have spent most of her tenure ignoring or opposing environmentalism, but she was also uniquely qualified, by comparison with most politicians, to understand it scientifically. She graduated from Oxford with a degree in Chemistry, where she worked under the supervision of future Nobel laureate Dorothy Hodgkin. On the other hand, she had done more than side with anti-environmentalist corporate interests in government; she had extended the deregulatory agenda further than most had ever imagined. Nicholas Ridley, her secretary of state for the environment, 1987–1989, 'occasionally referred to environmental groups as "extremists" and "pseudo-Marxists"' (McCormick 57). Thus, when she addressed global environmental issues such as ozone depletion and climate change in a series of speeches and interviews in the late 1980s, it puzzled both acolytes and critics: was this a sincere change of direction motivated by a strong grasp of the evidence, or was it political opportunism of some kind? The former interpretation came to seem implausible given the lack of concerted action over the next two years, whereas the latter ran counter to her fearsome reputation for 'conviction politics'. In any case, environmentalism was hardly a live issue when she first addressed it; as Andrew Marr recalls, her speech to the Royal Society was expected to be such a non-event that 'no television cameras were sent to record her speech and the prime minister had to read it by the light of wax candles held over her head in an ancient hall' (Marr 480). She did go on to replace Ridley with Chris Patten, who was much more open to the environmental lobby. Nevertheless, Margaret Thatcher was evicted from Downing Street by her own party in November 1990, not long after the publication of a white paper on the environment that humiliated Patten and betrayed little evidence of her Damascene conversion.

Margaret Thatcher did much to unfetter and embolden corporate anti-environmentalism, as *The Times* editorial on the white paper frankly acknowledged: '[Conservatives] oppose green policies because, in the corridors of Whitehall, they are not free agents but regard themselves as delegates of interest groups: the oil and gas companies, the motoring lobby, road builders, and that sternest of all short-termers, the Treasury' (McCormick 170). Nevertheless, Thatcher's environmental legacy remains deeply ambiguous. Over three terms, her government eviscerated trade unions, forcing several into mergers that mitigated their narrow sectional interests. In principle, their declining influence ought to have allowed Tony Blair's New Labour to espouse environmental causes less equivocally, although the reality was less encouraging. She took credit – in her Royal Society speech, for example – for environmental initiatives that actually started life as European Directives, while at the same time solidifying the association of 'Brussels' (site of the European Union's parliament) and interfering environmentalists. Whatever her motivation, Thatcher's surprise intervention in 1988 legitimized global environmental concern to a remarkable degree, even if it did not displace the major preoccupations of politicians altogether. Robinson argues, moreover, that 'the 1980s saw much of the environmental movement adapt to Mrs Thatcher's version of popular capitalism. The rise of "green" consumerism … has to some extent been a compromised response to Thatcherite policy and philosophy' (191). Thatcher's dominance interacted with exogenous factors like the growing power of the European Commission and the emerging scientific consensus about global warming to reshape both environmentalism and opposition to it.

The Wildlife and Countryside Bill was introduced in the Lords, not only because of Parliamentary timetabling but also because environmental issues were not seen as *political* in November 1980. Ten years later, when Thatcher left office, such a belief would have seemed ludicrous. Robinson's conclusion, in *The Greening of British Party Politics*, is that, despite the disappointment of environmental idealists, 'the framework of the existing party political system is appropriate, and broadly speaking, the diversity amongst environmental groups is well matched with the variety of political ideologies' (228). Another way to put this is to say that, while the evidence of comprehensive 'greening' of party politics at the end of 1980s was patchy, to say the least, Thatcher's revolution had clearly politicized the environment in ways that continue to reverberate through the climate debate today.

Climate scepticism in the UK: What we know

'The Armstrong and Miller Show', a popular British comedy show, included a sketch about climate change in the programme broadcast on 12 December 2010 (mbalax32). Torrential rain can be heard outside a suburban home where a couple is sitting reading on a sofa. The man gets up and walks over to the window, then turns to his wife and comments: 'Well, whatever happened to global warming, eh?' Suddenly a red X appears on screen, and a stentorian public service announcement begins:

> Stop! From October 1st, if you say 'Whatever happened to global warming, eh?' whenever it's a bit cold or wet, you could be cooling off in a prison cell. [Leaflet is seen coming through letterbox.] This leaflet is being sent to every household in Britain. You have until September 30th to learn the difference between climate, a long-term term trend averaged over many years, and weather, which is what's going on outside the window right now. [Couple is seen earnestly reading leaflet.] Make sure you study it. Because if you don't, the next shower you get

caught in could be in the prison washblock. [Menacing prison inmate is seen throwing a bar of soap to the floor.]

The man is now depicted turning from the window again, saying: 'Look at this weather, eh? Still, I'm sure it'll all average out statistically to indicate a long-term warming trend.' A big green tick appears on screen, and the man's wife smiles awkwardly towards the camera. The sketch concludes with the voiceover and onscreen slogan: 'Global warming quips – get acclimatised.'

The butt of the satire seems obvious: the habit, common to lay sceptics and warmists alike, of mistaking individual weather events for climate trends. Framing the satire in the style of a public service announcement, though, focuses attention on the intrusive, overweening moralization and bureaucratization of individual behaviour by a new regime of climate governance. Banning feeble sceptical jokes is just the kind of thing the nanny state *would* do.

Armstrong and Miller's sketch speaks to a dramatic shift in the cultural and party politics of climate change between 1990 and 2010, from a marginal concern of a few scientists and environmentalists to apparent hegemony. As we will see, there were actually two periods in which 'global warming', as it was initially known, had a high profile: 1989–1992, when the IPCC's First Assessment Report (FAR) was published and the Rio Earth summit took place, and 2006–2010, which saw the climate documentary *An Inconvenient Truth* (2006), the IPCC's AR4 (2007) and the Climate Change Act (2008). Climate scepticism lagged behind in both instances: Richard D. North and Wilfred Beckerman published sceptical books in 1995, and the great majority of the texts discussed in detail below date from 2008 to 2010. Scepticism in the 1990s portrayed global warming as a wacky, extremist belief, whereas second-wave scepticism, as we might call it, differed rhetorically by positioning itself predominantly as 'heresy,' reflecting the perceived dominance of a scientifico-political consensus about climate change in the UK. Nevertheless, the modest changes in British GHG emissions and the near-total disappearance of climate change from the political agenda at election time suggest that it is a rather thin hegemony by contrast with Germany, where climate change is less often challenged, and the United States, where there has never been a consensus and partisan conflict prevails. This section explains the emergence of a thin hegemony of climate governance in terms of party political competition, media attention and public opinion.

The first wave of global climate activism was stimulated by scientific concerns articulated in the IPCC's FAR, and channelled primarily through the United Nations Framework Convention on Climate Change, which began holding annual Conference of the Parties (COP) meetings in 1995.[2] British political parties had begun to take notice of environmentalism in 1989, when the Green Party won 14.5 per cent of the popular vote (but no seats), its best-ever result in percentage terms. A flurry of pro-environmental statements followed in 1990, including the Conservative's *This Common Inheritance*, and the party manifestos for the 1992 election gave significant additional space to environmental issues – especially the Liberal Democrat party, which is most directly threatened by the Green vote. Still, as Neil Carter observes:

> The Labour and Conservative parties have made no concerted effort [up to 2006] to promote the environment during an election campaign. Even in 1992, when the environment figured strongly in all the main party manifestos, neither major party emphasized it in its press conferences.
>
> (Carter 'Party Politicization' 748)

The Conservatives won the election, and Labour lost it, with barely a mention of climate change.

John Major's government (1992–97) was hampered by its small majority and the rise of Euro-scepticism in both the Conservative Party and the British media, although John Selwyn Gummer was a surprisingly effective secretary of state for the environment who unified a hodgepodge of regulatory acts and agencies in the environment agency. The UK signed the Kyoto Protocol in December 1997, but climate change was a low political priority throughout the decade because the decline of manufacturing and the shift from coal to natural gas led to falling GHG emissions even without concerted effort. Both Labour and the Conservatives pursued a policy known as 'preference accommodation': 'they moved their rhetoric and policies closer to the preferences of those voters wanting greater environmental protection' while avoiding competing with each other by proposing 'costly environmental protection policies which could alienate large numbers of voters' (Carter 'The Politics of Climate Change in the UK' 424). Whereas American sceptics began seriously to mobilize in the mid-1990s, neither advocacy nor opposition had particular salience in the UK until later.

Tony Blair's New Labour, elected in 1997, might have been expected to follow the path of environmental modernization touted by social democratic parties in Northern Europe. Blair had reduced the formal influence of trade unions on party policy and made enthusiastic, if infrequent, references to 'green issues'. The government committed to ambitious GHG emissions reduction targets: 20 per cent from 1990 levels by 2010, and 60 per cent by 2050. However, Michael Jacobs's Fabian Society pamphlet 'Environmental Modernization: the new

Labour agenda' noted in 1999 that 'New Labour is not comfortable with the environment as a political issue', and so 'there has been no "ideological narrative", no "story to tell", of the kind which New Labour has developed in other fields' (Jacobs 1, 6). As Carter points out, Blair's Chancellor Gordon Brown weakened a proposed climate change levy on polluting industries in the face of determined opposition, and then, in September 2000, protests by truckers and farmers derailed the 'Road Fuel Escalator', a policy introduced by the Conservatives to reduce transport emissions by increasing excise duties by 5 per cent on road fuel annually. The fuel protests began as a failed Conservative Party stunt, but later escalated into an extremely disruptive blockade of refineries by tractors and trucks. Thousands of petrol stations closed, hospitals cancelled non-essential operations and supermarkets began to run out of food. For the first time since the 1992 withdrawal of the pound sterling from the European Exchange Rate Mechanism, the Conservatives were ahead of Labour in the polls ('Drivers Kept Waiting as Shortages Ease'). Moreover, environmentalist protestors who had opposed road-building during the 1990s did not turn out to oppose the farmers and truckers. Blair's New Labour, ever sensitive to the feelings and opinions of 'Mondeo Man',[3] suspended the Road Fuel Escalator and backed off environmental issues for several years thereafter.

The next peak of interest in climate change provoked most of the hostile responses we analyse below. Between the 2005 G8 conference in Gleneagles, Scotland, when Blair sought to assume the mantle of global climate leader, and the COP 15 Copenhagen climate summit in December 2009, attended by Blair's successor Gordon Brown, a remarkable series of developments occurred that brought about major legislative change and elevated climate change to the thin hegemony satirized by Armstrong and Miller. First, the government's Chief Scientific Advisor Sir David King claimed that climate change was a threat greater than terrorism. Blair, who won the 2005 general election with the lowest popular vote in British history, hoped to recover from the severe damage to his popularity and global stature caused by his participation in the 2003 US-led invasion of Iraq. Then, in December 2005, David Cameron became leader of the opposition Conservative Party, and embarked on a major rebranding to 'detoxify' it by moving closer to the political centre. He replaced Thatcher's torch logo with an oak tree, travelled to Svalbard in Norway to witness the apparent effects of climate change (and get a photo-op with sled dogs) and proclaimed that Britons could 'Vote Blue, Go Green'. Cameron's overhaul effectively sidelined prominent Conservative climate sceptics, who came to be more closely associated with the anti-immigration, anti-European Union UK Independence Party. Crucially, the re-alignment also forced Labour from its position of minimal accommodation into active competition with the opposition parties. The Conservatives, egged on by environmental NGOs, effectively set the pace for the government; as Carter explains: 'Several Labour Government climate initiatives were policies initially proposed by the Conservatives, including the Climate Change Bill, reforms of air passenger duty, feed-in tariffs and support for a new high-speed railway linking London to Birmingham and beyond' (Carter 'The Politics of Climate Change' 428).

Blair, keenly aware of the threat from a 'modernized' Conservative Party, helped to persuade the European Council in 2007 to adopt the '20-20-20 by 2020' targets, which mandated 'a unilateral 20% reduction target for CO2 emissions, a 20% share of renewable sources in energy consumption and a 20% improvement in energy efficiency – all by 2020' (427). Under his successor, Prime Minister Gordon Brown, the 2008 Climate Change Act (CCA) was passed with cross-party support. It places a legal duty on the secretary of state for the environment to 'ensure that the net UK carbon account for the year 2050 is at least 80% lower than the 1990 baseline' ('Climate Change Act 2008'). The CCA was, and remains, a tremendous accomplishment of British environmentalism, even if the political consensus that delivered it has since disintegrated.

Just five Conservatives voted against the CCA. Nevertheless, they represented an increasingly vocal, even vituperative, opposition to the consensus, much of it funnelled through the notoriously outspoken British tabloid media. Like the right-wing press, the CCA rebels were, with one exception, also 'Euro-sceptics' who campaigned for Britain to leave the European Union. The outsized role of tabloids in the UK means that most research on climate scepticism has come from scholars of journalism and environmental communications, who have largely confirmed what we might suspect about the relationship between the ideological orientation of a newspaper and its reporting of climate change (Boykoff and Mansfield; Boykoff; Painter). Two newspapers in particular gave credence to scepticism and failed to preserve the distinction between reporting and opinion pieces: 'In two right-wing newspapers with a combined daily circulation of 2.7 million (the *Express* and the *Mail*), between 48% and 50% of *all* the articles … included sceptical voices' (Painter 108). By contrast with observations of the broadsheet press in the UK and the United States, scholars found tabloid reporting did not become more accurate or less partisan over time thanks to the disproportionate contributions of specific individuals, including Michael Hanlon (*Telegraph, Express, Mail*), James Chapman (*Mail*) and Christopher Booker (*Telegraph*) (although Chapman later abandoned his scepticism)

(Boykoff and Mansfield). As Boykoff observes, British tabloids reported climate change with their trademark 'ingenious and pithy' (555) headlines and 'deliberately contrarian positions taken with ironic tones' (560), framing it through 'weather events, charismatic megafauna and the movements of political actors and rhetoric' (549). Over and over, global warming was dismissed as 'hot air from politicians': in a sardonic revision of Blair's argument for the Iraq War, Hanlon wrote in 2004 that 'for all their posturing over their green policies, Tony Blair and Michael Howard may find they have declared war on an enemy that doesn't exist and instead of weapons of mass destruction, we now have weather of mass deception' (quoted in Boykoff 564). Boykoff's close examination of a sceptical column in the *Daily Mail* concludes that 'through a combination of opinion-driven reporting with satirical tones, sensationalized villains (the Met Office as "so-called experts"), and sceptical claims and frames, the piece casts doubt on the legitimacy of scientific assertions, and specifically the veracity of claims regarding anthropogenic contributions' (564). Even as the thin hegemony in support of the IPCC was forming, climate scepticism – along with Euro-scepticism, often in the same newspapers – was bubbling away discontentedly.

The significance of the scepticism expressed by the *Mail* and the *Express* should not be exaggerated, even if the 2016 British vote to leave the European Union casts right-wing populism in a different light in retrospect. As Painter shows, *The Sun*, the largest tabloid by far, employed Jeremy Clarkson (see below) as columnist, but was run by James Murdoch, 'who is widely known to be concerned about global warming and has a background in environmental sciences'. Perhaps cognizant of its comparatively youthful readership, *The Sun* employs a dedicated environment editor and reports climate issues in a relatively unbiased way. *The Guardian*, a liberal newspaper, has put climate change at the centre of its reporting: 'Since 2008, the paper and online site has had a team of six full-time environment correspondents, two editors, a dedicated picture editor, and two production journalists' (95). Moreover, as Gavin Marshall's analysis of the reporting of the Copenhagen conference reveals, the overall salience of climate change is never very great: his graph comparing Google Trends searches on 'football', 'X factor'[4] and 'climate change' shows the latter as a flat line running very close to the Y axis. Even Copenhagen and Climategate barely register.

A study of British media (including advertisements and websites) commissioned by the left-leaning Institute for Public Policy Research (IPPR) usefully maps three dominant British 'discourses' of climate change at the peak of the period of party competition in 2006–2007: alarmism, pragmatic optimism ('technology will save us') and non-pragmatic optimism. The authors subdivide the latter into two categories, 'settlerdom' (an odd, unilluminating name) and 'comic nihilism':

> [Settlerdom] rejects and mocks the alarmist discourse – and with it climate change – by invoking 'common sense' on behalf of 'the sane majority' in opposition to 'the doom-mongers'. It dismisses climate change as a thing so fantastic that it cannot be true and reflects a refusal to engage in the debate. It is seen most clearly in the broadly rightwing popular press, but is also likely to be the stuff of pub conversations. It is significant because it is immune to scientific argument and its prevalence underlines that the task of climate change agencies is not to persuade by rational argument but to develop a new 'common sense'.
>
> 'British comic nihilism' is another evasive rhetorical repertoire. Its rejection of climate change is whimsical, unserious, blithely irresponsible – a sunny refusal to engage in the debate, typified by comic musings on the positive possibilities of a future with climate change. It is currently marginal, seen in just a few places in the middle-class press and radio. But it is potentially important because it is a very British repertoire (self-mocking and contrary, dealing with adversity and threat by use of humour).
>
> (Segnit and Ereaut 7–8)

In keeping with their remit – to ask 'how are we telling the climate change story and can we tell it better?' – Segnit and Ereaut recommend 'treating climate-friendly activity as a brand that can be sold' (9), which seems to be at odds with their assertion that scepticism is 'likely to become increasingly marginal in the face of mounting evidence' (24) and their doubt about the efficacy of 'residual models of public service or campaigning communications' (9). Most importantly, they recommend 'treating climate change as beyond argument': 'The "facts" need to be treated as being so taken-for-granted that they need not be spoken' (25). In a 2007 follow-up paper, they claim this objective has already been achieved: 'There is now a broad consensus that climate change is happening and that man is at least partly responsible for it' (94). Given that all the texts discussed below date from 2008 and after, it seems clear that scepticism was alive and kicking. In fact, in the years following passage of the CCA, British public opinion moved *away* from acceptance of anthropogenic climate change. What happened?

A 2014 longitudinal analysis of public opinion surveys proposes a four-way periodization:

> (1) 1980s and early 1990s, showing increases in knowledge and awareness; (2) mid-1990s to the mid-2000s, a period marked by growing public concern but also variability in opinion; (3) mid- to late-2000s, showing declining public

> concern and increasing skepticism in some nations, with polarization of viewpoints within and between nations; and (4) 2010s, which so far suggest possible stabilization of public concern about climate change. (Capstick et al. 45)

Although the long period of growing public support for climate mitigation was manifested in the CCA, opposition grew too, especially in the late noughties[5]: scepticism about the warming trend rose from 4 per cent in 2005 to 15 per cent by 2010, and increasing numbers of Britons apparently came to suspect that the seriousness of climate change was exaggerated (Whitmarsh). Studies found that generalized scepticism was higher in the UK (44 per cent Eurobarometer) than the EU average (30 per cent), but also suggested a porous distinction between active scepticism and uncertainty (Poortinga et al.). Although political affiliation was a significant factor, as in the United States, British sceptical publics tended to be older, poorer, less educated and less certain than warmists – quite different to McCright and Dunlap's wealthy, college-educated 'cool dudes' (McCright and Dunlap). Poortinga and colleagues conclude:

> The finding that climate scepticism is associated with attitudinal uncertainty, ambivalence, and conflicting cognitive-affective responses suggests that most climate sceptics may not hold their views very strongly. So, perhaps in contrast to the caricature of a dogmatic sceptic who is "'waiting to pounce on any scientific uncertainty'", climate sceptical publics seem to be less opinionated than non-sceptical publics.
>
> (1021)

Scholars have attributed the growth of British scepticism to the 2008 financial crisis; the failure of the 2009 Copenhagen conference; the near-simultaneous release of the hacked 'Climategate' emails; a downturning political and media 'attention cycle'; and a succession of cold, snowy winters. A German study of shifting attitudes in Hamburg suggests a mere reversion to the mean after a few years of elevated concern (Ratter, Philipp and von Storch 7). By contrast with these efforts to explain short-term fluctuations in poll numbers (Ereaut and Seignit discern an emerging consensus in the course of just a year!), Stuart Capstick and colleagues have ingeniously re-analysed six data sets from 1997 to 2010 in order to discriminate between temporal scales of public opinion change: 'relatively short-lived movements in attitudes as revealed by survey data and influenced by transitory phenomena; slower shifts in public discourses that track changing cultural contexts; and enduring ways of understanding climate change that are tied to longer-term ethical foundations' (Capstick, Pidgeon and Henwood 726). Looking beyond the fluctuations, they find that 'the personally and socially relevant aspects of climate change have gradually found purchase in people's understanding of everyday life' (745). Far from appearing 'malleable and capricious' (746), respondents across the surveys increasingly accept responsibility for addressing climate change, even as they acknowledge 'pressures' from other areas of their lives. Moreover, the re-analysis found encouraging evidence in all six data sets of a durable ethic of intergenerational equity and 'stewardship' of the nonhuman world. A superficial reading of British opinion trends might conclude scepticism is on the rise, but in fact it seems to be fracturing into a constellation of more or less justified concerns about media representation, scientific process, the limits of human nature, the reliability of climate models and the economic, cultural and environmental cost of transitioning from fossil fuels to sustainable energy. Indeed, one might well argue that Britons are maturing into a properly critical, ambivalent relationship with their climatically altered future. The sceptical texts discussed in the next section have facilitated the shift, willy-nilly.

Climate scepticism in the UK: An ecocritical analysis

Several strands of British culture and politics have been traced that bring us to the brink of the late noughties and the era of thin hegemony. First, there is the satirical depiction of straitlaced, straight-faced Romantic environmentalists in Byron and Wilde. Second, there is the historical strength of apolitical conservationism in the UK from the late nineteenth to the late twentieth centuries, which aligns with Capstick, Pidgeon and Henwood's finding of durable intergenerational concerns in British publics. Third, we have seen that, under the pressure of Thatcher's ideological Conservatism, environmentalism became politicized and Europeanized, thereby greatly increasing its influence, but also eliciting a counter-reaction, mainly from right-wing conservatives. This process clearly parallels the emergence of Republican anti-environmentalism in the United States during and immediately after Ronald Reagan's presidency, albeit that the British counterpart was coloured by Euro-scepticism. Finally, a growing consensus including all three national political parties, all but one broadsheet newspaper, many business leaders, and Sir David Attenborough, led – under the specific conditions of Cameron's attempt to outflank New Labour – to the 2008 Climate Change Act and the apparent hegemony of pro-IPCC politics.

The texts discussed in detail here, barring a couple from the 1990s, belong to the efflorescence of climate scepticism in the years from 2008 to

2015. Before examining them, it is worth rehearsing some of the evidence they adduce in support of their self-conception as 'heretics' confronting an oppressive orthodoxy. Al Gore's documentary *An Inconvenient Truth* (2006) was immensely influential in the UK, prompting the Labour Department of Education to distribute copies of the DVD to all British schools. Stewart Dimmock, a school governor from Kent, took the DfE to court, claiming the film contained 'scientific inaccuracies, political propaganda and sentimental mush' (Peck). A High Court judge refused to ban the film, but required teachers using the film as a resource to draw attention to what *The Telegraph* called its 'Nine Inconvenient Untruths'. Two years later, the newly created Department of Energy and Climate Change funded TV advertisements that narrated a climatically altered future, complete with weeping rabbits and drowning puppies, in the form of a bedtime story that would terrify children (JoetheElectrician). At the end, the little girl asks plaintively, 'Is there a happy ending?' In 2011, an independent report on science programming, commissioned for the BBC Trust, warned against the 'false balance' that could give 'undue attention to marginal opinion'. The report was welcomed by climate scientists, but was read as 'muzzling' climate sceptics (Rao). Not only had all three national political parties committed to dramatic cuts in GHG emissions, but the nation's broadcaster was keeping them off the air and children were being – as they saw it – indoctrinated with global warming alarmism.

A particularly striking example is provided by 'No Pressure', a four-minute film written by Richard Curtis and Franny Armstrong for the climate charity 10:10, which was withdrawn from YouTube on 1 October 2010, the day of its release. 10:10 invited people and businesses to pledge cuts of 10 per cent of their carbon emissions in the year 2010. In the withdrawn advert, schoolchildren, office workers and footballers are depicted being told about the 10:10 campaign, and largely agreeing to support it. The small number of holdouts in each group, including the football coach, are then graphically blown to bits, their bloody remains splattering everyone around. At the end of the film, its narrator Gillian Anderson is also blown up for refusing to take the pledge. Much like Armstrong and Miller, 'No Pressure' appears to take aim at climate sceptics who think there is 'no pressure' to act, while at the same time attempting self-deprecating satire of environmentalist intolerance. Only the first aspect was addressed by climate sceptics such as James Delingpole, who claimed, with characteristic hyperbole, that 'the environmental movement has revealed the snarling, wicked, homicidal misanthropy beneath its cloak of gentle, bunny-hugging righteousness'.[6] Having satirized environmentalists for being humourless, climate sceptics were now chastising them for attempting humour – though to be fair, the film is simultaneously gross, politically incoherent and only mildly amusing. The more important point, for our purposes, is that 'No Pressure' sardonically acknowledges the hegemonic status of climate change in British culture at that moment, even as it stages, with cartoonish violence, the imagined punishment of those who fail to connect their knowledge to their behaviour.

The place of 'global warming' in sceptical texts was somewhat different during the 'first wave' in the 1990s. Already, there were the inevitable puns, as in the title of a booklet published by the 'Institute of Economic Affairs', a conservative think tank: *Global Warming: Apocalypse or Hot Air?*, by Roger Bate and Julian Morris.[7] Also, the critique of 'eco-doomsters' is to the fore in Wilfred Beckerman's Preface, which sardonically alludes to the puritanical message of environmental 'preachers' (Bate and Morris 5–6). The condescending tone of the Preface is not shared by the pamphlet, which is simply a brief, sceptical summary of climate science in the 1990s that focuses on the acknowledged crudity of climate models at that time, drawing reassurance from Richard Lindzen's informed, but generally contested, assertion that 'negative feedbacks' in the climate system would outweigh 'positive feedbacks'. Bate and Morris claim, on this basis, that 'the overall effects of GHG [greenhouse gas] emissions are unknown but are unlikely to be seriously good or seriously bad, because the global ecosystem appears to be "engineered" for stability' (27). Their confidence aligns with the 'myth of nature' defined as 'individualist' in John Adams's influential *Risk*:

> Nature benign: nature, according to this myth, is predictable, bountiful, robust, stable, and forgiving of any insults humankind might inflict upon it … Nature is the benign context of human activity, not something that needs to be managed. The management style associated with this myth is therefore relaxed, non-interventionist, *laissez-faire*.
>
> (Adams 34)

Adams's other 'myths of nature' depict it as 'perverse/tolerant' (i.e. resilient, up to a point – the 'hierarchist' perspective); 'capricious', according to fatalists; and 'ephemeral' or fragile, which is the typical assumption of environmentalists.

For Bate and Morris, benign nature aligns with the virtue of unimpeded markets: they call for the elimination of distorting fossil fuel subsidies because 'free markets in energy will not only be efficient, but will also alert us to changes in environmental conditions – via the price mechanism – far faster than any model might do' (42). In fact, climate change is a perfect example of an economic 'externality' from the perspective of fossil fuel or nuclear power stations. Regardless, Bate and Morris insist that both the climatic and the economic future are unknowable, but thanks to the alleged stability of 'the global ecosystem' – a claim at odds with the expressed views of many paleoclimatologists (Pearce) – they are confident both will be fine.

The title of Wilfred Beckerman's own book, *Small Is Stupid: Blowing the Whistle on the Greens*, suggests a rather more caustic tone than he actually adopts. Unlike much later British scepticism, Beckerman's tone is witty, self-deprecating and rationalistic, as when he admits his limitations in relation to climate science:

> Not being a scientist – or even a rock star, a politician, a diplomat or related to any Royal Family – it might be thought that I am not qualified to express any view about global warming. But I would hate word to get around among my colleagues at Oxford that I was reluctant to write about a subject simply because I did not know much about it. And, fortunately, one does not need to know much about it in order to learn that the really top scientists in the climatology field are acutely aware of the gaps in their understanding of the process of climate change.
>
> (Beckerman 80)

Beckerman acknowledges that 'the world is facing serious environmental problems' (3) – indeed, he was appointed by the Labour politician Anthony Crosland to the Royal Commission on Environmental Pollution in 1970 – but is perceptively critical of 1970s environmentalists' failed prophecies and misunderstanding of the nature of 'resources': he prints a table of 'known reserves' of resources from the Club of Rome's *The Limits to Growth* (1970) alongside the equivalent figures from 1989 under the sardonic heading 'How we used up all the resources that we had and still finished up with more than we started with' (53). His sharpest criticism – albeit still conveyed with the bemused restraint of an Oxford don – is reserved for Integrated Assessment Models (IAM), which yoke climatic and economic simulations:

> There are several very complicated computerised models on the market for making the requisite predictions. But in fact none of them is necessary. It can all be done on the back of an envelope, or even in one's head.
>
> (90)

Given that humans occupy almost every climatic zone on Earth, and have frequently migrated voluntarily across far greater temperature gradients, he asserts that the economic impact of the 2.5°C of warming projected over the twentieth century will, for most countries, be either favourable or negligible. At worst, the people of Bangladesh might have to be compensated for the loss of 20 per cent of their country (94). Beckerman's lack of confidence in IAMs is counterpointed by unerring faith in the wisdom of the free market. He advocates that we remove fossil fuel subsidies, keep researching the global climate system, resist 'pressures from semi-hysterical eco-doomsters' (103) and focus on 'more urgent environmental problems, particularly those in developing countries' (102) until sensible, gradual mitigation policies and effective zero carbon technologies emerge.

Richard D. North's *Life on a Modern Planet: A Manifesto for Progress* (1995) shares Beckerman's disdain for 'doomster' Greens, while approving of 'the generalised ecological and environmental concern almost everyone now feels', which he dubs '"green" with a lower-case g' (North 8). Like Beckerman, North has impressive form as an environmentalist: he wrote a series of books in the 1980s on conservation and farming, and admits that he 'was probably thought of as a propagandist for the cause' (1). The strength of his sceptical book lies in how its detailed case studies of specific environmental incidents, such as the 1993 *Braer* oil spill and the 1976 Seveso dioxin release,[8] draw attention to gaps between scientific knowledge and the publicity campaigns mounted by Greenpeace, which North describes as 'a campaigning organization with a long record of being cavalier with evidence' (103). His scepticism regarding global warming is sensitive to the risk of 'hype' (63), but open-minded towards the scientific consensus then emerging. North's own conclusion is shaped by paleoclimatic evidence of the volatility of the global climate system, which he calls a 'temperature rollercoaster': 'If this sense of a white-knuckle ride and its acceleration do not suggest the need for precautionary response, it is hard to see when such a response would be justified' (69).

The dominant sceptical positioning in the first wave in the UK, then, is a 'balanced' (North and Beckerman's favourite adjective) accommodation with moderate environmentalism, combined with a clear – albeit respectful – marginalization of 'eco-doomsters'. This generation allies itself with 'greens' against 'Greens', which threatens to upset the typology of Segnit and Ereault's discourse study above: the disparagement of doomsters places North and Beckerman in the 'settler' subsection of non-pragmatic optimism, but their overall orientation is clearly pragmatic optimism. We can see from the modesty of their scepticism that global warming was then nascent as a political issue, and far less polarized.

Whereas 'balance' was the watchword in the 1990s, 'reason' fulfilled that role for North and Beckerman's inheritors in the second wave: former Chancellor of the Exchequer Nigel Lawson and science writer Matt Ridley, whose book *The Rational Optimist* (2010) is not discussed here. Lawson's *An Appeal to Reason: A Cool Look at Global Warming* (2008) repeats 'rational' and its cognates so often it recalls the relentless tolling of a church bell on a Sunday morning. The IPCC is described as being 'biased', but at the same time 'authoritative and influential' (12), and so although Lawson repeatedly stresses the acknowledged uncertainties of climate science, he largely confines his critique to impact and policy scepticism. Based on the 'conventional wisdom', he sums up the threat of climate change in economic terms:

> On the most pessimistic assumptions, and on the basis of the majority view of the science of global warming, the existential threat confronting the world today, from which the planet must be saved, is that, a hundred years from now, the people of the developing world may not be 9.5 times as well off as they are today, but only 8.5 times as well off. (Lawson 53)

Sir John Houghton published a scientific critique of *An Appeal to Reason* in *Nature*[9]; for our purposes, it is important to note, with Richard D. North, that Lawson's 'tone isn't quite right' because of 'the way his general bounciness alternates with occasional whining' ('The Social Affairs Unit – Web Review … '). For example, Lawson notes the deaths of 15,000 'very elderly people', most of them in France, in the heatwave of August 2003, then goes on to counter that 'I spent the summer of 2003 in south-west France myself, and found it perfectly tolerable, but it was clearly a hardship for some' (34). He often trades on his experience in government, as when he admonishes:

> As is frequently the case in government … we are faced with the task of deciding, rationally, the most sensible policy course to take against a background of fundamental uncertainty. We need to avoid being paralysed into complete inactivity. But we also need to avoid being panicked into what could be disastrously damaging action. In many ways the decision to invade Iraq is an instructive parallel (with the government's alarmist Stern Review playing the role of Mr Blair's notorious 'dodgy dossier').
>
> (21)

Political point-scoring aside, Lawson's arguments are at their strongest when he attacks the 'scam' (77) of cap-and-trade, and when he explains why climate change adaptation has good prospects, not the least of which is that it is 'essentially a matter of a large number of local and practical measures, which require no international treaty or worldwide agreement for their implementation' (43). Curiously, though, he treats adaptation as if it is in direct competition with emissions reduction ('mitigation'), and writes about the latter in apocalyptic terms:

> For a start it would mean unwinding the industrial revolution and returning to a pastoral society. But that would indeed be only a start. For man began messing about with the planet when he ceased being a hunter-gatherer and invented farming. So agriculture ... would have to go too.
>
> (45)

Lawson's exaggeration is a useful reminder that environmentalists are not the only ones with a record of failed prophecies; conservative and corporate rhetorics, from Bryant and May's defence of white phosphorus to ICI's attempts to block regulation of CFCs, have often warned of economic collapse if specific activities are curtailed. When it turns out that 'environmental regulation [is] a little cheaper than they thought' (North 65), their dire prognostications tend to be forgotten, whereas those of environmentalists are endlessly recycled. Richard Lambert, chairman of the Confederation of British Industries, is hardly a hair-on-fire Green, but even he criticizes Lawson's 'airy generalisations' (Lambert) in his review of *An Appeal to Reason*. Lawson may be the inheritor of North and Beckerman's pragmatic optimism on a philosophical level, but his uneven style and exaggerated anxiety about emissions cuts are symptomatic of his relatively weak control of the non-economic material, as well as the wider polarization and politicization of climate change during the noughties.

As discussed in the Introduction, 'response scepticism' is a relatively recent addition to the typologies of environmental communications scholars (Capstick and Pidgeon 391). In the British sample, 'doubts commonly expressed by participants around the value of action taken to address climate change' and 'doubts around human nature and the human condition' were more strongly correlated with unconcern about climate change than were 'epistemic' doubts about the science itself (398), which suggests to the authors that response scepticism develops out of a 'wider sense of fatalism or resignation'. Though widely influential, such fatalism is seldom articulated by sceptical literature, which tends to be written – ironically enough – by those with a passionate interest in the subject. John Gray's *Straw Dogs* (2002), a bestselling work of popular philosophy, is unusual in this regard. Gray never questions the science of climate change, but he dismisses the possibility of concerted action to prevent it because it depends, he thinks, on moral capabilities that human primates –

technologically advanced but morally stunted – can never marshal. Citing James Lovelock's assessment of humans as a disease of the earth, which he calls '*disseminated primatemaia*', Gray asserts, in characteristically blunt, assertive terms, that humans are incapable of destroying their 'host', the earth, and will 'never initiate a symbiosis with' it (8). He reaches the bleak conclusion:

> Humans are like any other plague animal. They cannot destroy the Earth, but they can easily wreck the environment that sustains them. The most likely [outcome is that] *disseminated primatemaia* is cured by a large-scale decline in human numbers.
>
> (12)

Gray's perpetual overstatement of the evidence that Humanism is a delusion, pure and simple, is bolstered by his epigrammatic, aphoristic style, which conspicuously apes that of another great anti-humanist, Friedrich Nietzsche. Nevertheless, I myself have struggled over many years to answer Gray's basic case, which is that technological progress (including in our destructive capabilities) is cumulative, whereas moral progress is fragile and reversible. Scientists see further by 'standing on the shoulders of Giants', as Isaac Newton modestly admitted, whereas moral wisdom has to be learned afresh, all too unreliably, by every human being.

Gray pursues anti-humanism with unusual rigour, rejecting any and all routes to 'the salvation of mankind', and predicting – like Michael Crichton and Charlton Heston (see chapter 2) – that

> *Homo rapiens* [*sic*] is only one of very many species, and not obviously worth preserving. Later or sooner, it will become extinct. When it is gone the Earth will recover. ... The Earth will forget mankind. The play of life will go on.
>
> (151)

Wisdom consists in acknowledging the meaninglessness of action. Gray concludes:

> Other animals do not need a purpose in life. A contradiction to itself, the human animal cannot do without one. Can we not think of the aim of life as being simply to see?
>
> (199)

Environmentalists are well aware that fatalism stalks their ventures. Several commentators have acknowledged that climate change challenges 'the limits of our cognitive and affective capacities' (Jamieson 8; Hamilton; Clark *Ecocriticism on the Edge*); the activist George Marshall wrote a book called *Don't Even*

Think about It: Why Our Brains Are Wired to Ignore Climate Change (2014). These authors, reasonably enough, treat fatalism as a psycho-social problem to be solved – with manageable actions, say, or positive news about climate activism. The deepest irony, though, is that taking Gray seriously opens up a yawning existential chasm beneath all our hopes, with long-term, large-scale endeavours the first to fall in. There can be a few environmentalists who have never peered into it; in this sense, we are all sceptics at times.

Capstick and Pidgeon found that 65.1 per cent of their sample agreed that 'people are too selfish to do anything about climate change', while 53.2 per cent agreed that 'it is not in human nature to respond to problems that won't happen for many years' (396). I doubt very many of them had read *Straw Dogs*. A high proportion, though, would've seen Jeremy Clarkson on *Top Gear* or read his column in *The Sun* (later collected into books), making him arguably the most influential climate sceptic in the world. Clarkson epitomizes what Ereault and Segnit call 'comic nihilism', although the extraordinary popularity of his show (said to be the most-watched in the world) would seem to contradict their claim that it is a marginal repertoire. Clive Hamilton's preferred term, 'hairy-chested denialism' (Hamilton 123), captures Clarkson's overt (if often self-mocking) masculinity, though not the broad appeal of his hedonistic anti-environmentalism. Hamilton goes on to note:

> [Clarkson] has become notorious for green-baiting, deriding public transport, promising to run down cyclists and declaring: 'What's wrong with global warming? We might lose Holland but there are other places to go on holiday.' It's an opinion, or rather a sentiment, that has instant appeal to the segment of the population that feels cheated of its enjoyment by climate doom-mongering, particularly when combined with state nannyism. In this way, Clarkson transforms climate transgressors into victims of political correctness. For some, it validates their resistance to behavioural change, justifying their reluctance to take the bus, buy a smaller car or recycle waste.
>
> (124)

Clarkson's comic nihilism would not go far if he were not in fact funny. But he is. He veers between bullish *braggadocio* and ironic acknowledgement of failure – a popular T-shirt for *Top Gear* simply reads 'That's not gone well … '. He captures the virtues and limitations of the cars he drives with vivid, often sexual, similes, as in this description of the Audi R8 supercar:

> It's not the speed, though, that impresses you most of all – it's the way this thing feels through the corners. Driving most supercars, it's [*sic*] like trying to

> manhandle a cow up a back staircase. This is like smearing honey into Keira Knightley.
>
> (*Top Gear*, season 10, episode 2)

His stock in trade is comic hyperbole, which is perfectly suited to deflating what he sees as environmentalist (and other kinds of) alarmism. Here, for instance, he mourns the proliferation of 'elf and safety' rules,[10] concluding with swipe at his nemesis, *The Guardian's* environmental columnist:

> Already, in the period of Great Boredom, they've stopped us smoking, killing foxes, reversing without a banksman, playing conkers, enjoying bonfire night and taking toothpaste on an aeroplane. And now they are thinking of banning patio heaters, doing 30, and wearing hooded tops. Soon, it will be illegal to not be George Monbiot.
>
> (Clarkson *For Crying out Loud!* 309)

Clarkson here is Byron to Monbiot's Wordsworth. 'They' are the killjoys – bureaucrats from local councils, labour unions, Whitehall and the European Union – who seek to protect us from both our own stupidity and the worst excesses of unregulated corporations. Clarkson occasionally questions the science of climate change ('attribution scepticism') – what he calls the 'outdated and now completely discredited theory that man causes global warming' (Clarkson *Is It Really Too Much to Ask?*) – but much more often asserts that the subject is simply 'boring'. He has even proven willing to criticize Sir David Attenborough, Britain's only secular saint:

> My respect for The Attenborough as a broadcaster is boundless. He could tell me that I was a giant panda and I'd believe him. He could come on the television and say koala bears can fill in tax forms and I'd stroke my chin appreciatively. But when he comes on the television to say [actress] Sienna Miller's Range Rover has broken the Gulf Stream and overheated a guillemot, well, I'm sorry, but I just nod off. Because finger-wagging environmentalism, even from the God of the electric fish tank, is catastrophically boring.
>
> (79)

The escalating sequence of absurd claims attributed to 'The Attenborough' is worth pausing over. BBC Earth trades on the majesty and sublime improbability of nature, but Attenborough's 2006 intervention, 'The Truth about Climate Change', is a step too far, claims Clarkson. The comical impossibility of the claim that 'Sienna Miller's Range Rover has broken the Gulf Stream' (known in rhetoric as *adynaton*) draws attention to the supposed victimizing of 'middle class' indulgences, as opposed to 'fat lazy northerners who won't get off their arses and fit loft insulation' (Clarkson *Driven to Distraction* loc. 2083). More plausibly it acknowledges that attributing vast, long-term change to infinitesimal individual contributions seems unfair, as well as daft. On the first point, Dale Jamieson's careful assessment of climate ethics accepts that 'it is … not surprising that people do not see picking up their kids after soccer practice as reckless or negligent behavior' (152). The second is compellingly described by Timothy Clark – again, from a radically different perspective to Clarkson's – as a 'derangement of scale', in which the juxtaposition of a trivial daily action with the global, long-term impact to which it contributes disorientates us in a way that could easily spin-off into absurdism. Clark notes that climatic scale effects disrupt a dizzying array of everyday assumptions: 'Even as the global stakes become higher, the term "decision" must become diluted almost out of all recognition in relation to the kinds of daily banality implicated in climate change' (Clark 'Some Climate Change Ironies' 137). Clarkson's adynaton satirically diagnoses derangement of scale, but in place of Clark's challenging aporia, he concludes, unhelpfully, that we ought to dismiss the whole issue as 'boring'.

Despite their global popularity, and the commensurate impact of Clarkson's performance of anti-environmentalism, he and his flagship show *Top Gear* have received very little scholarly attention, even within media studies. Frances Bonner suggests the neglect is due to 'generic hybridity; conservative masculinity; anti-environmentalism; and, on the scholarly side, a nervousness about confronting a text that so relishes its reactionary politics' (33). Studies focus on the show's gender politics, specifically the 'Janus-faced' oscillation between traditional heroic masculinity – embodied in the silent 'superhero' Stig (a pseudonym that recalls the caveman in a popular children's book) – and the 'ironic, humorous and self-deprecating' anti-heroes Clarkson and Hammond, an oscillation that Angela Smith says typifies the 'new lad' of the late 1990s and noughties. Bonner confirms that 'freedom from all restraints is obviously [*Top Gear*'s] ideal' (38), but Kieran Tranter and Damien Martin develop the point that the presenters' seeming lawlessness *requires* the spectre of law for its risk-taking to seem appealing to other men. They note that Clarkson and Hammond's brand of 'combustion masculinity is about taking risks in cars and being seen in this risk-taking by other males' (Tranter and Martin 8). Where Clarkson's grumpy opinionated persona reigns supreme in his newspaper columns and books, his and Hammond's self-conscious 'boyishness' is counterbalanced on *Top Gear* by the presence of James May, or 'Captain Slow' as he is mockingly called by the other two. May's self-presentation is more 'hippy' than them; he betrays nerdy interests in technology and – crucially – he is the programme's resident environmentalist. Although his commitment is often set up to be teased and undermined, May's 'controlled, constructive and caring' presentation of what Tranter and Martin call 'hydraulic masculinity' ('hydraulic' as in construction machinery) provides something of an alternative to Clarkson and Hammond's 'onanistic male climaxing through risk-taking in cars' (16). They conclude that, despite its overt sexism:

> This is the purpose of Top Gear. It is men laughing with, and at, men role-playing a past masculinity. It shows the silliness, the out-of-time-ness, the past-ness of combustion masculinity.
>
> (16)

It is perhaps for this reason that, as Bonner found, *Top Gear* is popular with many viewers (including women) who don't share Clarkson's politics. Clive Hamilton admits:

> One does not need to be a petrolhead or into pimping one's motor vehicle to enjoy *Top Gear*'s fantasies. For some, it is not inconsistent to enjoy an evening watching Clarkson do donuts in a Mack truck and drive to work in a Prius the next day.
>
> (125)

If Hamilton is somewhat coy about whether he includes himself in this group, the present author is not. In its heyday, *Top Gear* was TV gold, and not only because it sustained the BBC financially more than any other programme. There are (whisper it) bad environmentalists who enjoy fast motorbikes, perhaps even 'pimping one's motor vehicle'.

Max Boykoff considers that Clarkson's global warming jibes betray naked self-interest: 'Under the guise of irony and cynicism, such Clarkson comments … effectively cohere with and sustain his political economic interests, be they narrowly perceived through the success of his BBC ode-to-automobiles program *Top Gear* or a penchant for market-led and anti-regulatory management of the environment' (Boykoff 561). If so, it is hard to account for the quite different perspective brought to the programme by Captain Slow. Boykoff underestimates Clarkson's broad appeal, which derives in part from his humorous, charismatic protest against the tendency to understand risk in purely negative terms. It is, as Adams points out, a widespread intuition outside academia:

> The starting point of any theory of risk must be that everyone willingly takes risks. This is not the starting point of most of the literature on risk.
>
> (15–16)

Clarkson's enthusiasm for risk-taking ought to both direct our attention to the pleasures that emissions mitigation really would endanger and alert us to the possibility that climate change itself might be neither 'boring' nor uniformly catastrophic, but rather an energizing challenge to human ethics and ingenuity.

Clarkson's comic nihilism is inimitable, fortunately, but that hasn't prevented less accomplished climate sceptics from trying to play the same tune. James Delingpole is obviously a Clarkson wannabe, as when he describes climate change as 'a threat so vanishingly small, it makes about as much sense as building garlic farms to ward off vampires, or blue whale shelters in case any stray cetaceans get sucked from the oceans by freak tornadoes and dumped over the British countryside during rain showers' (loc. 3794–96). His 2010 book *Watermelons* drags devil-may-care conservativism down to the level of largely witless sneering and relentless *ad hominem* attacks on climate scientists. Which is ironic considering Delingpole's seeming resentment at being treated as a fossil fuel company stooge. He denies being in the pay of the 'denial industry' in characteristically puerile terms:

> Equally, the fact that I am heavily in the pay of Big Koch – I'm not really: this is just a fantasy of mine, and I like saying 'Big Koch' even though the joke isn't as funny as it could be because the Koch brothers' surname is in fact pronounced 'Coke' – does not necessarily mean my argument is corrupt.
>
> (loc. 1110–13)

Delingpole's protestation that we should play the ball, not the man, would be more persuasive if he ever restrained himself in that regard.

He is more winning when he confesses to being shushed by his wife as he mutters sceptical observations about the Greenpeace videos at Glastonbury Festival (loc. 1241), and when he caricatures 'nice Al Gore with his frayed lovable air of some portly, slightly battered, once incredibly expensive teddy bear bought for one of the Rockefeller kids in the 1930s' (loc. 1722–23). George Marshall's generous assessment of *Watermelons* as 'the most entertaining attack on climate change as a belief system' is contestable – Richard Bean's *The Heretic* is much funnier and cleverer – but his conclusion is not: 'Delingpole has no interest in science or evidence, so this is just pure narrative-driven bile' (Marshall 245).

The book's argument, delivered with more verve than substance, is that the field of climatology, the whole IPCC and the UN COP process have been hijacked *in toto* by socialists whose sole interest is the destruction of capitalism, not climate science (watermelons: green on the outside, red on the inside, geddit?). To make the case for this strikingly silly, shallow and polarizing view, he draws liberally, though without acknowledgement, on the press releases of industry groups such as the 1990s 'Global Climate Coalition'. It was the GCC that alleged the IPCC's Second Assessment Report (SAR) had been single-handedly 'doctored' by Dr Ben Santer, a statistician, to foreground the 'political claim' of 'discernible human influence on global climate'. Delingpole uncritically repeats this point (loc. 908–22), despite Santer's own detailed responses to the allegation ('Climate Science Glossary – "Close Encounters of the Absurd Kind"'). Actually, clear acknowledgement of uncertainty *does* appear in the SAR's Summary for Policymakers along with the 'fingerprint' claim:

> Our ability to quantify the human influence on global climate is currently limited because the expected signal is still emerging from the noise of natural variability, and because there are uncertainties in key factors. These include the magnitude and patterns of long term natural variability and the time-evolving pattern of forcing by, and response to, changes in concentrations of greenhouse gases and aerosols, and land surface changes.
>
> (Houghton 5)

Poke at any individual example adduced by Delingpole in *Watermelons*, and you find him being, in his own phrase, 'economical with the *actualité*' (loc. 1261). Moreover, he continually equivocates between broad, Trumpian resentment towards the whole 'liberal establishment' and the more localized – though still unsubstantiated – accusation that the IPCC is lousy with socialists. He directs this argument, rather surprisingly, at 'you', an implied reader who is supposedly one of the socialists' 'useful fools':

> The last thing I want to do at this early stage is insult you by suggesting that you're gullible and thick. I think you've been brainwashed, that's all. (loc. 139)

The heretic pose is distinctively European for the simple reason that climate change is politically hegemonic in most European countries, albeit that Delingpole's idiom (choosing words like 'thick') gives it a self-consciously English spin. On the other hand, his paranoia about 'One-World Government' is uniquely American in origin (Marshall 18), as, arguably, is his absurd/terrifying moral dualism:

> There are no-half measures in the modern green movement. To join it simply because you like trees, flowers and birdsong is the rough equivalent of joining the Nazi party in the mid-1930s just for the smart uniforms, restaurant discounts and more efficient train timetables. Which is to say that the eco-Fascistic elements

> are not optional extras. The anti-capitalism, the hatred of economic growth, the curtailment of personal liberty, the disdain for the human race, the yearning for a One-World Government of rule by 'experts' – these are all as integral to watermelons as *Lebensraum* and extermination camps were to Nazism.
>
> (loc. 2986–90)

Climate activism has perhaps been subject to some left entryism, and the history of environmentalism is marred by misanthropic statements – probably because real environmentalists sometimes suffer misanthropic moods – but the claim that 'the eco-Fascistic elements are not optional extras' is demonstrably false, as well as insulting. The politicization of the environment described above is taken here to an appalling extreme. Delingpole's self-description as a '*South Park* Conservative' seemed engagingly eccentric in 2010; it looks very different in 2018 now that Delingpole is a contributor to the 'alt-right' 'Breitbart' website. That joke isn't funny any more.

So far, my analysis of British climate scepticism may have done little to dislodge the popular stereotype, not least because Clarkson in particular seems to revel in embodying it. The remaining texts, though, exemplify the diversity of British sceptical texts more effectively. The first, Philip Foster's *While the Earth Endures* (2009) announces its oblique approach to climate change on the first page:

> First and foremost I intend to preserve the integrity of the Word of God. But I am also going to depart from the current evangelical Christian consensus about the nature of the revelation given in the first chapters of Genesis.
>
> (5)

Far more than the ranting of a Smart Alec alt-right conservative, Foster's book came as a surprise. In keeping with its author's Cambridge degrees in biochemistry and theology, it veers quite suddenly between the supposed 'irreducible complexity' of DNA and extensive Old Testament exegesis on the seeming imperfections in God's creation. It devotes several chapters to confronting 'Young Earth Theory' with the 'absolutely overwhelming' (27) evidence that the universe is billions of years old, but then dismisses evolution as 'a piece of negative theology surrounded by truisms' (93). As well as being rambling, opinionated and very poorly copy-edited, Foster's book adopts an amusingly old fogey-ish tone, as when the paucity of information in Genesis regarding the Creation is turned into a virtue:

> It is the dull and lazy student who looks for easy ways out of doing his assigned work – it is the good student who works hard to learn for himself. At school,

> some text books used to have the answers at the back of the book – but that only spoils it! These days, I suppose, this is one of the dangers of the internet.
>
> (71)

Foster's usage of 'dull' in the sense of 'thick', not 'boring', is striking, as is the bespectacled vicar implied by the interpolation 'I suppose'. Elsewhere, he reminds readers interested in solar astronomy: '*Never* look the sun directly' (146).

Foster goes on to claim that, while God appears to concede physics and geology to the scientists (35–49), climate is in His domain:

> The Lord is in charge of the weather, no question. Today, in a humanistic and atheistic world, such an idea is regarded as merely quaint and pre-scientific. Like the builders of Babel, humans now think they are causing the weather.
>
> (122)

Foster's argument recycles all the sceptical talking points – Santer rewrote IPCC SAR, Rachel Carson is worse than Hitler, CO_2 is a fertilizer – up until the shocking *denouement*. Having proposed that the observed global warming trend is actually caused by the effects of cosmic rays on cloud cover – often known as the 'Svensmark effect' – Foster suggests that God controls the Earth's weather by causing supernovas:

> Like the cosmic rays setting out on their amazing journey through the Galaxy in order to reach this tiny planet and start a particular cloud formation to produce a particular rain storm with unerring aim. *He makes the wind His messengers, Flaming fire His ministers*, so these fiery messengers [cosmic rays] may serve other purposes of God.
>
> (213)

The changes in DNA required to bring about the irreducible complexity of the natural world, Foster asserts, are also brought about by means of the 'delicate molecular surgery of the cosmic ray' (216).

It is difficult to know how to respond to such an eccentric theory. Observing that multiple lines of scientific evidence cast doubt on the Svensmark effect seems beside the point ('Climate Science Glossary – Cosmic Rays'). Nor is it worthwhile to pour atheistic scorn on the notion that a divine being would need to interfere in Creation in such a roundabout way. Rather, one must skirt condescension and acknowledge the unique heterogeneity of *While the Earth Endures*: its earnest effort to integrate science and theology in an intellectually honest way. Foster may be right that we'd be 'freed from the *angst* of our age' (222) if we believed that the wonders of nature – which clearly captivate Foster as much as the present author – were the outcome of such a 'mind-boggling' (215) intervention. His faithful scepticism would be more reassuring than, say, Gray's enervating fatalism, but for this reader, sadly, it is simply incredible.

Martin Cohen's *Paradigm Shift* (2015) is at the opposite extreme to Foster, both philosophically and stylistically. The author is a jobbing philosopher, writing popular texts such as *Critical Thinking Skills for Dummies* (2015) and *101 Ethical Dilemmas* (2007), but his sceptical text is published by Andrews UK, which offers four e-book publishing 'packages' ranging from £75 to £500. Cohen enfolds climate scepticism within a broader questioning of scientific and other 'experts', but his careless treatment of complex issues undermines his attempt to bring acerbic epistemological scepticism to bear on climate science. Each chapter contrasts 'what we're supposed to think' with 'what you're not to say' on topics as wide-ranging as Darwinism, clinical psychiatry, evidence-based medicine, homeopathy, astrology and macro-economics. In every case, Cohen finds reason to doubt hegemonic views or boost those despised as 'unscientific' without avowing anything much himself.

Cohen's broad knowledge of the history of science provides him with some arresting examples. For example, he highlights the irrationality, occultism and politicking of such illustrious thinkers as Galileo, Newton and Descartes, but then concludes with a trivializing false dichotomy: 'So where's all this history pointing? Just once again to the conclusion that science advances by irrational and political devices, not by weight of "objective evidence"' (Cohen, loc. 1525–26). He broaches crucial issues, such as the creeping pathologization of mental distress (cf. Haslam), but then scuppers himself with flippant, implausible, trivializing analogies:

> It is not so long ago that medical experts travelled in wooden wagons painted with outrageous claims, dispensing coloured water in fancy bottles to cure various ills. Evidently, these were not real doctors but crooks and charlatans! But brightly painted wagons impressed people back then. Nowadays, doctors must train for many years and have lots of books and 'government advisories' to achieve the same effect. And modern-day coloured water is made by huge transnational companies with gleaming steel and glass-fronted laboratories. Yet, too often, neither the diagnoses nor the remedies are any better.
>
> (loc. 677–81)

'Too often,' Cohen's favourite weasel phrase, spares him the effort of properly explaining, justifying or quantifying the effects he describes. Instances of expert failure are indeed legion, but his accounts reveal that they are almost always noticed by other experts. So what are the proper limits and capacities of expertise? The more scientifically complex the field, the more brutally reductive is Cohen's treatment of it, as when he sums up chaos theory (now called complexity theory) as 'there are no rules!' (loc. 2491). By the time we get to climatology, any lingering trust in the author's accuracy has evaporated, so his banal, straw-man conclusion fails entirely to shock:

> The important thing, myth or science, call it what you will, is that you don't think that by calling it 'science' [climatology] becomes irrefutable. Because that it ain't. Even in the flexible world of climate science, there's no such thing as an 'average global temperature', nor even an average global CO2 level. The figures you arrive at depend on what you choose to measure, where you choose to measure it, and at what time. The selection of data is all.
>
> (loc. 2766–70)

Well, yes, of course, that is precisely the challenge of earth systems science. Does Cohen have any suggestions about how it could be improved? He does not.

Cohen draws extensively on the work of Paul Feyerabend, whose *Against Method* (1975) epitomized the spirit of the moment with its sceptical demolition of scientific authority. However, he acknowledges none of the cogent objections to Feyerabend's relativism, and offers no advances on his analysis. Writing in the *Times Higher*, Cohen claims to be an environmentalist disillusioned by the shift from local conservation issues to 'propaganda' about climate change ('Beyond Debate?'). It is a defensible position, which is maintained with far greater authority by Peter Taylor's *Chill*, discussed below. Cohen, though, adds little in terms of either style or substance.

Having saved the best until last, we arrive at the most entertaining and illuminating examples of British climate scepticism. The first, *The Real Global Warming Disaster* (2009), is by the *Daily Telegraph* columnist and founder of the satirical magazine *Private Eye*, Christopher Booker. The book benefits from a journalist's economy of phrase and eye for political poppycock, notably the deal Tony Blair made with Vladimir Putin to support Russia's entry into the World Trade Organization in return for ratification of the Kyoto Protocol. Given that the Protocol's baseline year was 1991, when polluting Soviet industries were still in operation, 'Russia would start off way below its Kyoto allowance and would thus be able to make billions of dollars a year under the UN's Clean Development Mechanism from selling those "carbon credits" which were a key part of the Kyoto system' (loc. 2290–91). He is amusing, as well as persuasive, on politicians' (of all stripes) lack of comprehension of the huge technical and economic challenges of decarbonizing the British energy supply, mostly with wind energy:

> It was hard to recall any issue on which British politicians *en masse* had ever become so detached from reality. Yet, with one or two exceptions, these Quixotic proposals were solemnly reported by the unquestioning media, without any hint that they were pure wishful thinking.
>
> (loc. 5912–14)

Booker recites the usual sceptical talking points about the corruption of the IPCC and the possible influence of the sun, but his underlying argument is quite fascinating and idiosyncratic. It extends the central claim of his 'gargantuan, sometimes absorbing and often blockheaded … book' (Kakutani), *The Seven Basic Plots: Why We Tell Stories.* As the title suggests, Booker argues – at numbing length – that all book and film plots can be reduced to just seven, including The Quest, Rags to Riches and so on. With the astonishing breadth of a book that took thirty-four years to write, Booker seeks to show that 'all kinds of story, however profound or however trivial, ultimately spring from the same source, are shaped around the same basic patterns and are governed by the same hidden, universal rules' (14). This plausible, if unoriginal, idea then forms the basis of a far more tendentious normative claim: that Western literature since Romanticism has gone wrong because it kept trying to depart from this archetypal pattern, in which the masculine and feminine principles are reconciled in the ideal balance symbolized in marriage. As a result, Booker suggests, we should see Steven Spielberg's movie *E.T.* as providing

> a more substantial ending than the plays of Chekhov, Proust, Beckett or any other story in this chapter. Because their pseudo-endings, going nowhere, are all that stories spun from the ego alone can ever hope to achieve.
>
> (454)

Combining conservative Catholicism with Jungian cultural analysis and a *soupçon* of evolutionary theory, Booker dismisses the entire Modernism tradition – and American culture, to boot – as essentially 'immature'. He repeatedly relies, without evidence, on the supposed adverse reaction of abstracted 'readers', although my suspicion is that Booker himself is the jilted bridegroom deprived of a proper conclusion:

> The archetype cannot be cheated. If it is defied, the story is doomed just to peter out, or to be forced into some implausible 'pseudo-ending' which leaves its audience curiously unsatisfied.
>
> (494)

Despite the inherent flaws in its argument, anatomized elsewhere (Mars-Jones), *Seven Basic Plots* is the foundation of the sceptical position of *The Real Global Warming Disaster*:

> We all of us, much more than we are consciously aware, see the world in terms of stories, 'narratives' which help shape the way in which we try to understand the world around us: explaining how it works, where we have come from and where we may be heading for. All ideologies in this way have their own narrative, and 'environmentalism' was no exception.
>
> (loc. 6647–50)

We agree. Indeed, the subconscious power of narrative is a truism of modern literary culture. Regardless of whether they concur with Booker's Catholic-Jungian interpretation of narrative archetypes, literary scholars ought to take his argument seriously as a test of their own faith in the shaping power of narratives. George Marshall presents psychological evidence that people will hang on to a compelling story even in the face of directly contradictory factual evidence, and concludes mournfully:

> This is why it is extremely hard for a deeply unengaging narrative based in fact to compete with a compelling narrative based in falsehood. 'The balance of evidence leads many climate scientists to suggest that our emissions may be damaging the climate' is, unfortunately, less inherently compelling than 'rogue scientists are conspiring to fake evidence in order to secure larger research grants'.
>
> (106–07)

He cites Booker and Michael Crichton (discussed in Chapter 4) as supporting evidence, but this book is full of other examples.

Here is the problem for ecocritics: if, as the Canadian indigenous writer Thomas King's oft-quoted line has it, 'the truth about stories is that's all we are' (2), how can we claim that climate change is, uniquely, exempted from this condition? To put it in binary terms, does scientific evidence count, or do we select what counts on the basis of largely pre-scientific commitments, as Booker argues? At the same time, though, Booker shies away from the relativistic implications of this position, not because sceptics have stronger evidence – *ex hypothesis*: they must select it on the basis of *their* own narratives – but because conservatives are apparently more likely to accept the wisdom of the archetypes. Environmentalism, for Booker, is not marked by biocentric care for the non-human world, but the narcissistic belief that humans possess god-like powers: 'Those affected by this new concern for the "environment" were coming to see mankind as a greedy and reckless cuckoo in the nest of creation, capable not just of wreaking immeasurable damage on all other forms of life but of destroying it altogether' (loc. 6130–32). On this view, which Booker shares with the Mormon radio host Glenn Beck, climate scepticism reflects an appropriate attitude of humility.

There is a puzzle, though, about the role of apocalyptic narrative in climate activism. Booker acknowledges that environmentalists'

> vision of the coming apocalypse conjured up by their prophets, such as Al Gore and James Hansen, and confirmed by those 'sacred texts' handed down by the IPCC, had much in common with ancient myths and Biblical tales of the world being visited with 'extreme weather events', plagues, fires, mighty winds and above all floods so immense that whole cities would vanish below their waves. (loc. 6682–85)

Given such ancient provenance, Booker ought to endorse such a 'basic plot,' and yet he complains, in racially tinged terms, that environmentalists are idolators thanks to the 'computer model [that] stands at the heart of the story like some mysterious fetish at the centre of a jungle clearing, attended by those modern versions of witch doctors who are the consecrated interpreters of its oracular powers' (loc. 6693–94). But the subterranean appeal of basic plots reflects a psychology of archetypal form, not content; whether the idol is Jahweh or HadCRUT ('Temperature') ought not to matter. Even though climate apocalypticism seems to fulfil his closure criterion, Booker seems willing to bend his own theory to suit his ideological orientation.

The Heretic (2011) is by far the funniest and most technically accomplished sceptical text in the British canon. Playwright Richard Bean already courted controversy with his satirical treatment of East End immigrants through the ages, *England People Very Nice* (2009). His sceptical play features a paleogeophysicist, Dr Diane Cassell, who comes under pressure from her boss, Professor Kevin Maloney, to delay publication of evidence that sea level has not risen at all in the Maldives. She exercises her tart tongue in lively exchanges with her anorexic daughter Phoebe and a clever young student and environmentalist, Ben Shotter (whose name recalls Dr Ben Santer, a climatologist discussed above):

> BEN: Look, if we double CO_2, we double temperatures, that's bare bait, man, and that is the end of the world. Common sense innit.
>
> DIANE: If common sense trumped science my mother would be running a nuclear power station. The relationship between CO_2 and temperature is not linear, it's logarithmic. Think of an example, from your own life perhaps, where doubling a variable does not double the effect.
>
> (Bean 39)

Diane receives death threats from the Sacred Earth Militia, whose undercover operative Mordoff, a Geordie ex-Marine from 'Site Services', is a working-class version of the Wordworthian Romantic of Byronic satire. During the course of the play, Ben learns scientific scepticism, and Kevin threatens Diane with sacking if she upsets the 'consensus'. Above all, Earth Sciences must not sacrifice its prestigious position within the modern university:

> KEVIN: It was the Arts forever, wasn't it, until in the sixties Sociology floated to the top like an aerated turd, hung around for a few years, before finally getting sucked down the tube of its own gaping fatuousness. Then in the seventies, the Psychologists took over the asylum. Boy did those tossers fancy themselves. But they could never nail anything properly down. One minute being mentally ill is a crushing personal tragedy, next minute it's a bit of a laugh and you should try to enjoy it. All that Psychology ever achieved was making bullshit respectable, which of course, paved the way for Media Studies and ten years of mind-numbing bollocks! So that day, last year, when Media Studies' top witch knocked on my door and begged me to let her first years onto your introductory Earth Sciences modular lecture, that was the moment I knew we'd finally arrived. It's official – we are the kings of the castle. Let's not fuck it up, eh?
>
> (35)

Where other climate sceptics merely assert that science is distorted by groupthink and professional opportunity, Bean's delightfully comic depiction highlights institutional pressures that will resonate with any British academic. In the context of the relentless audit culture and artificially induced competition within and among British universities, Diane's 'heresy' is refreshing:

> KEVIN: The 'Climate Change Research Unit' would service clients by –
> DIANE: – I'm not a sex worker.
> KEVIN: Listen! We are the Earth Sciences Faculty of YUIST for teaching, but *virtually* we are a separate budget centre, providing tools to the market.
> DIANE: What tools would I be selling?
> KEVIN: A computer model of sea level rise.
> DIANE: I'd rather sell the fluff from my naval [*sic*]. It'd be more use. After a couple of years they could knit a jumper.(33)

Bean's satire on the instrumentalization of the 'neoliberal university' is comparable to Laurie Taylor's *The Poppletonian* from the *Times Higher* in its skewering of the vacuous language and, arguably, intellectual conformity fostered by corporatization. It is deeply ironic that Bean's targets – the monetization of knowledge, the tyranny of Human Resources and the cant of 'student centred learning' – are themselves consequences of the neoliberalization of British universities initiated by the Conservatives and enthusiastically extended under New Labour.

The popular stereotype of climate sceptics depicts them as anti-scientific, but the truth is that British sceptics, like Michael Crichton (see Chapter 4), are more often disappointed scientific idealists. So it is with Diane Cassell, as she demonstrates in this exchange with the (real-life) BBC interviewer Jeremy Paxman:

> PAXMAN: Doctor Cassell, are you a global warming *denier*?
> DIANE: There is no evidence that CO_2 is responsible for twentieth century warming.
> PAXMAN: You're pretty much alone in this belief aren't you.
> DIANE: It's not a belief. I'm a scientist, I don't 'believe' in anything.(55)

With her sharp wit and fierce independence, Diane embodies a resilient modernist ideal of disinterested scientific authority – although she also loves her Jaguar XK8 and proclaims that 'cars are liberating, democratic and feminist' (97). By appealing to the evidence of a single salt-intolerant tree thriving on a beach in the Maldives in opposition to the IPCC's claims of sea level rise, moreover, Diane fulfils the empiricist orientation that Sheila Jasanoff includes in her characterization of the British 'civic epistemology' (Jasanoff 263). With superb if paradoxical intuition, Bean's play resurrects a myth of the scientist that, as we explain in Chapter 6, three decades of publicized climate science really ought to have vanquished.

The play's climax takes place at Diane's house as the Sacred Earth Militia closes in, intending to kidnap a climate sceptic. The usual sceptical talking points are gradually diluted by the accelerating action, although Diane squeezes in a comic tirade against environmental apocalypticism when Phoebe invites Ben for a romantic walk around a supposed medieval plague village:

> DIANE: Can you explain something to me Kevin? Every year Phoebe and I walk around Wharram Percy. *Every year* I explain to her that the residents left the village in the sixteenth century because there was a change of land use. The landlord wanted to graze sheep, which meant an end to arable farming, so everyone packed their bags and left to look for work elsewhere.
> KEVIN: How prosaic.
> DIANE: Yes. But this generation –
> PHOEBE: – it's not my generation that has fucked the planet.

DIANE: This generation, are disaster junkies. Armageddon in three acts.

PHOEBE: Fuck off.

DIANE: It's as if every last twitching synapse has been transplanted from the stolen corpse of a Hollywood screen writer. Why be content with 'a change of land use' when you can have the drama of 'wiped out by the Black Death'. Every day they wake up craving a narrative fix. When they see a photograph of a polar bear, hitching a ride on a passing ice flow [*sic*], they cannot see a wild animal at ease in its natural habitat. What they see is the last five minutes of Titanic! That one ton carnivore's contented yawn becomes Leonardo DiCaprio's hopeless scream as he drifts inexorably away from that posh girl who's normally in a corset.

BEN: Kate Winslet. (91)

The conservative objection to 'eco-doomsters' is familiar enough, and the hyperbolic satire recalls Clarkson and Delingpole. Unlike other sceptical texts, though, *The Heretic* memorably dramatizes the contrast between the misanthropy of the Sacred Earth Militia and the defiant humanism of Diane and the other characters. When Phoebe suffers a starvation-induced heart attack, Geoff Mordoff (who has been hiding in the house) abandons his plan to kidnap Diane and saves a life instead. The comic resolution is thereby juxtaposed directly with the would-be cruelty of the environmentalist 'disaster junkies'.

We can be more specific: Act Five conforms neatly to Booker's outline of the seventh basic plot, 'Rebirth', which he illustrates with the plots of *A Christmas Carol*, *Crime and Punishment*, and *Silas Marner*. The hero, on this view, is Ben, because he is the one who falls 'into the grip of an egocentric obsession, which renders him both unable to feel for others outside himself and also blind to the reality of what is happening to him' (203). Diane's coaching in scientific scepticism aligns with Ben's acceptance of Phoebe as a 'redeeming figure', leading to his internalization of his mentor's language and empiricist idealism:

KEVIN (to BEN): … Do you believe that we're warmer now than we've ever been?

BEN: Ever been, or in the Holocene?

KEVIN: Christ! You can tell he's one of yours [Diane's]. Of course, in the Holocene. Do you believe we're warmer now than we've ever been in the Holocene?

BEN: I'm a scientist, yeah. I can't allow myself to 'believe in' anything.

The last Act is redemptive on a number of levels: Phoebe is alive, not dead, and is about to marry Ben. Her pregnant body contrasts visibly with her anorexic state in the first four acts; indeed, she embodies both the redemptive figures identified by Booker, 'a Young Woman' *and* 'a Child' (204). Diane and Kevin have buried their differences, and are now romantically united, but their modes of transport to the church imply that each has retained her or his own distinct identity:

> KEVIN: Right! It's me and the bride in [Diane's] Jag, with the top down. You're driving the Prius, and Ben is on his bike.
>
> (113)

There is no direct evidence that Booker has seen the play, but it ought to be a favourite, corresponding as it does to his views on both 'satisfying' plots (that conclude with heterosexual marriage) and climate change.

The last text to be considered here is, in a number of ways, the most heterodox. It is also a demanding test of our resolution to be agnostic on the scientific issues. Peter Taylor's *Chill: A Reassessment of Global Warming Theory* (2009) engages in considerable detail with both climate science and the social context in which it operates. The author is, as he frequently emphasizes, 'a committed environmentalist' (P. Taylor 3) and 'leading advocate of *rewilding* policies in nature conservation' (n.p.), with experience of the use and abuse of computer models in political campaigns. Stylistically, the book substitutes a 'more-in-sorrow-than-in-anger' idiom of disappointment for the kind of sneering satire that typifies British scepticism. While some of its claims are all too familiar, the basic orientation of *Chill* is utterly different from all the others: expressly and persuasively eco-feminist, green and empirical, albeit not uncritically so. The book has made next to no impact with either sceptics or warmists as a result.[11]

Peter Taylor's experience has made him wary of the ways in which environmental issues – notably climate change – are 'scientificated', a problem we discuss in the penultimate chapter. Yet, unlike Cohen, he is no epistemological anarchist:

> In addition to my training in natural sciences, I have an abiding interest in how different cultures, including my own, perceive their environment. In my experience, the world of environmental perception always interplays with theories of causation, divinity and notions of purpose and progress. In 'western culture' these elements are separated, as if inhabiting unrelated compartments of the mind. Thus, with regard to climate change, the issue is regarded as 'scientific' as if there were some pure and objective compartment of knowledge unaffected by any of the other boxes into which some very powerful and pervasive human propensities have been so solidly put. Social scientists would beg to question

> such a reality, but I will address these issues only by way of a signpost to further enquiry. The main thrust of this book is to question the science on its own terms.
>
> (3)

With that caveat, Taylor effectively adopts the mantle of a one-man IPCC, reviewing both the Assessment Reports and their evidence base with painstaking thoroughness. He proposes 'a predominantly natural explanation for global warming' that is 'entirely tenable within the accepted bounds of science, with every tenet supported by peer-reviewed work in the specialist literature' (47). This act of supreme presumption is conducted with – for the most part – appealing modesty. At the outset he asks: 'Who am I to disagree with [the] apparent consensus?' (3). Throughout the book, his own rhetoric is cautious. More substantively, he argues that the IPCC process prematurely identified anthropogenic greenhouse gas emissions as the primary cause of warming in the 1990s, which imposed on the Earth systems science community a 'prior commitment' to climate model-based projections of further change. He observes that scientists seldom challenge findings of colleagues from other specialized fields, and, in the present political context, refrain particularly from drawing conclusions that might conflict with the IPCC consensus. For example, he analyses a series of papers that debate methods of measuring the Earth's total albedo, or reflectance, and its relationship to oceanic heat storage. It seems an arcane argument, but Taylor cites a claim that a 1 per cent change in albedo would be equivalent 'to the computed effect of a doubling of carbon dioxide levels' (62). He concludes:

> [There are] a number of papers that refer to a period of changing short-wave (SW) flux throughout the 1990s affecting the oceans' heat storage. The authors comment that these changes are 'not reconciled' with climate models that assume changes in LW flux are responsible for global warming. This is yet another example of low-key statements that are not overt criticisms of the current global warming hypothesis when in fact they are of critical importance and give rise, once more, to the ability of partisan commentators to argue that no real scientific dissent has been published or, as with the IPCC, that a consensus exists on causation.
>
> (66)

From a literary critical perspective, Taylor's habit of close reading 'against the grain' is both immediately recognizable and persuasive. Science and Technology Studies researchers would probably concur with Taylor's account of a politically enhanced version of 'black-boxing', in which knowledge artefacts imported from cognate scientific domains are 'taken for granted as completed projects, not as messy constellations' (Sismondo 85). From a scientific perspective, though, *Chill* would presumably be infuriating, given that Taylor – an outsider with no record of work in climate science – appears to question *either* the integrity *or* the intellectual rigour of any scientist who does not support his own view. Moreover, Taylor ignores the ways in which the IPCC deliberately, as Paul Edwards puts it, '*brings controversy within consensus*' (xvii) by inviting comments on draft reports from 'national governments and by stakeholders, including environmental groups and corporate organizations' (399). A 1999 change brought in review editors, who are not involved in the drafting, to 'ensure responsiveness to the comments and criticisms collected during review' (401).

Taylor's solar flux hypothesis is endorsed by many other sceptics, but *Chill* presents it in impressive detail. He constantly reminds us that he is citing 'new science' (103) and claims there is 'mounting evidence' in favour of his view (89). Taylor explains in gendered terms the difference between his focus on natural cycles, notably oscillations in teleconnected ocean currents, from climate models' attention to trends:

> Science has become mired in a polarized, left-brain view of the world, which even within its own terms of reference has made it blind to the operation of cycles, irregular periodicity, the mathematics of spirals and elements of chaos. It would be trite to say that these are all elements of a feminine mode of thinking but nevertheless true.
>
> (242)

Taylor's most persuasive arguments against the primacy of climate models, though, derive from his own experience in environmental activism. Where right-wing sceptics portray climate change as the continuation of a tradition of environmentalist 'doom-mongering', Taylor explains the disreputable history of computer models that repeatedly *underestimated* environmental risks, as in the case of polychlorinated biphenyl (PCB):

> Neither its eventual toxicity nor its propensity to be transported as a volatile substance from landfill in warm regions and to be later distilled into cold environments had been predicted by the models that justified its initial release.
>
> (252–53)

On Taylor's account, it was the repeated *failure* of computer modelling to anticipate future hazards that eventually prompted the European Union to adopt the precautionary principle towards potentially toxic substances.

Despite his deep scepticism regarding the reliability of prediction, Taylor makes one falsifiable claim: that oceanic oscillations and a solar minimum should lead to global cooling after 2009. The fact that the global mean temperature has continued to rise supports a higher estimate for climate sensitivity than 'a likely range from 0.56–1.0°C for carbon dioxide doubling' (223). To the extent that most warmists *and* sceptics maintain, 'it's the science, dummy', Taylor has already been proven wrong.

However, Taylor's counter-review of the IPCC in Part 1 of his book is balanced by a compelling consideration of social pressures on science and environmental policy in Part 2. For one thing, his scepticism about attribution does not translate into impact scepticism:

> The underlying message of the previous chapters is that dangerous climate change is an immediate problem that will inevitably get worse. It cannot be mitigated on any policy-relevant timescale.
>
> (333)

He shares this conclusion, if not the reasoning that led to it, with authors such as Clive Hamilton, Dale Jamieson and Mike Hulme. We need to take time to get policies right, Taylor argues, and focus on ecological and social resilience, rather than emissions reduction, in the meantime. His most emotive appeal concerns the vast impact of dramatic emissions reduction on the British Isles, which has been continually understated by environmental organizations. As he points out:

> That policy, enacted without stringent safeguards, would lay waste to the British landscape. That which I love, and which sustains me, would be turned into a technoscape of turbines, barrages, plantations and powerlines.
>
> (302)

He is not exaggerating. David Mackay, chief scientific advisor to the Department of Energy and Climate Change, prints a map of a future Britain where 300 gigawatts of energy (i.e. present consumption) is produced with no fossil fuel emissions (MacKay 215). It includes 52 new onshore wind farms, 100 urban waste incinerators, 40 nuclear power stations and 2,700 square kilometres of solar power sited in North Africa. None of the other five 'plans that add up' (212) are any more attractive: Plan E, an economically optimal solution with no imported electricity, envisages Britain with *ten times* as much nuclear power capacity as in 2007.

Having previously campaigned to strengthen local communities, environmental organizations now collude with government and corporate interests, claims Taylor, to override objections to 'clean energy' projects. Quite unlike Delingpole's socialist conspiracy, this suggestion aligns with the evidence already presented here about the politicization of the environment in the 1990s. For Taylor, the final irony is that climate change has led his fellow environmentalists to abandon their hard-won criticisms of potential bias and groupthink within scientific communities:

> These sorts of questions have become common ground when analysing the 'defence' industry, pharmaceuticals, pesticides, agrochemicals, nuclear and GMO industries, but the 'global warming' fraternity and its UN operation is placed beyond question. To even suggest that similar forces may be at work is to be denigrated and dismissed without argument.
>
> (294)

Has climate science been spared the kinds of critique levelled at, say, the biotechnology industry, simply because it is seen as ideologically aligned with scholars in Science and Technology Studies? Are climate models false friends? We return to these crucial questions in Chapters 6 and 7. At this point, we need only observe that *Chill* contradicts the assumption that environmentalists cannot be climate sceptics. It shouldn't be surprising: the impact of mitigation, on the British Isles at least, seems certain to be dire.

Conclusion

Throughout most of the twentieth century, environmentalism was culturally prevalent in Britain, but politically invisible. During the 1980s, Margaret Thatcher's ideological Conservatism elicited a more politicized environmental movement, which found a sympathetic audience in Brussels. In the early years of climate activism, British sceptics were mild and reasonable in their criticisms, but as successive IPCC assessments reported increased confidence in anthropogenic warming, the sceptical response became more shrill and defensive. During the pivotal period 2005–2010, a fragile warmist hegemony prevailed in British politics and culture, further polarizing of public opinion and prompting sceptics to proclaim their own 'heretical' character. Their authors largely conformed to the conservative white male stereotype, while the texts themselves recycled a small number of specific allegations and counter-claims: the apocalypticism of environmental organizations, the corruption of climate science and the IPCC, the Svensmark solar hypothesis and so on.

Beneath this veneer of similarity, though, I found considerable stylistic, generic and philosophical variety. Fatalism, a little-studied aspect of response scepticism, vies with the more familiar economic optimism of Lord Lawson's *Appeal to Reason*. Peter Taylor and Philip Foster both endorse the role of cosmic rays, but from radically different perspectives and to diametrically opposed conclusions. Both Jeremy Clarkson and James Delingpole purvey hyperbolic satire with a recognizably British cultural pedigree, but the latter laces his bile with conspiracy theories from across the Atlantic. And in Bean's *The Heretic*, British climate scepticism enjoys a unique literary accomplishment, much funnier and more effective, in its way, than warmist dramas such as *The Contingency Plan* (2009) or *Greenland* (2011).

In the aftermath of the passage of the Climate Change Act, warmist activism and sceptical outrage have been in relative abeyance. British political and social life have been dominated by financial crisis and austerity (2009 on), a referendum on Scottish independence (September 2014), a general election (May 2015), a further referendum on European Union membership (June 2016) and another snap election (June 2017). It is now clear that Brexit will consume almost all the energies of the British polity for years to come. Still, in a context where the CCA and the Paris Agreement commit Britain to climate mitigation policies, it may be that reduced political salience and a lower-temperature debate will provide opportunities for collaboration and practical problem-solving. Understanding sceptical perspectives is only the first step.

3

Klimaskepsis in Germany

Axel Goodbody

Climate scepticism in Germany – surely not?

Germans are proud of their country's reputation for environmental awareness and progressive green legislation, and not without justification. Over the last thirty years, Germany has led the way in reducing pollution from industry, transport and domestic heating, promoting recycling and reducing the volume of waste, decoupling economic growth from resource consumption and carbon emissions, and generally meeting the environmental challenges associated with population growth, urbanization and industrialization. The OECD called the country a 'laboratory for green growth' in 2012 and praised its 'proactive role in environmental policy within the EU and internationally'. Its energy policy in particular had 'a beacon-like character for many other countries around the world' (see Uekötter, ch. 1). The Green Party has governed at regional level and, in coalition with the Social Democrats, formed the federal government between 1998 and 2006. More importantly, many of its policies have been adopted by other parties since the 1980s and passed into legislation. Environmental problems are bipartisan issues in the Bundestag. Under both Social Democrat and Christian Democrat (Conservative) chancellors, Germany has set itself ambitious goals in climate policy, including reducing greenhouse gases by 40 per cent by 2020, and by 80–95 per cent by 2050. Germany has set the international standard with its accelerated timetable for transitioning from fossil fuels to renewables. The German *Energiewende*, a term variously translated, either (neutrally) as 'energy transition', (literally) as a 'turnaround' in energy policy, or (more grandly) as 'energy system transformation' or 'energy revolution', is more ambitious than the decarbonization strategies of most other nations, and differs from them in aiming to eliminate nuclear power as well as (ultimately) fossil fuels from the country's energy mix, and seeking to do so in significant measure by promoting the feeding of power generated by small producers from renewable sources into the grid (wind, solar and biomass). (See Hager and Stefes for an in-depth discussion of the *Energiewende* in international comparison.)

It is worth reflecting for a moment on the reasons for the strength of public support for these radical and expensive environmental policies. Cultural tradition and national identity have clearly played a role. The Germans' self-understanding as a people close to nature found expression in the eighteenth century in the writings of Johann Gottlieb Herder, and in the nineteenth in those of Ernst Moritz Arndt and Wilhelm Heinrich Riehl. The Roman historian and ethnographer Tacitus had described the Teutonic tribes in his *De origine et moribus Germanorum* (AD 98) as a forest-dwelling people, defending their freedom and integrity against the corrupting influence of surrounding nations. German self-identification with nature, and with forests in particular, has been referenced in paintings by artists from Caspar David Friedrich (*The Chasseur in the Forest*, 1814) to Anselm Kiefer (*Varus*, 1976), and a long line of German nature poets starting with Klopstock and Goethe, Schiller and Eichendorff have contributed to a sense of special affinity with the natural environment. Few participants in the environmental movement in the 1970s and 1980s were conscious of the historical links between their concerns and either Romanticism or the Life Reform Movement at the turn of the twentieth century, when interest in personal wellbeing went hand-in-hand with belief that it could be achieved through closeness to nature. However, the resonances with cultural tradition which environmentalism possessed undoubtedly helped to make it such a strong force in Germany, in comparison with its neighbours.

A second, more recent reason for the importance of nature and environment for Germans is the quest for a new, positive national identity since the Second World War. United in shame for the crimes against humanity committed in the Third Reich, Germans embraced green thinking, alongside liberal democracy and the social market economy, as an opportunity to recuperate collective self-esteem. Pride in the new self-image as a green nation also served to a degree as a substitute for the loss of geopolitical power and linguistic and cultural prestige. Americans may see themselves as 'nature's nation' (Perry Miller), but the democratic environmental patriotism which has provided a safe and acceptable form of collective identity in today's Germany is in essence anti-nationalistic and has pacifist leanings. The environmental movement gained significantly in strength from its overlap with the peace movement in the early 1980s, at a time when the arms race between the superpowers constituted a particular threat to the lives of the East and West Germans caught between them.

The Germans' tradition of regional allegiance and local belonging, which is reflected in the country's federal structure, also favoured the establishment of initiatives around local environmental causes. Conservation and environmental concern had roots in the Bund Heimatschutz (Association for the Protection of the Heimat, founded 1906), which sought to preserve regional architecture, customs and dress against the homogenizing influence of mass culture, as well as protecting natural monuments and endangered landscapes from industrial transformation, pollution and the loss of habitats. The Bund Naturschutz in Bayern (Bavarian League for Nature Protection), out of which BUND, the German branch of Friends of the Earth, grew in 1973, was founded in 1913, and the Weimar constitution of 1919 was the first that took protection of the natural environment into consideration. A final factor in Germany's leading position in matters environmental is the nation's consensual political culture and tradition of corporatist cooperation between politicians, industry and the unions, in which expert-driven regulation serves as a way around confrontational clashes. This distinctive 'civic epistemology' (Jasanoff) has facilitated cross-party agreement on major environmental issues and a buy-in of industry.

Cultural values, self-identity and political opportunities thus converged in the 1970s to the advantage of environmentalism in Germany, and whether because of the nation's strong Romantic tradition, its wish to reinvent itself after the Second World War or its inherited institutions and legal frameworks, the country acquired a reputation as a model of 'greenness'. However, a more nuanced assessment reveals tensions beneath the surface, and significant shortcomings. In the final chapter of his 'new history of German environmentalism', entitled *The Greenest Nation?*, Frank Uekötter has examined Germany's standing with respect to environmental politics, legislation, consciousness and behaviour. While he acknowledges that 'throughout the twentieth century Germany has been at the forefront of the global green movement' (viii), and environmentalism has effectively become a 'national code of conduct' (Umweltkultur), making it difficult for individuals to *not* be green, Uekötter notes contradictions between the Germans' self-perception as green and their actions, and a failure to meet some fundamental challenges. Germans build cars with large engines and drive fast (they still have no blanket speed limit on their motorways), but conceal the environmental impact by stressing how clean and efficient their motors are. In terms of lifestyle, they love foreign travel, and despite advances in vegetarianism, meat plays a central role in their diet. All but one of the country's major rivers are disfigured by engineering works to reduce flood risk and facilitate shipping. And most significantly, over 40 per cent of the electricity consumed in Germany is still generated from coal, and more than half of this from lignite (low-grade, highly polluting coal). As a result the country does not come off as well as might be expected in sustainability rankings and international comparisons of carbon footprint or environmental impact (see Burck, Marten and Bals).

The same mixed picture is found in terms of environmental consciousness. Germany may generate 23 per cent of its energy from renewables, thanks to generous fixed feed-in tariffs, but the price of energy is in consequence among the highest in Europe, which has led to discontent among consumers and in industry. There is also growing popular resistance to onshore wind farms and the pylons required to bring power generated in the north of the country down to the south, where much of it is consumed. A degree of public scepticism exists regarding ambitious environmental policies, which have not always been well conceived or implemented consistently, and this includes climate scepticism. While there is a broad consensus of public opinion on the reality of global warming, and general acceptance of the precautionary principle and the need to decarbonize the economy, sceptical views have been expressed historically by a minority, and increasingly since 2007–2008, when the financial crash coincided with a loss of public confidence in climate science following what has become popularly known as the 'Climategate affair' and the revelation of errors in the IPCC's 2007 report.

On the one hand, public opinion surveys such as the Eurobarometer indicate that Germans consider climate change very important: in 2015, after poverty (28 per cent), respondents in Germany considered climate change was the most serious problem facing the world (26 per cent, well above the EU average of 15 per cent). The vast majority (91 per cent) believed that it was important that their government should set targets to increase the amount of renewable energy used and improve energy efficiency (European Commission). Other surveys confirm the high level of German awareness: a Pew Research Center survey of global attitudes and trends in November 2015 found that 55 per cent of Germans were 'very concerned about climate change', in comparison with 41 per cent of citizens in the UK (Stokes, Wike and Carle). The political and ideological polarization that characterizes the United States, where one can make a good guess at a person's opinion on global warming by ascertaining their views on abortion, same-sex marriage and gun-control, is almost absent in Germany, where there is a widely shared sense of the intrinsic value of nature and inter-generational responsibilities, and religious fundamentalism (creationism) is insignificant (see Fröhlich 74f). Debates on climate change are in consequence less concerned with cultural values, and press reporting is less polarized and polemical.[1] The material interests of actors such as the energy industry, energy workers' unions and associated political groupings also exercise less influence in political debate. Germany does not have the extensive network of sceptics funded by lobbyists, foundations and think tanks close to the oil, gas and coal industries which are found in the United States, stirring up fears of economic damage, and presenting climate change as harmless and measures to counter it as unnecessary. Whereas US managers are expected to adopt an adversarial stance, and it does not cost them credibility, German concerns typically seek cooperation with government. As a result, few of the Germans who have voiced sceptical views appear to possess direct links with industry (see Fröhlich 53).

On the other hand, a comparative survey of climate and energy beliefs among the public in Britain, Germany, France and Norway carried out in June 2016 found, somewhat surprisingly, that the percentage of Germans who did not believe that the climate was changing (16 per cent) was higher than in Great Britain (12 per cent), France (6 per cent) and Norway (4 per cent). Germany and the UK also had the highest proportion of people sceptical about human activity as a cause for climate change (16 per cent and 14 per cent, respectively). And only one in four (24 per cent) in Germany thought that a large majority of scientists (≥ 80 per cent) agreed on anthropogenic climate change. Belief in a strong scientific agreement was higher in Norway, France and the UK, where 30–35 per cent of respondents thought that the consensus lay above 80 per cent (Steentjes et al. 18–21).

A television programme in the *Philosophical Quartett* series broadcast on the national network ZDF on the evening of 27 November 2011 says much about the nature of German scepticism. The talk-show host Rüdiger Safranski had invited the philosopher Peter Sloterdijk to discuss climate change with Gerd Ganteför, nanoscientist and professor of Experimental Physics at the University of Konstanz, and Frank Schätzing, author of the bestselling novel *Der Schwarm* (The Swarm, 2004). Ganteför, whose book *Klima. Der Weltuntergang findet nicht statt* (Climate. It's Not the End of the World) was about to be released, positioned himself as the voice of reason. He urged the public not to heed alarmist environmentalists, and to remember the uncertainty inherent in predictions of global warming and assertions about its causes and consequences. Claiming that global warming would actually bring significant benefits for Germany, he assured viewers that, whatever dangers it held in store, human ingenuity would negotiate them safely. There was in any case no point in the German public radically altering their way of life before agreement was reached for other countries to do likewise.

The choice of the novelist Schätzing as opponent, rather than a competent scientist or politician, is instructive. In inviting the author of a fantasy sci-fi thriller (which has sold 4 million copies and been translated into twenty-seven languages), which is principally concerned with the potentially disastrous consequences of large-scale exploitation of undersea resources, and only indirectly with climate change, Safranski chose a prominent representative of environmental alarmism, whose (fictional) prophecies of doom appealed to consumers' guilty consciences while entertaining them with sensational images of natural destruction. The premise of the programme, which was billed under the title 'Klimawandel – ein Glaubenskrieg? Wahrheitsfindung zwischen Wissenschaft und Ideologie' (Climate Change – a War between Rival Beliefs? Finding the Truth between Science and Ideology), was that supposed scientific facts about climate change had come to be treated as articles of faith, and needed to be challenged by enlightened citizens in a spirit of healthy scepticism and democratic action. Climate activism in general, and the dramatic scenarios of novelists and film makers in particular, were 'Volksverdummung' (dumbing down the nation), and manifestations of a 'deutsche Lust am Untergang' (German predilection for doom), against which individual 'climate dissidents' were courageously taking up arms.[2]

As Stefan Rahmstorf (discussed in the Introduction), spokesperson for the Potsdam Institute for Climate Impact Research and probably the country's best-known public scientist, subsequently wrote in a blog about the programme ('Die deutsche Lust'), it gave the impression that the physical phenomenon of climate change was no more than a quirk of the national psyche. Far from being characterized by a propensity to gloomy fatalism, German politicians and scientists were, he argued, at the forefront of constructive international efforts to address the problem of climate change. A guest contributor to the same blog had already pointed out (25 December 2011) that although Ganteför was referred to in the programme as a 'climate theorist', his professional expertise did not extend to climatology. The talk-show guest's assertions that climate change would not lead to an increase in hurricanes or droughts, or a significant rise in sea level, should therefore not be taken for the truth. Neither Safranski nor Sloterdijk intervened to correct Ganteför's claim that there was no need for action to mitigate climate change. Rahmstorf understandably concluded that the programme was less an attempt to establish the truth about climate change than an exercise in mocking the exaggerations of (literary) catastrophism.

This configuration of the climate change debate as one between misguided alarmists and rational sceptics reflects how some warmist overstatements had precipitated a backlash which threatened to affect public perception of the government's climate policy. Some at least of the arguments presented also suggest there is more to German scepticism than one might expect. In this chapter, I will outline the presence, extent and nature of climate scepticism in German politics, the media and online, analyse examples of the discursive construction of German climate sceptics' arguments in popular science and consider their treatment in literary fiction. I conclude by summarizing the key arguments of German sceptics, indicating features which distinguish scepticism in Germany from that in the United States and elsewhere, and suggesting that some climate sceptics at least have played a constructive role in German debates on climate change and that their arguments deserve a hearing as correctives to excesses of popular green feeling. But first, to place the phenomenon of German climate scepticism in a wider historical context, I will rehearse some of the critiques of earlier excesses of the environmental movement, tracing the outlines of three modes of anti- or post-environmentalist thinking in Germany.

Anti-environmentalism in Germany: An overlooked tradition

Exploration of anti-environmentalist thinking in Germany started in the early 2000s with research into environmental communication in science, politics and the media (Hornschuh 1st ed.). Since 2010 German environmental historians, social scientists and ethnologists (Frank Uekötter, Andreas Möller, Birgit Metzler, Werner Krauß) have begun to ask critical questions about the factors which contributed to the striking success of the German environmental movement in the 1970s and 1980s, and to consider the distorting impact of this success on subsequent debates.[3] This work coincided with the rise of Science and Technology Studies, and has been influenced by Bruno Latour's diagnosis of the absence of a clear separation between science and politics in modern society.

Climate scepticism is the most recent manifestation of a tradition of critical interventions in environmental debates going back to the 1970s, in which *Waldsterben* (forest dieback) played a central role. Birgit Metzler has demonstrated the interplay of scientific knowledge, politics and public opinion in environmental debates in her study of the acid rain scare which swept over West Germany in the first half of the 1980s, *'Erst stirbt der Wald, dann Du!'. Das*

Waldsterben als westdeutsches Politikum (1978–1986) (First the Forests Die, Then You! Forest Dieback as a Political Issue in West Germany, 2015). Waldsterben was less a physical reality awaiting scientific discovery and public recognition than a gradual incremental change, suddenly and arguably arbitrarily perceived as a crisis, a product of selective perception by the public, amplification by the media and self-interested instrumentalization by political actors. The damage is now thought to have resulted as much from frost and drought in the 1970s as from acid rain. But there remains to this day a degree of uncertainty about the causes of forest dieback, and whether disaster was averted by timely counter-measures or never actually constituted such a serious threat. The lower level of public concern in the countries bordering Germany, although their foresters witnessed similar phenomena, is explained at least in part by the special resonance of dying forests with German cultural values and tropes.

The conclusions which Metzler draws about how forest dieback became such an important matter of concern in the German-speaking world, why it remained so for so long and with what consequences are directly relevant to later debates on climate change. One of the most heated environmental debates in German history and five years of spectacular protest action were triggered by alarming reports by the forestry scientists in 1979–1980 that the nation's forests would suffer total decimation within a generation. A Hamburg senator caught the public mood with his assertion that Germany was facing 'an ecological Hiroshima' (*Spiegel* 'Wir stehen vor' 73), and the amplification and periodic repetition of the message by the press resulted in a decade of exaggerated public concern. The ailing health of the German forests was interpreted as a symptom of a broader environmental crisis, which was in turn seen as signalling the inherently (self-) destructive trajectory of modern civilization. By the mid-1990s, Waldsterben was being referred to by critics of its alarmist presentation in public discourse as a cardinal 'eco-error'.

The Brent Spar campaign is a second example of emotionally driven behaviour exceeding the rationally justifiable response to an issue: the extent and seriousness of potential marine pollution from deep-sea disposal of Shell's decommissioned oil storage buoy in 1995 was exaggerated in press reporting, on the basis of a greatly inflated estimate by the campaign organizers (Greenpeace Germany) of the amount of oil involved. Glossing over scientific uncertainty, loading environmental change with moral value and employing apocalyptic rhetoric in a succession of debates since that over nuclear energy in the 1970s laid the foundations for disenchantment with environmentalism, recalcitrance and polemic confrontation on later issues – thereby leaving the nation in what looks to much of the rest of the world like a time warp over nuclear power, and possibly also hindering progress towards a reasoned response to the challenge of climate change.

It is beyond the scope of this chapter to give a comprehensive account of critiques of the environmental movement in Germany. However, an outline of some of the main currents of thought from which it emerged is sufficient for our purpose. The first vocal critics of environmentalism were situated on the political left. There was some justification for their suspicion that environmental protest was, consciously or unconsciously, a distraction from socio-political exploitation and the class struggle. Concern for nature and the environment in Germany has, as already noted, roots in late nineteenth and early twentieth-century conservationist organizations which were politically conservative and anti-modernist. Worse, it was linked with the far right in the Third Reich, when forest romanticism and the idealization of rurality played a central role in Blood and Soil ideology. Nazis such as Walther Darré, Rudolf Hess, Fritz Todt and Alwin Seifert promoted organic farming, animal rights and alternative medicine, and sought to ban invasive species. Right-wing elements were largely excluded when the Green Party was founded in 1980. Environmental issues were combined with traditional left-wing policies, and the new green thinking drew principally on the utopian visions of a reconciliation of humanity with nature in Marx's early writings, and those of Ernst Bloch, Theodor W. Adorno and Herbert Marcuse. German environmentalism continued, however, to draw support from conservative critiques of consumer society alongside Marxist critiques of capitalism. Claims that it was a repackaging of totalitarian orientations and irrational dispositions ignored the grass-roots structure, radical democratic thrust and pro-science orientation of the Green Party. But it is no surprise that thinkers on the political left tended to see love of nature as bourgeois sentimentality, and nostalgia for a premodern social order, and to be suspicious that paternalism and prolonging social inequality were being cloaked in green ideas. A recurring argument of climate sceptics has been that decarbonization is being pursued by elites at the expense of the poor and developing countries.

The poet and essayist Hans Magnus Enzensberger, one of the most influential figures on the German cultural scene since the Second World War, formulated an in-depth leftist critique of the environmental movement in 1973. In his essay 'Zur Kritik der politischen Ökologie' (A Critique of Political Ecology, cited in the following from the English translation), Enzensberger accused the environmental movement of ideological blindness and naivety. The thinking of the different groupings of which it was made up was 'at once obscure and confused' (259):

green 'technocrats' (industrialists and state officials) were pursuing their own economic and political interests; the bulk of 'concerned citizens' were members of the middle class, whose main interest lay in protecting green open spaces and whose lack of political insight made them easy targets for demagogues; the 'eco-freaks', the hard core of the environmental movement, were for their part escapists who inclined ideologically towards obscurantism and sectarianism (261). The result was a confused alliance of political motivations and interests, and groups with differing socio-psychological needs, some of them driven to action by feelings of guilt and a quest for redemption, others delighting in the anticipation of a collapse of bourgeois order. Environmental thinking served the interests of company managers and investors in an eco-industrial complex; it prolonged colonial exploitation in a new guise; it facilitated the imposition of authoritarian political structures.

Ten years later, Enzensberger's journal returned to the subject. Issue no. 74 of *Kursbuch* (December 1983), entitled 'Zumutungen an die Grünen' (Provocative Questions for the Greens), presented a fundamental critique of environmentalism's normative turn by the ecologist Ludwig Trepl ('Ökologie – eine grüne Leitwissenschaft?' [Ecology – A Green Discipline Dominating Science?]), and an essay by Stefan Welzk calling ironically for people to learn to live without forests ('Fetisch Wald. Scherzo funèbre' [Fetish Forest: Scherzo funèbre]), alongside articles mocking alarmism, pointing to problems with land communes, critically analysing aspects of the green world view, and measuring the structures and achievements of the Green Party against its aspirations. In a piece entitled 'Keine Lust aufs grüne Paradies' (Green Paradise Not Wanted) the novelist and political commentator Peter Schneider summed up his aim as being 'den politischen Ansatz der Grünen und der Friedensbewegung gegen seine Ontologisierung verteidigen' (to defend the political project of the greens and the peace movement against its ontologization, p. 188).

A second group of critics of German environmentalism was primarily concerned with what they saw as its irrational pessimism, its debt to a problematic philosophical tradition and its participation in a worrying cultural trend. In the early 1980s popular and high culture in Germany were characterized by a fascination with natural and man-made disasters. Works of environmental non-fiction such as Hoimar von Ditfurth's popular science book *So lasst uns denn ein Apfelbäumchen pflanzen. Es ist soweit* (Then Let Us Plant an Apple Tree. It Is Time, 1985) and literature including Hans Magnus Enzensberger's epic poem *Der Untergang der Titanic* (The Sinking of the *Titanic*, 1978), Christa Wolf's narrative and accompanying lectures *Kassandra* (Cassandra, 1983) and

Günter Grass's novel *Die Rättin* (The Rat, 1986) painted the course of human civilization in overwhelmingly gloomy colours, culminating more often than not in a catastrophe wiping out the entire human race. A spring tide of popular apocalyptic writing was triggered by the threat of nuclear war when the arms race between the United States and the Soviet Union peaked in 1983, raising the possibility of the deaths of millions of Germans, who stood at the front line of East and West (see Lilienthal). The feeling that the end of the world was nigh was omnipresent in the press and on television and pervaded environmental discourse.

These fears might have been short-lived had they not resonated with what Klaus Vondung has called (10f) a 'fundamental leaning towards the apocalyptic world view', which has shaped German political movements and ideologies over the last two centuries, on the left as well as the right, and the strong German strain of cultural pessimism. Towards the end of the nineteenth century, Nietzsche looked forward to the complete destruction of an effete and corrupt civilization which had reduced human existence to a slow form of suicide. In the early twentieth century, Oswald Spengler's *Untergang des Abendlands* (The Decline of the West, 1918–1922) interpreted the age as rotten to the core, developed a cyclical theory of history and argued Western civilization was nearing the end of its own cycle. Sigmund Freud's view of history in *Das Unbehagen an der Kultur* (Civilisation and Its Discontents, 1929) was equally pessimistic, arguing that civilization was inevitably rendered neurotic by the repressions required to ensure its survival. Cultural frustration accumulated and threatened to explode into aggression and self-destruction. Since 1945 German cultural pessimism has divided into different strands, in critiques of technology (Martin Heidegger, Günter Anders), the media and the culture industry (Theodor W. Adorno, Max Horkheimer, Hans Magnus Enzensberger) and environmental degradation (Klaus Meyer-Abich, Günther Nenning). (See Bennett.) The environmental catastrophism of the 1970s and 1980s, when scenarios of the disappearance of the human race and restoration of the earth to its lost equilibrium became commonplace, was both literal and metaphorical, reflecting political circumstances and conforming to a familiar German pattern of thought. Variants of the narrative of the end of humanity as an act of avenging nature are present in the works of both major and minor novelists and essayists, before their first explicit connection with climate change in Anton-Andreas Guha's *Der Planet schlägt zurück* (The Planet Strikes Back, 1996).

Lawrence Buell has described 'apocalypse' as 'the single most powerful master metaphor that the contemporary environmental imagination has at its disposal'

(285), and narratives of nature's revenge in German fiction have served as a medium for a counter-discourse to the hegemonic understanding of nature as a resource to be freely exploited, challenging anthropocentrism and using the shock of exaggeration to warn against the self-destructive forces in modernity. However, the apocalyptic perspective is, as my co-author Greg Garrard has pointed out (2004, 86), associated with a social psychology of paranoia and violence, and extreme moral dualism, dividing the world into friend and enemy. It leaves little space for compromise or reform, and devalues common sense, pragmatic solutions. The apocalyptic narrative therefore came in for criticism in the 1980s by commentators such as Jacques Derrida and Susan Sontag. In Germany, apocalyptic thinking unhelpfully accentuated the divide between pragmatic rationalism and technological optimism on the one hand, and concern over dangerous technologies and human impact on the environment on the other.

The essayist Michael Schneider was one of the first German critics of catastrophism, taking issue with the seemingly fatalist, sometimes even nihilistic frame of mind of his fellow writers in essays such as 'Apokalypse, Politik als Psychose und die Lebemänner des Untergangs' (Apocalypse, Politics as Psychosis and the Playboys of Doom) and 'Die Intellektuellen und der Katastrophismus: Krise oder Wende der deutschen Aufklärer?' (The Intellectuals and Catastrophism: Crisis or Turning-point among German Enlightenment Writers? (34–133)). Another early critic of eco-pessimism was the sociological commentator and futurologist Matthias Horx, who was to go on to become an outspoken climate sceptic.

Ulrich Horstmann's essay *Das Untier. Konturen einer Philosophie der Menschenflucht* (The Monster. Outline of a Philosophy of Flight from Humanity, 1983) presented the most closely argued philosophical critique of contemporary apocalypticism. In the first instance, it was a satirical intervention in the debates on the dangers of nuclear war. Horstmann's provocative premise was that the goal of human civilization was self-destruction. Writing from a cool, 'anthropofugal' perspective, he took a detached look at human history and human nature, free of what he called humanistic illusions and sentimental attachment to our species. The environmental movement was not his main concern, but he wrote that it functioned, like humanism, as a sedative in what he saw as the final phase in the invention of weapons with the power to wipe out all life on earth.

Blending Schopenhauerian pessimism with Swiftian satire in a *reductio ad absurdum* of the apocalyptic thinking of the early 1980s, Horstmann argued that nuclear winter would return the planet to the stark beauty and pristine state it enjoyed for billions of years 'bevor die Folgen der Urzeugung und

Selbstbefleckung sein Antlitz so nachhaltig zerfraßen' (before the consequences of the primordial begetting of life and self-abuse corroded its face so lastingly, p. 79). Readers were initially baffled by his satirical fantasy of a world purged of human destruction. However, it was reprinted in 1985 and again in 2005, at a time when the apocalyptic tone (Derrida) re-emerged in literature, cinema, popular science, computer games and sociological analyses, in the context of global warming. (See Eva Horn's study, *Zukunft als Katastrophe/The Future as Catastrophe*.)

A third group of critics of the environmental movement consisted of disillusioned greens. In part this phenomenon reflected a predictable decline in interest from the high point of German environmental concern: the political and economic challenges of reunification in 1990 and the growing impact of globalization meant that ecological regulation was increasingly perceived as an obstacle to economic growth. The new groundswell of public opinion was picked up by comedians, for whom green activists became a target as grumpy spoilsports, and a market for eco-sceptical books emerged, although critics did not attain the prominence of their counterparts in the United States. At the same time, however, formerly committed environmental activists began to voice criticism of lazy green thinking, and what they saw as a tendency for people to jump to conclusions on individual issues which spoke to a popular environmental worldview. Edgar Gärtner, for example, was an environmental journalist with special knowledge of hydrobiology, who worked as chief editor for the German branch of the World Wide Fund for Nature (WWF) from 1993 to 1996. He left the organization when (in his own words) 'climate policy began to replace traditional conservation requests' (http://gaertner-online.de/profile-in-english/).[4]

The investigative journalists, columnists and popular science writers Dirk Maxeiner and Michael Miersch describe this trajectory from green activist to environmental renegade and climate sceptic in their book *Alles grün und gut?* (All Green and Dandy?, 2014). Having demonstrated against nuclear power, been involved in the Alternative scene, and campaigned for organic farming and nature conservation in the 1980s, they worked from 1989 to 1993 as editors for *Natur*, the most important European nature magazine of the time. As they write (294), they kept discovering that the doom and gloom stories expected of them were not borne out by the facts:

> Die meisten Skeptiker, denen wir begegnen, sind ehemalige Umweltbewegte wie wir, die sich an irgendeinem Punkt ihres Werdegangs in ein Thema vertieft haben. Bei einem war es der Walfang, beim Nächsten die Gentechnik, beim Dritten die Müllentsorgung – ganz egal. Zu diesem Zeitpunkt ahnten sie noch

> nicht, dass sie an der Tapete einer Weltanschauung kratzten. Und als sie weiter kratzten, kam ihnen die ganze Wand entgegen. (297)
>
> (Most sceptics who we meet are former members of the green movement like us, who have at some point in their development gone more deeply into a particular issue. In one instance it was whaling, in another genetic engineering, in a third waste management. It's the same in each case. At first they had no idea they were scraping at wallpaper which covered over a worldview. When they continued to scrape, the whole wall came down around them.)

Combining familiarity with mainstream research in disciplines ranging from history to biology, and economics to politics, as well as books by sceptical thinkers such as Bjørn Lomborg and Matt Ridley, with acute observation of the popular environmental movement in Germany, Maxeiner and Miersch's book on 'eco-optimism' (1996) and their lexicon of 'eco-errors' (2002) became bestsellers. They adopted a stance of critical enquiry, as dissenters from green dogma, exposing the falsehood of popular myths. They argued for instance that 'sustainability', once a progressive concept in management and environmental protection, has become 'ein nebulöses Weltbeglückungsmodell' (a nebulous panacea for putting the world to rights, *Lexikon der Öko-Irrtümer*, p. 230). The green movement no longer required that propositions be grounded in rational argument: it viewed humans as a danger for the planet, and sought to berate and regiment the public. Being green was a badge of moral probity, and no longer a matter of critical thinking or solving environmental problems. NGOs lacked a political mandate, but were becoming lobbyists for the eco-industrial complex and powerful international actors, thereby endangering democracy. Instead of pragmatically exploring options and seeking solutions to problems which brought more benefit than harm, improved people's lives and cemented social cohesion, Western eco-elites were imposing ideologically grounded choices on a suffering Third World, and blocking advances in food production and disease prevention. The German public's conscientious waste separation was a cathartic everyday ritual whose effectiveness was undermined by the subsequent mixing with non-recyclable waste. Rinsing yoghurt pots was the equivalent of liturgical foot-washing (28).

Maxeiner and Miersch pointed out that nature is always changing, and our very survival depends on changing it; that conservation is sometimes at odds with ecology; that humans should be viewed as creative problem-solvers and not just as consumers and destroyers; and that the German rejection of GM crops and stem cell research, while ostensibly grounded in science, results in part from a syncretistic green religiosity marred by strange aberrations. Writing with stylistic verve and at times mischievous exaggeration, they called for a new form of environmental policy, one based less on entrenched and gridlocked worldviews than rational and constructive action. Once imaginative protesters, the Greens were now driven by pathos and missionary zeal. Environmentalists were a priestly caste with a sense of moral superiority over their more materialistic fellow citizens. Climate catastrophe was the last refuge of the homeless Left (18).

Taken together, these three groups of critics have drawn public attention to genuine weaknesses of the environmental movement, in a spirit of concern over its failure to achieve fundamental aims. If at times they have reduced it to a caricature, they have at others made valid points, for instance about sentimental romanticism, the mindset of catastrophilia and moves to impose a rigid puritanical code of behaviour. The climate scepticism which has emerged in Germany in the twenty-first century grew in some measure out of this critical sympathy with environmental goals. It was a logical step for Maxeiner and Miersch to challenge popular assumptions about climate change, and dispute the need for a radical programme of economic reform and social re-education.

German scholars, too, have challenged environmentalism: historians such as Wolfgang Behringer and Frank Uekötter have distanced themselves from environmentalist alarmism, pointing out the mixed motivations of the greens, their ambivalences and blind spots, and how climate protection has developed into a moral crusade, trumping other legitimate environmental and social concerns. A comparable impetus underlies the work of the natural scientist Hans von Storch, the economist Hans-Werner Sinn and the political sociologist Ingolfur Blühdorn. The difference between their arguments and those of self-professing climate sceptics such as the historian Andreas Möller, the biologist Josef H. Reichholf, the physicist Gert Ganteför and the chemist Fritz Vahrenholt is sometimes a matter of degree rather than of kind. Independent voices such as Hans von Storch have been treated as sceptics by the advocates of climate protection, and as advocates by the sceptics (see Grundmann and Scott 234).

The emergence of climate scepticism in Germany

Two accounts of climate scepticism in Germany have been published to date: a fifty-page Working Paper 'Klimaskeptiker in Deutschland und ihr Kampf gegen die Energiewende' (Climate Sceptics in Germany and Their Fight Against the Energiewende, 2013), authored by Achim Brunnengräber at the Environmental Policy Research Centre at the Free University of Berlin, and Tanja Fröhlich's book

Klimaskepsis in Deutschland. Handlungsempfehlungen für Politik und Wissenschaft (Climate Scepticism in Germany: Recommendations for Action for Politics and Science, 2014). Both studies understand scepticism not in the narrow sense of denial of anthropogenic global warming, but as a range of positions querying the necessity for, or the nature of, climate protection measures. While they provide useful information on German sceptical actors and institutions, and their motives and arguments, their aim is less to understand the hopes and fears of sceptics than to assess their political influence and suggest strategies for limiting it.[5]

As in the United States, climate change had been debated in scientific circles since the late 1970s. In 1986 the Deutsche Physikalische Gesellschaft (German Physics Society) published a report warning of the threat it posed, and in 1987 the government set up a Parliamentary Commission of Enquiry to examine 'preventive measures to protect the Earth's atmosphere'. In the early 1990s, three institutions were founded to advise German policymakers – the Scientific Advisory Council on Global Change (WGBU), the Wuppertal Institute for Climate, Environment and Energy, and the Potsdam Institute for Climate Impact Research. Building on the reputation as a powerhouse of environmental initiatives which it had gained in the previous decade, Germany played a leading role in EU and international climate agreements at Rio (1992), Kyoto (1997), and in the EU emissions trading directive, and launched the Erneuerbare Energien Gesetz (Renewable Energies Act) in 2000.

Climate scepticism was relatively rare in Germany before the international furore over the hacking of emails from the University of East Anglia's Climate Research Unit in the run-up to the Copenhagen summit in December 2009, which was widely (although erroneously) understood as having exposed the doorkeeper mentality of cliques of researchers and the withholding of data that failed to support the consensus on global warming and its causes. At the same time, the hockey stick curve, presented by Al Gore and others as an icon of imminent catastrophe, seemed to demonstrate the political corruption of climate science: it had perhaps been unwise of the IPCC to make so much of this symbolic curve, which ignored the medieval warm period and the little ice age, thereby accentuating the impact of industrialization since the Second World War. A form of scepticism challenging the oversimplified interpretation of complex scientific findings in public debates on climate change and questioning the efficacy and cost-effectiveness of government policy has gathered momentum in Germany since 2007–2008. Despite the broad cross-party agreement on climate change, a handful of politicians have adopted sceptical positions, and sceptical articles have appeared at intervals in the press.

Climate scepticism is not official policy of any of the major political parties in Germany. The few openly sceptical politicians are to be found in the Freie Demokratische Partei (the Liberal Party) and the Christlich-Demokratische Union (Conservative Party). Their main concerns have been the economic impact of the proposed mitigation measures, energy security, the loss of individual freedom and the neglect of other social problems. The FDP in Saxony has been particularly pro-sceptical, with Holger Krahmer (Liberal MEP for Saxony 2004–2014) authoring two pamphlets about the 'inconvenient truths' about climate policies (2010 and 2011), and organizing an 'alternative climate conference' in Dresden to combat what he called 'media hysteria and green actionism' in 2012. Opposing environmental regulation as a brake on free enterprise, predicting the loss of jobs and emphasizing scientific uncertainty, Krahmer has dismissed forecasts of temperature rise as mere 'Kaffeesatzleserei' (reading tea leaves). Similar views have been expressed by the Christian Democrat parliamentarian Marie-Luise Dött.

While there is no organized populist anti-environmentalist movement in Germany, climate sceptics have found a home since 2013 in the Alternative für Deutschland party. The AfD claims that the impact of CO_2 on the climate is not proven, denies that the global temperature has risen in the last two decades, accuses climate scientists and the government of suppressing information on the benefits of warming, and demands a stop to subsidies for renewable energy.[6] The possible influence of sceptics over political decision-making has led the Greens to question the government about it in the Bundestag. Meanwhile in Austria, government concern over the disputation of climate science and rejection of climate policy was sufficient for a suite of 'CONTRA' projects to be commissioned from the Austrian Climate Research Programme, to examine the roles of interest groups (network analysis) and the media, the different kinds of scepticism and the impact of apocalyptic rhetoric.

The European Institute for Climate and Energy (EIKE), founded in Jena in 2007, is the only German organization of any significance to deny the existence of anthropogenic climate change. EIKE, which has links with the Heartland Institute and the Global Warming Policy Foundation in the United States, and related organizations in the UK, convenes climate and energy conferences, and campaigns against energy system change. The EIKE *Handbuch für Klimaskeptiker* (Handbook for Climate Sceptics) states:

> 'Es gibt einen weithin sichtbaren Berg von Beweisen für die Erderwärmung der 1990er Jahre, aber die These, dass CO_2 daran Schuld ist, ist dünn wie ein Fliegenbein und sie bröckelt schon bedenklich – wenn Klimaskeptiker nur

> einheitlich Druck machen. [...] Nicht das Klima ist bedroht, sondern unsere Freiheit! Umweltschutz: Ja! Klimaschutz: Nein!' (There is a mass of evidence for global warming in the 1990s, but the assertion that CO_2 is to blame for it is as thin as a fly's leg and crumbling alarmingly – or would be, if climate sceptics got together to apply pressure. [...] It's not the climate which is in danger, but our liberty! Environmental protection: Yes! Climate protection: No!)

Trend scepticism (denial that the global mean temperature is rising) is rare in Germany: the thinkers discussed here tend, like those examined in the chapter on French scepticism, either to attribute it to natural causes or to claim its impact will be benign. Most common is the argument that the urgency of Klimaschutz – literally 'protecting the climate': the term was coined in analogy with the compounds 'Naturschutz' (nature protection, or conservation) and 'Umweltschutz' (environmental protection), and embraces efforts to prevent climate change as well as adapt to its effects – has been exaggerated and attempts to do so are either doomed to failure or disproportionately costly. There has been significant distrust of the motives behind the government's *Energiewende* programme, which was introduced on the advice of the Scientific Advisory Council, and in particular of the ambitious socio-ecological transformation of German society outlined in its 2011 report, *Welt im Wandel: Gesellschaftsvertrag für eine Große Transformation* (A Changing World: A Social Contract for a Grand Transformation).

Turning to the media, climate change was first brought to the attention of a wider German public by the *Spiegel* (a weekly magazine founded in 1947, modelled on *Time*, renowned for its aggressive exposés of government malpractice and scandals, which was for decades required reading for Germany's left-liberal intelligentsia) in a sensational lead article, 'Das Weltklima gerät aus den Fugen' (World Climate Out Of Control), published in August 1986. The message was underlined by a dramatic cover image of Cologne cathedral, symbol of the German nation as well as Catholicism, half-submerged in floods, bearing the caption: 'Ozonloch, Polschmelze, Treibhauseffekt: Forscher warnen. Die Klimakatastrophe' (Ozone Hole, Melting Poles, Greenhouse Effect: Researchers Warn of Climate Catastrophe). The term 'climate catastrophe' had been coined by the Arbeitskreis Energie (Energy Working Group) of the Deutsche Physikalische Gesellschaft – a body with a long-term interest in nuclear power – in a report written only months after public confidence in the nuclear industry had been shattered by the Chernobyl accident. The hypothesis of climate change was swiftly treated as fact, and the story drowned out the scientific findings it was based on in dramatizations and premature claims to certainty. Climate scientists began to be cited in the press saying the Germans would not see another white Christmas, prophesying climate wars, and warning of an unstoppable flow of climate migrants into Europe. A grand narrative of doom was circulated over the next decade, which climatologists, physicists and biologists were dragged into supporting, willing or not. When the river Elbe burst its banks in the once-in-a-century flood of August 2002, it was acknowledged that there was no scientific proof of a link between the floods and climate change. But the probable principal cause of the extensive damage (building on flood plains) was ignored: the high-energy way of life in Germany was blamed, nature was striking back.

Climate scepticism was in no small part a response to such exaggeration. The *Spiegel* again laid the foundations for the new trend, switching from environmental alarmism to scepticism in 1995 with a cover announcing what it saw as the country's drift from environmental protection into 'eco-madness' ('Feldzug der Moralisten: Vom Umweltschutz zum Öko-Wahn' (Moralists on the Rampage: From Environmental Protection to Eco-madness, 25 September 1995)). Some articles asserted the Germans had united in a chorus of 'Gutmenschen' (do-gooders) conscientiously separating their recyclable waste, boycotting environmental delinquents and lamenting the 'ecological collapse' as a way of salvaging their consciences. Others commented acerbically on the number of people incapacitated by their sufferings from imaginary forms of chemical pollution, carcinogenic electromagnetic smog and diffuse anxieties about the future. It was to be a decade, however, before this disenchantment with environmentalism became visible in *Spiegel* reporting on climate change. The move towards climate scepticism is visible in an article entitled 'Klima inszenierter Angst' (A Climate of Stage-managed Fear) in January 2005. The authors, Hans von Storch and Nico Stehr, challenged the view that climate change was the greatest problem facing the planet. They wrote that the fearmongering prophets of doom would do well to remember that there had been many extreme weather events and changes in the climate in the past. The media's sensationalist presentation of the recent floods amounted to a dangerous distortion of knowledge, in which some scientists were complicit: science was losing its ability to advise the public objectively. By 2010, the *Spiegel* was adopting a position of outright, polemical scepticism (see Evers, Stampf and Traufetter). The magazine *Focus* featured a cover story 'Es wird wärmer – gut so!' (It's Getting Warmer – And That's Great!) in November 2010, listing likely gains from global warming and playing down the losses (Pantle). By 2012 the tabloid *Bild*, which had published a series of sensationally alarmist articles in Spring 2007, was writing of 'die CO2-Lüge' (the CO2 lie) and describing climate catastrophe as 'Panik-Mache der Politik' (a political scare tactic).

While the *Tageszeitung* (which often supports the Greens) and the broadsheets *Die Zeit*, *Financial Times Deutschland* and the *Süddeutsche Zeitung* have maintained a generally critical stance towards climate sceptics, some of the more conservative papers, popular dailies and weekly magazines have been open to argument and counter-argument. The weekly *Die Welt* published an article entitled 'Der heilige Krieg der Klimaskeptiker' (The Holy War of the Climate Sceptics) on 5 September 2007, which disqualified climate sceptics as delusional agents of neoliberalism, but balanced against it a second, neutral article by Matthias Armborst, 'Die Bewegung der Klima-Skeptiker formiert sich' (The Climate Sceptic Movement Is Forming), and prepublication of an extract from Dirk Maxeiner's sceptical book *Hurra wir retten die Welt!* (Hurray, We're Saving the World) under the header 'Wider die Ökodiktatur' (Against Eco-Dictatorship).

While affirming the scientific consensus on climate change, the *Frankfurter Allgemeine Zeitung*, which reflects the views of the business community, has sought to strike a balance between warnings and scepticism. In April 2007 it published an article by Christian Bartsch suggesting concern over the climate had turned into irrational hysteria ('Wider die Klimahysterie. Mehr Licht im Dunkel des Klimawandels' [Against Climate Hysteria. Shedding More Light on the Darkness of Climate Change]). In August of the same year, the paper gave a full page over to a riposte by the combative spokesperson for the Potsdam Institute for Climate Impact Research, Stefan Rahmstorf ('Klimawandel: Deutsche Medien betreiben Desinformation' [Climate Change: The German Media Are Misinforming the Public]). Rahmstorf argued that so-called climate sceptics were taking the public for a ride, and the media were guilty of failing to check the facts. A few weeks later, the *Frankfurter Allgemeine* permitted seven of the sceptics who Rahmstorf had singled out for criticism to respond in a co-authored article. 'Wir müssen Urängste relativieren' (We Must Relativize Deeprooted Fears) formulated a cogent defence of the right to express doubts and challenge the scientific and political establishment's narrative of climate change. The goal of the government's climate policy was far-reaching reform of German society and the economy. Anyone daring to question the wisdom of this was being dismissed as immoral. Rahmstorf, a media star on whose every word the captains of industry, the NGOs, the chancellor and the general public were all hanging, might as well consider his mission accomplished were it not for the miserable handful of whingers and killjoys who stood in the way of his 'Endsieg', that is, final victory in the climate debate. (The term recalls the Third Reich.) Rahmstorf had admitted to suppressing unwelcome reporting, the sceptics claimed, and blacklisting journalists who insisted on researching matters for themselves. He was effectively conducting a Jihad, wilfully misquoting opponents. The authors of the article were not 'climate deniers', but ordinary citizens, as keen as anyone else to bring about the transition from fossil fuels to renewable energy. But they had experienced eschatological hysteria before, and knew it when they saw it. Climate catastrophe had become a secular religion, subsuming quite different issues in a grand narrative of guilt and atonement, contributing to the catastrophilia which plagued the nation, and leading to a ban on new ideas. Weather and climate were among the oldest objects of fear: whoever exercised control over their interpretation could do anything. Religions and dictatorships had lived from them. So today's fears must be democratized, moderated and relativized. The authors asserted their right to doubt. They were only a small marginalized minority, but someone must hold open the doors to a sceptical understanding of the world against the 'gleichgeschaltete öffentliche Meinung' (ideological alignment of public opinion [another term from the Third Reich]). The article exemplifies the ambivalence of German scepticism as a whole: the polemical implication that Rahmstorf was acting like Goebbels's propaganda machine or Al Qaeda in his policing of public statements on climate change was outrageously inflammatory, and distracted from the many valid points touched on.

A year later, the *Frankfurter Allgemeine* attacked the climate protection measures of the green regional government in Baden-Württemberg in an article 'Grüne Revolution. Die herzliche Ökodiktatur' (Green Revolution. The Cheery Eco-dictatorship), which was also outspoken in associating environmentalism with totalitarianism, but did not directly reference the Nazi past. Winand von Petersdorff wrote of 'eco-tyranny': regulations on biofuel, the eco-modernization of residential buildings and costly subsidies for renewable energy were robbing consumers of their freedom of choice. The drivers of Porsches, people going on foreign holidays and meat eaters were being pilloried. The fossil-fuelled German economy was being presented as ethically unacceptable: 'Die Transformation zur Klimaverträglichkeit ist moralisch ebenso geboten wie die Abschaffung der Sklaverei und die Ächtung der Kinderarbeit.' (The transformation to climate compatibility is being treated as a moral imperative comparable to the abolition of slavery and the proscription of child labour.)

Apart from political pamphlets, the press, and to a lesser extent TV, the internet and popular science books have served as the most important platforms for German sceptics. Internet discourse, which is characterized by an absence of provisionality, doubt and self-questioning, exacerbates polarization by acting as an echo chamber. 'Geht die Welt unter?' (Is the world coming to an end?), for instance, the Forum gegen die Irrlehren von Treibhauseffekt und Klimaschutz (Forum Against the False Teachings of Greenhouse Effect and Climate Protection) asks:

> Der Treibhauseffekt wird stärker.
> Es wird immer wärmer.
> Die Pole und Gletscher schmelzen.
> Der Meeresspiegel steigt.
> Der Golfstrom wird versiegen.
> Dürren und Überschwemmungen nehmen zu.
> Die Klimakatastrophe ist da.
> *Und Sie sind schuld, weil Sie CO_2 produzieren!*
>
> Glauben Sie all das auch? *Dann liegen Sie falsch.* Diese Seite unternimmt den Versuch, Sie über einen der am weitesten verbreiteten Irrtümer aufzuklären – nämlich über das Märchen von der Klimakatastrophe und ihre angebliche Ursache, die vom Menschen erzeugten 'Treibhausgase'.
> (http://www.klimaskeptiker.info/)
> (The greenhouse effect is growing. It is getting warmer and warmer. The poles and glaciers are melting. The sea level is rising. The Gulf Stream will soon stop circulating. Droughts and floods are on the increase. We are witnessing a climate catastrophe. *And it's your fault, because you are producing CO_2!* Do you believe all this? *Then you've had the wool pulled over your eyes.* The purpose of this webpage is to enlighten you on one of the commonest mistakes today: the fairy tale of climate catastrophe and its supposed cause, man-made 'greenhouse gases'.)

Blogs emerged in the early 2000s as a counter-sphere of public communication which could no longer be ignored. As the climate change ethnologist Werner Krauss has pointed out in an article presenting eight widely read German blogs ranging from advocacy through 'honest brokerage' to scepticism, they have the potential to play an important role in climate debates as a forum for dialogue between scientists and an interested lay public. Sceptical bloggers write of the 'climate lie' and of the *Energiewende* as the product of a global green conspiracy. Facts are often manipulated. Nonetheless, if one disregards such polemics, blogs cite many of the somewhat justified criticisms of environmentalism and climate policy which have already been noted. German internet sceptics, by contrast with their American counterparts, often support what they see as genuinely sensible and necessary environmental protection measures, while opposing 'climate protection', that is, measures seeking to reduce CO_2 in the atmosphere. The money would be better spent, they claim, feeding the world, promoting health and providing affordable energy. Their principal criticisms are directed against what they see as the influential German 'climate change industry', messianic politicians, a bloated bureaucracy bent on further growth, conservationist groups spreading panic in order to gain social influence and deluded idealists.

At a time when it appeared that the information released to the public was being controlled and the disclosure of data was selective, blogs written by retired men with technical and scientific training, committed postdocs and concerned citizens constituted an alternative voice to what the bloggers saw as the cartel of scientific journals and the one-sided media. Hans von Storch's 'Klimazwiebel' (see http://klimazwiebel.blogspot.co.uk/) in particular sought to serve as an archive of dissident views, a workshop for ideas and a cross-disciplinary forum for argument. Von Storch argues that German sceptic bloggers have made the scientific and political establishment recognize that climate science is 'post-normal', in the sense of being characterized by uncertainty of knowledge, concerning social values, involving high risks and potentially necessitating urgent solutions. They have brought home to policymakers the failings of procedures in climate science for managing uncertainty and the reluctance to acknowledge social motivations for supposedly objective findings. In his opinion (perhaps downplaying the problem of filter bubbles), blogs ensure all voices are heard. By challenging assumptions about the causes and extent of warming trends and hasty forecasts about their social impact, they contributed to embedding contemporary debates on climate change in a larger story of the history of climate, its impact on human culture and human interventions in climate. (See the special number of the journal *Nature & Culture* on *Postnormal Science: The Case of Climate Research*, edited by Krauss, Schäfer and von Storch.) Popular science performs a similar social function, bridging the gap between scientific writing as a professional medium of scientific research and the realms of popular political and cultural discourse.

Scepticism in popular science

Since the 1970s popular science books introducing recent research in physics, biology and other complex subjects to a general readership have topped the bestseller lists. The popularization of science is not merely a mediation of established authoritative knowledge for a passive, ignorant public, to be judged in terms of how accurately it conveys ideas and concepts: it is also a form of knowledge production, inasmuch as it tells stories of scientific discovery, explores the consequences of scientific facts for people's lives and makes them meaningful for readers (see Leane). Using narratives and metaphors to condense and communicate complex issues and simultaneously engage with readers, the authors of non-fiction books on the environment have sparked debates over the place of humans on earth and the ethics of our actions. The book which arguably exercised the greatest influence over the international environmental movement was a work of popular science, Rachel Carson's *Silent Spring*.

In the last fifteen years, dozens of accounts of climate change written for a non-specialist readership have been published in Germany – in some cases American and English works in translation, but in others, German originals. These have contributed to shaping public views on the reality of global warming, the extent of its anthropogenic dimension, ways of mitigating and adapting to it, and our responsibility towards future generations and other species. While only a minority of the German popular science books on climate change express sceptical views, the genre has provided climate sceptics with a medium in which they can develop their arguments at greater length and with greater sophistication than in the press and in blogs. Beginning in 2007 with Kurt Blüchel's *Der Klimaschwindel* (The Climate Hoax), Hartmut Bachmann's *Die Lüge der Klimakatastrophe* (The Lie of Climate Catastrophe) and Joseph Reichholf's *Kurze Naturgeschichte des letzten Jahrtausends* (Short Natural History of the Last Thousand Years), sceptical popular science books have challenged and provided alternatives to the generally accepted 'social facts' pertaining to climate change (the sociologist Emile Durkheim's term for the collectively recognized metaphors, images and symbols which acquire normative force, determining the public's interpretation of and response to social issues). The more polemic titles are the product of small specialist publishers such as the TvR Medien Verlag in Jena and the Kopp Verlag in Baden-Württemberg (a publisher of right-wing esotericism, populism, extremism, pseudoscience, conspiracy theories, wellness, survival skills and self-defence), but others have been brought out by well-known publishing houses.

The most serious exposition of scientific facts, measurements and predictive models, theories and solutions is found in *Die kalte Sonne. Warum die Klimakatastrophe nicht stattfindet* (2012, published in London in English in 2013, and by the Heartland Institute in America in 2015, under the title *The Neglected Sun: Why the Sun Precludes Climate Catastrophe*). Its authors are Fritz Vahrenholt and the geologist and palaeontologist Sebastian Lüning. Vahrenholt can be described, like Maxeiner and Miersch, as an environmental renegade. After studying chemistry, he worked at the Environmental Protection Agency in Berlin and co-authored a highly regarded book on the chemical accident in

Seveso in 1978. *Seveso ist überall. Die tödlichen Risiken der Chemie* (Seveso is Everywhere: The Deadly Risks of Chemicals) is still in print. Vahrenholt joined the Social Democratic Party, became a prominent environmental spokesman and served from 1991 to 1998 as Senator for Environmental Affairs in the city of Hamburg. However, after commissioning controversial waste incineration plants, he fell out with the Party and went into industry, spending stints on the Board of Deutsche Shell and the wind turbine manufacturer Repower. By the time of writing in 2012, he was CEO of the green electricity company Innogy, a renewable energy subsidiary of the giant RWE concern, one of Europe's five leading electricity and gas companies, with interests in oil, gas and lignite production, and electricity generation from gas, coal and nuclear power.

Despite these links with the energy industry (which he openly acknowledges in *Die kalte Sonne*, pp. 10 and 12), it would be wrong to dismiss Vahrenholt, honorary professor at the University of Hamburg since 1999, as a mouthpiece of either the fossil fuel or the renewable energy lobby. *Die kalte Sonne* is no mere promotional pamphlet. Nor is it, with its over 350 pages of text, 70 further pages of references and its many graphs presenting data, a bedside book for the average climate denier. The authors accept the existence of global warming, but argue (citing, among hundreds of other studies, French volcanologist Vincent Courtillot's work on solar cycles as the cause of climate change – see Chapter 5) that most of it derives from the variation in the Earth's distance from the sun on its elliptical orbit (the Milankovic cycle), the fluctuation of solar irradiation in cycles which have caused the earth's temperature to rise and fall in the past and other natural factors such as volcanic eruptions. While not disputing the greenhouse properties of CO_2, they hold its importance has been grossly exaggerated. In addition, they argue that since 1988 we have entered a cooling phase which will last for several decades. This gives us time to wean ourselves off fossil fuels and restructure the economy on a sustainable basis, without the necessity for hastily adopted, poorly thought-out measures such as carbon trading. They call instead for a reorientation of energy policy to promoting efficiency, and for allocation of the vast sums earmarked for carbon trading to more urgent social and ecological needs of the burgeoning world population. In sum, the negative effects of global warming have been exaggerated, there is no need for significant climate action in the next thirty years and the 'climate chancellor' Angela Merkel's policies are naively idealistic.

Die kalte Sonne attracted considerable press attention and social media approval. Stefan Rahmstorf and other defenders of mainstream climate science therefore went to some lengths to refute its authors' scientific arguments.

Vahrenholt and Lüning selectively cite sceptic scientists and interpret the results of recognized authorities in such a way as to support their own views. (Some of the latter subsequently defended themselves vigorously against this use of their work.) Their description of themselves as 'climate realists' and guardians of the real truth about global warming must be taken with a pinch of salt. However, the book is largely free of polemics: comparisons of the Energiewende with the Soviet Union's planned economy in the 1920s and 1930s and Mao's Great Leap Forward (328) is an anomaly. And the alternative energy agenda of gradual transition to renewables which Vahrenholt and Lüning outline, one combining climate protection in the longer term with economic prudence and fairness towards developing countries, no longer seems so far from mainstream political opinion.

Gerd Ganteför's *Klima. Der Weltuntergang findet nicht statt* (Climate: The End of the World Is Not Happening) is a second non-trivial account of climate change by an independently minded scientist. Ganteför's position has already been outlined above: he accepts global warming but queries its attribution to human activities, and above all challenges alarmist assessments of its impact. His book, which is based on a lecture series he gave at the University of Konstanz, but written for lay readers, was published by Wiley-VCH, a specialist in the provision of scientific, technical and specialist information for researchers and professionals, including a popular series, 'Erlebnis Wissenschaft' (Science as Adventure). It is more personal, provocative and humorous than Vahrenholt and Lüning's book. The hint in the text on the back cover that the author will expose climate change as a myth is compounded by the satirical adaptation on the front cover of the familiar environmentalist icon of the polar bear, perched on a block of melting ice, hapless victim of global warming. Here, three polar bears are paddling happily in a warm sea under a rainbow, off the shore of a tropical island.

Critiquing both activist hysteria and the conspiracy theories of more extreme sceptics, Ganteför promises reliable orientation, based on scientific fact, and the exposure of urban myths. He takes issue with the miserabilist doomsaying and suicidal mix of guilt, fear and despair which he sees as rife in Germany, arguing that climate change will bring as many advantages as disadvantages. His principal message is to control population growth, produce enough energy to keep it cheap and permit a decent standard of living for all, and adapt to the inevitable global warming. Indeed, we should enjoy its benefits while they last: in the longer term it will get colder. The earth's temperature has always fluctuated, and we are nearing the end of an interglacial warm phase: glaciers may one day extend as far south as Cologne again. Without the greenhouse effect, he reminds us, the average surface temperature today would already be minus 18°C.

Klima uses short semi-autobiographical, semi-fictional narratives in boxes interspersed throughout the book to enliven the factual exposition. The adherents of popular environmentalism are chided here for their intolerance of anyone questioning the logic of their actions. In the context of discussion of the opposition to wind farms, the disillusionment of a young environmentally minded engineer called Florian is described, when he discovers that politicians are more concerned with winning the next election than solving the problem of providing clean energy. Florian, whose name suggests natural innocence, reappears in other stories, gradually learning the ways of the world. As a climate scientist, for instance, he learns that he has to package his results and doctor his graphs in order to obtain funding. The book ends with a brief excursion into a distant fictional future. In a letter written at the end of the current Climate Optimum, when global warming has ceased to balance out the gradual cooling from natural causes, a future Florian considers the prospect of returning to the temperatures we have today. He depicts the horror scenario of a world in which Greenland, Siberia and the Antarctic will become uninhabitable again, and the Sahara will revert to desert. The environmentalists, he writes, are clamouring for new coal power stations to prevent the level of carbon dioxide in the atmosphere from falling.

Irony and satire play a central role in Dirk Maxeiner and Michael Miersch's *Lexikon der Öko-Irrtümer. Fakten statt Mythen* (Lexicon of Eco-Errors: Facts Instead of Myths, 1998) and *Alles grün und gut?* (2014). We have already seen how these self-styled 'eco-optimists' became critics of the environmental movement and came to deconstruct popular views on climate change as part of a wider exposé of the contradictory statistics, questionable suppositions and improper generalizations lying behind alarmist headlines. The chapter on climate change in the *Lexikon der Öko-Irrtümer*, the longest of fifteen entries, opens with telling examples of exaggeration and oversimplification by Greenpeace, WWF, Al Gore and the German press, and goes on to show how ancient patterns of cultural interpretation of natural disasters and changes in the climate are being perpetuated in contemporary climate discourse. Maxeiner and Miersch dispute the melting of the polar ice caps, the rising sea level, the increase in extreme weather events and the contribution of anthropogenic CO_2 to global warming. In short, there is no evidence, they claim, that human activity is impacting on the global climate, and we are heading, if anything, for a new ice age rather than global warming.

Their position changed by the time they came to write the parts of *Alles grün und gut* concerned with climate change (Chapters 2 and 3), sixteen years later.

In the meantime Maxeiner had published a short book on the subject, *Hurra. Wir retten die Welt! Wie Politik und Medien mit der Klimaforschung umspringen* (Hurray, We're Saving the World: How Politics and the Media Are Taking Liberties with Climate Science, 2007). This carefully researched and well-written book makes for an interesting read, illustrating its arguments with historical examples and allusions to people and places. Although he holds that there remains a significant degree of uncertainty as to the causes of climate change, Maxeiner now accepts the greenhouse effect, and that CO_2 contributes to global warming; his target has become 'climate indoctrination'. Exploring psychological, social and political reasons for climate alarmism, he argues that a seamless transition from climate discourse to religious discourse has resulted in climate change being framed, like earlier natural catastrophes, as punishment for a sinful way of life. Doubters are being stigmatized as 'deniers', consciously referencing the Holocaust. The sceptics are champions of reason and of freedom in the face of a looming eco-dictatorship. Maxeiner devotes short thought-provoking chapters to climate change as a scapegoat distracting from more pressing but intractable social and economic problems: the decimation of tropical rainforest and overfishing as the real culprits of species loss; the failings of carbon trading (which he sees as no more than a sale of indulgences, a granting of ecological absolution); the use of climate protection as an excuse for pursuing dubious geoengineering fantasies; and ecologism as a form of religiosity, reflecting a persistent longing for salvation at a time when the established faiths have lost their hold. Wind turbines are replacing church spires. The book ends with a Who's Who of the top twenty-five scientists in climate debates, which includes a few outright climate sceptics (Richard Lindzen and Fred Singer), but also a larger number of American, German, French and Israeli scientists who disagree significantly with aspects of the IPCC reports.

Alles grün und gut revisits these arguments, asserting on the one hand that climatologists have little real knowledge of the consequences of global warming, and on the other that it has other causes than carbon emissions (deforestation, intensive agriculture, overgrazing, urban conglomerations and methane from stock raising). Maxeiner and Miersch warn of the limitations of climate modelling and the tendency to ignore regional differences. Climate has become the index of all anthropogenic influence on nature, leading us to ignore the detrimental effects of other human activities. The threat of climate catastrophe has become a system of belief, endowing pointless actions with social meaning. The Freiburg Eco-Institute, the Wuppertal Institute for Climate, Environment and Energy, and the Potsdam Institute for Climate Impact Research are all guilty of alarmism, by propagating the notion of 2°C as the maximum tolerable rise in global temperature. Maxeiner and Miersch argue that German energy policy (the *Energiewende*) is driven by irrational desires. After Fukushima, 513 of the 600 members of the Bundestag voted in May 2011 to reinstate the phase-out of nuclear power which had originally been introduced by a Social Democrat/Greens coalition in 2000, and reversed by Angela Merkel (in coalition with the business-friendly Liberals) in late 2010. The result? The landscape was being destroyed by farmers growing maize as biofuel and erecting wind turbines. By 2014 there were 500 German Citizens' Initiatives opposing the construction of wind farms. Subsidies for renewable energy were nothing less than a transfer of money from ordinary people to landowners, businessmen and investors. The authors assert that Germany should acknowledge its mistake and pursue cheaper, more socially equitable and environmentally friendly options.

The standard German sceptic argument that environmentalism has become a secular religion, playing on public feelings of guilt and desire for redemption, is developed into a little story in the introduction of Hartmut Bachmann's *Die Lüge der Klimakatastrophe*. It is the early sixteenth century, and a poor peasant is struggling to pay his annual dues to the local convent. The man has been injured in an accident and his family is on the brink of starvation. Having sold a goose at the fair, he is on his way home with the money for the convent, when he is accosted by mendicant monks. They persuade him to part with his hard-earned pence in return for a certificate promising that his time in Purgatory will be shortened, and his soul will go straight to heaven when he dies. Climate protection measures are presented as a swindle comparable to the peddling of indulgences, over which Luther broke with the Church of Rome. Innocent German citizens are being 'fleeced', and climate sceptics combating environmentalists' capitalization on public fears, deception and manipulation of information are courageous Lutheran reformers.

Scepticism in literature

The press and broadcasting, social media and popular science are probably the principal sources of information to which ordinary Germans turn to understand climate change and climate politics. But storytelling is, as we can see in this and the other chapters, present here alongside the facts and discursive arguments, in fictional narratives as well as accounts of historical events. Novelists, dramatists and poets are experts in storytelling, and in Germany as elsewhere, they have engaged with climate debates. On the one hand, public views and choices are reflected in the situations and outcomes they depict and the images they provide. Sketching scenarios and experimenting with the consequences of perceived patterns of behaviour, authors have explored the political, ecological and ethical implications of the whole range of social responses to climate change. On the other hand, stories also have the ability to open readers' eyes to different ways of seeing the world. Novels invest events with meaning and value by associating them with pre-existing desires, fears and patterns of perception. This can of course serve to reinforce dominant narratives. However, working with personalization, dramatization and emotional focalization, some writers have sought to distribute readers' empathy in new ways, leading them to break down existing habits of thought and identify with new perspectives. As Bernard Harrison has commented: 'The peculiar value of literature in a culture such as ours, the thing which really does make it essential to a civilised society, is its power to act as a standing rebuke and irritant to the dominant paradigm of knowledge' (Harrison 4).

Only a very small number of the 150 or so English language climate change novels identified by Adam Trexler and others are classifiable as sceptical, Michael Crichton's *State of Fear* (2004) being the best known. Writing at a time of what he saw as alarmist exaggeration, when climate scientists were still widely viewed as saintly truth-seekers, Crichton attacked the perceived fuelling of public fears of devastating climate change and the turning of science into an article of blind faith (see Chapter 4 for an in-depth analysis). German authors of climate fiction have, like their American and British counterparts, on the whole responded to climate change with alarm and regret, and sought to encourage their readers to take action on the climate. They have also tended to reinforce the widely felt sense of guilt and anticipation of punishment (sometimes, but not always, followed by redemption).[7] German literary production is typified by the alarmism of Frank Schätzing's blockbusting eco-thriller, *Der Schwarm* (2004, translated as *The Swarm*, 2006), the jeremiad of Ilija Trojanow's poetic *EisTau* (2011, translated as *The Lamentations of Zeno*, 2016), and the educational thrust of Claus-Peter Hutter and Eva Goris's book for young adults, *Die Erde schlägt zurück: Wie der Klimawandel unser Leben verändert* (The Earth Strikes Back: How Climate Change Is Altering Our Lives, 2009). While the public's reluctance to face the challenge of climate change features in these books, German novels have yet to be written which explore climate scepticism, either as a socio-political phenomenon or as a psychological disposition, as directly and perceptively as American author Barbara Kingsolver's *Flight Behavior* (2012).

The German public's disillusionment with climate politics after the so-called Climategate affair and the collapse of international negotiations at the Copenhagen conference in December 2009 is, however, reflected in three popular novels: Sonja Margolina's thriller *Kaltzeit* (Glacial Period, 2013), Nele Neuhaus's regional crime novel *Wer Wind sät* (Those Who Sow Wind, 2011) and Sven Böttcher's science thriller *Prophezeiung* (Prophecy, 2011). I shall look at these briefly in the following, before examining in greater detail Christian Kracht's and Ingo Niermann's more imaginative approach to fictionalizing climate scepticism in *Metan* (Methane, 2007).

The author of the self-published novel *Kaltzeit* is a journalist and writer of Russian Jewish origin, who studied biology and ecology and has combined this field of interest with writing on post-Soviet Russian politics. In 1995 she published a provocative non-fiction book denying climate change, *Die gemütliche Apokalypse: Unbotmässiges zu Klimahysterie und Einwanderungsdebatte in Deutschland* (The Comfortable Apocalypse: Disrespectful Remarks on Climate Hysteria and the Immigration Debate in Germany, 1995), and in September 2017 she defended Donald Trump's position on climate change in a piece in the *Neue Zürcher Zeitung*. The characters relating to climate change in *Kaltzeit* are Tanja, a Russian-born biologist living in Germany (a partially autobiographical figure), Professor Siegfried von Castorp, a physicist who played a leading role in stoking public fears of climate change in the 1980s and has become the Director of the Institute for Climate Change, and Robert, an idealistic young physicist working for Castorp.

Castorp, who is concerned for the future of climate change research (that of his institute as well as his own career) because of growing public distrust of climate science, disapproval of the high price of energy necessitated by the government's subsidies for renewable energy and rejection of the disfiguration of the landscape with wind farms, sends Robert to find out what is going on at a conference organized by German climate sceptics. Robert meets Tanja there, who turns out to be a leading climate sceptic and a thorn in the side of the climate research establishment. He learns that the data on which the Institute's influential climate models are based – and beyond that the government's famous *Energiewende* [Energy Turnaround] – are unreliable. Margolina names the foreign climate scientists Michael Mann and Phil Jones, and quotes from genuine emails hacked from the Climatic Research Unit in 2009. She summarizes the content of scientific papers challenging the evidence for global warming over the last fifty years, disputing the role of carbon dioxide, and arguing that natural causes such as solar flare activity are being ignored. The novel ends counterfactually, with the vindication of the sceptics. A leading sceptic researcher is awarded the Nobel Prize, and Castorp commits suicide on a research trip to the Antarctic. The readers learn that Castorp had originally taken up the cause of climate change to deflect public anxieties about nuclear power, and never entirely believed in it. A highly intelligent man whose ambition and arrogance led to his lonely and pathetic end, he stands in contrast to Robert, whose journey from blind faith in scientific and political practice to scepticism is traced sympathetically.

Margolina's novel is thus overtly didactic, inserting scientific information directly into a narrative with obvious positive and negative role models. It conveys key sceptical arguments, but it blends the real and the fictional in ways likely to mislead uninformed readers. The plot maintains suspense throughout, but the characters are two-dimensional and the love story is clichéd. An unusual feature is Margolina's leftist framing of climate politics. Climate scepticism is presented, through a series of allusions to socialism and class warfare, as a struggle for social justice and Enlightenment reason against an ideology imposed by powerful exploitative elites. In an epigraph, Bertolt Brecht's exhortation of workers to check the bill before paying it from the poem 'Lob des Lernens' (In Praise of Learning) is cited, and Tanja sings lines from Brecht's 'Lied vom Klassenfeind' (Song of the Class Enemy) which imply that in time climate sceptics will unite and triumph over the forces of obscurantist climate science and politics. Tanja asks Robert whether he has noticed that many German climate sceptics are former citizens of the German Democratic Republic. This fact, which might, if true, be explained as a consequence of residual anti-Western feeling in a generation which was marginalized after Reunification, is interpreted by Margolina as a result of experience which has made them more sensitive to flaws in dominant ideologies than the average West German. Climate policies are commonly associated with Communism in the public mind, not only in the United States but also in West German publications (see Mann), but here they are approached from an anti-capitalist standpoint.

Neuhaus's *Wer Wind sät* is a relatively complex work by a professional writer of crime novels. It is more informative and entertaining, and less polemic. Addressing a popular readership whose trust in climate science is shaken after Climategate, and who question the need for the German taxpayer to fund the government's costly subsidies for renewables, it depicts a world in which entrepreneurs in renewable energy are bribing individuals in state and local authorities to provide the positive evaluation reports required to obtain permission to construct wind farms, and resorting to illegal means to undermine the citizens' action groups opposing them. At the same time, however, the Citizens' Initiative opposing the proposed wind farm in the Taunus near Frankfurt around which the action is centred is anything but a happy community of environmentally committed idealists: its leaders turn out to be pursuing material interests and personal vendettas. Corrupt practices in eco-business and the instrumentalization of public fears of climate change by scientists and politicians are balanced against ruthless egotism and manipulation of the media by eco-activists. All the main actors are flawed characters, guilty of dishonesty, lack of regard for friends and colleagues, and neglect of partner or family responsibilities.

The author appears to accept the need for measures to combat climate change, while directing her readers to look beyond surface appearances in both climate action and opposition to renewables. However, this changes towards the end of the book, when the existence of an international conspiracy to conceal the absence of scientific evidence of global warming is alluded to as a 'bigger story' behind the crimes committed. In an Epilogue, news of the Climategate affair is interpreted as confirmation of the views of climate sceptics. In a note at the end of the volume, Neuhaus states that Climategate is the only historical fact alluded to in her otherwise fictional story. The persons, events and institutions described are freely invented, and it was not her intention to discredit or defame real persons or institutions (560). The 'climate pope' Dirk Eisenhut, Director of the 'German Climate Institute' is, however, like Margolina's Siegfried von Castorp, in some respects a fictionalized portrait of Hans-Joachim Schellnhuber, Director of the Potsdam Institute for Climate Impact Research, or perhaps rather of its principal spokesman, Stefan Rahmstorf. Neuhaus writes of 'lies' in the latest IPCC report (381), and asserts that the climate sceptics have gathered 'cast iron' proof that climate data has been manipulated for the last ten years (382), in a deliberate deception to uphold the hypothesis of climate change, stirring up public fears out of greed and desire for influence. The readers are told that the head of the IPCC has been involved in deals worth billions which depended on IPCC recommendations: Eisenhut is implicated and will probably have to resign (557).

Research suggests that the readers of fiction generally assume the reliability of facts presented as the truth, and that this is an important part of their reception of novels (Hahnemann). Neuhaus's casual introduction of departures from factual truth in her account of Climategate and her wish-fulfilling punishment of prominent German members of the 'internationale Global-Warming-Fraktion' (international Global Warming Faction, 557) are therefore problematic. But her book exemplifies the ability of fiction to challenge and destabilize the consensus of the political elite, and is a salutary reminder of the unwisdom of epistemic overconfidence.

Sven Böttcher's *Prophezeiung* presents a similar but more extended and sophisticated scenario of concealment of the uncertainty of climate science and the corrupt pursuit of self-enrichment by elites, framed in a narrative of their gradual revelation by an initially naïve and idealistic young female climate scientist. By- now familiar features include passages summarizing dissident arguments about climate change, and critical portraits of a 'climate pope' and a band of misguided eco-warriors. A key difference from *Kaltzeit* and *Wer Wind sät* is that climate change is not denied here; its causes are merely disputed. The action is set some decades into the future. The earth is warming in unpleasant ways (incessant rain and a plague of insects in northern Europe, and drought in the south). The heroine of the novel, the climate scientist Mavie Heller, makes two discoveries: the change in the climate is mainly due to a sudden increase in solar irradiation (although the problem is aggravated by an increase in the level of carbon dioxide in the atmosphere), and there is a sinister conspiracy by individuals seeking to derive financial and political advantage from its consequences. Professor Fritz Eisele, a superstar of climate science who travels around the world finding ever new, more elegant and politically persuasive turns of phrase to communicate the findings of climate science to politicians and the public, is revealed as deviously manipulating industrial bosses and political leaders so as to maximize the profits of his own clandestine investment company. He withholds information gained from a powerful new integrated meteorological program which would enable the lives of hundreds of millions of unsuspecting people to be saved. However, it turns out in the end that there are flaws in the software algorithms, which have skewed its predictions. The rain stops and the floods recede in a final scene echoing the Biblical Flood. A quiet hero emerges in the figure of Thilo Beck, a seemingly dull and pusillanimous scientist who had refused to allow himself to be swept away by financial temptations, the quest for power or fear of the future.

As well as challenging the claims of climate scientists to be able to predict the future reliably, Böttcher draws attention, in a sub-plot involving a vain celebrity scientist who threatens to seek a solution to the problem by triggering a volcanic eruption with nuclear detonations, to the dangers of machismo proponents of geoengineering taking advantage of the situation to realize their sci-fi dreams. A group of internet-savvy eco-activists thirsting to inform the global public about the impending climate catastrophe only makes the situation worse, by precipitating chaotic mass emigration from the regions worst hit by the change. Other figures include a Rawlesian prepper and a rich playboy who is only temporarily weaned from his position of implicatory climate scepticism by his sister's murder. The book combines a critique of public blindness to the need for climate action (selfish consumerist citizens' hedonistic disregard for climate change) with distrust of climate scientists advocating political action, and exposure of the dangers of fantasies of technological control.

The breadth and seriousness of the author's research into climate debates are evident in the acknowledgements at the end of the book. Alongside Wally Broecker and Robert Kunzig's *Fixing Climate*, which explores the possibility of abrupt climate change and puts forward a geoengineering solution, James Lovelock's bleak forecast and advocacy of technological solutions, *The Vanishing Face of Gaia*, Fred Pearce's alarmist *The Last Generation* and David MacKay's measured *Sustainable Energy without the Hot Air*, the list includes Nigel Lawson's sceptic *Appeal to Reason* and Christopher Booker's *The Real Global Warming Disaster*. Böttcher also cites Webster Griffin Tapley's conspiracist account of the 09/11 attacks, James Wesley Rawles's practical guide, *How to Survive the End of the World as We Know It*, Shaun Chamberlin's *Transition Timeline*, and critiques of politics and the media by John Pilger and others. *Prophezeiung* is in many ways a balanced and successful dramatization of climate change debates.

The final novel to be examined here, *Metan*, merits fuller presentation and discussion because of the unconventional satirical strategy it adopts in fictionalizing climate change. Billed on the back cover as 'die unglaubliche Wahrheit über den Klimawandel' (the unbelievable truth about climate change), this short prose work (88 pages of text, followed by 41 pages of captionless black and white photographs loosely associated with the narrative) is less an expression of climate change denial than one of ironic detachment from the earnestness and heat of climate debates at the time of writing. In this it reflects the profession of cynical disregard for social inequality and political injustice for which Christian Kracht is known. Kracht and Niermann take global warming as a given and acknowledge its transformative consequences. However, pointing out that methane is a more active greenhouse gas than carbon dioxide, and focusing on the methane produced by the digestive systems of an ever-larger population of humans and cattle as a prime cause of global warming, they provocatively advocate its active promotion through 'methanization' of the earth's atmosphere.

In addition to displacing carbon by methane emissions, the authors integrate familiar sceptical arguments in the text. The readers are told that the 'Kritiker des Klimawandels' (critics of climate change), who warn of rising sea levels, coastal flooding and desertification, overlook the fact that vast new areas at the poles will become accessible to agriculture (29). Climate change cannot be halted. Rather than heeding the population of the Maldives, Kracht and Niermann argue, we should follow the example of the Netherlands, a world leader in both the production of methane and the building of dykes. But they go further, arguing that adaptation is no more than a stopgap measure. We should therefore do what we can to accelerate global warming. We should burn up the world's reserves of oil, thereby bringing modern civilization (and the human race) to an end – and in doing so enabling a new, more intelligent species to emerge, whose physiology is compatible with an atmosphere in which water and oxygen have been replaced by methane.

Kracht and Niermann playfully develop a fanciful variant of Lovelock's Gaia hypothesis, which enlists myth in a conception of the earth as an organism capable of regulating its own environment. Methane is described as the breath of god, an all-pervasive divine spirit: the worship of the sun god throughout the ages and cultures was 'indirectly a cult of methane' (28). It is personified as a 'Methangetüm', or methane monster.[8] Parts of the book read as a parody of popular scientific accounts of climate change (there are no notes or references, but the book includes a wholly superfluous index of places, names and associations); at other moments Kracht and Niermann satirize the genre of sensationalist political exposé. As if this were not enough, *Metan* is also a spoof on occult conspiracy thrillers such as Dan Brown's *Da Vinci Code*. The omission in the title of the 'h' which is present in the normal spelling of the German word for methane is explained in a passage suggesting it is an anagram of 'atmen', German for 'breathing' (16). 'Metan' is printed on the dust cover in a modern Gothic typeface of the kind associated with neo-Nazi groups, hinting at a link with their efforts to revive Germanic paganism, and the occultist preoccupations of certain right-wing paramilitary groups. A note on the back cover announces:

> Spannend geschrieben, zwingend recherchiert und mit eindrucksvollen Fotos versehen, enthüllt Christian Krachts und Ingo Niermanns *Metan* eine Verstrickung kosmischen Ausmaßes. Das Buch hat eine Tragweite, welche Wilsons und Sheas *Illuminatus*-Trilogie, Stephen Hawkings *Eine kurze Geschichte der Zeit* und Edward Bulwer-Lyttons *Das kommende Geschlecht* bei weitem übertrifft.
>
> (Thrillingly plotted, compellingly researched and illustrated with impressive photos, Christian Kracht and Ingo Niermann's *Metan* exposes an embroilment of cosmic dimensions. The implications of *Metan* far exceed those of Wilson and Shea's *Illuminatus* trilogy, Stephen Hawking's *Brief History of Time*, and Edward Bulwer-Lytton's *Coming Race*.)

A series of political conspiracy theories are interwoven in the framework narrative of the authors' ascent of Mount Kilimanjaro in a party of tourists (whose increased flatulence at high altitude furthers the methanization of the atmosphere). These conspiracist fantasies are taken to wildly implausible extremes, through Quixotic invention and exuberant construction of alleged connections, in order to fit the history of the last fifty years into a narrative of progressive methanization. The readers are told, for instance, that Japan, Australia (which harbours ambitions to conquer India, build an empire and dominate the Pacific), South Africa and Switzerland (which has a secret atom bomb) are, as proponents of nuclear energy, enemies of methane. Saddam Hussein, secretly an agent of the 'methane monster', worked hand in glove with the Israelis and invaded Kuwait to be able to burn its oil wells and refineries, and boost the methane content of the atmosphere. The maverick American political activist and conspiracy theorist Lyndon LaRouche is repeatedly referenced. Embroidering on reality in the spirit of LaRouche, whose movement disputes the existence of anthropogenic climate change and advocates technological solutions to (naturally caused) global warming, Kracht and Niermann have LaRouche ally with Eugene Terre Blanche, the white supremacist founder of the Afrikaner Resistance Movement, to launch an atom bomb on Kilimanjaro, so as to reactivate the dormant volcano and reduce solar radiation by emitting clouds of soot and sulphur dioxide into the atmosphere. The conspirators' aim is to draw a line under the culturally degenerate and genetically moribund human race, and enable a new, better humanity to emerge, at the very place where *homo sapiens* originated. However, they are overheard by the omnipresent methane monster and outwitted: in the explosion vast quantities of subterranean methane are also released.

More a scurrilous pamphlet framed as an autobiographical travel narrative than a novel, *Metan* combines the disregard for the distinction between historical reality and imagination and the playful treatment of secret codes which characterize postmodern conspiracy fiction with parodic passages of natural science (e.g. explaining the origin of life on earth through a 'self-sacrifice' of methane). It simultaneously echoes the idea of a master race in possession of a mysterious energy force for which the Theosophists valued Bulwer-Lytton's Victorian tale. An initially bewildering piece of writing, *Metan* gains meaning if we see it as simultaneously a dismissal of the conspiracy theories prevalent in some climate scepticism and a critique of climate alarmism. This does not mean that Kracht and Niermann deny global warming or the dangers it brings. The production and worship of methane can be read as a metaphor for global capitalism, touristic consumption, military-industrial destruction of the environment, the dissolution of democratic structures and moral degeneration.

Farting our way into extinction, we humans are too dumb to realize we are destroying the atmospheric basis of our existence. *Metan* exemplifies the camp take on public issues which characterizes its authors' work, in which moral values are subordinated to an aesthetic of dandyism. It shares with Kracht's other novels a concern with style which has won him critical acclaim; an ambivalent fascination with popular culture and Western consumerism; and an interest in alternative and reimagined history, existential ennui, and courting political controversy. Kracht's pastiche of alarmist environmental non-fiction is a taboo-breaking work of eco-blasphemy making light of eschatological thinking, comparable to Horstmann's satirical attack on nuclear apocalypticism in the 1980s. Both works provocatively envision a return to the inorganic, playfully critiquing the latent will to catastrophe which Peter Sloterdijk sees as pervading modernity. Published in February 2007, at the height of emotional public feeling about climate change, *Metan* made a unique contribution to the literature of climate scepticism, adding postmodern pastiche to a field dominated by action novels and science thrillers.

Key characteristics of German climate scepticism

Climate scepticism in Germany has taken a wide range of forms and adopted different standpoints. It would be wrong to claim that all German sceptics share the same motivations or behave in the same way in their interventions: on the web there is evidence enough of the vociferous, polarized argument, paranoid mindset and conspiracist theories found in other countries. However, this is not the whole story: it has been my aim to show that there is also a significant body of climate sceptic writing which makes a valuable contribution to debates in Germany, and deserves to be engaged with. The key arguments of these sceptics have been

- the continuing uncertainty of scientific knowledge as to the extent of climate change and its causes
- the tendency of the prevailing discourse to distort and exaggerate the risks associated with climate change
- the hypocrisy of policies serving to cement first-world domination and benefit the rich and business at the expense of the poor, while calling for individuals to forgo simple pleasures of consumption
- unthinking public acceptance of green ideology where critical analysis is needed, and the naivety of well-meant eco-warrior activism

- the dangerous propensity of over-ambitious projects, be they technological or social engineering, to bypass democratic control
- the willingness of natural scientists to allow themselves to be drawn into pronouncing on matters of political choice, thereby undermining the objectivity and authority of science
- the need for rational optimism and hope rather than despair.

By contrast with most Anglophone sceptics, German climate sceptics see themselves not as enemies of the environmental cause, but as its critical friends; not as climate change deniers, but as sceptics in the sense of challenging unfounded assumptions and demanding evidence-based policy. They regard themselves as unjustly stigmatized and treated as dangerous, although they are in reality a small and beleaguered minority (German scepticism is not, as in America – see McCright & Dunlap – a significant counter-movement to reflexive modernization) that lacks the prominent supporters enjoyed by sceptics in other countries. The Umweltbundesamt (Federal German Environmental Agency) described Maxeiner and Miersch, alongside Vahrenholt and Lüning, and Günter Ederer, as 'climate change sceptics' in a booklet published in 2013, stating that they regularly published 'Beiträge [...], die nicht mit dem Kenntnisstand der Klimawissenschaft übereinstimmen' (contributions which [...] do not conform to the current state of knowledge; Lehmann 112–13). The journalists applied for an injunction to stop distribution of the publication, arguing that they had denied neither the existence of climate change nor its anthropogenic causes, and merely pointed out scientific uncertainties and criticized aspects of the IPCC's reports. However, the Administrative Court in Halle and the Higher Regional Court in Magdeburg rejected the claim, commenting that the publication served to counter 'postfactual discourse' (see Miersch's detailed announcement of the court finding on the EIKE website in March 2017). In a sense, however, the sceptics have won the day: by 2013 much of Germany's vaunted energy transition was effectively stalled by concerns about the cost and the impact on the economy. The focus of government policy on greenhouse emissions as if they were all that mattered was, in Frank Uekötter's words (168), an 'intellectual monomania at odds with the best traditions of environmental thinking'. Maxeiner and Miersch are not the only sceptics who regard themselves as proponents of a measured, rational and pragmatic response to climate change and other environmental problems, and as such a necessary corrective to eco-hysteria and the emotional intensity of green fundamentalist positions on issues from nuclear power and forest dieback to GM crops, fracking and climate change.

German climate scepticism is in part a reaction against the ambivalent fascination with catastrophe which has been particularly strong in the German-speaking world (see Gerstenberger and Nusser). German climate sceptics present themselves as realists in the face of an irrational green apocalypticism, and as defenders of freedom of thought against ideology. Some are former environmental activists who became disillusioned with the hailing of scientists as oracles for a society unsettled by climate change, as prophets and political cue-givers, rather than as providers of specialist factual knowledge. However carefully popular interviewees such as Mojib Latif, Hans Joachim Schellnhuber and Stefan Rahmstorf hedged their statements (for instance on whether storms and floods were manifestations of climate change), the media, politicians and the public saw them as confirming a deep-rooted suspicion that humans were enemies of the planet. In rejecting this 'horizon of expectation' (Hans Robert Jauss), climate sceptics have served as agents of critical self-appraisal of the environmental movement.

The German climate scepticism examined here has rarely been a matter of wilful ignorance, deliberate deception or even contrarian intransigence. If it is 'denial' (a term which I have avoided because in the German context it suggests an analogy with Holocaust denial, implying that climate scepticism is a deliberate misrepresentation and distortion of facts for ideological reasons, immoral and punishable by law), then only in the sense outlined by the ethnographer Kari Norgaard in her study of climate-related attitudes and behaviour in Norway. Norgaard understands 'implicatory denial' as a product of cognitive dissonance: it is an unconscious suppression of the truth to defend a collective identity as a pro-environmental people against the distressing reality of Norwegians - and Germans - high-energy, consumer-capitalist way of life.

Achim Brunnengräber ends his report on climate scepticism by noting that in Germany as elsewhere, sceptics have developed a narrative of the threat to freedom, and the self-interest and corruption of climate scientists, which builds their sense of identity. Opposing the general consensus on climate change has undoubtedly functioned as a tool for the identity construction of certain individuals and groups. Tanja Fröhlich, who participated in meetings and events organized by climate sceptics as part of her research, comments (53) that the people she met were rarely in the pay of energy companies. They were often retired, and comfortably off. They did not seem to be acting out of fear that their living standard would suffer if climate regulation measures were introduced, nor to be motivated by the allergic reaction many Americans have to what they see as efforts to restrict their liberty. Nor were they primarily driven by affiliation with a political party or ideology. Many had a scientific training, and some appeared to be seeking compensation for lack of professional recognition. Climate scepticism tended to be part of a more general anti-establishment feeling, and associated with an 'outsider' mindset. In terms of regional distribution, there seems to be a concentration of climate sceptics in Thuringia and Saxony, areas of the country formerly in communist East Germany, which have become a focus for disaffection with Western liberal political values and structures, despite the equal presence of marginalized social groups in other parts of the country.

The central narratives of German sceptics have nevertheless been those of rational enlightenment and social justice: defence of reason against deception and manipulation by the ideologues and 'high priests' of environmentalism, and resistance against economic exploitation and political domination by a self-serving elite. As the meteorologist Hans von Storch and the cultural anthropologist Werner Krauß have written in *Die Klimafalle. Die gefährliche Nähe von Politik und Klimaforschung* (The Climate Trap. The Dangerous Proximity of Politics and Climate Research, 2013), sceptics are performing an important social function, as mouthpieces for an alternative understanding of climate rooted in a long history of popular perception, which must be taken into consideration if climate protection measures are to gain public acceptance. Von Storch and Krauß do not subscribe to doom and gloom forecasts of the collapse of international trade and steep increases in carbon emissions. Nor, however, do they believe that binding international agreements will bring about a significant reduction in global emissions. They rather put their faith in the pragmatic activities of individual nations and cities, increases in efficiency and regional adaptation measures to climate risks. If these are to succeed, it will be necessary to admit all to the table and make space for their different perspectives, approaches and alternative knowledge claims.

4

Climate Scepticism and Christian Conservatism in the United States

George B. Handley

Since the findings of climate science were first brought to the attention of US Congress in the 1980s, climate scepticism has exercised a persistent and authoritative influence over American policymakers and the general public, and has been the object of more academic attention than in any other country (see Introduction). Although directed at a new phenomenon of climate change, this scepticism emerged from a Cold War discourse that sought protection for the free market, promoted technology as a means to liberate humankind from the contingencies of nature, celebrated American exceptionalism and argued for the nation's Christian origins. Because concern about climate change, along with the policies its advocates sought to implement, came predominantly from Democrats, climate change was framed as a direct challenge to these primary values of American conservatism. As a preemptive attack on a predominantly liberal (in the American sense) climate change movement, American companies, central players in the fossil fuels industry and charitable foundations have financed a host of conservative think tanks (CTTs) to raise doubts about climate science, stall political action and solidify scepticism as conservative dogma.[1] The sceptical discourse issuing from CTTs has had wide influence in the Anglophone world, as well as in countries such as Norway and the Netherlands where English is widely spoken.

In the cultural arena, scepticism has taken many forms and has enjoyed access to various media, most notably conservative cable news and talk radio. Conservative favourites such as Glenn Beck, Bill O'Riley, Pat Robertson and Sean Hannity have fanned the flames of climate scepticism and helped to make it a central position of the Republican platform. In print media, major news outlets such as the *Wall Street Journal* (*WSJ*), as well as myriads of state and city papers, have featured opinions and syndicated Op-Eds by the likes of George F. Will and Charles Krauthammer who have raised questions about climate models, the costs of climate mitigation to the middle class and the increasing size of government. At the same time, it is not uncommon for the *WSJ* and Fox News to provide solid reporting about climate science and the impacts of climate change outside their 'opinion' sections (Painter and Ashe 7). CTTs such as the Heartland Institute, the Competitive Enterprise Institute (CEI), the Cato Institute, the Heritage Foundation, the Energy and Environmental (E&E) Legal Institute and others have sponsored or been affiliated with authors publishing monographs that also raise doubts about climate science. Among many such publications are Chris Horner's *Red Hot Lies: How Global Warming Alarmists Use Threats, Fraud, and Deception to Keep You Misinformed* (2008). Horner, an affiliate of the CEI and E&E Legal and a member of President Trump's EPA (Environmental Protection Agency) transition team, is a well-known sceptic and frequent commentator on television. Roy Spencer, a climate scientist at the University of Alabama who has collaborated with CTTs on the lecture circuit and on sceptical documentaries, authored *The Great Global Warming Blunder: How Mother Nature Fooled the World's Top Climate Scientists* (2012). Marc Morano, mentioned in our Introduction, has authored the book *The Politically Incorrect Guide to Climate Change* (2018), which adds to his already extensive record as an aide to Rush Limbaugh and James Inhofe promoting climate change scepticism through abrasive and contentious rhetoric. Lawrence Solomon's edited collection, *The Deniers* (2008), provides chapters by authors who raise concerns about natural cycles, computer models, the politics of scientific consensus and other matters. Like other sceptics, Solomon is motivated by a desire to avoid what he considers to be dangerous mitigation efforts and exaggerated claims of warmists, most evident in his book title that proudly contrasts the label of 'denier' with the book's scepticism. More recently, in the age of an increasingly democratized media, sceptics have gained a significant following on blogs such as *Climate Depot* and *Watts Up With That?*, websites that do battle with their warmist counterparts such as *Sceptical Science* or *Desmog Blog*. Documentaries have flourished as well, often as a riposte to Al Gore's well-known *An Inconvenient Truth* (2006), including such titles as *The Changing Climate of Global Warming* (2011) and the British documentary that has had much airplay in the United States, *The Great Global Warming Swindle* (2007).

If the continued obsession with Al Gore among sceptics is any indication, Gore's activism on the climate, starting with his service as a Democratic senator in the 1980s and then as vice president and as a presidential candidate, helped to solidify climate change as a partisan issue in the United States. As a film that is part autobiography and lament regarding the 2000 election and introductory lecture on climate change, *An Inconvenient Truth* embeds the subject within the story of the partisan struggle for the White House. What is obvious, then, though still in need of explanation, is that American climate scepticism is consistently identified with the political right while climate warmism – that is, a concern about the possibility or even the inevitability of environmental and human cost due to anthropogenic climate change – with the political left. It is distinctive in this regard: attitudes towards GMOs and vaccinations, for example, are not strongly partisan in the United States. As Gore began his campaign to fight climate change in the early 1980s, Ronald Reagan and his controversial Secretary of Interior James Watt helped to break with the bipartisan legacies of the 1960s and 1970s regarding the environment, giving the Republican Party a much more pronounced anti-environmental agenda. By the time of Newt Gingrich's 1994 Contract with America, the process known to political scientists as 'ideological sorting' was well underway: environmental concerns were increasingly understood to be liberal concerns. Since then, with the rise of cable news and eventually of social media, environmental issues have been increasingly mediated by this partisan and identitarian filter. The compromises that characterized the most important environmental legislation of the 1960s and 1970s are now anathema to both parties, making common ground on environmental issues especially challenging to identify and progress unlikely. Climate change has been so thoroughly politicized by the partisan divide in the United States, it is as hard to separate the scientific basis for concern about climate change from a liberal orientation to the world as it is to separate concerns about the costs and effectiveness of mitigation from conservative convictions. This makes conservatives as hesitant to accept the implications of the science as it does liberals to admit the costs and difficulties of mitigation.

This politicized framing of climate change trades in stereotypes: the people-hating climate activist who never met a tree (or a regulation!) he didn't want to hug and the flat-earth climate denier who rejects Darwinism along with the IPCC, treasuring illusions over empirical reality. To understand the roots of scepticism, I attempt to avoid stereotypes by identifying its patterns of logic as well as its surprising contradictions. Many, if not most, sceptics focus their doubts on the effectiveness of proposed climate mitigation efforts, some to the point of offering apocalyptic narratives about the risks of mitigation that in their minds outweigh the risks posed by the exaggerated claims of climate science. Others offer critiques of the ideological and emotional appeals of climate catastrophism and the tendency of warmists to identify severe weather events as evidence of climate change in support of their preferred policy changes. Environmental concerns are often seen by conservatives as exploited by liberals so as to undermine American ideals of liberty and free markets. For this reason, climate sceptics almost universally share suspicions that scientists and politicians are exploiting fears about impending disaster to promote an anti-capitalist, big spending and big government agenda that will result in excessive regulations that threaten fundamental American freedoms, even the market economy itself. As George Will famously said, 'There is a name for the political doctrine that rejoices in the scarcity of everything except government. The name is environmentalism' ('Fossil Fuels Belie Environmentalism').

There is no doubt, of course, that climate change as a political problem has thus far proposed predominantly transnational and big government solutions. It is hard to say, however, if the complex and global nature of climate change always necessitates such policies or if climate change policy has thus far simply been promoted by liberals rather than conservatives. A blurb to Chris Horner's books highlights this partisan framing:

> The occasional unguarded scientist candidly admits the need to twist the facts to paint an uglier picture in order to keep the faucet of government money flowing. In the name of 'saving the planet,' anything goes. But why the nasty tactics? Why the cover ups, lies, and intimidation? Because Al Gore and his ilk want to use big government at the local, state, federal, and global level to run your life, and they can brook no opposition. But the actual facts, as *Red Hot Lies* makes clear, aren't nearly as scary as their fiction.

Chris Horner taps into an anxiety that helps to explain why among the many cultural forms of climate scepticism, we find fiction thrillers, most famously Michael Crichton's monumentally influential *State of Fear*, that are offered as counter-fictions to what is perceived to be the mad rantings of the left. So, if sceptics present the climate debate as a choice between fiction and reality, they also present it as a choice between ideology and science. Sarah Palin captured this rhetoric when, in the same breath as insisting that there was 'no real consensus' on the climate, she argued that 'policy should be based on sound science, not politics' ('Sarah Palin'). And, of course, as we discussed in the Introduction, this only mirrors the posture of warmists who similarly mock the opposition's neglect of science and propensity for delusion. As we discuss further in Chapter 6, Palin's comment recalls an ideal conception of apolitical science that Science and Technology Studies (STS) scholars have repeatedly castigated as naive and uninformed about the real processes of scientific knowledge production.

Without clarity on what kind of authority to trust and why, it is not hard for an enquiring but relatively uninformed onlooker in the United States today to conclude after a quick google survey that climate science is, indeed, 'unsettled.' This is not to suggest, of course, that we can't navigate these waters to a successful orientation to empirical reality, nor that therefore both sides are equally wrong or equally right. It is merely to point out that despite scientific consensus on the climate, consensus is not obvious nor is it necessarily persuasive to everyone, least of all to those on the right who are repeatedly given reasons to be suspicious of both the science and the proposed mitigations. Climate change presents itself in the American mind as a profoundly unresolved, contentious and potentially risky debate, especially if citizens get it wrong, leaving the majority of Americans, as we'll see, distributed between 'alarmed,' 'concerned' and 'cautious,' with many still 'doubtful' and only a small minority (9 per cent) 'dismissive'. What this means for ecocritics is the importance of attention to discursive framing and the avoidance of polarizing language, as we suggested in the Introduction.

In my case, I will focus on the ways in which climate change is framed by religious questions of ultimacy that inform certain Christian ideas about the human place in the cosmos. While there is a great deal to document and say about climate change scepticism in the United States, I focus not only on the political assumptions behind climate scepticism but also on the ways in which scepticism taps into particular theological assumptions that activate a religious resistance. It is no coincidence that conservative Christians show the highest rates of climate scepticism in the United States. (It must be said, however, that warmists' own assumptions incline them to *believe* climate science, but that is a study for another time.) Religiously-inflected scepticism articulates human stewardship of the environment as a short-term responsibility to assure human flourishing and to maximize individual liberties, and entrusts uncertainties and externalities inherent in such a circumscribed set of responsibilities to the care of divine providence. Even when sceptics are not explicitly theological, their defence of free market capitalism and human autonomy is often inflected by a religious sentiment about the innate goodness of human nature that, when left free of external restraints, will use natural resources for their putative divinely sanctioned purposes. American climate scepticism has various manifestations, but in the majority of cases it is shaped by an ideo-theology that struggles to accept the reality of climate change because climate change challenges the presumed temporality of the American Christian nation and some cherished notions of individualism. Climate change also lays bare a universe of chance, tragedy and uncertainty that are anathema to a Creationist Christian theology, as we will see.

It is certainly easier to believe in anthropogenic climate change for those whose worldview already accommodates the idea that global cooperation is a value; that European social democracy is enviable; that large-scale government solutions can be good; or that human destiny is subject to chance but dependent on human will. In their understandable rush to frame the climate crisis as a moral issue in order to motivate action, warmists have at different times moralized almost every stage of human history and every economic activity, to the point of receiving criticism from sceptics for being the new Puritans. This moralizing, however, has outpaced warmists' willingness to seek to understand the ways in which human understanding of empirical reality is mediated by ideology and culture. Arguably, that is a kind of moral failure. If warmists want to insist on the morality of climate mitigation efforts, we must wrestle with the influence of culture and admit that individual belief in climate science isn't necessarily a hard-earned categorical virtue, nor is scepticism a categorical moral failure.

The present impasse in the United States on what is knowable about the climate motivates my consideration here of how cosmological narratives and moral discourses inform who citizens think they are, what their fundamental responsibilities are and how they interpret information about the world. As we noted in our discussion of Dan Kahan's research, cultural identity is at least if not more important than scientific knowledge or literacy as a predictor of attitudes about climate change. Moreover, such identities have presumptive ontological and cosmological dimensions, some of them explicitly religious. Again, this is not to dismiss the importance of understanding accurately the status of the science and of cultivating a capacity to be moved or changed by new data. It is merely to suggest that data will be better received if they are not framed in ways that are hostile to conservative Christian identities. An accurate understanding of the ideo-theology that informs climate scepticism is a precondition for such communication.

The culture of American climate change scepticism

The material benefits of industrialization in the United States became intoxicatingly evident to the generations that followed the Great Depression and the Second World War and provided an invitation for the rest of the world to aspire to similar conditions. A chief component of early scepticism about environmental problems was the confidence in the possibilities that technology might deliver citizens from biological limits and contingencies and provide an escape from the tragedies imposed upon us by the natural world. The great global struggle between communism and capitalism was presumed to be over in 1989, but the result may have merely been a shift into a new battle over the nature of the climate and the status of international scientific consensus.[2] The benefits of technology have continued to be patently and tangibly obvious, while their environmental costs have often been delayed or remote enough to deny or ignore. Indeed, because of the power of such illusions, as well as the scale of the material advantages enjoyed by many Americans, scepticism about the connection between the burning of fossil fuels and the warming of the planet has arguably been most adamant in the United States – the world's second largest emitter of greenhouse gases and one of the most religious populations among developed nations.

Climate change presents unique challenges to American culture, not the least of which is that it seems to ask a profoundly optimistic, future-oriented and individualistic American culture to think, as Michel Serres has argued, in terms of collective values and collective ethics and on a new temporal and spatial scale (78). I am speaking here of the difficulty of tracing, measuring and valuing individual choices and how they might impact an as-yet undetermined future not only for one's own community but for the planet collectively. In response to such challenges, many communities in the United States have resorted to familiar narratives about American exceptionalism and isolationism and about America's presumed role in Christian teleology, leaving climate change stuck in the intransigent culture wars that have defined US political culture since the 1960s. Climate change is often doubted in contexts where cultures are already feeling threatened by the phenomena of globalization, for example, whether globalization is experienced as a form of neo-colonialism, multi-national corporatism, faceless big government or pervasive secularism.

Across these various responses to climate change is a perception that climate change and traditional conservative values are incommensurable. In his study of Christianity's relevance to climate change, *The Future of Ethics* (2013), Willis Jenkins has suggested that resistance to climate change often stems from a suspicion that climate change condemns tradition for being inadequate in the face of a new reality. Jenkins insists, however, that confronting such inadequacy is the first step towards liberating creativity within a culture. Jenkins writes:

> There is more explanation for the problems we face than that we are failing to live up to our beliefs or that our worldviews are corrupt. Both of those things are continually true, but problems like climate change do not reduce to justice trespassed or nature violated .... Agents can learn new moral competencies, I argue, by participating in projects *that use their inheritances to create new responsibilities for unexpected problems*.
>
> (5)

Jenkins's point here is that while climate change is a moral issue, and it remains important that we work to increase our capacity to improve worldviews and our commitments to them, the complexity of climate change means we should be careful about reducing it to such fundamental human failings. He prefers instead an approach that highlights our capacity for change. After all, a culture is at its ethically strongest and most creative when it shows the capacity to face its inadequacies in the face of new problems. In this way it learns to survive and even thrive by reinvigorating traditions and values and finding ways to be ethical in response to new realities. There is, indeed, room within conservative Christian communities in America for addressing the reality of climate change. We need only consider the Evangelical Environmental Network and its focus on what they call 'Creation Care' or former South Carolina congressman Bob Inglis's non-profit 'republicEN', a group of conservative 'energy optimists' who are also 'climate realists'.[3]

Instead of finding recourse to such creativity, however, communities of climate scepticism have often reinforced their identitarian and ideological purity as a way to contest climate change as just the latest threat posed to the legitimacy of their existence. As I intend to show with various examples, this curiously risks a betrayal of their own most dearly held beliefs in the name of resistance to a (mis)perceived enemy. That is to say, the obstacles that climate change presents are formidable for any community, and the temptation may be to treat it suspiciously as a disguised *cultural* offensive. However, this is not because held or inherited values can't be adapted to the reality of climate change. To the degree that such creative work is eschewed in favour of an entrenched defensiveness, we see conservative Christian communities hardening their resistance, sharing values between political ideology and Christian theology and thereby becoming more resistant to the possibility that anthropogenic climate change is real. We end up with logic that amounts to saying that a conservative can't believe climate change is real because Al Gore is wealthy, or an isolationist can't believe it is real because the UN is overly bureaucratic, or that a Christian can't believe it because there is a sovereign God, or a libertarian can't believe it because wasteful big government has got us into financial debt. The dependent clause in each of these propositions can be valid claims, but an admission of the reality of climate change need not be a betrayal of those core beliefs.

The more climate warmists seek to shame and defeat the values that inform such attitudes, the more entrenched the conflict becomes. As Dan Kahan observes, even the claim of a '"97% consensus" of scientists effectively insults the conservative viewer with a "*do you get it yet, moron?!*" motif' ('Climate-Science Communication' 19). Climate change mitigation and Christianity can and need to get along. Wishing one or the other away only reinforces the conflict. When warmists position climate change as a challenge that *requires* betrayal of the fundamental values of a given community, this only further strengthens the very logic that informs the scepticism in the first place. The values that could have been adapted to become important allies in meeting the challenges of a warming planet instead become the energy behind deepening scepticism. What I am suggesting is that climate change is not merely a question about empirical reality and the status of science, but also a question of historical consciousness that easily obtains theological and cosmological dimensions. Mark Weiner has made a similar argument about Trumpism: 'As a framework for interpreting the past, climate change denial grows logically from the core metaphysical commitments of contemporary populist nationalism in its confrontation with trans-Atlantic, cosmopolitan, individualist liberalism' ('Climate Change Denial'). That is to say, climate scepticism stems from a way of life and a way of belief about the nature and temporality of the world, the boundaries of community, the historical past and the future. Climate change advocacy, of course, similarly stems from 'core metaphysical commitments' even if they are radically different from those that inform climate scepticism.

When advocacy comes from sectors of society that have already been identified as unfriendly (liberals, scientists, secularists, the international community and the like), sceptics can focus on the failings of the advocates rather than on relevant resources and inheritances that could be brought to bear to address the new problem. And when a sense of community, of nation or of religious identity is already firmly grounded in a bounded sense of identity, climate change directly challenges the existence of such boundedness. As Mark Weiner further explains,

> Contemporary climate science hints at a conception of 'the political' that transcends particularistic identity markers and encompasses humanity as a whole. This political community does not find its enemy in rival sovereign peoples which it keeps at bay through deals in which each side respects the territorial limits of the other. Rather it does battle with a global climatic process that even now is simultaneously affecting the historical course of all sovereigns.

Climate change, in other words, is most threatening to cosmologies that are highly invested in geographical and temporal boundaries that have been historically important in demarcating ontologies of identity. It is the possibility of an unbounded 'global political community' that is feared above all.

We can argue, then, that climate scepticism is one response among many to the broader challenge of an increasingly globalized world that requires cross-cultural respect and collaboration. There are certainly many parties who have failed to respond adequately to this challenge, and as Bruno Latour has argued, poststructural critics are among them, including of course ecocritics. Indeed, debates about the reality of climate change have exposed how the patterns of thought between conspiracy theories and critical discourse are disturbingly similar, as Latour acknowledges with dismay:

> Maybe I am taking conspiracy theories too seriously, but it worries me to detect, in those mad mixtures of knee-jerk disbelief, punctilious demands for proofs, and free use of powerful explanation from the social neverland many of the weapons of social critique. Of course conspiracy theories are an absurd deformation of our own arguments, but, like weapons smuggled through a fuzzy border to the wrong party, these are our weapons nonetheless. In spite of all the deformations, it is easy to recognize, still burnt in the steel, our trademark: 'Made in Criticalland'. (230)

In defence of what seems to be the equivalent of a mid-life crisis for a theorist, Latour assures us he has not lost confidence in criticism but he argues for a rethinking of critical strategies: 'The mistake we made, the mistake I made, was to believe that there was no efficient way to criticize matters of fact except by moving away from them and directing one's attention toward the conditions that made them possible' (231). 'The question,' however, 'was never to get away from facts but closer to them, not fighting empiricism but, on the contrary, renewing empiricism' (231). And so he argues instead for a form of criticism that aims at 'matters of concern' rather than 'matters of fact,' as a way to consider how and why our values move us to focus and place value on certain kinds of questions as opposed to others. For this reason, instead of focusing on the scientific errors or political history of scepticism, this study focuses on the matters of concern that have informed climate scepticism.

As long as conservative sceptics are told that they must think like Al Gore or a secular scientist and prefer, say, large-government solutions, climate change is a non-starter. However, when Pope Francis, or an evangelical climate scientist like Katherine Hayhoe, identifies Christian reasons to care and to act, climate change action on the part of Christians becomes a greater possibility. In our age of increasing polarization, liberals and conservatives alike have forgotten that cultures are adaptable and malleable entities that are subject to volition; they are neither inevitable nor fixed, and understanding their complex and particular forms of expression and something of their rhetorical power, as I hope to do here, hopefully provides an avenue for establishing real dialogue and productive change.

The demographics of climate change scepticism

It would help to start with a population-level picture of scepticism in the United States. According to a 2015 study of American attitudes about climate change conducted by Yale University's Program on Climate Change Communication, four in ten Americans are either 'extremely' or 'very' sure climate change is happening, while one in ten are 'extremely' or 'very' sure it is not (Leiserowitz 6). According to a 2018 update to this study, 72 per cent of Americans are either alarmed, concerned or at least cautious about anthropogenic climate change. In other words, a significant percentage of Americans are confused on the topic. In 2015, when asked to assume it is happening, 53 per cent of Americans believe it is human-caused, as opposed to 33 per cent who believe it is a natural cycle (8). About 57 per cent of all Americans are at least 'somewhat worried' about climate change while 16 per cent say they are 'very' worried.

As the graph in the figure below shows, as of 2018 the most dismissive of Americans make up a small percentage of the population, but when we consider this breakdown along with the fact that climate scepticism is a central tenet of the Republican Party at present, we face a situation in which the elected officials

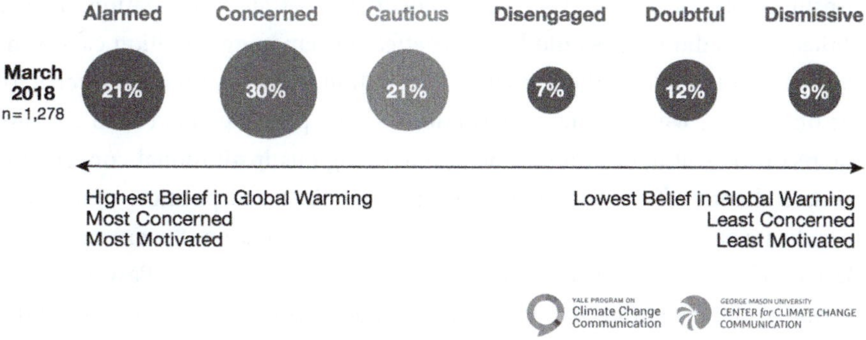

Figure Global Warming's Six Americas.

are poorly aligned with the feelings of their constituencies. Indeed, evidence suggests that political affiliation has more influence on attitudes about climate change than any other factor (Dugan 2015).[4] For this reason, many in the middle hesitate to form opinions or to see themselves as answerable to the problem in some way and instead defer to the discourse of their political leaders and the pundits on talk radio and conservative news channels. Christian conservatives rate among the least likely to believe that anthropogenic climate change exists or is a problem of concern. Rather than opening American Christians to creative and innovative and even faithful responses to the problem, the dismissive thinking of the most adamant sceptics tends to slow the capacity to respond and thus compromises both Christianity's integrity as a moral philosophy and the climate simultaneously. As the 2015 Yale study concludes:

> Together, the results demonstrate that many Americans who are not currently concerned about global warming, nonetheless believe we should care for other people and the environment, but have yet to recognize that reducing global warming will help both. As the majority prefer religious over scientific explanations, a moral perspective on global warming by religious leaders such as Pope Francis may reach segments of the U.S. public that have yet to engage with the issue. (Roser-Renouf et al. 'Faith, Morality, and the Environment' 5)

Some studies suggest that at present there is a strong correlation between religious belief and anti-environmental sentiment; but with the increased frequency of statements by ecclesiastical leaders and with more careful methods for measuring attitudes and practices with regards to environmental care, we have seen an explosion of institutional as well as grass-roots initiatives that promote concern for the environment among religious believers and provide compelling evidence that religion can have a more positive influence. As Charles Harper notes, congregations serious about reducing energy consumption could save 25–30 per cent. If half of all congregations in the United States did so, it would have the effect of removing a million cars from the road and would make available 13.5 billion kilowatt hours of electricity for other uses, without the construction of new power plants (5–26). While the record is still unclear about how much religious institutional concern for climate change affects believers' attitudes, practices and politics, signs seem to indicate an improvement. (This hope may be one reason, for example, that Barbara Kingsolver's novel *Flight Behavior* presents the figure of Pastor Ogle as pivotal to the resolution of a local environmental conflict.) It is no longer the case, if it ever was, that environmentalists and religious believers represent two incompatible groups.

Of course, religion has also provided a conduit for conservative political ideology to find its ways into the minds and hearts of believers through a kind of synthesis that has embedded traditional political conservative values within the worldviews of many Christians, challenging their ability to disaggregate religion from climate scepticism. And once citizens become locked in on their chosen political and moral authorities, their worldviews are under pressure to become increasingly hardened against the idea of climate science. Our attempt in this book to understand the cultural logic of this climate scepticism is based on the hope that change does not require wholesale alteration of worldviews but can be facilitated by greater understanding and employment of narrative to new ends. This approach envisages greater freedom and creativity for communities to imagine and enact a meaningful response to climate change based on a revised and reinvigorated approach to their own core traditions. In other words, the climate change movement and ecocriticism must be ecumenical to the bone. In the postmodern age of dispersed and disintegrated belief, there is great value in efforts through the arts, philosophy, political thought and religion to forge new cosmologies and worldviews, but given the persistence of traditional Christian beliefs in the United States at least, it would be just as important to rethink and repurpose those particular, inherited ideas.

Allow me now to turn to some of the more prominent narratives of climate change scepticism to understand why they have been adopted by Christians, even when those narratives threaten to contradict Christian beliefs.

An ideo-theology of American climate scepticism

A number of prominent Christians, including Pat Robertson, Sarah Palin and Oklahoma Senator James Inhofe, are known for claiming that climate change isn't real simply because it is a theological impossibility. There is perhaps no critic of anthropogenic climate change more brazen and proud of his minority status than Inhofe, repeatedly self-identified as a 'one man truth squad' ('Inhofe Speaks'). A highly influential climate sceptic, Inhofe has served as the chairman for the Senate Committee on Environment and Public Works. In his 2012 book, *The Global Warming Hoax: How the Global Warming Conspiracy Threatens Your Future*, and often in interviews, he cites the Bible to justify his scepticism: 'In the end, through all the hysteria, all the fear and all the phony science, what global warming alarmists have often forgotten is that God is still up there and as Genesis 8:22 reminds us, "As long as the earth remains,/there will be springtime and harvest,/cold and heat, winter and summer,/day and night'" (175). The British author Philip Foster, discussed in Chapter 2, uses this same verse from the King James translation as his title, *While the Earth Endures*, similarly signalling a confidence that the earth's destiny is underwritten by God and that climate change is therefore a cosmological impossibility. Elsewhere Inhofe adds some colour to this claim by saying, 'The arrogance of people to think that we, human beings, would be able to change what He is doing in the climate is to me outrageous' (qtd. in Johnson).

Inhofe shows how political ideology extends and colours a dominionist theology to such a degree as to make them indistinguishable and thus helps to solidify the moral urgency of climate scepticism. Inhofe entered politics because of a seemingly senseless regulation that prohibited him from moving a fire escape on a home he purchased in Oklahoma, a story of bureaucratic stupidity with which anyone can identify. If there is a distinction between such a senseless and freedom-restricting regulation and one that might be necessary to protect the freedom of those affected by environmental degradation, Inhofe does not say. Of course, the roots of such scepticism have a deep history in the United States. As Jacqueline Vaughn Switzer argues, American anti-environmentalism, particularly as it emerged as a form of resistance to the protection of public lands in the American West, has most often been about resistance to regulations that are perceived as threats to jobs and economic opportunities (6). Switzer notes that there are many and sometimes competing interests among environmental sceptics, including 'extractive resource industries like timber and mining, property rights activists (developers and individual landowners), recreationists, western ranchers and corporate farmers, businesspeople, and militia members and conspiracy theorists' (13). Inhofe's book was primarily motivated by the rising interest in cap and trade policies that he believed threatened 'hundreds of thousands of jobs, and [would] significantly raise energy prices for families, businesses, and farmers – basically anyone who drives a car, operates heavy machinery, or flips a switch' (ix). He further notes that liberal regulations (which appear to be any kind of regulation):

> would give our children a substantially depressed quality of life, forcing them to live in a less free, less prosperous America. My dream for my children and grandchildren is the same as the dream of parents all over America: that our kids will reap the many blessings of living in a free country and that their opportunities will be even greater than our own. (2)

Inhofe's cosmos is riven by a stark choice: either prosperity and a clean environment or protection of the environment at the expense of the economy.

Inhofe does not imagine or address a scenario in which the economy is protected at the expense of the environment or of any basic human freedoms, although Arlie Russell Hochschild cites several academic studies that contradict his assumption (258–59). As a result, whenever individuals or agencies, such as the EPA or the United Nations, are intent on defining and implementing models of sustainability, they are always perceived to do so unfairly at the expense of innocent victims who are just trying to make a living. There is no doubt that there are no easy solutions to rising emissions and mitigation may indeed be damaging in the ways he fears, but the assumption that any effort to establish sustainability for the planet 'would require nothing short of total control over the earth's resources' only obligates Inhofe, as he has done for the length of his career, to resist any and all regulations that pertain to climate change (214).

It is easy to attack Inhofe for his hypocrisy, for his failure to see the irony, for example, of claiming 'I've always said that when you don't have science on your side, when you don't have logic on your side, when you don't have truth on your side, you resort to attacks' (14) in a book filled with attacks on the character and intentions of Al Gore, on what he calls 'global elites', 'UN elites' and so on. Or his failure to acknowledge the irony of criticizing climate science for being influenced by or becoming a 'religion' when he quotes the Bible to justify his position and has liked to identify himself as a Christian in his many interviews and appearances when discussing his scepticism. But perhaps these charges of hypocrisy are, in fact, too easy. They are certainly not effective in changing anybody's mind.

I think what is perhaps most intriguing, and perhaps more effective to point out as a contradiction, is the high level of confidence his ideology has in basic human nature. Left alone to our own devices, human beings will always choose what is best, according to Inhofe. There is, in other words, no inherent fallibility in his human self-understanding that would seem to require a Saviour or a propitiation for human sin, despite his avowed Christianity. Inhofe's philosophy asserts an American individualism that papers over the rather serious Christian question of fallibility with the celebration and protection of individual freedom as its central and most holy tenet. Freedom obtains as the highest virtue because it is assumed that when left alone, the individual will always make the best choices, which is why, of course, regulation will always be the enemy. In this sense, it can and perhaps should be argued by theologians and philosophers who are interested in communicating environmental problems to conservative Christians that human beings cannot in fact be so trusted, and that at least some reasonable forms of voluntary self-restraint by way of democratically chosen regulations might be in order.

To the degree that Inhofe visits the biblical themes of greed, idol worship, exploitation of the poor or disregard for the divine creation of the world – themes that figure prominently in the writings of many ecotheologians – it is to suggest that such sins can only be found in contemporary environmentalism itself. He insists that nations, corporations and individuals should have maximum liberty to choose their own path of development as long as they 'must also live with the consequences of their decisions' (217–18). But due to his excoriation of regulation, this only suggests that he believes it is possible to foul one's own nest but not for degradation to go beyond self-harm. In his view, there is simply no having to live with the consequences of the decisions of others, no sense of a commons, let alone a tragedy of the commons. The only tragedy of the commons appears to be when regulation inevitably brings ruin to the economic commons. That is perhaps the reason why his fears grow in proportion to the scale in which he can envision the problem. In other words, he distrusts any authority outside his own imagined community of Christian Americans who are threatened by such policies because they are 'hard working, frontier spirited American[s] .... involved in an honorable profession, work[ing] harder than most, ... very religious, and provid[ing] jobs'. The UN, international treaties and political liberals are indifferent or antagonistic (3).

Other Christians have made similar theological cases against climate change. The Cornwall Alliance for the Stewardship of Creation, a Christian network of theologians, scientists and economists that is devoted to promoting what it calls 'biblical earth stewardship', condemns 'an environmental movement whose worldview, theology, and ethics are overwhelmingly anti-Christian, whose science and economics are often poorly done, whose policies therefore often do little good for natural ecosystems but much harm to the world's poor, and whose religious teachings undermine the fundamental Christian doctrines of God, creation, humanity, sin, and salvation' ('What We Do').[5] In short, this form of Christian climate scepticism depends on a notion of environmentalism as secular and anti-Christian. In its 2006 *Open Letter to the Signers of 'Climate Change: An Evangelical Call to Action' and Others Concerned with Global Warming*, the Cornwall Alliance asserts, in addition to claims about faulty science regarding global climate change,

> The stewardship God gave to human beings over the earth – to cultivate and guard the garden (Genesis 2:15) and to fill, subdue, and rule the whole earth (Genesis 1:28) – strongly suggests that caring for human needs is compatible with caring for the earth. As theologian Wayne Grudem put it, 'It does not seem likely to me that God would set up the world to work in such a way that human

> beings would eventually destroy the earth by doing such ordinary and morally good and necessary things as breathing, building a fire to cook or keep warm, burning fuel to travel, or using energy for a refrigerator to preserve food.'

The Christian mandate to care simultaneously for the earth and for the human family obviates here any environmental conditions that might require sacrifices or even tragic decisions in trying to strike that balance. In such defences of traditional dominionism, one rarely finds confrontations with the reality of American greed and overconsumption; the focus is instead always on necessities. Because of these implications of climate science, a less risky or less tragic interpretation of empirical reality is preferred.

One might argue that Grudem understands the difficult ethical implications of climate change better than he does his own Christian theology. He understands that climate change contradicts our traditional understanding of ethics that measures the proportionate consequences of our individual intentions and choices when made in full knowledge of potential consequences (see Jamieson). Among the more disturbing questions climate change raises are: How were we as a species supposed to have anticipated that this tremendous resource of fossil fuels that has provided the energy base for modern life, that has liberated so many from the harsh conditions of poverty and dependency, would become the greatest threat to our planet? How were we supposed to know that we ran such a risk? For believers in a sovereign God, the question is, why weren't we warned? And as Hannes Bergthaller has concluded, because our very idea of freedom and presumably of responsibility are both underwritten by fossil fuels, 'the understanding of freedom which co-evolved with the fossil fuel regime has now become an obstacle to its overcoming' (431). Climate change appears unprecedented and this is particularly challenging for a worldview that proscribes the unexpected. Grudem expresses a Christian nervousness about a cosmos in which human action has consequences beyond its intentions or in which humans must deliberate and act in a condition of relative ignorance.

At stake in this kind of scepticism, then, is the protection of a particular notion of a sovereign God and a related understanding of chance, accident and even tragedy. One resource that might help us to understand this notion is the website, *Answers in Genesis*, associated with Ken Ham and the Creation Museum in Kentucky, which attempts to defend the claim of a 6,000-year-old earth. The website provides videos and other resources to answer questions about science and the Bible, including questions about climate change, but also, interestingly, questions about the meaning of suffering and tragedy. Its climate change video, 'Global Warming: A Scientific Exposé of Climate Change', begins with the usual smattering of climate sceptics making arguments about the unreliability of the data, the shallowness of the evidence and the supposed political motivations behind the consensus. The video includes significant footage from the climate scientist Roy Spencer at the University of Alabama mentioned earlier and E. Calvin Beisner, the founder and spokesperson for the Cornwall Alliance (Oard and Lisle). Unlike other sceptical documentaries, though, the video adds a biblical justification by emphasizing the notion that God gives humankind dominion over the whole earth and that this dominion signifies His primary objective of human flourishing. Beisner, for example, notes that 'from the typical environmentalist perspective, the best environment is nature untouched by human hands. That's not a biblical perspective at all'. In such a tightly controlled universe as offered by *Answers in Genesis*, the concept of human dominion over the earth, rather than implying a sense of responsibility as it does for Christian ecotheologians, here implies a kind of insurance policy against environmental blunders and other unintended catastrophes.

The various speakers are clear to point out that they do not justify wanton abuse or 'desecration' of the earth but that just use of natural resources includes the need of developing nations to find cheap and available energy sources. What is significant here, however, is that this important question is raised to cast doubt on the entirety of climate science, as if to suggest that concern about climate change is inherently incongruous with a desire to solve the problem of human poverty. We are invited to 'reason through' the science to get to this conclusion, which ultimately means according to the video to choose biblical wisdom over scientific consensus. The documentary concludes by citing Inhofe's favourite verse, Genesis 8:22, which states, 'As long as the earth endures, seedtime and harvest, cold and heat, summer and winter, day and night will never cease.' Again, belief in God and belief in climate change are simply posed as mutually exclusive beliefs. For *Answers in Genesis*, it is heretical to believe that climate change could be anything other than the result of direct, divine sovereign will, since the idea of anthropogenic climate change suggests that we are both more responsible for the earth and yet less able to predict the consequences of our actions than we had thought.

It is not coincidence, then, that *Answers in Genesis* also defines human suffering in a universe tightly controlled by divine will. In a video about the meaning of suffering, 'A God of Suffering?', Dr. Tommy Mitchell interviews survivors of Hurricane Katrina and highlights the spiritual meaning of natural catastrophe as always reducible to a 'perfect creation' that was, due to Adam's fall, 'marred by sin'. Mitchell's theology proscribes the possibility of identifying specific causes for human suffering that might be avoided because, simply, 'there are no innocent people'. Unlike Inhofe's seemingly unlimited confidence in human nature, Mitchell believes like Voltaire's Pangloss that things will always happen the way that they are supposed to happen, since we are all to blame. He is so insistent on this tight causal link between all suffering and original and persistent human error that he cannot allow for the possibility of death and suffering at the time of Creation six thousand years ago. This is why he decries the irrationality and unfairness of the world proposed by evolutionists where life would have emerged from millions of years of violence: 'You've got one of two choices,' he insists,

> you've got no middle ground here. If you believe that over millions of years there's death and suffering and struggling and dying and things are just going to continue on the way they have always been, don't come to me and complain to me about my God because you have no leg to stand on. You have no basis for morality, you have no basis for judging God.

His theology must discount both the central role of chance in the distribution of suffering and, equally, its role in the creation of life. The paradox of expelling chance from the universe is that it also seems to expel human answerability for suffering. It is never clear what we can or should do in the face of suffering, since there doesn't seem to be such a thing as needless or avoidable suffering.

Mitchell seems to suggest that Creationists find the thesis of an earth formed over millions of years unacceptable, not necessarily because of their literal reading of Genesis and a belief in a six-day creation, but because a beneficent God couldn't possibly oversee millions of years of extinction, suffering and pain before human beings even showed up. Because in the Bible God pronounces the creation 'very good', Mitchell insists that it has to mean that there was no death and suffering at the beginning, even though the Edenic narrative suggests the inextricability of death and suffering with life and joy. Mitchell associates God's creative action with a kind of painless perfection. Claims about biological life to the contrary are unnecessary and erroneous temptations. In this way, Mitchell paradoxically ends up protecting his idea of God against the very world that God presumably created, and discounting the moral dimensions of human life that God seemed worried about in the first place.

It is not uncommon, of course, to hear similarly despairing language about inherent and categorical human failings by philosophers of the Anthropocene, and such rhetoric runs similar risks of implying that nothing could or should be done to make a difference. I am thinking of such thinkers as David Abram who in his 1996 book, *The Spell of the Sensuous*, argues that the very alphabet is a symptom of irreconcilable divorce from the intersubjectivity of human and more-than-human life forms, which thus seemingly leaves written culture with little hope of rescuing that connection to the physical world, even though that is precisely the aim of much environmental literature (including his own). Derrick Jensen's two-volume anarchist manifesto *Endgame* (2011) offers the metaphor that civilization is our 'Death Star' that must be destroyed. While this is, of course, a call to action, its implication is that our civilization is so profoundly rotten and the problems so pervasive, there are no grounds for hope in civilization as such. His argument might be considered a form of cultural scepticism that cannot accommodate the empirical reality of plural cultures and worldviews that will not go away, even though he insists they must. It also bears an uncanny resemblance to Michael Crichton's *State of Fear* in its appeal to the small elite minority who alone, because of their tough-minded confrontation with civilization's illusions, are capable of saving civilization from itself.

Thus, by suggesting that climate forcing is not just a function of fossil fuel use but also a symptom of something profoundly and categorically wrong about human civilization, these and other writers challenge our ability to see natural disasters or extreme weather events as anything other than evidence of the pre-ordained and inevitable consequences of inherent human failings. That is to say, these worldviews run similar risks of inspiring not action but a shrug of indifference. If sceptics fail to see evidence of the human hand in natural events, warmists run the risk of discounting the reality of natural disasters, chance incidents or the proverbial 'acts of God' as the insurance policy calls them. A belief in human fallibility, however, does not obligate us to see evidence of inevitable fallibility everywhere we turn. If there is moral urgency for change, it behoves warmists to conceive of the grounds for the possibility of human change and consider what narratives will most inspire citizens to change courageously in the face of a system of life that is subject to chance, accident, and vulnerable to tragedy. That is to say, if a Creationist narrative finds it difficult to account for the emergence of life and for a phenomenon like climate change, a worldview that accommodates climate change can still find it difficult to account for the diversity of cosmologies, the inherent complexity of climate change and the irreducible uncertainties of climate science. Impatient blaming and shaming of those who can't understand climate change similarly pretends that we can be confident in the direction of history if all of us would only assume the right beliefs. If environmentalism sees agricultural monocultures as damaging to the earth, perhaps they might also consider the dangers of ethical and spiritual monocultures.

The important point here is that for many conservative Christians doubts about the science only help to shore up a theological position that already proscribes the reality of climate change. In a survey conducted in 2016 by the Yale Program on Climate Change Communication, about 15 per cent of Americans believed that it is either definitely or probably true that 'God controls the climate, therefore people can't be causing climate change' (Roser-Renouf et al.). Tea Party members and Conservative Republicans are the most likely (38 per cent and 31 per cent, respectively) to believe that climate change is theologically proscribed and a full 30 per cent of registered voters who supported Donald Trump over Hillary Clinton. Oddly, about the same percentage of Americans (14 per cent) believe that climate change is a sign of the end of times (suggesting, of course, overlap) and 11 per cent believe that because these are the last days, we don't need to worry about climate change. It is not, in other words, a large minority. However, like the category of Americans (about 15 per cent) who simply do not believe climate change is real or human-caused, it is nevertheless a powerful and vocal minority whose certainty can have the effect of paralyzing a confused majority.

There are, needless to say, many religious responses that offer more hopeful readings of both the Bible and more trusting readings of climate science. Ecotheologians such as William Brown have challenged the assumptions and biblical claims of theologies of scepticism. Reading the book of Job in light of contemporary science, Brown concludes, for example, that 'Job comes to realize that the world does not revolve around himself, nor even perhaps around humanity. Creation is polycentric' (133). Brown and many others have argued for the moral imperative to care for future generations, to consider the sanctity of all life forms, and to live simply and consume modestly out of respect for the Creation and for the poor who suffer disproportionately the impacts of environmental degradation. As Pope Francis has argued, failing to 'acknowledge our creaturely limitations' leads to a distorted and exploitative meaning of stewardship (66). As he writes, 'Clearly, the Bible has no place for a tyrannical anthropocentrism unconcerned for other creatures' (68). Evangelical climate scientist Katherine Hayhoe also respectfully argues that the Bible teaches that we were made in the image of God:

> But then it tells us why: so that we humans could be responsible for every living thing on the planet. Now, some translations turn that into 'dominion' over the earth. But even so, would we respect someone who had dominion over a company or a nation and ran it into the ground? Of course not! All of us respect wise stewardship when it comes to being in charge of something. And that's

what Genesis is talking about. We are stewards or caretakers of the people, plants, animals and all living things on this planet. ('The Bible')

While Christian sceptics claim that because of Noah, God will not stop the turning of the seasons nor flood the entire earth again, she simply points out that neither is exactly what climate change threatens as a possibility. Instead she emphasizes scriptures that focus on the need in the last days to love and work for those less fortunate than ourselves and on why, therefore, many Christians can and do care about climate change. As she notes, objections 'have nothing to do with being religiously evangelical. They have everything to do with being *politically* evangelical'. Given our current politics in the United States, it is tempting to believe that many Americans do, in fact, prefer someone to run the country or the environment into the ground, but what is important here about Hayhoe is that we can identify the ways in which she appeals to the inner logic of evangelical life to help loosen the grip of conservative ideology and allow a different understanding of biblical wisdom to emerge. Indeed, let us be clear: there are better biblical answers to the meaning of suffering and to climate change than those provided by *Answers in Genesis*. Darren Aronofsky's film *Noah* suggests that it is a story about stewardship and about acting responsibly in the face of an evolved world subject to death and chance; the film seeks to balance the idea of divine sovereignty with the very real risks and obligations of acting ethically towards the physical world. In such a cosmos, climate change needs to be met with serious moral deliberation and scientific rigour.[6]

The nuances and rich morality of biblical narratives, however, are often lost on general audiences because of the challenge of reducing them to simple options and simple guarantees. In an editorial in a Utah paper, for example, one woman articulated her Christian climate scepticism this way: 'For those searching reasons for climate calamities worldwide, the Bible offers two options. First, nothing: It gives no reason, inferring that these things are natural for the planet. Second, the Bible tells us calamities come because of God's punishment for wrongdoing. Take your pick' (Openshaw). So Hurricane Harvey, for example, could only be interpreted as either utterly natural or totally divine, but never as a complex mix of human and natural forces witnessed by a compassionate rather than a punitive God. Indeed, the writer's theology proves convenient only for those unaffected by environmental degradation. It is hard, for example, to use this logic to explain why a family has been devastated by cancers caused by downwind radiation, or why only God or nature could be responsible for illnesses caused or exacerbated by increasing levels of air pollution. There is no room in such theology for human causes or even potential human solutions for the spread of such diseases as the Ebola virus. She insists that 'climate chaos' has been with us since the beginnings of human history, which is not in doubt, but concludes therefore that the efforts to mitigate climate change are a waste of effort and time. By asking us to assume climate change is either wholly natural or mysteriously but divinely mandated, she leaves little room for the possibility that humans are answerable for the climate. At the risk of falling into the pitfalls of proof texting, her argument is hard to square with the words in Micah that explain: 'The land shall be desolate because of them that dwell therein, for the fruit of their doings' (7:13).

In sum, even if it is not well considered or even well justified by scripture, doubt about climate change among American Christian conservatives is motivated by religious belief and, as such, it sees climate change as a direct threat to the authority of Christianity. Indeed, Christian conservative scepticism is paradoxically informed by a particular kind of trust. We might summarize these attitudes thus:

1) Human fate is in God's hands and the end is near. Humans cannot change the timing of God's plans nor is it likely that humans would have stumbled upon a problem that God could not have foreseen or forewarned them about. Besides, if the earth is going to die anyway, why worry ourselves that much or spend that much to take care of it for only a short while?
2) This also means that humans don't have sufficient power to influence the climate. That is God's prerogative. Natural events, then, are always expressions of God's will and symptoms of human fallenness but not the result of specific human actions, least of all those done in relatively benign ignorance of possible deleterious consequences. While it is imaginable that God punishes humans for sexual and other sins, overconsumption is not one of them.
3) God gave humans dominion, and while defenders of dominionism insist that this does not justify abuse of the earth, it does mean human flourishing always has a priority. Believers can identify worry over the fate of plants and animals as a lack of faith and as a failure to embrace the importance of people and families and the economies upon which they depend. Little attention is given to environmental degradation as a direct consequence of human choices.
4) The earth's resources are most likely unlimited because it is unthinkable that a just God would have placed humans on earth without sufficient resources for everyone. While wanton and excessive consumption is not

justified (albeit never defined), the middle-class American lifestyle is reasonable enough to expect for everyone.

5) Environmentalism and the science that backs it up emerged from the context of the secular counterculture of the 1960s and is a godless philosophy that is antithetical to religion, religious values and basic human freedoms. Its utopia is socialist and repressive of private property and individual self-realization.

Michael Crichton's *State of Fear*

Michael Crichton may very well be the Rachel Carson of climate scepticism. A singularly important author to Christian sceptics, Crichton has shown little interest in Christian cosmology but similarly rebuffs with almost giddy confidence what he sees as the paranoid catastrophism of climate science. As we will see, however, his critique of climate fear exhibits some paranoia of its own. If there is any question as to the importance of Crichton in American culture, I need only mention that his 2004 novel *State of Fear* earned him a call from Karl Rove and a private meeting with then President Bush. The novel also earned him a voice in a Senate hearing in 2005 and speaking invitations across the country on climate change, including at the influential American Enterprise Institute in DC. Portions of the novel are included as an appendix in James Inhofe's aforementioned book, *The Greatest Hoax: How the Global Warming Conspiracy Threatens Your Future*. It also won the 2006 Journalism award from the American Association of Petroleum Geologists (APG). (I note here the obvious: fiction is not normally considered journalism, nor is the APG normally invested in literary awards.) Of course, this positive attention was not without its counter-criticisms, including serious reprimands for the novel's poor use of science in the pages of *Nature, The New York Times*, from the Natural Resources Defense Council, the Union for Concerned Scientists, American Geophysical Union, and in other venues and from other individuals. In the midst of all this controversy, the novel made it to no. 1 on the *New York Times* bestseller list, and has since sold millions of copies. Crichton's popularity is, in other words, evidence of the powerful impact narrative can have on attitudes and behaviour, even if he is precisely the opposite of the kind of author that many ecocritics hoped would come along. Rather than revisiting the criticisms of his (mis)uses of science, I want to offer a critique of the novel's literary qualities and a reading of its moral logic to suggest that at least one reason he is more popular than the so-called cli-fi novelists is because he has an easier task. He is not arguing for a radically new paradigm of culture as many ecocritics and environmental thinkers seek to do, but is instead justifying trust in the direction of the earth's history by generating his own state of fear, not about the threat of climate change, but the threat of alarmists.

The novel is a thriller about ecoterrorism, positing the existence of a well-financed environmental organization, NERF, that has the support of a wealthy liberal donor, a team of liberal lawyers and the backing of Hollywood superstars who make appearances and speeches on its behalf. Unbeknownst to some of its supporters, however, NERF also benefits from and condones the violence perpetuated by an extremist environmental organization, ELF, that is engaged in a worldwide effort to create superstorms – with the help of obscure technocratic environmental engineering efforts – that will, by killing innocent people, serve to awaken humanity to the seriousness of the (non-existent) problem of climate change.

Crichton's doubts about climate change can be summarized briefly in the following seven points, some of which are logically incompatible or simply incoherent. My reader will note that there is no reference at all to Christian theology here. Indeed, it is the absence of such theology that most stands out when we consider his importance to Christian conservatives. Nevertheless, it is the conclusion of his worldview that most matters to Christian conservatives: suspicion towards climate science is total and proportionate to the absolute trust he believes we can have in the trajectory of the earth's history. Thus, for conservative Christian readers he inspires a kind of faith in divine providence that paradoxically leaves them in a state of perpetual fear.

1. Change is constant. Nothing we can do or have done will make even the slightest difference in the long run. We can't really manage anything well, and if history is an indicator, we never will. Nature is indifferent, violent and dangerous and has been long before human beings ever showed up on the scene.
2. The precautionary principle is bunk. This position seems at odds with #1. If change is constant and nothing we can do will make a difference, the justification for criticizing the precautionary principle for being inaccurate and unreliable would be that life is meaningless and nature directionless. He insists he isn't being nihilistic, but he doesn't provide reasons why we should ever care about our survival or our treatment of nature. He cites many examples when humankind has been needlessly cautious but none

when caution might have been called for. For Crichton, there seems to be no greater human shame than worrying about something that didn't turn out to be a problem.

3. We are inherently vulnerable to fear. The powerful will exploit climate change because of what fear garners them. This is an important critique of environmentalism and might even potentially open common ground with climate warmists, but it is not clear in the novel if any entities other than environmental organizations are interested in generating fear for gain. What about politicians? Corporations? Popular novelists?
4. We need civilization to protect us. This is at odds with #1, #2 and #3. Crichton is adamant that nature needs to be tamed, but given his view of natural change and his generally pessimistic view of human beings, it isn't clear why we should believe it is possible to trust civilization to do the job right.
5. Stoicism is a virtue. His is clearly a stoic worldview, but this seems at odds with #4 and perhaps with #3. Despite his confidence in civilization's capacity to tame nature, in his world the only heroes capable of saving us are stoic, manly, coldly objective and unemotional, and exhaustively familiar with scientific facts. Elite knowledge of scientific literature transcends the wisdom of institutions, history and global trends and is the only adequate way to protect ourselves from nature and from the clear and present danger of evil and conspiring men. Fearful, vain, feel-good and effeminate men are the enemy to good science. Tough, athletic but vulnerable (and physically attractive) women will conquer evil when matched with tough, athletic and almost unfeeling men.
6. Science is unreliable. At odds with #4, and #5. For Crichton as for most poststructuralists, science is perpetually susceptible to pollution by politics. He suspects that scientists are prone to bias psychologically; they are lured by easy research money; and peer review isn't rigorous enough. Like many other sceptics, Crichton believes that, because the IPCC interfaces between scientific working groups and UN member governments, the political contamination of climatology is near-total. And yet, as we discuss in Chapter 6, Crichton believes that only science can 'save us from politics', and then only if the norms of universalism, communalism, disinterestedness and organized scepticism, first outlined by Robert Merton in 1942, are fulfilled. In the Appendix to *State of Fear*, he claims: 'We still kill more than a thousand people each year for witchcraft. In my view, there is only one hope for humankind to emerge from what Carl

Sagan called "the demon-haunted world" of our past. That hope is science' (580). The great danger lies in the 'intermixing' of science and politics. Crichton is therefore a disappointed scientific idealist who believes in the power, rigour and rectitude of science, but is equally convinced that only a select few are capable of Merton's near-monastic discipline. Beyond the questions that might be asked of any norm-based account of science (REF Sismondo 27–35), we might ask: Given the potential social impact of both climate change and mitigation efforts, is chastely apolitical climate science even conceivable, let alone actionable?

7. Science is poorly understood. This is one of his more intriguing ideas but it is seemingly at odds with #6, since he draws on climate science selectively to show that the 'consensus' is biased. His point is that perceptions of environmental problems are managed by what he calls the PLM – the politico-legal-media complex – specialists, along with universities, in manufacturing fear to their own advantage by bending the science. In short, we need more 'true' scientists and fewer academics, lawyers and actors.

So why does Crichton hold such attraction for Christian conservatives? This is a difficult question to answer, but the answer may hold the key to understanding how centrally important cosmological trust is for American climate scepticism. Crichton's understanding of a violent and indifferent natural world is consistent with the evolutionary idea of a world 'red in tooth and claw' in Tennyson's famous characterization of Darwinian nature, and it is certainly at odds with the ideas we saw, for example, in *Answers in Genesis*. Even a fallen world is not as violent and indifferent on the scale imagined by Crichton, who is an evolutionist who fully accepts deep time. Indeed, Crichton is not known to have been religious or particularly Christian; he was sometimes described as a deist, but that might be overstating it. Trained in anthropology and medicine, Crichton advances a cosmology that is decidedly secular and derives his ethics from a rational, almost existentialist, surprisingly biocentric position. In a speech from 2003, he notes:

> But I think that you cannot eliminate religion from the psyche of mankind. If you suppress it in one form, it merely re-emerges in another form. You can not believe in God, but you still have to believe in something that gives meaning to your life, and shapes your sense of the world. Such a belief is religious. Today, one of the most powerful religions in the Western World is environmentalism. Environmentalism seems to be the religion of choice for urban atheists. Why

> do I say it's a religion? Well, just look at the beliefs. If you look carefully, you see that environmentalism is in fact a perfect 21st century remapping of traditional Judeo-Christian beliefs and myths. ('Remarks' 2003)

This is not an uncommon refrain in many circles of anti-environmentalism, and it is certainly an astute observation of the powerful ways in which religiosity in a postsecular age has been mapped onto contemporary environmentalism. However, as Mark Stoll has shown, environmentalism hasn't merely borrowed rhetorical strategies from religion. Contemporary American environmentalism owes a great deal to religious thought, particularly Calvinism, and it is no accident that a significant number of America's most famous environmental thinkers had strong religious upbringings and came from ministerial family lines (Stoll). It is especially ironic, then, that despite or because of its religious origins and despite the recent emphasis on environmental responsibility preached by many religious leaders worldwide, American environmentalism is now resented by many religious conservatives precisely because it directly competes for primacy as a theology and cosmology in the American imagination, often drawing upon similar conceits about the fallen nature of humankind, the declension of civilization towards degradation and apocalypse and the need for Jeremiads to awaken the slumbering citizens to their responsibilities. Crichton offers a similar tone and seems to have the academic chops to stand up to the nonsense of climate science (Harvard degree, scientific literacy, rugged, masculine individualism, and an all-out satirical view of liberals and Hollywood). He appears to speak the elite language of science but comes to very different conclusions.

The truth is, though, that Crichton is more dangerous to Christian thought than his many supporters seem to realize. He seems content to suggest that environmentalism is a religion in the same way that any religious belief has colonized the human mind, including Christian beliefs. In the same speech, he notes:

> I certainly don't want to talk anybody out of … a belief that Jesus Christ is the son of God who rose from the dead. But the reason I don't want to talk anybody out of these beliefs is that I know that I can't talk anybody out of them. These are not facts that can be argued. These are issues of faith.

Indeed, he seems inclined to a criticism of human epistemology that is akin to Noam Chomsky's notion of manufactured consent, except that his criticism is more anthropological than ideological and almost a form of biological determinism. For Crichton, we are hard-wired to believe erroneously, and it is only the elite few who inexplicably escape the illusions of others and have the masculine courage and stamina to face the hard truths that will save us. It is never clear, of course, why these select few are invulnerable to the failings of lesser mortals, but this has a striking resemblance to the Christian theology of Inhofe and others that insists on the fallenness of humankind but nevertheless remains unjustifiably, endlessly optimistic about (their) human freedom.

Given the strong critique of Edenic mythologies in environmental thought over the last few decades, it is interesting that Crichton's *State of Fear*, as well as *Jurassic Park*, similarly rejects naïve environmental assumptions about nature as Eden. His version of nature is more like a hell that will only burn you for romanticizing it. He takes us to the extreme and harsh conditions of Antarctica, the deserts of the southwest and the jungles of the Pacific Islands to drive home the point that nature is no friend. What is different, however, in Crichton's critique of simplistic ideas of nature as balanced ecosystem, as opposed to, say, ecologist Daniel Botkin's in *Discordant Harmonies* (1990), is that Crichton offers the most extreme and chaotic climates on the planet as spaces of dark immorality that need the taming effects of civilization. So, even though he offers a sobering and arguably accurate understanding of the indifference of nature, he tends to associate this darker ecology with certain geographies, races and forms of immorality that only an elite (and white) masculinity can vanquish. Although Joseph Conrad famously made the same mistake, Conrad's argument about human depravity and the challenge of judging it without hypocrisy did not, in the end, exempt anyone as a special kind of hero (not to mention that Conrad, unlike Crichton, was a gifted writer). In *State of Fear*, by contrast, the hero John Kenner is the triumphant 'knower,' as his name implies. He is also an international law enforcement agent with Tom Cruise looks and athletic abilities, capacious worldly knowledge and an extraordinary gift for lecturing at length with cool and detached mic-dropping arrogance, plus an uncanny resemblance to the authority conceded to (and claimed by) Crichton himself.

Indeed, even if we examine the novel independently of its political critique of environmentalism and climate science, it is hard to ignore its unidimensional characters and, consequently, its almost puerile morality. For example, Crichton offers the Hollywood actor Ted Bradley as Kenner's foil. As an actor who plays a liberal president on TV, he is clearly based on Martin Sheen. He is stupid, vain, weak, and his politics are a vacuous feel-good performance. He purports to value the ecological wisdom of indigenous people who live simple lives in small villages, but we are not surprised to learn that he has never ventured into any of them except during film shoots in developing nations in his actor's trailer.

Kenner insists that more barbarity and primitivism are found in these villages than any Hollywood actor could ever understand. We watch Bradley giving a feel-good lecture to school kids in Yosemite about the supposed 'balance of nature' and the great treasures of the Sierras. It's all very friendly at that point, but Kenner dresses him down on this and other occasions, showing his vastly superior knowledge of environmental issues and proving Bradley's hopeless naiveté. Kenner also turns out to be sexier, more athletic and endlessly capable of the most brilliant improvisation in desperate situations. His mission, after all, is to save the planet from ecoterrorists that Bradley is incapable of believing even exist. Bradley, Kenner and the other protagonists find themselves in the Pacific Islands in hot pursuit of the ecoterrorists, and as their situation grows ever more desperate, Kenner lectures him that civilization *protects* us from the indifferent violence of nature: 'Because what you see right now, all around you – this *is* nature' (527). Bradley, in other words, is a walking ism, everything that is wrong with green values.

Kenner always shows extraordinary resourcefulness, bravery and masculine toughness in the face of this dark nature, exemplifying a kind of masculinity that Bradley can only dream of (especially given that one of the novel's alluring beauties, Sarah, rebuffs Ted and is instead strangely attracted to Kenner). Sarah sees Kenner as a 'real man' (197) – that is an actual quotation. Although earlier in her life she had been distracted by a 'handsome young actor' and didn't really care to pay attention to facts, she was now thrillingly disillusioned by the sheer force of Kenner's capacity to dress down every climate change believer, including Peter, a NERF lawyer and the novel's undistinguished protagonist. '[Peter] was good-looking,' she observes, 'and he had the strong physique of an athlete. But sometimes he behaved like such a wimp' (322). When faced with the ELF conspiracy, she experiences nervousness and 'wanted someone competent to be with her. She liked being around Kenner. He was so knowledgeable, so skilled. He knew what was going on. He was quick to respond to any situation. Whereas Peter was a nice guy, but … ' (323). Peter eventually rises to the occasion, swapping his Prius for a pickup truck and learning to handle a gun, while Kenner is almost asexual, as befits Crichton's depiction of his stoic potency. Bradley gets his comeuppance, which Crichton has prepared his reader to hope for, in a scene in which he is slowly cut to pieces and eaten by the local cannibals, the *coup de grace* for his belief in the beneficence of Nature and 'primitive' people. As Greg Garrard has elsewhere noted of the novel: 'For some reason, we never meet an environmentalist who is (a) informed, (b) convinced of anthropogenically enhanced warming, and (c) not a murderous psychopath' (185).

As noted earlier, the novel has received most of its attention because of its position on climate change. Critics, pro and con, take notice of its many footnotes and graphs and its extensive bibliography, and either laud or lambast Crichton for his self-claimed 'Kenner' status, as the only one capable of staring down the world of illusions and deception that surrounds him. In all of the critical attention, however, there has scarcely been a word about the absurdity of the plot, the vapidity of his prose and the cartoonish qualities of his characters who wander his pages like tropes with legs. The book's huge popularity among climate sceptics suggests that their critical capacities have been smothered by distrust of Hollywood, mainstream politics, international cooperation and any science that fails to live up to Mertonian ideals of disinterestedness. Either that, or they are simply unfamiliar with quality literature.

Crichton's *State of Fear* seeks to dismantle our trust in authority, science and government while offering a stoic position of resistance that is authoritative, scientifically rigorous and trained by academic and government institutions. Similarly, he can write absurd plots and create empty characters but still have the moral gravitas of the social critic. The footnotes, the extensive bibliography and the author's manifesto at the back of the book expose the scaffolding of fiction in an almost Brecht-like manner, lending moral credibility to his status as an author of entertaining but not always plausible thrillers. In his insightful piece on Crichton in *The New Republic*, Michael Crowley suggests: 'By trashing the conventionally trained expert, Crichton has helped create an anti-intellectual ethos where the country's most powerful political leaders can embrace a science-fiction writer as a great authority.' Because he appears to be as wise as any scientist or intelligence officer, Crichton's distortion of reality doesn't look like the rabid imaginings of a paranoid but instead is offered as adding moral depth and seriousness to the playful rhetorical strategies of thriller fiction. He can criticize what he sees as the absurdity of climate change by simultaneously imagining implausible scenarios in which extreme acts of terrorism change, well, the climate. The trust he seeks to inspire in Kenner and in himself is in direct proportion to the fear he generates about the threat of climate change activism itself. Even if we assume that climate change is real and human-caused, for Crichton, the dangers climate change might pose to the human family do not compare to the threat posed by an ecoterrorist society, ELF, that is willing to kill innocent people by the thousands to create superstorms large enough to scare people into action.

Crichton constructs an elaborate, wildly implausible conspiracist fantasy from the familiar sceptical trope of environmentalists as pseudo-religious fanatics. *State of Fear* may be uniquely popular, but it is not one of a kind in this respect: radio talk-show host Glenn Beck has had a far less successful writing career than Crichton, but he is nevertheless the author of several bestselling books, including his anti-environmentalist novel (written with Harriet Parke) *Agenda 21*. Beck, a devout Mormon, tells the story of a future America that is without basic constitutional freedoms, where reproduction is entirely controlled and engineered because the earth and animals have priority. It is, in short, what Beck imagines as the trajectory of the UN sustainability goals and the global scare about climate change.

A product of the Earth Summit in Rio in 1992, the real Agenda 21 is a non-binding 350-page document that outlines sustainability principles for nations and communities worldwide according to concerns about climate change and related global environmental trajectories. In the eyes of its fiercest critics (almost all of them American), however, it was 'a plot to subjugate humanity under an eco-totalitarian regime' (Harman). Agenda 21 does raise serious questions about population levels and challenges some fundamental capitalist assumptions about private property and the use of natural resources; it is by no means ideologically neutral and is clearly at odds with a Christian conservatism. Thus, for reasons similar to Inhofe's wholesale rejection of regulation, Beck has long promoted the idea that Agenda 21 is based on 'anti-free market, anti-American views of the world' and 'will destroy America as we know it' (284, 294). His performances on radio and television inspired a writer, Harriet Parke, to co-author with Beck a novel that explores a nightmare scenario of the implementation of these goals worldwide. In his dystopian future, the 'Republic' rules tyrannically over its citizens by measuring their production of energy and by minimizing their impact on the environment, controlling their every move and quantifying their value solely on the basis of measuring individual energy production against energy use. Food has been replaced by nourishment cubes and running over a snake on your bike is punishable by death. Similar to Crichton, Beck offers an afterword in which he seeks to speak directly and with sober realism to his reader. In it, Beck makes this curious claim:

> Now, let me state the obvious: this novel is a work of fiction. But let me also state the controversial: it may not stay that way. Before all of the accusations begin about me promoting some kind of conspiracy theory, let me be clear: this novel plays out the ideas and concepts contained in the real Agenda 21 to their extreme ends. I do not really believe, for example, that people will be reciting pledges in honor of squirrels any time soon – but when animals and nature are valued more highly than human life, all kinds of absurd things begin to enter the realm of possibility. (280)

As with Crichton's use of graphs and footnotes in a thriller novel, Beck's fantastical imagination allows him to use a double standard of plausibility: he can defend himself against charges of implausibility by insisting that it is just fiction and then simultaneously warn us that conspiratorial actors in the world might render real what was only intended to be a silly fiction. Beck's refusal to take responsibility for his own distinction between fact and fiction maximizes the conspiratorial fear that he can claim he isn't peddling. As we saw with Horner's claim of Al Gore's fearmongering, he abdicates responsibility for his own fictionalized worst-case scenario and blames instead the 'fictional' claims of climate science. As Jonathan Haidt and others have noted, it is always easier to use critical suspicion to identify the political motivations and implicit bias of the other side than it is to engage in rigorous self-critique. This might also help us to understand why both authors use science fiction and fantasy as a rhetorical framework for the presentation of a supposedly serious political and scientific critique of what they perceive to be extremism. Of course, without any check against their own paranoia, there are almost no limits to the extremes to which they can imagine the enemy will go, and similarly no limits to the trust they ask us to have in their judgements. Their arguments would not be taken seriously in more traditional academic and political circles, but that is precisely the point. The academic standards and peer-review practices, which conservatives believe provide rhetorical cover for academics' own ideological preferences, are here replaced by absurd dystopian fictions.

To return, finally again, to Crichton, let us remember that Crichton's understanding of nature has more in common with dark ecology than with the Christian right. For example, he is harshly critical of Edenic ideas of natural harmony that ignore the findings of ecology and biology and cosmology. When Ted Bradley tries to persuade a group of schoolchildren that redwood trees are 'the guardians of the Earth' who lived in America 'before anything' (401), he is put straight – at length – by Jennifer, a beautiful, brilliant, professionally sceptical lawyer. Far from being 'primeval sentinels', she observes, the redwoods are 'merely the last in line' in a continuous, long-term process of change that was helped along by humans:

> Indians set fires … [so] there were only islands of old-growth forest in the midst of plains and meadows. The forests that the first Europeans saw were hardly primeval. They were *cultivated*, Ted. (405)

Jennifer's attack on simplistic notions of Nature's harmony and the 'Ecological Indian' are well-founded scientifically, but would not come as a surprise to any educated environmentalist. Indeed, it is hard to see how Crichton concludes that ill-informed romantic environmentalism is linked to climate science or activism at all. It is all too obvious that the inherent uncertainties and complexities of science in general, and of climate science in particular, do not play well in the public sphere of culture wars and policymaking. As a result, warmist cli-fi narratives have struggled to avoid didacticism and characterizations that easily distinguish the good guys from the bad guys: just as Ted Bradley is an easy satire of the Hollywood environmentalist, the vice president in the apocalyptic climate movie *The Day After Tomorrow* (2004), who physically resembles then-Vice President Dick Cheney, is made to recant his climate scepticism in a moment of public shaming at the end. Only rarely do climate fictions, notably Barbara Kingsolver's *Flight Behaviour*, succeed in conveying the difficulty and ambiguity, as well as the empirical validity, of scientific work.

Crichton's larger point is that violent and unpredictable change is inherent to the planet's deep and ancient history, from which he concludes that no human-caused change of any kind should be cause for concern. This supposedly amoral dark ecology is central to his entire project and worldview. In *Jurassic Park*, for example, he develops an entire ethic of macho stoicism out of the story of the Earth's origins and our small and brief moment on it. Consider this passage as recited by Charlton Heston in a phone call he made to the Rush Limbaugh Show in 1995, which has gone viral on the internet, appearing in several versions on YouTube and becoming ubiquitous on sceptical blogs and web pages ('Heston Reads'). Adapted from *Jurassic Park*, the passage is a fatalist manifesto, functioning as a mic drop for sceptics who simply wish to end the debate.[7]

> You think man can destroy the planet? What intoxicating vanity. Let me tell you about our planet. Earth is four-and-a-half-billion-years-old. There's been life on it for nearly that long, 3.8 billion years. Bacteria first; later the first multi-cellular life, then the first complex creatures in the sea, on the land. Then finally the great sweeping ages of animals, the amphibians, the dinosaurs, at last the mammals, each one enduring millions on millions of years, great dynasties of creatures rising, flourishing, dying away – all this against a background of continuous and violent upheaval. Mountain ranges thrust up, eroded away, cometary impacts, volcano eruptions, oceans rising and falling, whole continents moving, an endless, constant, violent change, colliding, buckling to make mountains over millions of years. Earth has survived everything in its time. It will certainly survive us. If all the nuclear weapons in the world went off at once and all the plants, all the animals died and the earth was sizzling hot for a hundred thousand years, life would survive, somewhere: under the soil, frozen in Arctic ice.

> Sooner or later, when the planet was no longer inhospitable, life would spread again. The evolutionary process would begin again. It might take a few billion years for life to regain its present variety. Of course, it would be very different from what it is now, but the earth would survive our folly, only we would not. If the ozone layer gets thinner, ultraviolet radiation sears the earth, so what? Ultraviolet radiation is good for life. It's powerful energy. It promotes mutation, change. Many forms of life will thrive with more UV radiation. Many others will die out. Do you think this is the first time that's happened? Think about oxygen. Necessary for life now, but oxygen is actually a metabolic poison, a corrosive gas, like fluorine. When oxygen was first produced as a waste product by certain plant cells some three billion years ago, it created a crisis for all other life on earth. Those plants were polluting the environment, exhaling a lethal gas. Earth eventually had an atmosphere incompatible with life. Nevertheless, life on earth took care of itself. In the thinking of the human being, a hundred years is a long time.
>
> A hundred years ago we didn't have cars, airplanes, computers, or vaccines. It was a whole different world, but to the earth, a hundred years is nothing. A million years is nothing. This planet lives and breathes on a much vaster scale. We can't imagine its slow and powerful rhythms, and we haven't got the humility to try. We've been residents here for the blink of an eye. If we're gone tomorrow, the earth will not miss us.

It is worth pausing over the rhetorical excesses of this passage. The hectoring didacticism is evident from the outset: 'Let me tell you … ', then 'Do you think … ?' Crichton-Heston proves cavalier with facts too: there were both cars and vaccines one hundred years ago; UV is lethal to many organisms, though it may accelerate mutation rates. And who is the beleaguered implied listener to this elliptical history of deep time? None other than the environmentalist, castigated in *State of Fear* for his cruel inhumanity, who turns out to be more naively humanistic than Crichton-Heston, the thoroughgoing inhumanist. The environmentalist is shamed for his sentimental attachment to *this* assortment of plants and animals, this particular collection of naked apes, his belief that any of this *matters*. Such pontificating is at once sophomoric and intellectually respectable, thanks to such figures as the poet like Robinson Jeffers, the existentialist filmmaker Werner Herzog and the philosopher John Gray, British author of *Straw Dogs*. Like climate scepticism, it is a male preserve.

Heston's rendition of the passage practically made Rush Limbaugh swoon about the assurances of divine providence, despite the decidedly atheistic cosmology articulated in it. Indeed, that is the central puzzle of American climate scepticism: that a macho dark ecology should appeal to Christian conservatives even though its negative theology ought to be anathema to them. Limbaugh responded to Crichton-Heston by reiterating that the very existence of God proscribes the possibility of climate change:

> But without question on Earth Day and every day, we owe our deepest gratitude to one inventor who is without equal. As long as men and women inhabit the earth, our very existence will be tied to his remarkable and unequaled creations, too numerous to mention, too complex to ever fully understand. He is known by thousands of names, but we call him God, the sole creator of the heavens and the earth. What incredible arrogance to believe that we limited human beings can destroy that which we cannot even begin to understand, much less create on our own, and that is earth and all of its glories. ('An Earth Day Salute')

Was he not listening? Crichton-Heston's keynote was death, not wonder; the process was creative-destructive change, not 'unequaled [presumably unchanging] creation'; and puny man was an absurd contingency, not the godlike meaning of it all.

The only way to reconcile these utterly disparate cosmologies is to note their joint fascination with inhuman justice. Limbaugh apparently accepts the scientific narrative of the origins of life (or at least chooses not to contest it when Moses himself calls in), but he overlays it with a theology that underwrites our complete and radical freedom from any contingencies, from any unforeseen consequences or from any painful responsibilities we might bear as God's chosen species. Heston-Crichton's cosmology seems to abjure justice – all is chance and change – but then smuggles it back in as the poetic vindication of dark ecology. If life is meaningless, the snuffing out of mankind ought, *ex hypothesis*, to be merely meaningless too, and yet deep time comes to *judge us* for our 'vanity' and 'folly'. So even though Crichton offers little by way of Christian cosmology, his is a universe in which tragedy is never a real possibility because we always get what we deserve. Crichton's universe is just, even if cruel. His cosmology is despairing and hard-nosed, inasmuch as it accepts our inevitable mistakes, but then shrugs in the face of ozone depletion or climate change because deep time, refracted through Crichton-Heston inverted romanticism, cancels out meaning and mocks our concern. This is the surprising but important common ground between the tight, controlling sovereignty of the God of a young earth and Crichton's conservative fatalism: utter confidence that the direction of the cosmos is guaranteed and for the best, coupled with a seemingly limitless capacity to imagine conspiracies that would undermine that confidence.

What is especially ironic is that a scientific version of the origins of life, precisely of the kind summarized in Crichton's passage, has been advanced by environmentalists as well, as a kind of narrative that will motivate ethical behaviour on behalf of the fabric of the whole of life. For example, Richard Williams summarizes the history of the earth and our impact on it in the hope that rational people in possession of the correct information will adopt a scientific cosmology as indicative of empirical reality and consequently adopt an ethics appropriate to that information. He notes that 'widespread acceptance of the Earth Narrative is critically important because it provides *Homo sapiens*, the most intelligent species yet to evolve on earth, with an objective understanding of their place on the planet and in the cosmos' (43). Armed with such an understanding, Williams simply assumes that human rationality will inevitably inspire correct choices. However, in an American context this approach to climate scepticism ignores a need not for data but for stories and cosmologies that mesh with a particular inherited worldview. Williams's own cosmological hope is that the scientific story all by itself, without any religious dressing, teaches that we belong to the earth, that we are part of a biotic community and that we must learn to work in relation to the whole. But is this really the case? Doesn't Crichton prove that this is not inevitable? Crichton at least understands that we are not wired to be so rational, except that he never seems to apply such evolutionary rules to himself or to those who think like he does. As Michel Serres argues, science is an epistemology in the indicative mood (what *is*), whereas religion is one example of an epistemology that operates in the imperative mood (what *ought to be*). We need both moods.

Because we are small and insignificant, Crichton seems to suggest, we should neither care about nor react to the possibility of our own degradation of the planet. And there is even worse news: according to Kenner, 'There can be no action without harm' (487), so there is simply no way to avoid environmental damage in any case, but at least our actions will always be inconsequential. Crichton has unleashed, quite intentionally I think, a veritable existential crisis, a tsunami of dark ecological *angst*, which can be survived only with the help of tough-minded hyper-masculine courage with plenty of utterly objective scientific knowledge at its disposal.

The irony is hard to miss: his case against environmentalism relies on the same state of fear that the novel suggests environmentalism has created. His recourse is to a story of ecoterrorism so violent that it can create massive glacier collapse, super lightning storms that kill children and massive waves to flood the California coastline, just to get people to believe in climate change. He imagines that we can change the climate violently, suddenly and artificially so as to disprove the idea that we can do so subtly, slowly and unconsciously, and to scorn, further, the belief that it would matter even if we could. So, the fear that environmentalists want us to have about our capacity to effect climate change is defused by being projected, simply, onto environmentalists themselves.

Scepticism of this sort resists anthropogenic climate change because it relies on a conception of a cosmos protected from the possibility of tragedy, that is, from the possibility that the free exercise of individual autonomy would ever result in unanticipated, unjust or disproportionate consequences. A Christian conservative, already predisposed to be suspicious of a faceless and increasingly bureaucratic society that long ago lost respect for religious values can find inspiration from a novelist of thrillers who provides the appearance of scientific and intellectual rigour and rugged, masculine heroism to shore up his threatened identity. Much like President Trump, the appeal is obvious, but the alliance seems destined to be catastrophic; that man is not your friend.

Conclusion

It was originally our intention, as co-authors, to seek out and highlight the diversity of climate scepticism in four different nations. In their own ways, British, French and German scepticism have yielded some pleasures, as well as surprises. The same could scarcely be said of American scepticism, which proved to be tedious, repetitive, predictable and paranoid. Perhaps the dominance of CTTs and their press releases has precluded any other sceptical cultural response; there is just no more to be said. Perhaps the acute polarization of American culture deters talented writers and artists from exploring sceptical perspectives. Perhaps they are all too busy blogging and trolling. The attention here to Crichton's strange relationship with Christian conservatism makes a virtue of adversity, illuminating one, if only one, important dimension of sceptical culture in the United States.

I have identified the rhetorical and ideological strategies that block serious engagement with the reality of climate change for Christian conservatives by promoting an ideo-theological case for scepticism that then inures such scepticism and embeds it in identitarian and moral discourses of radical certainty and trust. This curious synthesis of Christian theology and libertarian ideals renders individuals and cultures resistant to open and sincere dialogue and assessment of information with regards to the matter. This ideo-theology undergirds the seemingly endless rounds of debate in the United States about whether or not sun spots, water vapour feedbacks, unreliable measurements, computer models and excessive costs of mitigation are the real problem and about what the proper role of government is, and why conservative Christians seem reluctant to wrestle with such biblical ideas as justice, judgement, concern for the poor or any obligation to define and enact stewardship of the Creation. Because conservative Christians feel the impact of secularization keenly, there is already a built-in feeling of being embattled that only makes it easier to feel proud for going against the grain of whatever consensus there might be on climate change. And it is the joy and relish with which Crichton bravely and blithely goes against the grain that inspire his admirers.

Crichton, like many other sceptics, wants to insist with numerous examples in his appendix that the true spirit of science is scepticism and that therefore finding oneself in a small minority of scientific opinion is no shame, although he never supplies examples of when it might be foolish. Indeed, the harshest sceptics of climate change convey an almost gleeful pleasure in being a miniscule minority, working against the grain of accepted opinion. The harder warmists push with their own appeal to facts, data and reasoning and the more they might want to shame climate sceptics as flat-earthers, the more besieged and justified sceptics can feel. If there is a 'Christian' response to such a dilemma, it is what we have argued in the Introduction: to resist the temptation to further polarize the problem. Warmists who do not want to understand the particularities of providential evangelism and prefer to imagine that it defines all of Christianity imply, if not explicitly conclude, that Christianity needs to be abandoned. In so doing, they miss the opportunity to turn attention to the concerned but uncertain American majority and help them to confront their doubts, one uncertainty at a time, and to reconsider their own traditions and worldviews to find the faithful creativity needed to respond.

Christianity is not as incompatible with climate science as some might think, but the reaction against that perceived threat has created a kind of false consciousness for many conservative Christians. On the other hand, the challenges that climate change poses to the middle-class American lifestyle and its free-market capitalism are real, and the prospective costs and sacrifices are no doubt steep and will be unevenly distributed. Wyoming's per capita GHG emissions, the highest of any American state, are *1550 times* those of Vermont, the lowest (Friedrich et al.). Broad swathes of the country, especially in the south and midwest, rely on the internal combustion engine for leisure as well as transport: besides the F150 in the driveway, there may be a motorhome, a speedboat, an ATV or a snowmobile in the garage. Carbon pricing and other mitigation measures quite genuinely put such pleasures, enjoyed or aspired to by millions of Americans, in peril. Nevertheless, it would be unfortunate if these challenges collapse the robust discussion that is needed into the same old cultural war about the legitimacy and viability of Christian beliefs in the age of the Anthropocene. Clearly some Christian responses, most notably the Pope's, have identified the need for sacrifice, the need for an ethics of the future and of caring for the most poor as grounds for a response to the crisis of climate change. However, these biblical responses only highlight the ideological tensions that remain unresolved about the proper role of government and the delicate balance between individual liberties and the collective good. But if conservative Christian communities can feel faithful to their own tradition in the difficult work of meeting such biblical injunctions about the need to care for the poor, for the Creation and for future generations, then dialogue and agreement on some fundamental facts become possible, as well as perhaps greater collaboration.

The collective impact of humankind acting as a geological force changes the game for every culture and poses real challenges to traditionally held views of human autonomy and definitions of freedom. When identity is under siege, it is natural and normal for the defences to go up, but as these readings demonstrate it is also possible that those defences, when adhered to for too long and only as a reaction to circumstance, risk betraying the very identity that was defended in the first place. Indeed, as we saw in both Tommy Mitchell's and Crichton's different versions of fatalism, a negative protectionism that seeks to defend individualism only risks erasing autonomy altogether and defeating the meaning of moral choice in the face of struggle with the natural world. I would argue that for warmists and sceptics alike betrayal of what one adheres to becomes a real possibility when fear of threats posed to self or community grows greater than the love for oneself or for one's community. And when those defences grow thin, recourse to resources that help to amend and shore up a cosmological narrative that can sustain a categorical and outwardly aimed suspicion becomes a vital strategy. At root in much American climate scepticism, then, is an unspoken suspicion that the tradition to which one adheres has no adequate resources to respond to the problem, which helps to explain the desperation to meld and synthesize cosmologies - even such ill-sorted ones as Crichton-Heston's bizarre alliance with Rush Limbaugh - to create an ideo-theology that will allow an identity to survive.

This defensiveness is not only unproductive, it is unnecessary. There are ample resources within Christianity and within every society to remake and revitalize human community in light of new phenomena without having to betray or distort tradition beyond recognition. Such work will no doubt require reimagination and adjustments, but when those creative adjustments are made with clear-eyed and loving self-scrutiny, they are not defensive acts of blinding retrenchment but rather powerful expressions of the freedom and autonomy of the human imagination. This arguably does more to preserve human freedom than a defensive position precisely because it starts with a fundamental, sobering acknowledgement of the contingencies of the biological context in which human choices are made.

5

Climato-scepticisme in France

Stephanie Posthumus

During the French presidential campaign, Emmanuel Macron made the following controversial statement at a televised event on 4 February 2017: 'Il n'y a d'ailleurs pas une culture française' ['There is moreover not one French culture'].[1] Unsurprisingly, Macron was subsequently attacked by defenders of 'French culture' who retorted that the Musée du Louvre, the Bibliothèque nationale de France and the Opéra National de Paris were all examples of France's highly regarded and well-established culture. But if Macron had wanted to say there was no French culture, he would have said: 'Il n'y a pas **de** culture française.' In other words, the grammatical structure of the sentence refuses the kind of interpretation that was taken up and widely spread by the French media. As the subsequent sentence of Macron's speech clearly demonstrates, he was speaking about cultural diversification in France: 'Il y a une culture en France. Elle est diverse, elle est multiple' ['There is culture in France. It is diverse, it is multiple']. In the end, the debate did little, unfortunately, to challenge the notion of culture as a collection of canonical works, art, music, from the past; in other words, the notion of high culture.

Whatever one thinks of Macron's pragmatic neoliberal politics, I begin with his words because they trouble the idea that 'French' exists as a single, homogeneous block of traditions, habits and ways of thinking. I am not interested in being the gatekeeper of what is French and what is not. On the contrary, I use the term 'French' in this chapter to speak of a loosely held together and constantly evolving assemblage of terms, ideas, thinkers, places and responses. In part, I refer to the notion of French with language in mind – which is why I have kept citations in the original French whenever possible – but I remain aware of the kinds of power that are deployed to bolster claims about language use. For example, when French is used to counter the hegemony of English, it is seen as a form of cultural resistance. But when it is considered in the history of colonial expansion, it becomes the powerful tool of the oppressor.

While this chapter's main objective is to survey the (hi)stories of climate scepticism in France, it will also explore how the notion of 'French' is reinforced or complicated by this debate. How do climate sceptics identify as 'typically' French? How is their climate scepticism constructed by the media as 'French'? How is the notion of French used in comparative, cross-national analysis of climate scepticism? How are differences mapped back onto specific traits or socio-historical events? By carefully contextualizing my responses to these questions, I hope to avoid the danger of 'making other' (Abu-Lughod) in my analysis of anti-environmental sentiment and climate scepticism in France.

A brief prehistory of French climate scepticism

Scepticism has a long history in France. Before making the fundamental claim, 'I think, therefore I am' (*Discours de la méthode* (1637)) [Discourse on the Method], René Descartes instituted doubt as the quintessential philosophical method. Since one can be absolutely certain of nothing, thinking must start with absolute doubt. This method quickly became one of the three pillars of the French philosophical tradition along with rationality and dualism. Certainty of anything but doubt became a sign of ignorance or simple-mindedness. French literature, too, has been imbued with the spirit of sceptical doubt. Denis Diderot's *La Promenade du sceptique* [The Sceptic's Walk] – written in 1747 but not published until 1830 because of its heretical attack on the church and religious belief – set the tone for intense questioning of entrenched social beliefs. A form of cultural critique, literature was given the express task of revealing and ridiculing unquestioning faith in church or state.

Placing French climate scepticism in this 400-year-long intellectual history is both useful and problematic. Can an attack on climate change science really be traced back to Descartes's method of doubt or Diderot's disdain for Christian dogma? Not directly, no. But it is helpful to keep these historical figures in mind when examining examples of anti-ecological sentiment in France. Intellectuals such as Claude Allègre, one of the most mediatized French climate sceptics, often identify with historical figures who attempted to overturn truths espoused by the majority. Allègre even claims that doubt is specific to the French philosophical tradition: 'Le doute méthodique, n'est-ce pas un illustre français – René Descartes – qui l'a inventé ? Doit-on en France être condamné pour cela ?' (*L'Imposture climatique* 25) ['Did not a famous Frenchman – René Descartes – invent the method of doubt? Should one be condemned in France for that?']

The pro-/anti-nature debate in France dates back to the eighteenth century that pitted Jean-Jacques Rousseau – the tortured Romantic who preferred wandering the countryside to the French *salons* of the time – against his former teacher Voltaire – the satirical polemist who enjoyed rubbing shoulders with European aristocracy. In his response to Rousseau's philosophy of *le bon sauvage* [the noble savage], Voltaire wrote:

> Il prend envie de marcher à quatre pattes quand on lit votre ouvrage. Cependant, comme il y a plus de soixante ans que j'en ai perdu l'habitude, je sens malheureusement qu'il m'est impossible de la reprendre. Et je laisse cette allure naturelle à ceux qui en sont plus dignes, que vous et moi. (Letter to Rousseau, dated 30 August 1755). ['Reading your book makes one want to walk on all fours. However, it's been almost sixty years since I abandoned this habit, and so I feel, sadly, that it is impossible for me to do so again. I leave this natural posture to those who are worthier than you or me.']

The caustic, often humorous, tone of Voltaire's retorts can be heard in climate sceptic debates in France today. Moreover, rationalist thought – like the kind upheld by Voltaire in opposition to Rousseau's Romanticism – is often cited by climate sceptics as foundational to critiquing (overly political) environmentalist agendas.

The history of pro-/anti- nature attitudes in France cannot however be reduced to the opposing positions of Rousseau and Voltaire. Nineteenth-century anarchist geographer, Élisée Reclus rejected both Rousseau's Romanticism and Voltaire's rationalism in his view of ecology. As early as 1875, Reclus writes about 'unifying physical and economic data with a view to studying interactions between man and its natural environment' (Guest 76). Rather than separate nature and man, Reclus spoke of 'their cohabitation and dialectical interaction' (Guest 77). While much less known today than his American counterpart Henry David Thoreau, Reclus, too, mixed an ecological view of the world with revolutionary politics. As a libertarian, he participated in the Paris communes and refused the idea of democracy as a path to universal freedom: 'Voter, c'est abdiquer, c'est renoncer à sa propre souveraineté. N'abdiquez donc pas, ne remettez donc pas vos destinées à des hommes forcément incapables et à des traitres futurs. Ne votez pas !' (1855) ['To vote is to abdicate, to renounce one's own sovereignty. Do not abdicate, do not put your destiny in the hands of clearly incapable men, future traitors. Do not vote!']. Because Reclus remained anti-establishment until the end, his outstanding work in human geography and ecology was conveniently 'forgotten' by academics for many years.

And yet it is a revolutionary spirit similar to that of Reclus's that energized the movements of May 1968.[2] Although the claims of students protesting the elitism of French universities and the demands of unions striking in favour of improved labour conditions were more red than green, the seeds of political ecology were planted in the late 1960s. Student leaders and participants such as Daniel Cohn-Bendit and Brice Lalonde went on to become prominent green politicians. As Roger Cans explains in his short history of the ecological movement in France: 'Les enragés de mai ont déroulé un tapis rouge sous les pas des futurs écologistes' (110) ['The rebels of May 68 rolled out the red carpet for the feet of future environmentalists']. Despite early exposure to the far left, political ecology and more specifically green parties in France did not necessarily take up the socialist agenda. I will discuss this in more depth later in the chapter, but it is an important point to be making here: there is no pro-nature left and anti-nature right schism driving climate scepticism in France. Instead, there are shifting alliances on a micro-political scale with scientists and intellectuals momentarily taking up positions on the right or the left depending on what brings the most public attention.

May 1968's socio-economic upheaval and unrest on a national level was echoed in following years by more environmentally oriented causes in local settings. For example, sit-ins and demonstrations were organized at Larzac in the 1970s to protest against the government's proposed expansion of a military base. Local farmers came together with anti-capitalists, feminists and environmentalists at different Larzac gatherings over the years to continue their protests until 1981 when President François Mitterand finally abandoned the government's plans. The Larzac movement remains a highly regarded example from which many contemporary eco-movements in France draw inspiration: for example, the *Zadistes* who protested the building of a new airport in the rural area of Notre-Dame-des-Landes in 2009 (the name *Zadiste* comes from the abbreviation *Z.A.D.*, or *zone à défendre* [Zone to Defend]); the underground actions of *faucheurs volontaires d'OGM* [GMO volunteer reapers] who have destroyed Monsanto crops in different areas around France since the early 2000s; the *alter-mondialistes* [alter-globalizationists] whose movement began in 2003 at Larzac with the gathering of 200,000 people to protest the widening socio-economic gap between the North and the global South.

The 1970s Larzac movement also contained the key characteristics of what historian Michael Bess has identified as France's 'light green society': a strong attachment to a long agricultural past and a mix of nature-culture politics. According to Bess, France has developed a shallower, but wider, environmentalism

– hence, the adjective light-green – than other Western European countries because of its commitment to rolling farmland and *le petit paysan* [the small farmer], on the one hand, and its embrace of new technologies such as the Concorde, the TGV and more importantly nuclear power, on the other. France's light green society exemplifies, Bess argues, the happy marriage of modernity and ecology, giving birth to a nature-culture sentiment that sustains many different urban and rural ways of life. Bess concludes that France, 'a country with few surviving wildernesses and a great variety of partially humanized *paysage* [landscape] – may turn out closer to the shape of things to come' (294).

In 1971, France became the first Western European country to create a *Ministère de la protection de la nature et de l'environnement* [Ministry for the Protection of Nature and the Environment]. Even if Robert Poujade, the first minister, had little room to make real changes under moderate conservative President Georges Pompidou who loved driving, highways and fast cars, the Ministry was created to make a strong statement to the French people. Poujade explains that he found the word environment in an American or British newspaper and decided to adopt it even if it was considered to be an Anglicism at the time:

> Quand on l'a utilisé en 1971, les gens sont tombés des nues. Heureusement, l'appellation du ministère incluait les termes « protection de la nature »; cela ils comprenaient, mais « environnement », ils ne connaissaient pas. C'est un terme anglo-saxon démarqué du français. (52)
>
> ['When it [the word "environment"] was used in 1971, people were completely taken aback. Fortunately, the ministry's name included the words "protection of nature"; this they understood, but "environment," they didn't understand. It's an Anglo-Saxon term, different from French.']

Under Poujade's direction (1971–1974), the Ministry combined old attitudes about nature with new concerns about environment: urban parks were created, policies to clean up water and air were established and laws to reduce urban noise pollution were introduced. Despite its name, the Ministry clearly understood nature not as a wilderness to be protected – as per the American model – but as human habitat.[3]

It is from the perspective of nature and culture as necessarily imbricated that the French Green Party – *les Verts* – emerged in the 1980s. Although eco-thinker René Dumont had run for the presidency back in 1974 and eco-candidates were on the ballot from the municipal to the European level throughout the 1970s, an official party was not created in France until 1982 and *les Verts* not until 1984.

Part of the party's success during the eighties and nineties can be explained by the increasing anxiety about nuclear power plants. But the party had difficulty becoming a major figure on the French political scene with support at the presidential level at 3.8 per cent in 1988 and no legislative seats won until 1997. This difficulty can be explained in part by the party's refusal to make alliances with either the right or the left. As the then leader of *les Verts,* Antoine Waechter, stated early on in the game: 'Ni droite, ni gauche, l'écologie n'est pas à marier.' ['Ecology will not be married, neither to the right or the left.'] For the early *Verts,* this meant that a new political paradigm was needed, one that was radically different from what had preceded it, and one that did not adhere to the rules of political posturing.

Such an approach was more or less successful in the following years. By 1994, under the leadership of Dominique Voynet, the Greens decided to side with the socialist left to gain more support for their campaigns. Over the years, debate continued to rage about how 'leftist' green parties needed to be. For example, Brice Lalonde established his own Green Party, *Génération Écologie* [Ecology Generation] in 1991 that adopted a more centrist and at times right-leaning politics. This lack of a firm position on the left-right political spectrum meant, for some, that the Greens had succeeded in making environmental issues a widespread, non-partisan issue in France (Bess). For others, the centralization of environmental issues weakened the Greens as they became less and less distinct from the socialist left and the republican right (Sainteny). In the end, France's Green Party was most successful at European Parliament level, holding seven seats in 1997, its strongest year until 2010 when it merged with the European Greens, reflecting the general trend towards transnational ecological politics.

In the face of an emerging green politics in the 1960s and 1970s, French philosophy remained unmoved to say the least, with well-known thinkers rejecting outright both nature and *éco-pensée* [eco-thought]. For example, existentialist philosopher Jean-Paul Sartre exhibited a deep dislike of the natural world. One need only read the description of Roquentin's appalled fixation on a tree root in Sartre's novel, *La Nausée* (1938) [Nausea], to understand the existential *malaise* [discomfort] brought on by 'raw' nature. Jean Baudrillard's postmodern thinking goes further, exposing the world of pure representation into which the referent has completely collapsed. According to Verena Andermatt Conley, Baudrillard is 'the prototype of the brilliant *persifleur* whose world of simulacra does away with what seems to be an old-fashioned and hopelessly antiquated, indeed pre-electronic, materiality' (9). Such attitudes towards nature on the part of highly respected French philosophers and theorists have no doubt contributed to the impression that France harbours much anti-environmentalist sentiment.

Direct attacks on ecological thinking do not, however, become officially written into French intellectual history until 1992 with the publication of Luc Ferry's *Le Nouvel Ordre écologique* [The New Ecological Order]. Even if other anti-ecological books were appearing on bookstore shelves at the time, including Gérard Bramoullé's *La Peste verte* (1991) [The Green Plague], Yves Lenoir's *La Vérité sur l'effet de serre. Histoire d'une manipulation planétaire* (1992) [The Truth about the Greenhouse Effect. History of a Global Manipulation] and Philippe Paraire's *L'Utopie verte écologie des riches, écologie des pauvres* (1992) [Green Utopia. Ecology of the Rich, Ecology of the Poor], they did not have the same impact as Ferry's book.[4] There may be a couple of reasons for this: (1) Ferry was already a well-known essayist and philosopher, having published *La Pensée '68* (1985) [May 68 Thought] in which he and Alain Renaut critiqued leftist intellectuals who had participated in the student uprisings of May 1968; and (2) his book, *Le Nouvel Ordre écologique* [The New Ecological Order] attacked ecological thinking not only because of its supposed fascist tendencies, but also as a means of defending the French tradition of secular and universal humanism.[5] Lumping together thinkers as diverse as Aldo Leopold, Hans Jonas and Michel Serres, Ferry's book equated deep ecology or *écologie radicale* with a dangerous return to a state of (animal) nature. Reasserting the dualist logic of the Moderns, Ferry argued that humans must detach themselves from nature if they are to gain access to the arts, culture, beauty and ethics.

Despite what was largely a reductive reading of environmental ethics and animal rights, Ferry's book had a long-term negative effect on the development of *éco-pensée* [eco-thought] as an academic discipline in France. In a 2008 interview, French philosopher Catherine Larrère spoke of the 'censoring effect' that Ferry's book had throughout the 1990s in France. Emerging philosophers feared that any association with ecological issues would marginalize their work as mere 'applied ethics' or worse as 'anti-humanist' and 'anti-French'. It has only been since 2005 or so that disciplines like environmental history, environmental philosophy and ecocriticism have come to be recognized as valid subjects of enquiry in France.[6]

Attributing so much weight to a single book in the prehistory of climate scepticism may seem disproportionate, but Ferry does not disappear from the anti-ecological scene after publishing *Le Nouvel Ordre*. On the contrary, his voice is heard again and again on the same stage as France's most vociferous climate sceptic, Claude Allègre. Although it may be coincidental, Ferry held the position of *Ministre de la Jeunesse, de l'Éducation nationale et de la Recherche* [Minister of Youth, National Education and Research] from 2002 to 2004, two years after Allègre (1997–2000). Both Ferry and Allègre were nominated by right-wing UMP President Jacques Chirac. Later, Ferry more clearly aligned himself with Allègre, defending the climate sceptic in 2010 in an article in *Revue de la presse*, '"L'Imposture climatique" et l'indignation des belles âmes' ['The Climate Imposture' and the Indignation of the Noble-Minded'] and again in 2015 in *Le Figaro*, 'Claude Allègre vu par Luc Ferry' [Claude Allègre as Seen by Luc Ferry]. Moreover, it is not difficult to hear the echoes of Ferry's 1992 attacks on deep ecology's fascist tendencies in Allègre's repeated warnings against an 'écologie totalitaire' ['totalitarian ecology'] in his 2010 book *L'Imposture climatique* [The Climate Imposture].

The term *climato-scepticisme* does not appear in the French press until 2007, relatively late compared to Australia, Britain and the United States. But if one takes a longer view of anti-ecological attitudes that predate the use of the actual term, the year 1992 was pivotal. On the one hand, the Green Party was gaining more and more votes. On the other, intellectuals and scientists were mobilizing against what was seen as a rising ideological eco-order. As sociologists Hélène Guillemot and Stéfan Aykut explain:

> On peut faire remonter la généalogie du climatoscepticisme hexagonal à 1992. En réaction au Sommet de la Terre de Rio, se constitue une mouvance intellectuelle et politique s'opposant à une « écologie irrationnelle » au nom d'une « écologie scientifique ». Elle se manifeste par la publication d'ouvrages comme *Le Nouvel Ordre écologique* du philosophe Luc Ferry, et par des initiatives tel l'appel d'Heidelberg, signé par près de 4000 scientiques dont 72 Prix Nobel, qui dénonçait « une idéologie irrationnelle qui s'oppose au progrès scientifique et industriel ». (75)
>
> ['The genealogy of French climate scepticism can be dated to 1992. In response to the Rio Earth Summit, an intellectual and political group came together to oppose "irrational ecology" in defence of "scientific ecology." Expression of such an idea can be found in texts such as philosopher Luc Ferry's *Le Nouvel Ordre écologique* and in initiatives such as the Heidelberg Appeal, signed by over 4,000 scientists, including 72 Nobel Prize winners, who denounced "irrational ideology that opposes scientific and industrial progress".']

While I wholeheartedly agree with Guillemot and Aykut's genealogy of climate scepticism, their description of Ferry's book needs to be corrected. *Le Nouvel Ordre* is not defending scientific ecology against irrational ecology. In fact, the book speaks very little of science. However, Ferry does argue in the final chapter of his book for what he calls 'democratic ecology', that is, ecology based on the humanist ideals of liberty, beauty and finality (258–62). According to Ferry, humans must maintain their position above nature: 'L'homme peut et *doit* modifier la nature, comme il peut et doit la *protéger*' (247; italics in the original) ['Man can and *must* modify nature, just as he can and *must* protect it.'] However un-ecological the first part of this claim may seem, Ferry establishes a precedent when he qualifies his ecology as democratic and dismisses other ecologies as radical or irrational. As I will explain later, French climate sceptics do not throw the ecological baby out with the bath water; instead, they prioritize their ecological issues as the 'right' ones and dismiss climate change as the 'wrong' one.[7]

Climate scepticism can be seen as the most recent manifestation of what is an evolving climate change controversy. In their 2012 article, sociologists Stefan Aykut, Jean-Baptiste Comby and Hélène Guillemot offer a comprehensive snapshot of the 'career' of climate change in France (158).[8] While drawing on Science and Technology Studies (STS) to analyse this 'public problem', the article does not reduce climate change to a social construction. On the contrary, Aykut, Comby and Guillemot assert the importance of framing climate change with respect to different actors, stakeholders and discourses to better deal with its present and future effects. Comparing articles published in three major French newspapers from 1988 to 2012, they identify three phases in the career of climate change: (1) the first phase (1988–2001/2) when climate issues were identified as largely international, with France participating in global summits (where there was much room for disagreement and debate); (2) the second phase (2002/3–2008) when the issues became more domestic, with France creating its first comprehensive climate action programme and placing emphasis on individual moral choices (where there was less room for debate and controversy); and (3) the third phase (2009 to the present) when the issues give rise to more diverse controversies, with a broader group of visible actors both within and outside the scientific community participating in the debate (the emergence of climate scepticism per se in France).

While I will be focusing largely on the last two phases in my discussion of French climate scepticism in the next section, it is helpful to keep a longer view in mind. Looking back over the history of anti-nature and anti-ecological sentiment in France, one can see the emergence of three important characteristics: (1) the use of a sarcastic, at times, *persifleur* tone to critique pro-nature sentiment; (2) the dismissal of ecological science that becomes too embroiled in political affairs; (3) the method of doubt as central to scientific and intellectual thinking more broadly in France.

Climate scepticism in France: An overview

Comparative studies of attitudes towards climate change in different countries tend to offer a generalized summary of national differences. Toussaint Nothias and James Painter conclude that climate change is 'not subject to the same degree of intense political controversy' in France, that 'climate sceptics are present [...] but nothing like as consistently vocal a force', and that 'opinion polls normally show that the French public is more convinced by the science of climate change and the need to do something about it than in the UK and the USA' (89). Reasons given for these differences vary from one scholar to the next. Some have remarked on the small number of right-wing liberals who are both pro-free market and anti–big government in France, and others on the fact that the French media takes largely the side of climate change scientists. A more telling explanation can be found in a point I made earlier about environmental issues being non-partisan in France. While socialist centre-left President François Hollande successfully introduced environmental reforms and carbon tax initiatives, so did his republican predecessor, Nicholas Sarkozy, who pushed hard to launch the *Grenelle de l'Environnement* [Grenelle Environment] in 2007. Even parties on the far right in France such as the National Front have been heard favouring the reduction of greenhouse gases (Nothias and Painter 91).[9]

What then is driving the controversy? Initial assessments tend to identify individual motives and underscore 'une irrépressible mise en avant des ego' (Godard 61) ['an irrepressible show of egos']. The leading scholar of climate scepticism in the United States, Naomi Oreskes, points out that climate sceptics in France are for the most part 'scientifiques âgés, qui ont eu énormément de succès à l'apogée de leur carrière et qui à présent reçoivent de moins en moins d'attention' (47) ['aging scientists, who had great success at the height of their career and are given much less attention now']. It is true that the debate in France has been dominated by older, male scientists who published widely in the 1980s and 1990s and were well respected in their fields.[10] Specific to the French context is the fact that the two most mediatized French climate sceptics – Claude Allègre and Vincent Courtillot – are both trained geologists, the former a geochemist and the latter a volcanologist. Even if other voices have since joined the climate sceptic debate in France – mathematician Benoît Rittaud, economist Rémy Prud'homme, science historian François Ewald,[11] to name a few – geologists have dominated the scene in France. According to Antonin Pottier, research funding for geologists diminished at the same time that ocean and atmospheric sciences were emerging. Climatologists were seen as the new players on the block, and their methods such as computer modelling were looked upon with suspicion: 'Climate models impinge on territories where other disciplines claim legitimacy, leading to competition between different epistemic cultures' (Aykut, Comby and Guillemot 169).

French climate scepticism cannot be reduced, however, to a schoolyard spat between a small group of geologists and climatologists. The controversy began in the sacred halls of the *Académie des sciences* when in 2007 Vincent Courtillot was invited with his co-author Jean-Louis Le Mouël to publicly defend an article they had published in *Earth and Planetary Science Letters*, which argued that solar cycles were the driver of climate change. While in the United States, climate scepticism has been driven by conservative think tanks funded by multi-national oil companies, it first appeared at the very heart of the scientific institution in France. Environmental journalist Stéphane Foucart identifies this factor as specific to the French context:

> Ce sont les hautes instances scientifiques elles-mêmes qui, sous l'influence d'un petit groupe de chercheurs tendent à renvoyer dos à dos les climatologues et les climato-sceptiques [...] Situation extravagante et qui n'existe à peu près nulle part ailleurs. En France, le flou est entretenu, ou au moins permis, par les garants mêmes du savoir. (*Le Populisme* Kindle, Loc. 10 per cent)
>
> ['Under the sway of a small group of researchers, prominent scientific authorities have themselves tended to dismiss both climatologists and climate sceptics [...] A ludicrous situation that exists almost nowhere else. In France, uncertainty is maintained, or at least permitted, by the guarantors of knowledge.']

To understand how climate scepticism came to be taken so seriously by the Academy, it is helpful to consider the larger context of climate change as a public controversy in France.

In the 1990s, two separate groups emerged in France with expertise in the area of climate change issues. The scientific group, *l'Académie des sciences*, published dry, factual reports about global warming for their colleagues and peers, while the executive group, the GIES (*Groupe interministériel sur l'effet de serre*) [Interministerial Group on Global Warming] which later became MIES (*Mission interministériel de l'effet de serre*) [Interministerial Commission on Global Warming], reported directly to the president about socio-economic effects of climate change:

> En France, expertises scientifique et technique, d'une part, politique, d'autre part, sont soigneusement séparées. L'Académie des sciences et Yves Martin [GIES/MIES] représentent deux sources de légitimité différentes,

> mais complémentaires dans le processus politique français. Ils incarnent le désintéressement et l'excellence par leur statut et garantissent ainsi l'objectivité du processus d'expertise. (Aykut, 'La Construction' 104)
>
> ['In France, scientific and technical expertise, on the one hand, political expertise, on the other, are deliberately kept separate. The Academy of Sciences and Yves Martin [leader of GIES/MIES] represent two sources of legitimacy, different but complementary in the French political process. They epitomize neutrality and excellence because of their status, and thus guarantee the objectivity of the process of expertise.']

When a peer-reviewed article disputing anthropogenic climate change was published in 2005 in a scientific journal by a renowned French volcanologist, it was the duty of the Academy to address the issue. And so, in 2007, esteemed researchers from the *Centre National de Recherche en Sciences* (CNRS) and the Academy attended a series of debates between climate sceptic scientists and climatologists. This problematically placed two kinds of science on the same footing, disguising the fact that climate change was not the area of specialization of climate sceptic scientists.

The debate quickly moved from the halls of the Academy to more public venues because of the tireless efforts of geochemist Claude Allègre who enthusiastically supported the work of his friend Courtillot. In 2006, Allègre wrote a newspaper column about climate change for the popular press *L'Express* in which he raised doubts about diminishing snow caps in the Himalayas. But it was not until Allègre published *L'Imposture climatique ou la fausse écologie* [The Climate Imposture or Fake Ecology] in 2010 that climate scepticism came directly into the media spotlight in France.[12] Even though this happened at a later date in France than in the United States, it immediately captured the public's attention because of the legitimacy and loudness of the speakers involved. Media coverage of climate scepticism in France is unique in that it gives prominence to a select few voices, and so has 'the highest level of visibility for individual sceptics' (Grundmann and Scott 231). As I noted earlier, Allègre held the position of minister of education in the 1990s and Courtillot was a well-established researcher within the Academy and the CNRS. Their 'autorité institutionnelle' ['institutional authority'] and their 'carrière au sein de l'administration' ['career in administration'] lent much weight to their objections (Aykut, 'La Construction' 105). In addition, the rise of environmental journalism in France throughout the 1990s meant that there was an informed, well-read audience able to respond immediately to the allegedly falsified scientific content of Allègre's book. Sylvestre Huet, environmental journalist for the left-wing newspaper, *La Libération*, published his rebuttal *L'Imposteur, c'est lui* [The Imposter, It's Him] soon after Allègre's book. This was followed closely by *Le Populisme climatique* (2011) [Climate Populism] written by *Le Monde*'s environmental journalist, Stéphane Foucart. Though both books strongly disputed Allègre's claims, they also increased the book's impact.[13]

While other climate sceptic books have since been published in France – a handful of which I will discuss in more detail later – much of the debate has moved to the internet.[14] For example, the *Association des climato-réalistes* [Association of Climate Realists] whose founding members include Courtillot and Rittaud regularly publishes monthly online bulletins that critique the politics and science of climate change issues in France and around the world. Spearheaded by 'big names' in French climate scepticism, this website has an extremely active online community. Another popular website, *La Pensée unique* [Single-Mindedness], created by retired physicist and former CNRS lab director, Jean Duran, adopts the slogan 'En matière de Sciences, le scepticisme est un devoir' ['In matters of science, scepticism is a duty']. In other words, Duran invokes '[le] réflexe de "scepticisme ordinaire" qu'il présente comme la première qualité du scientifique, en confondant le doute méthodologique que devrait pratiquer le chercheur avec un scepticisme général' (Godard 62) ['the habit of "ordinary scepticism" that he [Duran] presents as the scientist's main quality, confusing methodological doubt that should be practiced by all researchers with general scepticism']. Additional websites such as *Le Portail des climato-sceptiques* [Climate Sceptics' Portal], *Climato-optimistes* [Climate Optimists] and *Climat de terreur* [Climate of Terror] target a French audience, but largely repeat information found on Anglophone forums and blogs.

In addition to moving to the internet, climate scepticism no longer offers a strong united front in France since the almost complete disappearance of Claude Allègre from the media after he suffered a heart attack in 2013. No longer driven by a small group of vocal scientists, it has morphed into a more general critique of ecological catastrophism. Right-wing intellectuals such as Luc Ferry and Pascal Bruckner have taken up their own battleaxes to attack a politics of austerity and heavy-handed government interventionism that result from, according to them, a dogmatic response to climate change. While scientists like Courtillot and Allègre were for the most part attribution sceptics, questioning the causes of global warming, intellectuals like Bruckner are typically policy sceptics, refusing to believe that current patterns of consumption need to change. In *Le Fanatisme de l'Apocalypse* (2011) [translated into English as *The Fanaticism of the Apocalypse*], Bruckner shifts attention away from the question of climate change science in order to attack environmental thinking as a new form of religious belief. He defends technology and capitalism – his first chapter ends with a defence of the automobile as a symbol of liberty and his final chapter with an apology for consumerism as a form of spiritual 'blooming of the self' (Kindle, Loc. 95 per cent) – and his book is read widely.[15] What makes Bruckner's arguments appealing to readers is the fact that he denies environmentalism its sense of righteousness and its visions of future apocalypse. In addition, he traces his position back to Voltaire who embraced the 'good life' in opposition to Rousseau's call for a simpler life. Much like the British science writer Matt Ridley, Bruckner asserts that humanity will only free itself 'par le haut' (by moving upwards), proclaiming his faith in the human capacity to invent, meet new challenges and go beyond limits.[16]

The shift in climate sceptic discourse from questioning climate change science to critiquing climate change politics can also be seen in the work of Benoît Rittaud, whose relatively youth compared to the large majority of 'scientifiques âgés' (Oreskes) ['older scientists'] has made him something of a poster boy for French climate scepticism. As a mathematician and more generally an epistemologist, Rittaud rejects climate change models and climatology's methods in his book *Le Mythe climatique* (2010) [The Climate Myth]. Even though he is critiqued for parroting the ideas of other climate sceptics – 'Il faut ainsi noter l'ampleur des phénomènes de reprise servile d'arguments et de références venus des États-Unis' (Godard 60)[17] ['It is therefore important to note the widespread phenomenon of servile repetition of arguments and references from the United States'] – he gives a French spin to his book by carefully engaging with tone and narrative techniques. Witty, well-read and poised, Rittaud has appeared on French television in debates against well-known climatologists such as Jean Jouzel. But Rittaud's position seems to be broadening out from that of attribution sceptic. In his most recent book, *La Peur exponentielle* (2015) [The Exponential Fear], he turns his attention to the cultivation of public fear that drives, he asserts, the politics of climate change. (Adopting a new target for his climate scepticism means that Rittaud does not have to address the fact that five years after his climate myth book, climatology's supposed 'faulty models' have accurately predicted some of the effects of global warming.) In *La Peur exponentielle*, Rittaud continues to play the 'science' card, using the mathematical concept of the exponential to explain fearmongering around global warming. But his position is more that of the intellectual as public figure than that of the scientist contributing to an epistemological debate. In this way, he models the transformation of climate sceptic discourse in France from scientists like

Courtillot and Allègre to intellectuals like Bruckner and Ewald, from the halls of the Academy of Sciences to the general public.

While advocates of climate change politics have certainly dominated the scene in France – with media stars such as Nicholas Hulot being the most prominent[18] – their tactic has often been to beat the drum of disastrous future scenarios. French climatologist and glaciologist, Jean Jouzel, also former vice-president of the IPCC in the early 1990s, has consistently been the voice of such dire warnings. The prologue to his most recent book, *Le Défi climatique* (2014) [The Climate Challenge], speaks of climate change as 'trop rapide pour que l'espèce humaine puisse s'y adapter sans souffrances' ['happening too fast for the human species to adapt without great suffering'], and asserts that 'il n'y a pas d'autres issues possibles' (n.p.) ['there are no other possible solutions']. However, it is not only climate sceptics and anti-ecological intellectuals who have become quite critical of these dire tones. Leftist intellectuals such as Isabelle Stengers have argued, for example, for a less reactionary, less globalizing response to the 'intrusion of Gaia'. In *Au temps des catastrophes* (2009) [In Catastrophic Times], Stengers speaks against both unlimited capitalist growth and imposed global eco-measures; she calls instead for experimenting with new modes of thinking and politicizing in local contexts, something she experienced personally during the 'GMO event' in France (*In Catastrophic Times* 35–36).[19] While taking planetary climate change very seriously – she warns against 'not paying attention', 'stupidity' and the dangers of not doing anything (quotes taken from her chapter titles) – Stengers concludes hopefully with the following conviction: 'Joy is what makes me bet on the future in which the response to Gaia would not be the sadness of degrowth but that which conscientious objectors to economic growth have already invented' (*In Catastrophic Times* 156).

New groups are emerging in France to take up the call for a more creative, experimental, response to climate issues. While extremely critical of anxiety-provoking environmentalist discourse, *néo-écolos* do not dispute the fact of global warming. In this way, they steal some of the rhetorical fire from climate sceptics while still advocating for changes to Western lifestyles of overconsumption. Using humour and lighthearted critique, groups like *Génération Cobayes*, or the 'Guinea-Pig Generation' in English, cultivate an 'écologie souriante' (Berland) ['smiling ecology'] that undermines the oppositional narrative of 'écologie démocratique' ['democratic ecology'] versus 'écologie totalitaire' ['totalitarian ecology']. As digital natives, these groups utilize social media much more playfully and subversively than climate sceptics do.[20] In addition, they organize public demonstrations to poke fun at anti-ecologists, but do so satirically, using slogans such as 'CO_2, j'en veux!' ['We want CO_2!'] 'Monsanto Président' ['Monsanto for President'], 'Les engrais, c'est le progrès!' ['Fertilizer as progress!'] and 'Sauvons la bourse, pas les ours!' ['Save the Stock Exchange, not the bears!']. On a different note, eco-documentaries like *Demain* (2015) [Tomorrow] highlight the many examples of communities around the world that are already making some of the radical changes needed to face climate change. These new voices of satirical optimism and joyful ecological awareness have done much to weaken the authoritative, institutionalized and, at times, unimaginative arguments of climate sceptics and warmists alike in France.

French climate sceptic texts: An ecocritical analysis

A socio-historical overview is necessary for understanding the emergence and development of climate scepticism in France, but a closer reading of individual climate sceptic texts reveals more culturally specific differences. Although not literary in the received sense, these texts adopt techniques for engaging readers that go beyond the simple presentation of scientific facts and arguments. While sociologists analyse climate scepticism as one of the evolving discourses about climate change, and environmental journalists refute climate sceptics' inaccurate scientific claims, ecocritics have the tools for analysing climate sceptic texts in terms of narrative framing techniques and modes of expression. In this way, ecocriticism creates a space where climate sceptic texts are taken seriously while also having their rhetorical strategies challenged, where the textual 'appeal' of climate scepticism is better understood in terms of culturally specific tropes and touchstones.

To some extent, the French texts I will be considering invite such an ecocritical reading because of the ways in which arguments are presented as part of a larger *histoire*. For example, Allègre begins *L'Imposture climatique* [The Climate Imposture] by referencing 'une histoire unique, improbable, fantastique, et pourtant bien réelle' (7) ['a unique, improbable, fantastic, and yet real story'], a story about 'un commando d'hommes – les uns scientifiques, les autres politiques' (7) ['a commando of men – some scientists, others politicians']. He uses the term *histoire* to dramatize the account of the rise of the IPCC he is about to give but also to sow doubt in the reader's mind about the neutrality of such a group. Similarly, Rittaud starts his book by speaking of the emergence of climatology as 'une histoire tragique et belle' (*Le Mythe* 12) ['a tragic and beautiful story'] as a way of undermining truth claims about anthropogenic climate change.[21] But the term *histoire* means both story and history. This second meaning invites the reader to interpret these texts as part of the history of climate change and part of the history of science as social discourse. While the word is meant to be understood negatively, it opens up a conversation about the history of science in the public sphere, a point to which I will come back later in the chapter.

French climate sceptics pay careful attention not only to the 'what' of the story they are telling, but also to the 'how'. For example, the paratext – the supplementary materials that are part of a book's presentation such as the cover page, title, front matter, back matter and footnotes – play an important role in creating a narrative frame and establishing a relationship with the reader. Rittaud includes an *avant-propos* in which he speaks honestly about his career as a mathematician. Likewise, Allègre uses a prologue to reassure the reader that he is not *anti-écolo*, that he did much to introduce laws against air and water pollution in France in the early 1990s. This paratextual matter allows the climate sceptics to clearly state their legitimacy as actors in climate change controversies and anticipate objections that could be made, for example, about being anti-environmentalist. To further strengthen the pact with the reader, Allègre's book adopts an intimate often humorous tone, playing up the conversational side of the interview format with emotional asides included in parentheses (such as '(*sourire de Claude Allègre*)' (23)) ['Claude Allègre smiles']. Rittaud, too, interrupts the telling of the 'story' to address his reader directly – 'lecteur' (11, 13) ['reader'], 'reprenons' (14) ['let's start again']. Both Allègre and Rittaud are clearly aware of the importance of increasing readability and appealing to a larger public.

As a literary critic, I have to admit that it is more entertaining to read the climate sceptic texts than the rebuttal texts (or rather, not all climate sceptic texts, but the ones I have singled out here). Rittaud begins his book with an example of a previous 'hoax' in the history of science when a handful of astronomers asserted in the nineteenth century that valleys on Mars were actually canals, vestiges of former human or alien life. He compares these beliefs to current theories about climate change and predicts the latter will soon be disproven much like the earlier explanations about signs of life on Mars. Anticipating the reader's objections about using history to establish his analogy, Rittaud quotes late-nineteenth and early twentieth-century French poet and philosopher Paul Valéry: 'L'histoire justifie ce que l'on veut. Elle n'enseigne rigoureusement rien, car elle contient tout, et donne des exemples de tout' (22) ['History proves whatever one wants. It teaches strictly nothing, because it contains everything, and has examples of everything']. Again, Rittaud reinforces the pact with the reader by admitting the problems with his astronomy-climatology analogy while also demonstrating that even a mathematician has a well-developed general literary culture.

This careful attention to form is not, however, what sets French climate sceptics' texts apart from those of their Anglophone counterparts. Such an assertion would be too generalizing and too reductive.[22] What can be seen as specific to French climate sceptic texts are the tropes that have tended to dominate the debate. First, I will examine the recurring notion of the *imposture* which is used to refer to the act of trickery, intentional or not, in climate change controversies.[23] From the Latin word *impostura*, the word is related to the verb 'to impose', and thus closely linked to the second trope, that of *ordre* in the sense of a group of people driven by a set of beliefs or ideology. French climate sceptics claim to be fighting a global environmentalist order that bolsters its position by using the faulty reasoning of science imposters. They see their role as combating this *ordre* (ideological battle) and exposing the *imposture* (scientific territory).[24]

One of the most well-known French literary examples of the imposter is undoubtedly Molière's *Tartuffe*. First performed in 1664, the play tells the story of a supposedly religious and devout man, Tartuffe, who ingratiates himself as a guest into the home of Elmire and Orgon. Friends and family see through Tartuffe, but not the head of the household, Orgon, who remains under Tartuffe's spell throughout the play. Mocking both the religious community and the bourgeoisie, Molière's play stirred up quite a bit of controversy in its time and remains highly popular to this day. Moreover, it inscribed the figure of the Tartuffe into the French imaginary to the extent that the word can be found in the dictionary to refer to a hypocrite. By entitling his book *L'Imposture climatique* [The Climate Imposture], Allègre is most certainly appealing to this practice of calling out the duper. He asserts that climatologists are intentionally tricking the public, pretending to do real science when their results are based on fabricated models and uncertain predictions. In Molière's play, it is King Louis XIV who intervenes when it looks like Tartuffe will end up with all the household's possessions. The problem with playing the monarch, as Allègre seems to want to do, is that this power, too, can be suddenly overturned (as the French monarchs painfully discovered during the French Revolution).[25]

By using the term *imposture* in his title, Allègre calls out a kind of knowledge construction that is unable to 'free itself' from political and social uses, that remains 'mired' in human interests and partiality. This practice of policing the borders of science brings to mind a text with a very similar title published at the height of the science wars in the 1990s. In *Impostures intellectuelles* (1997) [translated into English as *Fashionable Nonsense: Postmodern Intellectuals' Abuse of Science*], physicists Alan Sokal and Jean Bricmont castigate thinkers such as Gilles Deleuze, Julia Kristeva, Jacques Lacan and Bruno Latour for their use of scientific concepts and terms of which they have no 'real' understanding. The book builds on an earlier hoax: Sokal's publication of an article in the peer-reviewed journal *Social Text* that was, the author later revealed, a string of terms from quantum physics and complexity theory meant to confuse the reader. According to Sokal and Bricmont, literary scholars and philosophers, or the humanities more generally, lost their way when they began using concepts from the pure sciences. In other words, disciplinary borders needed to be respected.

A similar viewpoint about defending science's borders drives part of the controversy about climate change in France. Allègre denounces climatology as a pseudo-science because it has gotten 'mixed up' with politics (see also Rittaud who uses the term *climatomancie* [climatomancy] to decry climate change predictions used for socio-political ends). Allègre's book participates in a larger conversation about the limits of scientific discourse, about who is qualified to discuss science outside of the lab and about the ends to which scientific data and theories can be applied. Like Sokal and Bricmont, Allègre sees himself as reasserting the traditions of French rationalism and objective knowledge. But climate sceptics like Allègre and Rittaud are not the only ones critiquing science when it becomes too embroiled in socio-political debate. While supporting climate science as a legitimate field of enquiry, Stéphane Foucart, too, disparages the coming together of science and politics. He dates this problematic 'marriage' back to 2007 when Al Gore and the IPCC were awarded the Nobel Peace Prize conjointly. Foucart goes so far as to call this 'la grande erreur du comité Nobel' ['the Nobel committee's great error']: 'Les scientifiques étudiant le climat sont devenus, dans l'esprit d'une bonne part de la population, des idéologues au service d'une cause' (*Le Populisme* Kindle, loc. 2 per cent) ['Scientists studying climate became, in the minds of much of the population, ideologists working for a cause'].

In his 1990 book, *Le Contrat naturel* [translated into English as *The Natural Contract*] – a text involved in earlier eco-controversies in France as one of the main targets of Luc Ferry's *Le Nouvel Ordre écologique* [The New Ecological Order] – French philosopher Michel Serres examines the epistemological implications of the emergence of climate change: 'Global history enters nature; global nature enters history: this is something utterly new in philosophy' (*The Natural Contract* 4). In the face of this novelty, Serres lays the theoretical foundations for a natural contract that will allow humans to live symbiotically with the earth. But more important to my argument here is Serres's analysis of the intertwined stories of science and the law since the trial of Galileo:

> The sciences begin in such legal actions; they enter history through the courtroom door. [...] The internal history requires a judgement of truth, a decision about whether Anaxagoras and Galileo and Lysenko are wrong or right [...] The external history has the sciences join or develop into schools or pressure groups, and it demands that their truth be socially canonized. Individuals or associations appear before a given court, and fragile truth is thereby reinforced [...]. In the final analysis, there is no general history of science that is not judicially recorded. No science without trials; no truth without judgements, whether internal or external to knowledge. Its history can't do without tribunals. (*The Natural Contract* 62)

Rather than decry such entanglements, Serres posits that we can never have science without the socio-judicial processes that establish what constitutes truth at a given time in a given place; scientific knowledge has necessarily emerged within the *polis*.

While such assertions may seem quite commonplace after the rise of STS and the work of Bruno Latour (a former student of Serres), climate change controversies continue to resurrect the spectre of pure scientific knowledge untouched by political bias. This may be because of the strength of a second trope that has dominated anti-environmentalist critiques in France since the early 1990s: the idea of an *ordre écologique* [ecological order]. Unfortunately, Ferry's characterization of ecology as radical militancy, as a return to fascist or totalitarian order, continues to be heard over and over again in climate change controversies in France. Much too reductively, Allègre affirms: 'Je soutiens que la tendance profonde de l'écologie politique est d'être totalitaire' (26) ['I maintain that political ecology's underlying tendency is towards totalitarianism']. Later, he uses the expression 'totalitarisme climatique' (94, 110, 140) ['climate totalitarianism'] to warn readers against a system that has no tolerance for those who challenge climate change theories. Finally, he describes a future 'écologie totalitaire' ['totalitarian ecology'] at which time earth will be run by a global governing body of technocrats who make decisions for all citizens based solely on saving the planet (264). Such reductive appeals to the trope of a totalitarian order are in part to be expected in the work of climate sceptics. But they also appear in defences of climatology and climate change politics. Recently republished in paperback, Foucart's book carefully counters many of the arguments put forward by climate sceptics like Allègre and Rittaud.

Yet Foucart, too, speaks of an ecological order that was instituted when the Nobel Prize was given to the IPCC:

> Il a renforcé l'idée fausse que la climatologie est un ensemble de sciences militantes, tendues vers le même objectif que celui des ONG environnementalistes: asseoir un nouvel ordre écologique. Nouvel ordre impliquant un changement civilisationnel radical, une mutation profonde des modes de vie qui ont cours en Occident. (*Le Populisme* Kindle, loc. 2 per cent)
>
> ['This reinforced the wrong idea that climatology is a collection of militant sciences, working towards the same goal as environmentalist NGOs: the establishment of a new ecological order. A new order requiring a radical change of civilization, a profound transformation of current Western ways of living.']

Foucart redraws the lines around science, admonishing climatology to stick to its field of expertise and stay out of politics. According to Aykut, one of the particularities of climate change controversy in France is exactly 'cette défense de la Science (avec un grand "S") contre une idéologie dangereuse et obscurantiste issue de la "deep ecology" anglo-saxonne' ('La Construction' 88–89) ['this protection of Science (with a capital "S") against a dangerous and obscurantist ideology arising from Anglo-Saxon "deep ecology"']. Given that Foucart denounces Ferry as a 'philosophe climato-sceptique' (*Le Populisme* Kindle, loc. 81 per cent) ['climate sceptic philosopher'], it is unfortunate, to say the least, that he cultivates the same fear of an ecological order. This trope is clearly deeply rooted in the French environmental and anti-environmental imagination.

Rather than build walls around scientific knowledge, other voices have emerged in France that acknowledge climatology's increasing role within the political sphere. In *Climat: le vrai et le faux* (2011) [Climate: the True and the False], climatologist Valérie Masson-Delmotte targets a more general audience to explain the scientific and political challenges of climate change. However, she states in the book's foreword that it is better to keep these two kinds of challenge separate: scientific issues have to do with understanding and predicting climate change, and political issues with taking action and adapting to climate change. Oceanographer and climatologist Éric Guilyardi and his sister Catherine Guilyardi, a journalist, take a different approach. In their co-written book *Que feriez-vous si vous le saviez? Des climatologues face à la désinformation* (2015) [What Would You Do If You Knew? Climatologists Facing Disinformation], they acknowledge the responsibility of the scientist to transmit knowledge and the journalist to produce information about climate change. Narrating a climatologist's daily life in the laboratory and describing the constant pressure faced by environmental journalists to produce the next big story, the book aims to educate the general public about climate change as a social problem. Its use of the first-person pronoun, alternating between the brother's and sister's perspective, demystifies Science (with a capital 'S') and embraces the model of embedded, embodied, situated knowledge.

Fictionalizing climate change controversies: A few examples

Whereas examples of climate fiction abound in contemporary Anglophone literature, the topic of global warming has appeared only intermittently in French contemporary literature, at least as far as adult fiction is concerned. As scholars of *littérature pour jeunesse* [children's literature] have noted, climate change has been taken up quite quickly and extensively in children's and young adult fiction in France. Pedagogical and at times moralizing, eco-literature for a younger audience does not shy away from teaching a lesson or conveying a political message to its reader. In adult literature, on the other hand, the *roman à thèse* [didactic/thesis novel] fell out of fashion not long after Jean-Paul Sartre's theorizing of *la littérature engagée* [engaged literature] in *Qu'est-ce que la littérature?* (1948) [translated into English as *What Is Literature?*]. The rise of the *Nouveau Roman* [New Novel] in works by Alain Robbe-Grillet, Jean Ricardou and Nathalie Sarraute sidelined the question of literature as a means for authentically representing the socio-historical real and foregrounded the practice of writing as producing its own kinds of reality.

The *ère du soupçon* [era of suspicion] so prevalent in French literary circles from the 1950s until the early 1980s continues to inflect attitudes towards politically engaged literature. Even though many contemporary novels adopt a *retour au réel* [return to the real] (Vercier and Viart), they do so with caution, often from an historical or autofictional approach. Climate change remains a topic that is difficult to tackle in the novel because its ethical and political stakes are so high. Most of the case studies I will consider here use satire to fictionalize climate change and so distance themselves from calls for radical lifestyle changes. The few texts that do portray climate change seriously use a form other than the novel such as the *bande dessinée* [comic book] or science fiction and thus avoid the accusation of reducing fiction to a *roman à thèse* [didactic/thesis novel].[26]

The relative absence of French climate fiction does not mean that novelists are not aware of or engaged with environmental issues or more specifically the problem of global warming. In the 25 December 2014 issue of *La Libération*, the directors of the *Maison des écrivains et de la littérature* (MEL) [Writers' and Literature House] in Paris made a strong statement about literature needing to respond to climate change. They then invited well-known authors such as Pierre Bergounioux, Éric Chevillard, Michel Deguy, Maryline Desbiolles and Olivia Rosenthal to write short literary pieces in response to the following questions:

> Face à la menace, maintenant si précise, du changement climatique, face à l'espoir aussi que représente la mobilisation mondiale sur ce sujet, que peut la littérature ? Se fera-t-elle entendre ? Que peuvent les mots face aux désastres annoncés ? Témoigner ? Émouvoir ? Faire prendre conscience ? Pousser à la réflexion ? Que peut encore le langage dans ce monde de l'image, de l'immédiateté, dans l'urgence où nous sommes ? Si la littérature n'est pas que divertissement et loisir, si elle participe, du plus intime, de l'aventure humaine, elle ne peut tout simplement pas rester indifférente. Ses forces, même si maigres en apparence, ne doit-elle pas les mettre toutes entières dans la balance, pour peser contre la fatalité, la lâcheté, la tristesse d'un monde sans possibles ? (Gouttebaron and Boudier) ['In the face of the threat of climate change, now so real, but also in the face of the hope that global mobilization around this subject represents, what can literature do? Will it be heard? What can words do in the face of predicted disasters? Witness? Move deeply? Bring about awareness? Encourage reflection? What can language do in the world of images and immediacy, given the urgency we are facing? If literature is not just entertainment and leisure, if it participates in the most intimate of human adventures, it cannot remain indifferent. Should its forces, however weak they seem to be, not be measured in order to tip the scales against the inevitability, cowardice, sadness of a world without possibilities?']

In total, thirty-one authors participated in the yearlong MEL event, and their texts were read aloud to the National Assembly on 15 November 2015 in support of the then upcoming United Nations Climate Change Conference in Paris, France (COP21).[27] The written texts range from brief philosophical essays to poetry, from short stories to personal letters written to future generations. To some extent, the diverse modes of expression adopted by the authors who participated in this event illustrate the continued difficulties of integrating climate change into the more traditional form of the novel in France.[28]

One genre that has emerged in France to take up environmental issues related to plants, animals and human habitat more generally is the eco-thriller. In *Poison vert* (2002) [Green Poison], *H_2O* (2004), *Mort sur la forêt* (2007) [Death above the Forest], Patric Nottret develops the character of Pierre Sénéchal, a detective fighting eco-crimes such as the cloning of dangerous tropical plants, the spread of genetically modified soy-destroying insects and the strange reappearance of the previously extinct dinosaur-fish, coelacanth. Published by a well-known French publishing house, Éditions Robert Lafont, these novels have yet to win a literary prize or attract the attention of literary critics writing for *Le Monde des livres* or the magazine *Lire*. A much more widely read eco-thriller is Jean-Christophe's *Le Parfum d'Adam* (2007) [Adam's Perfume]. In the novel, two American detectives, former CIA agents, are fighting an ecoterrorist group, the New Predators, who are conspiring to wipe out the world's poorest populations by developing a new cholera strain to be released in the waters of the Rio de Janeiro's favelas. In the novel's postface, Rufin cites Luc Ferry as one of the most direct influences on his thinking about the dangers of eco-politics. His novel clearly promotes Ferry's idea that a militant ecological order is driven by irrational thinking and global-scale violence and should be rejected in favour of a more tempered response to environmental issues. As a member of the *Académie française* and a former French ambassador, Rufin models a response to environmentalism that is rooted in a traditionally French humanist, secular republicanism.

Much less embedded in the French institutional and political system, Russian-born, French-speaking novelist Iegor Gran has been building his literary *oeuvre* on social critiques of political correctness. In many of his novels, the satirical mode is used to target commonly held views of the left; for example, his novel *O.N.G!* (2003) [NGO!], which won the literary prize for Black Humour in France, recounts the increasingly violent encounters between two neighbouring NGOs, the one environmental (*La Foulée verte*) [Green Stride/Momentum], the other humanitarian (*Enfance et vaccin*) [Childhood and Vaccines]. The two groups' idealistic hopes of 'saving the world' are reduced to petty, vengeful acts that escalate over the course of the story and eventually lead to the imprisonment of one of the members of the environmentalist group for attacking a woman from the humanitarian aid group. To some extent, Gran's writing can be placed in the lineage of satirical writing dating back to Voltaire's novel *Candide* (1759) that tells of a young optimist who, after encountering multiple hardships, gives up the hope of creating the best possible world. Similarly, Gran portrays the disillusionment that follows from experiencing the difficulties humans have in overcoming self-righteousness and one-upmanship.

More specific to the topic of fictionalizing climate change controversy, Gran's novel *L'Écologie en bas de chez moi* (2011) [Ecology Below My Place] pokes fun at environmentalists who aim to reduce global warming by implementing token actions such as turning off lights, driving hybrid cars and using recycled toilet paper. With his usual biting tone, the narrator mocks events like European Bike Week, Earth Day, the Paris Sustainability Show that his friend Vincent regularly attends, but that do not, in the end, require Vincent to make any real changes to his bourgeois lifestyle: 'Le sacerdoce de l'environnement remplit le calendrier. [...] La pratique d'une religion prend du temps [...] Vincent n'est ni moine ni un intégriste. Il est pratiquement croyant – dans la mesure où sa foi n'empiète sur sa mode de vie' (30–31) ['The calling to be an environmentalist makes for a full calendar. [...] Practicing a religion takes time [...] Vincent is neither a monk nor a fundamentalist. He is a practical believer inasmuch as his faith does not encroach on his lifestyle']. But Gran's satirizing of Vincent, as a prime example of an eco-Tartuffe, is not a gratuitous fictionalizing gesture. Even if such a person does not exist in Gran's life, he wrote the book based on an incident that happened in his own life. After publishing a critique of Yann-Arthus Bertrand's eco-documentary *Home* in the daily newspaper *La Libération*, Gran was bombarded by letters and emails from readers accusing him of anti-environmentalism. This *fait divers* [news item] is recounted in the opening chapters of the book as the catalyst for the subsequent estrangement between the narrator and his friend Vincent.

The book blurs the line between fiction and non-fiction further in its attack on environmentalism. Gran includes his original newspaper article at the end of the book as a 'Bonus'. He reinserts lines comparing Bertrand's film and Nazi propaganda film-maker Leni Riefenstahl's work that had been deleted by the *Libération*'s editors. Although Gran never identifies himself as the narrator of the book, the story is told from the first-person perspective and so reduces the distance between the reader and the author. In addition, the book is full of footnotes that constantly interrupt the plot. At first, this seems reminiscent of Michael Crichton's novel, *State of Fear* (2004), in which footnotes are used extensively to dispute climate change findings. But where Crichton cites scientific articles, Gran uses footnotes (over a hundred of them!) to mock the ecological wave that has flooded social media, popular culture and advertising, Hollywood movies and even literary studies. The targets of Gran's cutting social commentary are numerous; no stone of eco-political correctness is left unturned, from sustainable development in Third World countries to 'greenwashing', from Nicholas Hulot and Al Gore to COP 21, from the fourth IPCC report to the famous hockey stick graph curve.

The novel is clearly meant to engage in *humour noir* [black humour], that is, a rhetorical mode that critiques commonly held beliefs from a position of detachment, bitterness and at times amusement.[29] For the narrator, this also means targeting unfounded climate sceptic claims; he scoffs at his dentist's explanation of Greenland's name as proof of climate change cycles (77–78) and then speaks of 'freeing himself from his own side's stupidity' (82). At times, the reader is overwhelmed by the narrator's derision and searches for evidence of a lighter humorous touch or a more sincere tone. It's not until the end of the novel that a partial response is given to the question of what is left standing in the wake of *humour noir* [black humour]: the narrator offers a glimpse of his belief in humanity's capacity for invention, creativity, innovation and civilization, the so-called 'ABCs of humanism' (123). Despite his pessimism in the face of increasing eco-zealotry and fears of global apocalypse, the narrator speaks of turning the page, writing other books, moving on to other subjects. The reader is left to conclude that literature has a role to play, however small, in challenging hegemonic views and holding open alternatives.[30]

Philippe Vasset's *Le Journal intime d'une prédatrice* (2010) [The Diary of a (Female) Predator] also relies heavily on satire as a mode for fictionalizing climate change, but the novel's main target is capitalism's far-reaching death grip on the planet. For the 'Ice Queen' – the moniker given by the media to the head of the multinational company ICECAP – global warming represents a multitude of moneymaking opportunities such as the creation of an Arctic amusement park, new terrain for mining and drilling, and ice-free global shipping passages. The 'female predator' of the story is portrayed as the epitome of advanced global capitalism that destroys every living thing in its path. And yet the third-person narrator of the story through whose eyes we view the main female character (which raises the question of how this story is the 'diary of a female predator') remains sympathetic to his boss, her weaknesses, her failed attempts to appear fearless. When, at the end of the novel, ICECAP stocks plummet because of a possible scandal involving the Ice Queen, it is the narrator who responds to her silent supplication for death, putting his hands around her neck and strangling her.

Vasset is not critiquing advanced capitalism's total lack of concern for life in order to convey an environmentalist message about caring for the earth. In the novel, those working to slow climate change are driven by the same desire as the Ice Queen: to get rich. The company THINICE, run by the Ice Queen's arch-enemy, invests heavily in emissions trading and new technologies for carbon capture. The novel bleakly portrays the current world economic system, leaving the reader with little hope for the future. Yet literature is still held to its role as social critique. Like Gran, Vasset mixes fictional characters with real events and people, including references to then Canadian Prime Minister Stephen Harper, Russian scientists working on cloning the woolly mammoth and proceedings of the UN Climate Change Summit in

Copenhagen. In addition, Vasset experiments with the novel's form. Two-thirds of the story is told in parenthetical 'asides' that convey the narrator's thoughts about the main character. The other third is different characters' direct speech, company memos and letters, and fictional news articles. Completely stripped of descriptive passages, the novel reads like a collection of voices filtered through a strangely disembodied narrative consciousness. Even if climate change serves largely as a plot device, Vasset invents a form that mirrors the effects of advanced capitalism on human behaviour and experience.

Another subgenre that has emerged in the last few years in France is the 'eco-farce' that uses climate change as a source of humour. Augustin Guilbert-Billetdoux's *Le Messie du peuple chauve* (2012) [The Bald People's Messiah] is an example of such a text. The first part recounts the existentialist musings of the protagonist who discovers he is going bald. Treating his physical condition as a mortal illness, he stops working and begins spending more and more time online exchanging messages with other balding men. To convey the seriousness of his 'physical condition', the protagonist heads to a UN climate change summit in India where he hopes to find the largest possible audience for his message. The power struggles and petty squabbles of various climate change stakeholders take up the entire second part of the novel and are narrated using the same deadpan humour as the first. In the end, the novel creates a perplexing analogy between the protagonist's overblown reaction to going bald and the UN's response to climate change catastrophe.

A much more successful eco-farce is Joël Baqué's *La Fonte des glaces* (2017) [Melting Ice] that is funny and ironic without any of the heavy-handedness of Gran's *humour noir* [black humour]. In Baqué's novel, the protagonist, a retired butcher whose life is reduced to a monotonous daily existence after his wife passes away, stumbles upon a taxidermied emperor penguin in a thrift store. He immediately falls in love with the animal and sets up his attic as a 'cold room' for other stuffed penguins that he calls his 'Dream Team'. But this is not enough to satisfy his love for a species going extinct. He travels to Antarctica and then northern Canada, experiencing one surprising adventure after another (including an intimate encounter with an emperor penguin looking for a mate). Even if the protagonist is eventually caught up in the green washing machine – he becomes a mediatized figure for 'Save Our Future', an NGO front for a company using melted iceberg water to produce a new beer – Baqué's text explores the affective and emotional ties of an individual to an iconic species in the era of the sixth great extinction.

While these contemporary novels use humour and satire to represent climate change, science fiction has tended to adopt a more serious attitude towards environmental issues. In *Le Procès de l'homme blanc* (2005) [The Trial of the Whiteman], Yann Quero imagines life on earth in 2143 when climate change has forced humanity to live in a few small pockets on the Asian continent. Leaders of the only remaining functioning state, the Republic of Singapore, attempt to prosecute the 'White Man' for bringing about such a catastrophe. In *L'Avenir ne sera plus ce qu'il était* (2010) [The Future Will Not Be What It Was], Quero situates the story in a much nearer future. On 1 January 2036, alien spaceships land on earth to warn humanity that global warming is threatening life on the planet. The aliens offer to help reduce the effects of climate change, but they are suspected of an ulterior motive: wanting to sterilize humans. Until the end of the story, the reader is left wondering whose side the aliens are on. In both these science fiction adventures, Quero avoids the dangers of an apocalyptic narrative while portraying (more or less successfully) the many complex socio-political threads of a truly global, even interplanetary, crisis.

In *Saison brune* (2012), available in English as *Climate Changed: A Personal Journey through the Science* (2014), Philippe Squarzoni explores the hybrid possibilities of an autobiographical graphic novel. Combining personal anecdotes, interviews with climatologists, explanations of environmental policies and ethical reflections, Squarzoni dives into the contradictions at the heart of individual consumer capitalist behaviour and global climate change issues. With an endorsement by Jean Jouzel and stark black-and-white images, the graphic novel conveys a largely pessimistic message: 'Of course we'll make this transformation one day. We'll do it because we have reached the limits of our natural resources. Or because the warming will suddenly cross a threshold, and a brutal climatic phenomenon will hit us hard. We will accomplish this change under the worst conditions. Forced by circumstance. And way too late' (Squarzoni 455). Taking climate change seriously means in this case adopting the most realistic view possible according to climate change scientists. Even if the novel ends with the question of how not to end on such a dark note, Squarzoni leaves the reader with the work of imagining alternative futures.

From (overly) satirical to (overly) realist, the few French contemporary texts that touch on climate change reveal the limits, dangers and potential of fictionalizing its ethical and political stakes. They challenge the limits of 'literary fiction' by finding other ways 'to imagine the unthinkable beings and events of this era' (Ghosh 33), but without really portraying a new reality in which 'non-human forces have the ability to intervene directly in human thought' (31).

Given the important theoretical work on non-human agency by thinkers such as Bruno Latour, we might ask why French contemporary literature continues to uphold a largely human-actor view of climate change issues.[31] Without hazarding an answer, I point back to the division of knowledge and ethics that has characterized attitudes towards environmental controversies in France. If government deals with policy and scientific institutions with technological solutions, individuals are not required to change their way of living or thinking about the environment. And yet a radical shift in the imagination is what is needed to flourish – and not just survive – in a post-capitalist world.

Conclusion

Climate scepticism no longer echoes in the halls of France's most esteemed scientific institutions. While the year 1992 was key in terms of anti-ecological sentiment in France, the years 2007–2010 were the most important for French climate scepticism. Even as online sites such as *La Pensée unique* [Single-Mindedness] and the *Association des climato-réalistes* [Association of Climate Realists] continue to stir up impact and policy climate scepticism, the most vocal figures such as Claude Allègre have disappeared from the political stage. It's true that a few centre-right intellectuals such as Luc Ferry and Pascal Bruckner tirelessly uphold the principles of progress and reason in the face of what they see as rising eco-dogmatism. But their philosophical arguments lack depth and originality when compared to those of Isabelle Stengers and Bruno Latour, who address the problem of growing barbarism and global eco-modernism, respectively.

A more worrisome trend is the shift from print newspapers and magazines to online news sites whose coverage of climate change issues tends to be more limited. As a recent study of the media coverage of COP 21 demonstrates, BuzzFeed and Vice (as well as their respective equivalents in other languages) homed in on one or two issues during the summit, about which traditional media had presented a more complex view, including water scarcity, the use of renewable energy, health impacts and food security, to name a few (Painter, Kristiansen and Schäfer).[32] By targeting the single, attention-grabbing image, social media simplify and even distort the complex social problem at hand. This is true of both anti- and pro-environmentalist websites (see, for example, *National Geographic*'s video of a starving polar bear that went viral in early December 2017). Readers can counter these effects by engaging with a wide range of texts outside their linguistic, cultural and political comfort zones. Part of the process of moving beyond the internet's echo chambers is being exposed to a polyphony of discordant voices. For ecocritics, this means reading texts like Baqué's *La Fonte des glaces* [Melting Ice] or Vasset's *Le Journal intime d'une prédatrice* [Diary of a (Female) Predator] that satirize climate change politics.

As for the current eco-political climate in France, there has been a subtle shift to a more global environmentalism since Emmanuel Macron's election as president in May 2017. Affirming his role as the 'saviour' of the Paris COP 21 climate accord after Donald Trump withdrew his country's support, Macron created the 'Make Our Planet Great Again' research fund. With a budget envelope of 60 million euros, the fund aims to lure American scientists who want to work on climate change issues to France. It can accommodate from 30 to 50 research projects of up to five years (so far, 18 American scientists have been accepted). Riffing on Trump's campaign slogan – 'Make America Great Again' – the fund clearly appeals to an Anglophone audience in order to promote a global ecological view of the planet. Macron is manoeuvring France into the position of main player on the world stage of climate change politics (in part to fill the void left by the United States). However, he does so by partially turning his back on the cultural tensions that continue to simmer in France (McCauley).

It is at this point that cultural ecocriticism intervenes to expose a problematic appeal to global environmental politics that glosses over social identities and differences. The objective is not to argue once again for culture over nature, as if ecocritics had not already fully exposed the pitfalls of such dualist thinking. Rather, it means analysing the ways in which climate change is embedded in different socio-cultural contexts, in which social and environmental issues are bound together. In a discussion with Bruno Latour and Baptiste Morizot, French philosopher Pierre Charbonnier explains that a new 'land/earth' politics is needed for considering climate change and social identities conjointly.

> Nous avons toujours sous les pieds la même planète, mais plus tout à fait la même terre. Et avec cette transformation, ce sont nos relations sociales et politiques qui elles aussi prennent une nouvelle forme. Cela s'ajoute à l'équivoque que recèle la terre depuis plus longtemps: elle est à la fois ce dont on vit et là où l'on vit, ce qui donne les fruits qui garantissent la reproduction des individus et des groupes, et ce qui conditionne une partie de leur identité. Les frictions induites par cette équivoque sont parvenues aujourd'hui, sous la pression du changement climatique, à un seuil critique. à tel point que nous sommes sans doute poussés à modifier nos repères intellectuels, la boussole conceptuelle qui nous a servi, depuis l'avènement de la modernité, à nous repérer dans l'espace politique. (228)

[We still have the same planet under our feet, but no longer exactly the same land/earth. And with this transformation, our social and political relationships are also taking on new forms. This adds to the ambiguity the land/earth has harboured for an even longer period: it is both that from which one draws life and the place where one lives, that which gives the fruits that guarantee the reproduction of individuals and groups and that which conditions a part of their identity. Under the pressure of climate change, the tensions arising from this ambiguity have reached a critical threshold, to the point that we must now modify our intellectual references, the conceptual compass we have been using since the birth of modernity to find our bearings in political space.]

6

Science and Technology Studies, Ecocriticism and Climate Change

A mapping of the environmental humanities would have more trouble drawing some borders than others. Multidisciplinary critical animal studies overlaps ecocriticism of an activist orientation, whereas environmental history thrives nearby with relatively little commerce. Science and Technology Studies (STS), another agglomeration, might seem to share interests with ecocriticism, such as the cultural place of scientific knowledge, and yet there have been few systematic attempts at interdisciplinary study to date. In a 2001 article, STS scholar Bruce Clarke critiques ecocriticism's at times unquestioned use of scientific theories as objective truth and explains the work of Bruno Latour and Michel Serres as models of a more socially complex understanding of the sciences. Similarly, ecocritic Ursula Heise asserts that ecocriticism must at some point confront 'science's claim that it delivers descriptions of nature that are essentially value-neutral' (4). A few figures from STS, notably Donna Haraway, Bruno Latour and Karen Barad, feature in ecocritical texts of a 'new materialist' bent, but the fundamental epistemological challenges have seldom registered.

Climate change, in particular, is a given in ecocriticism; the main question is how literature might help raise awareness and deepen consciousness of climatic risks. While it might be true to say, in an ideal world, that 'ecocriticism is not the literary critical department of the IPCC' (Garrard 186), that is how researchers in the field have largely behaved. STS scholars, as we will see, treat the IPCC as an object of study, seeking to improve its effectiveness with their analyses. This chapter, then, brings an agnostic STS perspective to bear on climate science, eliciting contrasts with ecocriticism that may nudge the latter in new directions.

Fearful symmetries and false equivalence

In the course of our research, we noticed many symmetrical claims made by both warmists and sceptics:

- *Ad hominem* attacks on the integrity or intellectual capacity of opponents.
- Allegations of conspiracy on the other side, such as Oreskes and Conway's *Merchants of Doubt* and James Delingpole's *Watermelons*; Claude Allègre's *L'Imposture climatique* [The Climate Imposture] and Sylvestre Huet's *L'Imposteur, c'est lui* [The Imposter, It's Him].
- Claims of motivated reasoning against opponents. Myanna Lahsen notes, 'Like their contrarian counterparts, advocates point to the extra-scientific factors propelling their opponents while shunning recognition of the fact that they themselves are similarly influenced by values, beliefs, and interests' (550). Each side believes in their own devotion to rationality and to rigorous science while the other slides into emotionalism, ideology and fear.
- Representation of one's own position as 'David' battling the 'Goliath' of Big Oil/Big Eco, as claimed by British motoring journalist Jeremy Clarkson: 'The eco-ists have the ear of the prime minister, the leader of the opposition, the whole of the BBC, most of the country's newspapers, every single university campus and nearly every government in the world. Whereas I have the ear of the Ford Capri Owners Club. Which is comprised of half a dozen men in Dennis Waterman-style leather bomber jackets' (77).
- Complaints of severe harassment heard from warmists (Powell), sceptics (Booker loc. 6608) and 'moderates' like Hans von Storch: 'As a scientist, I strive for independence from vested interests. I am in the pocket of neither Exxon nor Greenpeace, and for this I come under fire from both sides – the skeptics and the alarmists – who have fiercely opposing views but are otherwise siblings in their methods and contempt' (Storch).
- Accusations of anthropocentric arrogance, long levelled by environmentalists against Christians and humanists, are now fired back by sceptics (see Chapter 4). Marc Morano quotes geologist Robert Giegengack: 'The Earth is fine. It has been around for four and a half billion years. It was here before we were here. We can't save the Earth' (59).
- Reality of a knowledge-action gap, albeit one that sceptics celebrate: 'Fortunately, the gap between rhetoric and reality … is far greater than I can recall with any other issue' (Lawson 103).

- Satirical representation of 'carbon offsets' as equivalent to medieval indulgences (Delingpole loc. 3710; Monbiot 'Selling Indulgences'); of 'eco-asceticism' as a form of *macération* [scourging of the flesh] (Bruckner).
- Acceptance of an idealized conception of science, as seen in responses to the 'Climategate' emails (discussed below): 'Scientists and their critics alike interpreted the stolen emails as embarrassing deviations from the alleged social demands of a consensual, objective, and accessible science. They referred to "dogma" and "interests" as sources of corruption in science and appealed to "openness" and "transparency" as a means to resolve disagreement' (Ramírez-i-Ollé 402).
- Dismissal of the IPCC as 'political', either because it is run by socialists or because its consensus-seeking mandate marginalizes more alarming projections; the 'grande erreur' of the Nobel committee when deciding to award the 2007 Peace Prize to the IPCC (Foucart).
- Claims from both sides that if we but 'follow the money', we can identify the economic motivations for concerns or doubts about climate change.

Claims may be symmetrical simply because contending parties agree – that carbon offsets assuage guilt without reducing emissions, for example. Moreover, such symmetries may be characteristic of impassioned debate in general; it is human nature to claim that *my* views are informed by logic and evidence, whereas *yours* reflect naked self-interest (Haidt 98–99). Symmetrical accusations of anthropocentric *hubris* probably reflect little more than poor definition of the terms involved. The knowledge-action gap and the sense that opponents are fantastically well-resourced, as well as conspiratorial, seem quite distinctive, though. Both warmists and sceptics expend significant effort quantifying the financial resources ranged against them, which are taken in the first place to encompass the fossil fuels industry and in the second, climate activism and publicly funded climate science in their entirety. Thus, an academic study of the role of Conservative Think Tanks (CTTs) in supporting climate scepticism claims that 'the self-portrayal of sceptics as marginalised "Davids" battling the powerful "Goliath" of environmentalists and environmental scientists is a charade, as sceptics are supported by politically powerful CTTs funded by wealthy foundations and corporations' (Jacques, Dunlap and Freeman 364). James Delingpole acknowledges the role of CTTs, but claims the vast funding of universities, environmental organizations and the United Nations shows that '"Big Eco" is a rather more significant player in the AGW propaganda game than anything Big Carbon can muster' (loc. 1174). Is there anything to choose between these symmetrical claims?

We address the question of competing *interests* below, but there is clearly a risk of false equivalence here. Tenured academics (i.e. not British scholars) are not *employees* in the way that Heartland Institute advisors are; they ought in principle to be more independent. Furthermore, direct funding of advocacy organizations (warmist or sceptic) is very different to expenditure on satellites and ice-core studies, all of which gets lumped into the 'Big Eco' category. *Pace* conservative American suspicion of 'government-funded research', the latter is distributed by means of highly competitive anonymous peer review, which is imperfect insurance against bias but still distinct from political lobbying. Having said that, both sides have reason to think themselves underdogs: we are all reliant on a fossil-fuelled economy, giving us good reason to ignore the 'inconvenient truth', and there is, at the same time, a strong *cultural* bias against corporations, as Delingpole observes:

> However independent-minded and politically acute we may think we are, we're all prey to certain cultural attitudes so deeply ingrained that we're probably not even aware of them. One of these is the popular notion that funding from Big Business (Big Oil, Big Carbon, Big Koch …) is tainted, compromised and almost inevitably corrupting, while funding from a nature charity, or even from a government agency with a nice-sounding concept like 'Environmental Protection' in its title must be well over 3,500 times nicer.
>
> (loc. 1228–32)

Modern culture, especially the sector ironically dubbed 'social' media, facilitates cycles of outrage and harassment that make everyone involved in the debate feel like a 'persecuted minority'. The crucial question for climate politics is how to counteract that damaging tendency.

A small contribution would be to question *apparent* symmetries that conceal objective differences, such as Big Oil versus Big Eco, but acknowledge genuine symmetries, such as the universality of motivated reasoning, group dynamics and the cultural cognition of risks. Dan Kahan and colleagues, who have demonstrated that improved science literacy actually *increased* political polarization in an American study group, emphasize that

> a hierarchical individualist who expresses anxiety about climate change might well be shunned by his co-workers at an oil refinery in Oklahoma City. A similar fate will probably befall an egalitarian communitarian English professor who reveals to colleagues in Boston that she thinks the scientific consensus on climate change is a hoax.
>
> (734)

The risk of ostracism, in each case, is far greater and more salient than any probable, immediate climatic or economic risk to the individual – especially if stigmatizing, polarizing language continues to be the norm in climate activism and sceptical counter-activism.

Scholarship can make a contribution by addressing obvious biases. As discussed in the Introduction, warmism is so seldom questioned as a social, psychological or cultural phenomenon that symmetrical treatment is striking when it does occur, as in Lorraine Whitmarsh's observation: 'It should also be noted … that this research equally highlights the ideological basis of belief in (as well as denial of) climate change, since high proenvironmental values and left-of-centre political views predispose individuals to believe in the reality and severity of climate change' (698). To take an example from our own field, ecocritics are fully aware of the limitations of apocalyptic rhetoric; in the name of symmetrical analysis and depolarization we ought to explore openly our agreement with climate sceptics when they criticize 'climate alarmism'.

Perhaps the most persistent symmetrical claim is that the opposition has been corrupted by interests. If it were true, it could seriously distort both climate science and politics. Luckily, such claims can be checked, to a reasonable degree, to see if the apparent symmetry is real. The warmist claim is supported by research that tracks the relationship of specific authors (most of them American or British) to CTTs (Dunlap and McCright; Dunlap and Jacques; Oreskes and Conway), although the correlation has weakened in recent years and the conspiracist argument itself has been sharply criticized (Grundmann). It doesn't seem to be considered that individuals with sceptical views are invited to work or publish with CTTs, rather than having developed their views as a result of such relationships.

As regards the credibility of the IPCC, Sonja Boehmer-Christiansen, a rare example of an openly sceptical STS scholar, argues that scholarship should attend to the question: 'Who is likely to gain from emission reduction?' (70). Her answer claims that climate scientists, environmental organizations, government and inter-governmental bureaucracies, and renewable and nuclear energy corporations used the IPCC to universalize their sectional interests:

> The global warming threat was constructed in the 1980s by a coalition of interested parties offering expertise and technologies to solve the problem. The climate threat, like the limits to growth scare beforehand, offered new opportunities to environmental bureaucracies and professionals who found the proposed solutions empowering. A belief system was provided by

> environmental religiosity, while science, engineering, and economics provided the rationalizations from which global and selected national bureaucracies would derive authority for promoting technological change, 'greenmailing' opponents, and raising revenue.
>
> (88)

In particular, she presents evidence that the IPCC's representation of scientific uncertainty has consistently been driven by political, not scientific, considerations.

Boehmer-Christiansen's assertions should be taken seriously, even if her rhetoric (such as referring to funding agencies as scientists' 'paymasters' (402)) sometimes undermines her diagnostic purpose. Simon Shackley and Tora Skodvin go one better, taking the question of interests seriously enough to look closely at both Boehmer-Christiansen's argument and the processes of the IPCC. They point out that:

> There is a serious circularity in the argument. How do we know that increased funding is the driving force? Because there has been an increase in funding!
>
> (Shackley and Skodvin 176)

In fact, funding to specific institutions and organizations fluctuates, just as one would expect in a competitive environment. Moreover, it is unclear from Boehmer-Christiansen's analysis whether self-interested scientists are the driving force of the IPCC, or 'pawns in a battle of political heavyweights' (177). Shackley and Skodvon respond to her uncertainty manipulation claim by narrating a fascinating argument among scientists and governmental representatives about the Global Warming Potential (GWP, a key numerical quantity used in climate models) of methane during the development of the Second Assessment Report (1994). Crucially, their detailed analysis does not dismiss the notion that interests were in play, but it does highlight the heterogeneity and mutability of those interests (see also Sismondo 50–52). For example, there were participants who opposed a more 'politically useful', less conspicuously uncertain, representation, as well as those who supported it. The arguments presented at the meeting traversed matters of technical science, policy representation and IPCC process. Shackley and Skodvin's judgement on the methane GWP episode is more nuanced than Boehmer-Christiansen's assertion that homogenous, unidirectional interests bias the IPCC towards greater certainty:

> Clearly, the boundary between what was an issue for science and what was an issue for policy was not at all obvious and subject to negotiation. In fact the position of that boundary depended to an extent on how scientists thought policy makers

> distinguished between science and policy themselves and in the implications of that for the use of GWPs in policy making in certain industrialized countries. In making these judgements the scientists acted themselves as unofficial policy makers.

Paul N. Edwards's fascinating history of climate modelling, *A Vast Machine* (2010), reveals in still greater detail how computer models, far from manipulating data in the service of political interests, are required to *elicit* usable data from vast reams of patchy, heterogeneous weather records:

> All modern climate data are modeled in a variety of ways to correct systematic errors, interpolate readings to grids, and render readings from various instrument types commensurable. *If we cannot trust models without evidence, neither can we trust evidence without models.*
>
> (412)

Given the complexity, recursivity, global interconnectedness and intense scrutiny of the climate knowledge infrastructure Edwards describes, and the '*proliferation within convergence*' (436) of climate images (including, crucially, climate sensitivity estimates) it yields, the notion of 'science' obediently yielding 'rationalizations' for environmental religiosity is frankly absurd.

These scholarly depictions of climatological knowledge production do, admittedly, contravene the fiction of the disinterested scientist, as well as the clear distinction between hypothesis and evidence required by Karl Popper's influential falsificationist philosophy of science. They are also more complex (and interesting) than the simplistic, *ex post facto*, conspiratorial narrative constructed by Boehmer-Christiansen and borrowed by many other sceptics. Detailed, questioning attention to the IPCC must honestly acknowledge *both* its hybrid scientifico-political character *and* the ways it has changed in response to fair criticism over successive iterations. Edwards, who has studied the IPCC more closely than any sceptical writer, concludes:

> Despite its imperfections, [the IPCC's] exhaustive, multiple-level, highly transparent review process remains the best approach we have for evaluating climate knowledge. It brings controversy within consensus, it limits bias, and it connects the world's far-flung climate science communities in an ongoing process.
>
> (429)

Given important differences between the scientific and lay understanding of 'uncertainty' (Shackley and Wynne; Zehr), as well as the inherent complexity of earth systems science, conveying the present state of knowledge is fiendishly difficult. Nevertheless, the IPCC process has continually revised both its processes and its conclusions, and not always towards greater alarm: AR5, for instance, revises the lower bound of *likely* equilibrium climate sensitivity downward from 2°C to 1.5°, which is hard to comprehend if warmist interests rule supreme ('IPCC, Intergovernmental Panel on Climate Change').

The truth is, as we have sought to show here, that conspiracist and *ad hominem* attacks, of whatever orientation, consistently underplay internal dissension and conflicting interests. Even the 'fossil fuel industry' is fractured between coal, oil and gas, between traditional and 'tough' sources of oil, and between the differing priorities of state oil companies and their transnational private competitors, not to mention the seemingly contradictory behaviour of players in the fossil fuel industry who invest in renewable energy or promote large-scale sustainable developments. STS research tends to emphasize the 'external' factors that shape scientific enquiry, including economic and political interests, but does not, for the most part, deny the importance of 'internal' disputation and consensus regarding data, models, physical laws and research methods (Hacking 90–91). Our methodological agnosticism towards climate scepticism likewise brackets 'internalist' scientific issues, such as 'the problem of the mode of existence [...] of neutrinos, genes, fossils, ['global climate'] or other scientific creatures' (Stengers 25), paying attention instead to external matters of rhetoric and framing that could equally well be applied to warmist literature. By contrast, popular exposés of climate scepticism, such as *Merchants of Doubt*, critique it in externalist terms, while accepting internalist arguments for the warmist position. STS-informed scholarship would be symmetrical, unlike most ecocritical and environmental communications research to date, *and* more attentive and sceptical than most 'sceptical' treatments of the influence of external factors on climate science.

A related, and equally tenacious, sceptical claim is that the climate issue has *politicized science* in favour of warmism, memorably captured by Nigel Lawson as 'the PC [political correctness] at the heart of the IPCC' (105). Contrarily, there is evidence, highlighted by climate activists, that the IPCC's consensus-building approach, combined with its embedded science-policy interface, introduces a bias *against* acceptance of extreme climatic risks ('Climate Science Glossary – IPCC Consensus'). A similar bias may affect the media, contrary to sceptical claims of doom-mongering: a US study found news outlets were reluctant to credit 'worst-case scenarios', and concluded that 'if reporters wish to discuss "both sides" of the climate issue, the scientifically legitimate "other side" is that, if anything, global climate disruption may prove to be significantly worse than has been suggested in scientific consensus estimates to date' (Freudenburg and Muselli 483). More interesting, for our purposes, are the arguments from STS scholars and environmental humanists that climate change is eroding a boundary between science and politics that was always fictitious, and that a challenge to the 'scientification' of environmental issues was long overdue. At stake in both the critique and the celebration of politicization is Robert Merton's influential delineation of the ideal scientific ethos in 1942, with its norms of 'universalism, commun[al]ism, disinterestedness, and organized scepticism' (Sismondo 23). The sceptical politicization claim is, in this instance, the *inverse* of the STS position, which welcomes open acknowledgement of the politics of science.

In the Anglophone world, the popular stereotype of climate sceptics is that they are uniformly 'anti-scientific', but our research reveals a far more complex picture.[1] As Ted Nordhaus and Michael Shellenburger point out:

> The conventional wisdom is that environmentalists and global warming deniers like best-selling novelist Michael Crichton disagree over the value of science. But both share most of the same beliefs about Science and the need for it to stay clear of values and politics. This statement – 'Because in the end, science offers us the only way out of politics. And if we allow science to become politicized, then we are lost' – was uttered by Michael Crichton, but it could just as easily have been uttered by most environmental scientists.
>
> (139)

Crichton's idealism can be criticized for only seeing bias on one side of the argument, but we must still ask whether or not scientific objectivity is either achievable or desirable. Crichton's view is shared by many working scientists, which has made it more difficult for the IPCC to recruit to its working groups (Shackley and Skodvin 177). Moreover, despite the pervasive commercialization of American university science in the wake of the 1980 Bayh-Dole Act, the norm of disinterestedness remains a strong, if remote, regulative ideal in American science, as Sheila Jasanoff has argued:

> Pure science is another American Eden. Its loss is perpetually mourned; attempts to regain the forsaken state of grace are a recurrent national project, even an obsession. In the politics of science, the rhetoric of the fall harmonizes with that of restoring science's purity, especially when scientific knowledge is imported into complex social and political contexts. Notions of science's platonic specialness abound in the discourse of public policy, expressed in binary oppositions between good or sound science and science that is substandard because it is biased, not objective, or tainted by interests.
>
> (228)

All the while though, STS scholars like Bruno Latour have questioned the 'modern constitution' that divides science and politics, matters of fact and matters of value, truth and opinion. From this perspective, the problem is not the advent of politicized science, but the mistaken belief that there was ever any other kind, and Merton's norms represent a disreputable *ancien régime* in which idealized Science (as opposed to the messy, diverse business of the sciences) was empowered to inform and regulate politics without ever being contaminated by it in return. Environmentalism accepted too easily this regulatory role for Science as a way to short-circuit democratic debate, 'introduc[ing] nature into political preoccupations that had earlier been too exclusively oriented toward humans' but '*continu[ing], alas, to use nature to abort politics*' (Latour, *Politics of Nature* 19).

The problem with the IPCC, especially in its first few iterations, was that it aimed to 'scientificate'[2] climate change by *feeding* supposedly value-free scientific knowledge into an intensely political international process of negotiation. The failure of that effort to deliver the desired outcomes is seen as confirming what STS scholars like Latour already suspected:

> Conceptions of politics and conceptions of nature have always formed a pair as firmly united as the two seats on a seesaw, where one goes down when the other goes up, and vice versa. There has never been any other politics than the politics of nature, and there has never been any other nature than the nature of politics.
> (*Politics of Nature* 28)

This view does not imply that scientific knowledge is *reducible* to political preference; rather it means that the science–policy nexus must be sliced and diced in different, less dualistic, ways. For one thing, Latour's analysis demands that we come to terms with the *irreducibility* of dissensus:

> Every ecological crisis opens up a controversy among experts, and these controversies generally preclude the establishment of a common front of indubitable matters of fact that politicians could subsequently use in support of their decisions. In the face of this familiar situation … two attitudes are possible: we can wait for the sciences to come up with additional proofs that will put an end to the uncertainties, or we can consider uncertainty as the inevitable ingredient of crises in the environment … The second attitude has the advantage of replacing something that is not open to discussion with something that can be debated, and of binding together the two notions of objective science and controversy: the more realities there are, the more arguments there are.
> (*Politics of Nature* 63)

While climate scientists continue to seek 'additional proofs' (though, really, how many more Assessment Reports do we need?), it must also be accepted that 'climate change' has a broad range of meanings that cannot be determined or constrained by geophysical sciences alone.

Mike Hulme, founding director of the Tyndall Centre for Climate Change Research, comes to this very conclusion in *Why We Disagree about Climate Change*, a wide-ranging critique of scientification from an influential climate scientist. Hulme avows that 'the idea of climate exists as much in human mind and in the matrices of cultural practices as it exists as an independent and objective physical category' (28). He contrasts the 'wicked problem' of climate change with the superficially similar issue of stratospheric ozone depletion: where the latter was eminently suited to scientification and political resolution by the 1987 Montreal Protocol, the former is strikingly different in terms of 'the causes, consequences and actors involved' (292). The IPCC/COP process, which aimed to introduce a similar intergovernmental protocol in Kyoto, underestimated the pre-existing salience of climate:

> Humanity has a very long cultural history of understanding the idea of climate and of experiencing its sensual intimacy. There is no such cultural or sensual history of relating to stratospheric ozone. While both phenomena are largely invisible to our senses, revealed through the constructions of environmental science, climate and ozone occupy radically different sites and fulfil quite different roles in our cultural imaginations.
>
> (292)

From the STS-informed perspective Hulme adopts, climate change is a perfect example of what Silvio Funtowicz and Jerome Ravetz call 'post-normal science' (PNS), where 'facts are uncertain, values in dispute, stakes high and decisions urgent' (744). By contrast with 'normal science', as described by Thomas Kuhn, PNS is guided by a new methodology in which

> uncertainty is not banished but is managed, and values are not presupposed but are made explicit. The model for scientific argument is not a formalized deduction but an interactive dialogue. The paradigmatic science is no longer one in which location (in place and time) and process are irrelevant to explanations. The historical dimension, including reflection on humanity's past and future, is becoming an integral part of a scientific characterization of Nature.
>
> (740)

Funtowicz and Ravetz recommend that, under the increased pressures of PNS, it will be vital to *extend* legitimating processes such as peer review to a broader constituency, albeit with the proviso that 'with mutual respect among various perspectives and forms of knowing, there is a possibility for the development of a genuine and effective element in the life of science' (741). As we have seen in our studies of climate scepticism, respect is rather thin on the ground.

It is particularly ironic that PNS, which was precisely intended to integrate incommensurate perspectives, itself became embroiled in the polarized debate. James Delingpole's *Watermelons* goes out of its way to attack Funtowicz, Ravetz and Hulme for supposedly admitting that

> 'Climate change' ... has little if anything to do with 'science' as you or I might understand the concept. It's not a genuine problem to be solved, but a handy excuse – with a fashionable green patina – to advance a particular social and political agenda under the cloak of ecological righteousness and scientific authority.
>
> (loc. 1816–19)

This from an author whose whole thesis is that Anthropogenic Global Warming (AGW) theory has little or nothing to do with science (loc. 1966). The honest effort to turn down the rhetorical temperature and move beyond a narrowly scientificated argument is depicted as a sneaky attempt to dispense with Mertonian norms of scientific probity. Ah well, it was worth a try.

Ravetz himself posted a discussion of PNS on the sceptical website wattsupwiththat, and was shocked by the fury of some of the responses. Ravetz's post in fact challenges the validity of climate models and agrees that the 'Climategate' emails, hacked or filched from the Climate Research Unit at the University of East Anglia in 2009, reveal 'the contradictions between scientific probity and campaigning zeal' (Ravetz 150). But where Ravetz claims that 'the combination of non-critical "normal science" with anti-critical "evangelical science" was lethal' (151) – in other words, climate science was not post-normal *enough* – his sharpest critics allege that 'post-normal science is one of the manipulative arts that Machiavelli would have been proud of' (154). In a reflective essay on the exchange, Ravetz acknowledges how PNS might be seen as extenuating scientific fraud:

> This [sceptical attack on his own work] does not deny that much or most of climate science, recognising and coping with deep scientific uncertainties, is sound; it's the policy-relevant core, that we might call 'global-warming science', that is perceived as rotten. So all of my methodologising, Mike Hulme's sociologising ... are quite beside the point. The damning facts are in, and they

> are either recognised or denied. On that basis it is easy to suppose that I am a sophisticated apologist for the enemy, and that all my uncertainty-mongering effectively provides a licence for those bad people to dissemble and deceive. (156)

The more expert committees exonerate the UEA Climate Research Unit (CRU) scientists (there have now been nine investigations in total ('Climate Science Glossary')) the wider the supposed 'whitewash' of nefarious activity extends, according to sceptics. In their strongest forms, such claims are indefensible: the main allegations of conspiracy and fraud depend on highly selective quotation and interpretation of a tiny proportion of the 1,073 emails. Even so, the CRU scientists' reluctance to release data sets and their efforts to marginalize divergent perspectives are obvious, and the toe-curling exchange about how they could secure prizes for one another is deeply unedifying. In that context, it is not surprising, although it is disappointing, that Climategate continues to be rehearsed endlessly as a 'smoking gun' rather than a teachable moment for all concerned.

The climate science community took heed of the episode, making more data sets publicly available and reconsidering peer-review policies, in what science journalist Fred Pearce calls 'a sea-change from the days in the CRU bunker'. Climate geeks of whatever persuasion can now create their own graphs of temperature change and Arctic ice from the data sets, thanks to www.woodfortrees.org, a self-funded, independent website created by a British software developer. STS scholars who took the opportunity to review their relationship to climate science concluded that social scientists had been too unwilling to subject it to critique for fear of 'abetting distorting backlash campaigns that often depart from indications of weaknesses in climate science and associated institutions, however big or small' (Lahsen 551). Myanna Lahsen's detailed examination of *Merchants of Doubt*, for instance, pointedly argues that Conway and Oreskes dismiss criticisms of climate models by sceptics that, in more scholarly contexts, the latter author has explored in detail (Lahsen 553; Oreskes, Shrader-Frechette and Belitz; Oreskes, Stainforth and Smith). She presents a persuasive argument that the *lack* of STS discussion of climate science could help to engender mistrust in sceptical (in the broad sense) publics:

> The US public is right to believe that scientific experts still are arguing about ACC in terms of its likely extent and impacts. They are even smart to believe that, because they see beyond what they are being told by powerful and prestigious scientists and analysts; they may rightly perceive logical inconsistency when

> advocates of concern [admit] that scientific research always involves doubt, that scientists by nature are inclined to question, that scientific findings involve evidence the details of which remain unclear and can be falsified by new discoveries and, on the other hand, suggest that the science is settled and that scientists all agree about ACC – as if dissent does not exist, also outside of the small faction of contrarians. They may even have read scientific analyses of how the dynamics of decision making and consensus formation processes can tend to engender belief polarization, overconfidence and marginalization of skeptical arguments, and how this also happens within the IPCC … and around the science it assesses.
>
> (554)

Scholars such as Roger A. Pielke Jr., Stéfan Aykut, Werner Krauss and Hélène Guillemot analyse climate scepticism within the larger context of climate change as an evolving public controversy. Identifying the science/politics nexus as their object of study, they consider a wide variety of actors whose positions cannot be reduced to 'for' or 'against' climate science (though Pielke himself has been labelled a denier). As Guillemot concludes at the end of her study of the reshaping of scientific fields and epistemic cultures brought about by climate change controversies, 'Ce n'est pas la confiance dans la réalité du changement climatique, mais le cadrage même du problème qui est en cause ici' (349) ['It is not confidence in the reality of climate change that is called into question here, but the framing of the problem itself.'] Their approach clearly counters the polarized positions of those who reveal the 'falsehoods' of climate scepticism and also those who chastise climate change science for getting too 'mixed up' with environmental politics (Foucart).

We discuss the '97% consensus' claim in the last chapter. For the moment, we need only agree with Lahsen that scepticism is actually *sustained* by an idealized conception of climate science, which is then all too vulnerable to disruption by evidence of competing interests, modelling limitations, science-policy negotiations, vexed uncertainty judgements and so on (see also Wynne). As in our discussion of Boehmer-Christiansen's critique of the IPCC above, we suggest that the solution is not to assert, ever more stridently, 'settled science, nothing to see here', in the hope of fending off or silencing sceptics. Rather, it lies in detailed, agnostic and symmetrical treatment of both warmist and sceptical positions, so as to, in Lahsen's words, 'open up [climate change] to broader public debate and decision-making in ways that give proper weight to scientific reason and evidence while also recognizing the political and economic dimensions that [scientification] obfuscates, but which are inescapable' (556) As we have argued, notably in Chapter 4, such an approach also helps us to talk more openly about the implicit values and cosmologies that are brought to bear in the *interpretation* of climate change, including by ecocritics who seem unwilling to acknowledge the contingency of their own spiritual and political worldviews. Climate change is 'inescapably' a literary and cultural phenomenon, as well as a political and economic one, but ecocritical treatments have always been asymmetrical and unselfconsciously committed, until now.

Sceptics, of course, quoted hacked CRU emails selectively to emphasize transgressions of Mertonian norms. One particular email, from Professor Phil Jones, was recycled endlessly: 'I've just completed Mike's Nature trick of adding in the real temps to each series for the last 20 years (ie from 1981 onwards) [and] from 1961 for Keith's to hide the decline' (cited in Ryghaug and Skjølsvold 300). There were numerous responses from the scientific community, predominant among them some acknowledgement of 'shortcomings' or 'human failings' combined with *re-assertion* of climate science as 'ideally resulting from an accumulative consensus generated by socially detached individuals who strive to make data available to non-scientists' (Ramírez-i-Ollé 401) – the Mertonian ideal, in short. What both attackers and defenders of the CRU miss is that the hacked emails *themselves* reflect considerable debate about the legitimacy of combining a mix of pre-1961 and proxy records with the 'real temps' (i.e. modern instrumental record). Again, detailed attention by STS scholars highlights a more plausible and intriguing process than the simplistic conspiracy 'revealed' by sceptics, in which 'consensus' – a public performance of unanimity – had to be painstakingly constructed through a complex, recursive set of methodological and rhetorical arguments among a group of scientists with clearly divergent views (Ryghaug and Skjølsvold 302). Marianne Ryghaug and Tomas Moe Skjølsvold conclude not that lay publics are 'ignorant fools' who ought to be patronized and ignored but that we can all learn from the Climategate emails how science in-the-making actually works:

> [Climate] debates are performed in much the same way as is reported in many ethnographic studies of scientific work. Unfortunately, many journalists seem unaware of such work and have judged the e-mail conversations on a kind of Boy Scout image of science. Thus, they appear to be surprised that scientific facts are made and not just discovered, that they emerge as products of deliberation and persuasion, that methodological doubts may be resilient, and that scientists' trustworthiness is important. Thus, in the long run scientists may be better served by greater openness with respect to the actual practice of science, rather than upholding the conventional image of cool, restricted display of instrumental rationality.
>
> (302)

The central question for STS, and for ecocritical practice attuned to it, is how to question the 'Boy Scout image of science' in such a way as to secure broader respect for, and participation in, climate knowledge-making.

STS scholarship has vacillated, all along, between celebration of its own irreverence towards the idol of Science and tetchy explanation of why it is not, after all, 'anti-science' (let alone anti-Reality). Bruno Latour's mournful, defensive reflections in 'Why Has Critique Run Out of Steam?' acknowledge the pleasure of subversion, but focus on answering the more serious charge:

> While we spent years trying to detect the real prejudices hidden behind the appearance of objective statements, do we now have to reveal the real objective and incontrovertible facts hidden behind the illusion of prejudices? And yet entire Ph.D. programs are still running to make sure that good American kids are learning the hard way that facts are made up, that there is no such thing as natural, unmediated, unbiased access to truth, that we are always prisoners of language, that we always speak from a particular standpoint, and so on, while dangerous extremists [i.e. climate sceptics] are using the very same argument of social construction to destroy hard-won evidence that could save our lives.
>
> (227)

Latour laments that 'no matter what we do [in STS], when we try to reconnect scientific objects with their aura, their crown, their web of associations … we always appear to weaken them, not to strengthen their claim to reality' (237). Why, in principle, should reuniting science and society be understood in terms of contamination, rather than celebration? Well, Latour is being a little disingenuous about STS, which has overwhelmingly preferred 'debunking' to boosting scientific prestige (Hacking 35–62). More frankly, Isabelle Stengers acknowledges: 'Nothing is more difficult than to accept the necessity of complicating a struggle that is already so uncertain, grappling with an adversary able to profit from any weakness, from any naïve goodwill' (23). Our procedure in this book consciously extends goodwill to climate sceptics – some will say too much – but not, given our extensive acquaintance with its canon, naïveté.

Perhaps ecocriticism, which nailed its green colours to the mast from the outset, should steer clear of STS for fear of recapitulating its seeming complicity with 'dangerous extremists'. In other contexts, scholars have pushed back against scientification and technocratic framing of environmental issues:

> Questions of value, difference, and competing worldviews must be *re-enlivened* as crucial parts of the conversation. We need a politics of environmental difference.
>
> (Åsberg, Neimanis and Hedrén 76)

Indeed, but will this conversation include conservatives and climate sceptics?

We suspect that ecocritics will share our willingness to complicate the 'Boy Scout image of science', and we recall that our study has elicited the diversity concealed behind stigmatizing monikers. Were ecocriticism to ally itself with STS, it would attend symmetrically to anti-environmental and environmental cultures, validating conservative perspectives and critiquing alarmism where appropriate. Where, for example, are the ecocritical treatments of Naomi Oreskes and Erick Conway's *The Decline of Western Civilization*, which proclaims its scientific plausibility despite projecting a climate sensitivity higher than at least 95 per cent of the model runs used by the IPCC? STS-informed scholarship would, moreover, invite questioning of the ways ecocritics tend to align activism and research, suggesting instead that ethical commitments ought to be kept at a self-conscious distance from cognitive efforts to understand and interpret diverse cultures of nature. Moreover, such agnosticism ought to alter our pedagogy, especially but not only in institutions with a politically diverse population. What would happen if we taught *The Heretic* alongside *Flight Behaviour*? Given the reality of polarization, perhaps we should leave jokes about Donald Trump at the door? Just as STS profitably turned Climategate into a teachable moment that told us more about climatology than either the sceptics or scientific Eagle Scouts supposed, climate change scepticism could be an opportunity for ecocriticism to reconsider, and reconfigure, its relationship with teaching, activism and environmental science.

7

What We've Learned from Climate Sceptics

It would be pointless to undertake all this analysis without acknowledging how engaging with climate scepticism has changed our minds. As Jonathan Haidt, a leading advocate of viewpoint diversity and perspective-taking, argues:

> A good place to look for wisdom ... is where you least expect to find it: in the minds of your opponents. You already know the ideas common on your own side. If you can take off the blinders of the myth of pure evil, you might see some good ideas for the first time.
>
> (*The Happiness Hypothesis* 242)

In some cases, these are ideas we had already encountered, but dismissed or failed to take fully seriously. In others, they are ideas that were not found *in* our sceptical texts, but occurred to us while reading. Certainly, there was no shortage of 'talking points' – criticisms addressed years ago and long-refuted arguments, some over two decades old – but there were also more or less compelling claims that demand to be aired in conclusion.

We also make space here for differences in what was learned depending on the specific contexts of climate scepticism we each examined, and the interests we brought to bear on these contexts. The importance of the points below varies in terms of their relevance to the cultural and national climate scepticism under consideration. We will take the time to identify disagreements between our ways of coming-to-terms with climate scepticism, 'honouring divergence', 'gathering around it to think and hesitate together' (Stengers, *In Times* 143).

We will start with the less compelling claims.

Environmentalists hate fun

Po-faced nature-lovers have been the butt of jokes for centuries. Ever since the 1970s boom in environmental jeremiads, alleged humourlessness has combined with fearmongering to form a deeply unattractive stereotype. It's not only conservative anti-environmentalists who warn about the risks of a political strategy focused on negativity. Ted Nordhaus and Michael Schellenberger argue that environmentalism has thrived in periods of optimism and economic growth and warn that the movement has 'saddled us with the albatross we call the politics of limits, which seeks to constrain human ambition, aspiration, and power, rather than unleash and direct them' (17). They go on to complain that 'no single word better describes the ethics of environmentalism than "sacrifice"' (124), so what can we offer that doesn't sound like 'a lifelong global celery diet' ? (Prugh, Costanza and Daly 41)

Nothing could be less fun than compulsory humorousness. Still, Michael Branch has made a brave attempt to respond to the 'abhorrent condition of jokelessness in which we [environmentalists and ecocritics] reportedly find ourselves' (377) in 'Are You Serious? A Modest Proposal for Environmental Humour'. Without humour, and without the related capacity to unleash ambition and creativity, environmentalism will fail to motivate social change effectively. Vibrant environmentalist groups in France like *Génération Cobaye* are well aware of the need for an 'écologie souriante' ['smiling ecology'] and effectively use social media like YouTube videos to promote a politically engaged, humorous take on issues related to fossil fuels and global warming.

Reds under the bed

Are environmentalists 'watermelons' – green on the outside, but red in the middle? It's a prevalent claim among Anglophone sceptics that both reflects and reinforces political polarization. Admittedly, there are individual examples of obvious left entryism, such as the Lacanian-Leninist cultural theorist Slavoj Žižek, who seems interested in climate change only to the extent that it is the crisis that really, finally destroys capitalism (38). Green parties in all the countries surveyed here have tried to position themselves as 'neither Left nor Right but forward'. But, just as sceptics tend to the right, environmentalists are typically left-leaning. Whether they 'start' as socialists and discover the environment later, or simply acknowledge that environmentalist policies often require regulation, remains an open question. Until and unless conservatives become more vocal and engaged with the challenge to promote effective mitigation legislation, the political discourse surrounding climate change will remain decidedly on the left. Climate warmists, despite any political differences they might have with such proposals, ought to welcome them into the discussion.

This changes everything

The notion of socialist conspiracy gains credibility when one reflects on the scale and scope of changes required to reduce GHG emissions substantially and quickly. Popularizing treatments of climate change, such as *An Inconvenient Truth*, have tried to avoid freaking people out by emphasizing small changes in behaviour or consumption patterns, while major institutions such as the European Union have touted financial instruments such as carbon credits. The business-as-usual strategy itself has prompted response scepticism across the political spectrum (Van Rensburg 5). Citizens of wealthy countries who see climate change as a threat to their way of life – at least some important aspects of it – are correct. Marc Morano argues:

> The climate agenda literally impacts every aspect of your life. The purported solutions to this non-problem will affect what kind of lightbulbs and appliances you are allowed to buy, the size of your home and how it is heated and air conditioned, how you travel, the food you eat, the clothes you wear, and how many kids you can have.
>
> (2018, 8)

The *environmental* impact of decarbonization on both densely populated regions and wildlands selected for renewable energy projects would be immense. Environmentalists may not mind if Americans and Canadians can no longer run pickup trucks, Greyhound-sized RVs, ATVs and motorboats, but what about 'fossil freedoms' – forms of social emancipation underwritten by cheap oil (Bergthaller)? How should we respond to what Isabelle Stengers calls the 'intrusion of Gaia' (characterized by James Lovelock as 'her' revenge) knowing that the struggle is not between humans and the earth, but with the political and economic systems that gave rise to global warming?

The politicization of science

This issue is addressed in Chapter 6, where we acknowledge that climate change has eroded the perceived boundary between politics and science. From a scholarly perspective that boundary was largely fictitious all along. It is worth asking, though, whether we would continue to be calmly agnostic if we *opposed* the economic interests seen as 'corrupting' the science, as in the case of biotechnology.

Galileo, Galileo: The trouble with consensus

Environmental activists have set great store by the quantification of the consensus among climate scientists. But hasn't there been scientific consensus before that turned out to be wrong? Does science operate by consensus? Is there, in fact, the kind of consensus that is claimed? And, even if there were, will it move us to individual and political action?

The first claim is clearly true. The campaign against dietary fat began, according to Martin Cohen, with a single researcher in the 1950s, whose minority position developed into a solid consensus over two decades in the face of conflicting evidence (loc. 686–709). A German meteorologist, Alfred Wegener, claimed in 1915 that all the present continents had once been fused in one, which he called 'Pangaea'. His heterodox theory of 'continental drift' (later renamed 'plate tectonics') did not fully displace the prevailing consensus for well over half a century, and then only because the older generation died or retired (Bryson 173–81). The widespread idealized conception of Science, moreover, depicts it as progressing by means of 'organised scepticism' (Merton) or 'falsification of hypotheses' (Karl Popper), which implies scientific consensus really *ought* to be vulnerable and fleeting. Climate sceptics like to adduce examples of scientific heretics like Galileo who either overturned a consensus or succeeded in imposing a false one. Even if such parables usually turn out to be more ambiguous than they seem, they reproduce a heroic scientific narrative with much wider appeal than the messy reality of the production of scientific knowledge (see Chapter 6).

Environmental organizations are selectively respectful towards scientific consensus: Greenpeace rejects the 'release' of all Genetically Modified Organisms, even though the US National Academy of the Sciences consensus statement found no evidence of risks to human health or the environment.[1] Scientific consensus is not politically decisive. Nevertheless there have been numerous attempts to quantify it among climate scientists (Anderegg et al.; Cook et al. 'Quantifying the Consensus'; Oreskes; Verheggen et al.), all of which have come up with figures in the 90–100 per cent range (Cook et al. 'Consensus on Consensus'). *The Guardian* newspaper runs climate articles under the heading 'Climate Consensus – the 97%', a figure derived from Cook's 2013 paper, confirming its supposed persuasive value ('Climate Consensus – the 97% | Environment').[2]

The '97% consensus' reassures those already disposed to accept the IPCC position, and perhaps sways the undecided. To sceptics, though, it must seem as improbably high as the electoral results of Kim Jong-Un (100 per cent), Bashar al-Assad (97.6 per cent) or Kurbanguly Berdymukhamedov of Turkmenistan (97 per cent) ('The World of 100% Election Victories'). Cook's 97 per cent figure also invites closer inspection of his paper's methodology, which Richard Tol found severely wanting. Pearce and colleagues note the irony that, far from securing assent, efforts to quantify consensus 'invited intense scrutiny to the judgments underpinning their claim, and generated further doubt' (2). Furthermore, Dan Kahan's research emphasizes that non-scientists experience the 97 per cent consensus claim primarily as corroboration or as a challenge to their cultural identity. In his critique of an Organizing for Action video, Kahan notes that a conservative viewer will most likely respond to it as a personal slight, not a rational argument (18): 97 per cent consensus is 'a bumper sticker, and it says "fuck you" on it' (Vaidyanathan).

Climate sceptics can read

We discussed stigmatizing language in the Introduction, but it is important to return to an obvious point: sceptics can read what is said about them. The dominant academic account of popular climate scepticism goes like this: fossil fuel-funded conservative think tanks (CTTs) disseminated deliberate untruths to confuse the lay public about the extent of scientific consensus on climate change, and it is this that has successfully delayed concerted political action. We agree this is an accurate account of the origins of climate scepticism in the Anglophone countries we discuss in this book. But what if obdurate scepticism were, in part, a *response* to climate science, governance and activism? Put it together: the Climategate emails appear to show CRU scientists imposing groupthink on their field; the IPCC is accused of marginalizing dissenting positions and admits publishing an unsubstantiated alarmist claim; major news organizations such as the BBC abandon the balance norm in climate reporting; and climate activism in turn depicts dissenters as idiots who might deserve, a would-be satirical British video suggests, to be blown to pieces. A warmist documentary from the height of the climate wars was actually entitled *Age of Stupid* (Franny Armstrong, 2009). No wonder some sceptics have adopted the valorized role of heretic.

Both activists and scholars chastise climate scientists who concede too much to sceptics. A remarkable article criticizing the 'seepage' of non-scientific arguments into the scientific domain argues, 'In response to constant, and sometimes toxic, public challenges, scientists have over-emphasized scientific uncertainty, and have inadvertently allowed contrarian claims to affect how they themselves speak, and perhaps even think, about their own research' (Lewandowsky et al. 1). Specifically, Lewandowsky and colleagues suggest that climate scientists permitted 'contrarian' perspectives to infiltrate their science insofar as they discussed the supposed 'pause' or 'hiatus' in global mean surface temperature increases after 1998 – even if they did so to dismiss its significance. Giving 'unwarranted attention and credence' to contrarian arguments or individuals so as to avoid seeming arrogant or elitist is listed as one of the ways that seepage could occur (4). Their argument depends on two assumptions: that there was never any 'methodological or empirical argument' (5) that could justify talk of a hiatus (although they do acknowledge 'a slowdown, if you will' (6)); and that contrarian arguments must *ex hypothesis* come across the boundary from 'non-science', rather than from within. The first assumption is well-supported, but the second is never directly addressed. Lewandowsky and colleagues conclude with an extraordinary plea for intolerance of heterodoxy:

> We can do more to ensure that we do not inadvertently allow contrarian, skeptical, and denialist claims to seep into our thinking, leading us to overstate uncertainty, under-communicate knowledge, or add credence to erroneous claims by spending undue amounts of time responding to them, much less 'explaining' phenomena that do not even exist.
>
> (10)

Regardless of whether 'we' take their advice and somehow shut alternative perspectives out of our minds, such policing reinforces the sense that warmists cannot stand dissent. Moreover, *intolerance breeds scepticism* in turn as dissident scientists such as Judith Curry and Lennart Bengtsson have avowed. Lewandowsky and colleagues' assumption, not entirely unwarranted, is that sceptical arguments are simply intentional obfuscation. But one must ask: isn't that always a risk? Is tolerance for a disingenuous point of view the worst mistake we can make? The risk seems to be the point. We won't know where the bridges could be built until we start assessing the distance to the other shore.

The identity of 'climate sceptic' is what Ian Hacking calls a 'reflexive kind', a class of beings that responds to the fact of its having been classified in a certain way (102–05). All the texts discussed here ask to be read as evidence of that reflexivity, whether their tone is jeering, defiant or rationalistic. CTTs have participated in framing the sceptic identity, deliberately politicizing it and aligning it– in the United States especially – with cultural conservatism; we might say, with justice, that they started the process of polarization. It is nonetheless incumbent on scholars to do whatever they can to reverse it, avoiding stigmatizing language and polarizing framing of social and cultural research, thereby helping to re-align climate scepticism with the great scientific and philosophical tradition from which it takes its name.

Don't trust the models

The phenomenon of climate change is elicited from many species of computer models, including data models required to assimilate heterogeneous information about past weather from a wide range of proxies and instrumental records into homogenous climatic data sets, but the most contentious are General Circulation Models (GCMs) and Integrated Assessment Models (IAMs). GCMs project probable trends in Global Mean Surface Temperature (GMST) in response to changes in greenhouse gas emissions, while IAMs purport to simulate how geophysical and socioeconomic changes will interact far into the future. The reliability of GCMs (thirty-five of them in total) is estimated by comparing their ability to 'hindcast', or reproduce, past climatic changes once factors such as solar output, volcanic eruptions, greenhouse gas emissions and El Niño events are incorporated. Scepticalscience.com emphasizes that 'all the models are unable to predict recent warming without taking rising CO2 levels into account' ('Climate Science Glossary – climate-models-intermediate'). Short of postulating an as-yet-unknown factor and given acknowledged limitations in relation to specific factors and feedbacks (cloud formation, oceanic oscillations, biogeophysical processes etc.), GCMs have projected GMST and continental-scale changes in temperature and atmospheric humidity more accurately than sceptics assert. Nevertheless, ethnographic study of GCM-building scientists has noted 'the ambivalent and flexibly used identity of modellers as to whether they are builders of predictive truth generating machines (their main policy and funding identity), or of heuristic devices for aiding research' (Shackley and Wynne 125). Myanna Lahsen's study, which included six years of fieldwork, noted frequent contention – as well as productive collaboration – between modellers and empirical meteorologists. She suggests, 'Compared with modelers, the empiricists may at times be in a better position to identify model shortcomings because of their deeper knowledge of empirical processes simulated by the GCMs, and because of their lower psychological and professional investment in the models' (Lahsen 915). Her research confirms sceptics' suspicion that groupthink is a risk in such a specialized scientific community, but also affirms that it is regularly challenged from within and without.

Paul N. Edwards details the painstaking, decades-long research programme required to wring 'global climate data' from the forbiddingly 'noisy', patchy records of maritime logs, weather charts, ice cores, tree rings and satellite sounders (e.g. 312–317). He explains the increasingly sophisticated methods that have been devised to control for 'artifactual elements in both theory and observation' (282), including ensemble forecasting and perturbed-physics model runs. He concludes:

> It's not that climate simulation models are perfectly reliable, any more than weather forecast models always get it right. Instead, it's that the simulations already include a lot of data in their parameters; they are precisely *not* pure theories, but theories already partially adjusted to the conditions we observe in the real world. That's model-data symbiosis. So whether we are looking at data images or model projections of climate futures, we will always experience them as probabilistic, as shimmering rather than fixed.
>
> (352)

Edwards reports that, as of 2013, perturbed-physics models designed to explore possible errors in parameterizations always returned equilibrium climate sensitivities (see below) of *at least* 1.9°C, and often much higher (355). Scientific confidence in the direction of travel is extremely high.

At regional scales, though, and in relation to changes that matter to humans and other animals (such as precipitation), the models are essentially useless. Demetris Koutsoyiannis and colleagues compared predictions by six GCMs with actual climatic indicators at eight stations distributed around the world, and found that, while 'GCMs generally reproduce the broad climatic behaviours at different geographical locations', they are 'irrelevant to reality' at annual and climatic (30-year) scales (Koutsoyiannis et al. 682). Adding more factors, such as future changes in emissions or land-use, multiplies the uncertainties. IAMs link GCM projections to socioeconomic models to try and provide policymakers with cost-benefit analyses of mitigation and adaptation over the coming decades – and centuries. John Adams points out, though, that the benefits of emissions will largely accrue to different people than those bearing the costs of climate change, and in quite different forms. Of multi-century projections, he observes:

> 300 years ago the US dollar did not exist and most of the North American continent was still owned by the Indians. One way of appreciating the magnitude of the task that the greenhouse economists have set themselves is to imagine them transported by time machine back to 1693, and set the task of doing a

> cost-benefit analysis of the European conquest of North America – with the net present value of the conquest calculated in 1693 wampum.[3]
>
> (Adams 175)

IAMs can only model what can be quantified, leading to unavoidable systematic exclusion of cultural and political changes, even though 'historical examples … illustrate the importance of culture and institutions in the interpretation of, and response to, environmental change' (Shackley and Wynne 123). Oreskes and colleagues insist that regional-scale uncertainty and inability to predict major non-linear events, such as rapid break-up of continental icesheets or methane clathrate release, show that relying on adaptation rather than emissions reduction is extremely unwise (1025–26), but they assume that the costs of precautionary action are solely economic, as well as politically manageable. They may well not be.

Living with uncertainty

The likely response of global mean temperatures to rising carbon emissions (often expressed as 'equilibrium climate sensitivity') is known within certain bounds: a doubling of CO_2 will lead to at least 1.5°C of warming, likely 2–4.5°C, with 3°C being considered the most likely. Depending also on the pace of change, below 2° would pose few problems of adaptation, whereas over 4° would be catastrophic. Climate scientists have developed techniques to narrow (or 'constrain') the range as much as possible but remaining geophysical uncertainties and lacunae in the observational record could make a sharper picture unattainable – until it's too late. For sceptics, uncertainty justifies inaction.

Despite the efforts being made to constrain the projections, some warmists, such as the economist Paul Krugman, also emphasize uncertainty:

> Now, despite the high credibility of climate modelers, there is still tremendous uncertainty in their long-term forecasts. But … uncertainty makes the case for action stronger, not weaker.

Krugman points out the risk – considered extremely low but not negligible – that smaller increases in GMST could trigger disastrous feedback effects. This, though, sounds like a 'heads I win, tails you lose argument': more certainty (of mid- to high-climate sensitivity, anyway) strengthens the case for action, *and so does less certainty*. As Judith Curry points out, Krugman's argument implies that 'the [sceptical] merchants of doubt are now climate policy action's "best friends"'

('Uncertainty, Risk, and (in)Action'). She contends that climate scientists can never completely tame the 'uncertainty monster':

> Given the complexity of the climate problem, expert judgments about uncertainty and confidence levels are made by the IPCC on issues that are dominated by unquantifiable uncertainties.
>
> (Curry and Webster 1672)

It is tough for the non-specialist reader to follow the arguments between Curry and her critics (Hegerl et al.). So what is a concerned citizen and literary critic to do?

It helps to understand the irreducible limits to knowledge of our climatic future. As we saw in the discussion of models, adding complexity typically increases uncertainty. For that reason, says Jeroen van der Sluijs, efforts to 'exorcise' the uncertainty monster are doomed to fail: 'For each head climate science chops off the uncertainty monster, several new monster heads tend to pop up' (89). Seeking to channel and domesticate the monster, by determining who qualifies as an 'expert' and then quantifying 'consensus', is also ineffectual. Van der Sluijs admits that those who 'embrace' the monster include ideologically motivated sceptics but he insists:

> The IPCC process should be open to such sceptics … [because]the unpleasant way in which the game is played and the mixture of valid and ungrounded criticisms that it produces is the price that has to be paid for the key advantage for quality control of the identification of weak spots in the knowledge base.
>
> (91)

Van der Sluijs's preferred method of dealing with the uncertainty monster is 'assimilation', which implies revising our assumptions and expectations of science (specifically post-normal climate science), and 'learn[ing] to live with ambiguity and pluralism in risk assessment' (91). In effect, he recommends we accept what is known as 'epistemic scepticism', rather than seeking to combat it. Such scepticism is widespread: 'Doubts about climate science in particular may also be reflections of a more universal belief among the public that there are clear limits to the levels of knowledge that scientists actually possess in the domain of socio-technical risks' (Capstick and Pidgeon 398).

We would add that what is missing when we focus exclusively on *scientific* uncertainty is a discussion of values, an admission of the criteria we bring to bear in making judgements and the inherent risks of such a fundamental enterprise. Obsession with the data may serve to shield us from such vulnerable conversations as they essentially pertain to the humanities: who are we as a species and what are we doing here? Where do we want to go? As Daniel Sarewitz has argued:

> We are not suffering from a lack of objectivity but from an excess of it. Science is sufficiently rich, diverse, and Balkanized to provide comfort and support for a range of subjective, political positions on complex issues such as climate change .... Arguing about science is a relatively risk-free business; in fact, one can simply mobilize the appropriate expert to do the talking and hide behind the assertion of objectivity. But talking openly about values is much more dangerous because it reveals what is truly at stake.
>
> (90–91)

Psychologist Dylan Evans thinks we need to calibrate our 'risk intelligence' by seeking out a wide range of perspectives. Climate change, he says, is a signal example of 'probability neglect': 'When a hazard stirs strong emotions, people ... tend to factor in probability less, with the result that they will go to great lengths to avoid risks that are extremely unlikely' (Evans 13). Reading this book should have started re-tuning your risk intelligence, and helped you begin to assimilate the uncertainty monster.

Recalibration returns us to the values and narratives – worldviews – that frame our interpretations of the world. For us, this exercise in reading scepticism has exposed the culture of warmism as such. That is, in sceptics' persistent attention to certain predilections among manifestations of climate alarm, it reminds us that climate change is never a culturally or politically neutral question, even if sceptics' depictions of scientists and environmentalists are often stereotypical themselves. Climate positions are culturally embedded, of course, but least visible to those who passionately advocate one position or another. Although passion is not wrong or dangerous, scholars who are also devoted to climate action need to show sufficient detachment to engage in criticism, including self-criticism, in order to identify where we go from here.

Climate scepticism is transnational but culturally embedded

Identifying national similarities and differences across cultures of climate scepticism runs the risk of oversimplifying and distorting a complex picture by reducing the range of standpoints and forms adopted in each country to a handful of salient features. We would however like to offer some tentative observations comparing France and Germany, and then the UK and the United States.

Despite significant differences, climate sceptics in France and Germany have more in common with each other than with those in the United States, or even Britain. Climate scepticism emerged in both countries as a significant phenomenon around 2007, later than in Britain and America, largely as disputation of the need for a radical socio-ecological transformation rather than as trend (literal) or even attribution scepticism. Although public concern over global warming and its consequences has declined in France and Germany since 2010, the overall level of scepticism in the press and political discourse remains low, and the cross-party consensus on climate politics means there is little sign of the growing polarization of opinion seen in the Anglophone world. Climate change is not a touchstone for opposing worldviews.

Comparative studies of climate change politics in the two countries, like those of sociologist Stefan Aykut, have drawn attention to the institutional differences that, Sheila Jasanoff shows, give rise to distinct 'civic epistemologies': climate science and politics are regarded as the business of a technocratic and political elite in France, whereas they emerged as topics of public debate in Germany where non-political experts have been directly involved in the discussion of science and the formation of policy. However, French and German sceptics share, broadly speaking, fundamentals in both the arguments they present and the writing strategies they adopt. Positioning themselves as the voice of reason, common sense and objective knowledge, they oppose Romantic pro-nature sentiment and the philosophy of deep ecology. They speak out against catastrophism as a popular distortion and exaggeration of the risks associated with climate change and describe themselves as eco-optimists trusting in the ability of humanity to meet the challenges of global warming. Sceptics on both sides of the Rhine criticize the blurring of the distinction between science and politics and the way green 'dogma' abandons critical analysis of environmental problems for an unquestioned ideology.

At the same time, while we have noted the existence of a number of sceptical thrillers and science fiction novels, the bulk of sceptical writing is essayistic non-fiction in France, and popular science in Germany, and even sceptical novelists blend fiction with reality by introducing real people and institutions, facts and factoids into their works. We have observed a preference of both French and German sceptics for humour and satire, much like their counterparts in the British Isles: irony and sarcasm debunk the high moral claims of the greens. Writing with stylistic verve and aphoristic eloquence, they typically delight in paradox, subversive playfulness and mischievous exaggeration, with a number resorting to parody and black humour, to disrupt readers' acquired perceptions of the right way to address climate change and provoke them into reflection on alternatives.

However, such similarities do not make for a unified Franco-German front. On the contrary, we found no evidence of collaboration between climate sceptics in the two countries, despite the fact that many are scientists who might circulate in similar academic settings. Language is an obvious impeding factor (only a handful of the French and German texts have been translated into English). Another may be the different traditions from which climate scepticism emerges in both countries: a critique of cultural pessimism in Germany and a defence of secular humanism in France; a reaction against simplistic thinking and naïve activism in Germany and an adherence to methodical doubt in France; German sceptics' self-understanding as guardians of pragmatic realism and French sceptics' as proponents of rationalism. While these differences are not determining, they have allowed climate scepticism to follow separate discursive and political paths in the two countries.

Specific socio-historical factors have also affected the emergence of cultures of climate scepticism in each country. *Der Spiegel*'s 1986 cover image set the alarmist tone for climate advocacy in Germany. Sceptical critiques of the fascination with apocalypse, as well as their calls for a more eco-optimist view, are in part a response to this earlier portrayal of climate change. Moreover, quite a few of the climate sceptics in Germany have a strong track record as environmentalists themselves. In France, there was no single moment at which awareness about the state of the planet entered the public forum. Instead, climate sceptics drew on Luc Ferry's 1992 critique of an ecological order that would allow the State to implement totalitarian measures placing environmental concerns over social ones. Even if Claude Allègre worked to pass laws on air and water pollution, describing his position as that of 'true ecology', most French sceptics' engagement with environmentalism remains superficial if not contradictory (for instance in the refusal to give up 'the good life').

A closer look at individual texts in each country complicates this list of similarities and differences. On the one hand, the non-fiction writings of Maxeiner and Bruckner both critique green puritanism that exploits feelings of guilt and plays on a desire for redemption. But Maxeiner is a journalist well-versed in scientific debates, whereas Bruckner is a philosopher defending French secularism. Similarly, the over-the-top satire in Kracht's and Gran's fictional accounts of climate change clearly appeal to the reader's desire for a more lighthearted response to contemporary eco-politics, but they adopt very different forms in developing their satirical voice: Gran blurs the line between fiction and reality, addressing the reader directly, undoing the distinction between author and protagonist, and making extensive use of footnotes, whereas Kracht develops a world of multiple parody cynically ridiculing climate alarmism by substituting methane for CO2 as prime agent of global warming, and ultimately calling on humanity to make way for a more intelligent, less destructive species.

Given that climate scepticism fuses social and environmental perspectives, we are not surprised by such differences. French and German serve as 'language glasses' (Deutscher) through which the dominant eco-narrative is viewed in each country. So, even as global warming becomes the subject of further universalizing scientific studies and international agreements, it remains embedded in linguistic and cultural practices and meanings.

As Chapter 2 observes, British and American sceptics have much in common: they are quite consistently right-wingers and anti-environmentalists who recycle memes produced by CTTs on both sides of the Atlantic. 'Organised scepticism', which has seeded doubts about climate science and fostered polarization, is far more influential than it is in France or Germany, and the wide-open communication channels across the Atlantic ensure the two countries share a cultural history, to a degree. English/British nationalist and Euro-sceptic fervour, boosted by the smug, deluded assumption that the UK enjoys a 'special relationship' with the United States, aligns with American isolationism, although it falls short of President Trump's 'America First' assault on the international order. Evangelical Christianity is widely assumed to contribute a unique quality to American scepticism, so it was a surprise to come across Philip Foster's *While the Earth Endures*, which argues that God causes global warming by triggering supernovas. Still, the frumpy, bemused style of Foster's book and its publication by a tiny Christian press signal the eccentricity of the argument in a British context, whereas the infrastructure of American conservative media and publishing is immense and the leading Christian sceptic Jimmy Inhofe, discussed in Chapter 4, is a US Senator. A near-universal complaint, shared also with continental sceptics, is that climate science contravenes the ideal of apolitical science (see Chapter 6). However unjustly, the 'Climategate' emails were cited and recited by sceptics from all four countries to foster disillusionment with climate scientists, much as conservatives later made use of hacked emails from the Democratic National Congress to discredit Hillary Clinton's 2016 election campaign.

The differences between British and American scepticism are at least as striking as the resemblances, albeit that the lure of national stereotypes is strong here and furthermore our differing selections bias the contrast: Chapter 2 casts a wider net than Chapter 4. First: humour. It is by no means absent from American climate scepticism: Crichton's *State of Fear* takes great relish in dismembering the hypocrite Ted Bradley, and the author is surely winking when he assures us in his Author's Message, 'Everybody has an agenda. Except me' (574). Humour, though, is so fundamental to British scepticism it has its own taxon, 'comic nihilism' (Segnit and Ereaut 7–8). Clarkson, Delingpole, even Wilfred Beckerman's jokes not only subvert the zealous certainty of climate activists, but ironically undermine the masculine authority of the sceptics themselves. Self-deprecating humour is the stereotypical quality Brits most like to celebrate in themselves; in the case of climate sceptics, it is used – like the paradox of the trusted unreliable narrator – to reclaim, at a deeper level, the authority it appears to disclaim. Hard-won scientific authority scarcely stands a chance against a witty riposte.

The American rhetoric of the climate 'hoax' is distinct from the prevalent British sceptical identity as 'the heretic' primarily because climate change is more politicized in the United States – the liberals are trying to get one over on conservatives – but also because of conspiracist tendencies that have long prevailed in political discourse there. In fact, a transnational study published just as we were finishing this book shows that the United States is an outlier in this regard:

> The relationship between conservative ideologies and climate scepticism is unusually strong and consistent within the United States compared to other countries. For those who are embedded in US politics (and US-centric data sets), it is easy to see how one could reach the pessimistic conclusion that the debate around climate change is deeply mired in conspiratorial thinking and/or politically polarized 'culture wars'. However, … there is nothing inherent to conspiratorial ideation or conservative ideologies that predisposes people to reject climate science.
>
> (Hornsey et al. 619)

The drama of climate politics is played out openly in the United States, as Edwards points out: partisan politicians recruit scientists as 'expert witnesses' for televised Congressional hearings, with the result that '*two systems* [politics and science] *specifically designed to promote challenge-response-revision cycles multiply each other's effects*' (406). Britain's closed political system has helped maintain the thin hegemony, described in Chapter 2, against which climate heretics rebel. Backed by the Koch brothers and Fox News, American sceptics can hardly adopt the British pose of 'naughty boys', however hard they sell the fiction of a hostile, homogenous 'liberal elite'.

If British sceptical discourse is less heated, more blithe and irresponsible, than its American cousin, it is also conspicuously more literate than the examples discussed in Chapter 4. The sample size is tiny, of course, and our approaches are somewhat different, but Richard Bean's play *The Heretic* and Christopher Booker's theory of narrative archetypes are, in their different ways, artistically and intellectually credible responses to climate change. It is hard to think of American equivalents. Why have talented conservative writers – of which there are many – shied away from climate change? Why, moreover, have fiction writers of whatever stripe avoided characterizing climate sceptics? *State of Fear* may not include any credible, knowledgeable environmentalists, but Barbara Kingsolver's *Flight Behaviour* – the state-of-the-art in cli-fi – trivializes rural climate scepticism by blaming local TV weathermen. While serious Anglophone novelists always fear didacticism, the polarization of American politics may further deter imaginative engagement. Whatever the case, this seems a missed opportunity. More even than climate change itself, an acknowledged challenge to novelists (Ghosh), the fascinating diversity of climate cultures – including sceptical ones – cries out for fictional treatment. We hereby challenge American writers to step up.

Dissent is irreducible

Scientific consensus has not and will not eliminate disagreements about climatic risks and policy responses, not least because American warmists are no more scientifically informed than sceptics (Kahan 20). Much as Europeans like to look down on 'dumb Americans', 'cross-national differences in the fractions of populations that say climate change is a serious problem are not indices of scientific ignorance' (Jamieson 67). Our cultural comparison does not bear out the idea that less sceptical Germans are smarter than Americans; rather, we find that historical and political differences account for the civic epistemologies and related risk cultures of different countries. These broad influences interact with 'the particular contexts that individuals find themselves in: their personal experience of climatic danger; the way their affective and analytical reasonings operate; their placement of trust in experts; their values and their world-views' (Hulme 201). Worldviews shape, and are in turn shaped by, differing orientations (four, according to cultural theorists (Adams)) towards the management of risk. Add together the resilience of irreconcilable worldviews, the irreducible uncertainty of climate projections and the mass assent needed for democratic climate governance to make a difference, and it should be clear that neither scientification nor silencing organized scepticism will suffice. All is not lost, though: respecting political diversity, rather than trying to eliminate it, has an excellent record of success, as Haidt explains:

> If you put individuals together in the right way, such that some individuals can use their reasoning powers to disconfirm the claims of others, and all individuals feel some common bond or shared fate that allows them to interact civilly, you can create a group that ends up producing good reasoning as an emergent property of the social system.
>
> (*The Righteous Mind* 105)

A university could be such a site provided that viewpoint diversity is explicitly welcomed. It will not be easy, though. Polarization makes *rapprochement* more painful and unpopular, even as it makes it more urgent.

Dissent is internal

It cannot go unmentioned that the voices urging openness appear to come from the left-liberal side of the argument. With a few honourable exceptions such as Peter Taylor and Dirk Maxeiner, the sceptics we have encountered here seem to want to exacerbate polarization, not ameliorate it. Ironically, we did not learn respect for sceptical views *from them*.

Self-doubt is still less common in these texts than the desire for communication and compromise, and those are rare enough. To some extent, this is simply selection bias, in that the forms and genres surveyed here are more conducive to polemic than reflection. It is also, we want to say, the big lie that the supposed warmist/sceptic binary conceals. The truth can be glimpsed occasionally in population-level treatments of climate scepticism, such as Kahan's finding that 'for the vast majority of [his subjects] global warming elicits strong negative feelings, likely of fear or dread' *irrespective of whether they 'believe' in it* (25). Likewise, Michael Carolan's attempt to get 'behind' the quantitative, population-level findings of widespread scepticism ('climate change perceptions from … 10,000 feet' (319)) finds multiple examples of 'sociological ambivalence' in the Colorado citizens he interviews. Some respondents hold the 'seemingly irreconcilable views of being seriously concerned about climate change *and* believe that the media exaggerates its seriousness', which could lead to them being classified as either a sceptic or warmist, depending on the question and the context (Carolan 315). In other instances, respondents explain that they worry about climate change 'only a little' or 'not at all' to help 'resolve a tension between knowing climate change is real while feeling helpless about mitigating further effects' (316). His finding seems to support ethnographer Kari Norgaard's memorable conclusion, based on conversations with Norwegians, that 'apathy is the mask of suffering' (loc. 945). Carolan also notes, though, that his respondents themselves emphasized their own 'attitudinal instability'. By contrast, sceptical texts (and not a few warmist ones) stand out thanks to their bumptious self-confidence.

Typologies are too easily mistaken for reality, as Bruno Latour sardonically recalls:

> You can be at once and without even sensing any contradiction (1) an antifetishist for everything you don't believe in – for the most part religion, popular culture, art, politics, and so on; (2) an unrepentant positivist for all the sciences you believe in – sociology, economics, conspiracy theory, genetics, evolutionary psychology, semiotics, just pick your preferred field of study; and (3) a perfectly healthy sturdy realist for what you really cherish – and of course it might be criticism itself, but also painting, bird-watching, Shakespeare, baboons, proteins, and so on.
>
> (241)

If so, epistemic and response scepticism are prevalent not only because of the unique challenges posed by climate change, but because doubts about the human capacity for knowledge, wisdom and sustained moral action are ancient, ubiquitous and deeply plausible. The first step towards turning down the 'antagonistic cultural meanings' (Kahan 29) of polarized politics may be to recognize that we all, if we are honest, suffer the antagonism internally. 'Warmist' and 'sceptic' should be seen not as opposed identities but inner possibilities that are – now that a changing climate *is* our future – effectively permanent. The deepest fault lines are within.

The puzzle of sceptical literature

The pieces of the puzzle are, broadly, science, politics and the text. Without straying into climatological science, we have examined how these pieces fit together in each of the national contexts under consideration, stressing the distinctiveness of sceptical texts as well as their commonalities. British sceptics are more politically diverse than Americans, and the French and Germans are still more varied, although intriguingly there are disillusioned environmentalists everywhere. Criticisms of apocalypticism and environmentalist religiosity are widespread, too, although as Nordhaus and Shellenberger point out, 'Environmentalism doesn't work enough like a *church*' in terms of the kind of belonging and fulfilment it provides, let alone the commitment it expects (201). Some puzzles remain: why is climate scepticism deeply embroiled in left–right polarization in the United States, less so in the UK, and hardly at all in France or Germany (Hornsey et al. 616)? How does sceptical fiction differ from sceptical non-fiction in its portrayal of science as social discourse? How does the 'horizon of reception' of sceptical literature differ from one country to another in light of civic epistemologies? What impact does sceptical literature have on readers with varying degrees of climate science literacy? And why are virtually all of the sceptical writers, in all four countries, men?

Our analysis has acquainted readers with the diversity of sceptical literature, in Britain and Europe at least, and has puzzled over works that demand different forms of attention than 'quality writing'. Christian Kracht and Ingo Niermann's *Metan* cheekily challenges the moralization of climate with its call to accelerate global warming by maximizing capitalist production and consumption, but it does not meet any of the normal criteria of a major work. The popularity of some authors, for instance Crichton and Clarkson, is itself a puzzle; *State of Fear* is fairly exciting and *Top Gear* used to be funny and inventive, but their prominence seems exaggerated. The prospects for *singular* sceptical literature, in the sense outlined in the Introduction, are small, especially in the UK and the United States where political polarization seems to deter imaginative writing. However, there are more sceptical American climate change novels, in a broad sense, than space allowed us to discuss in Chapter 4. In genre fiction, Larry Niven's sci-fi novel *Fallen Angels* (1991) depicts, with humour and imagination, a future world in which a new Ice Age, initiated by declining solar activity, is exacerbated by misguided efforts to combat global warming. Ironically, 'the biggest environmental disaster in history was caused by environmentalism' (59): sci-fi fans form an underground resistance to the authoritarian green government, which has turned its back on technology. *Freedom* (2010) by Jonathan Franzen, an esteemed literary novelist, is an example of social and psychological realism set in the present. Franzen's principal protagonist, the partly autobiographical Walter Berglund, rebels against the subordination of other environmental issues (in particular the loss of the habitats of rare birds) to the reduction of carbon emissions. Similarly, the sympathetic protagonist in Joel Baqué's *La Fonte des glaces* allows the reader to experience some of the grief associated with the extinction of megafauna species while also revealing the questionable motives of green capitalism. Such texts are puzzling in the constructive sense that they fit into neither the climate sceptics' canon nor the category of warmist climate fiction.

If, as some scientists warn, the IPCC is actually too conservative, and if climate scepticism delays concerted global action beyond a tipping point that leads to catastrophe, it will have been an unimaginable cultural crime. At what price will our empathy have been bought then? A more scientifically probable outcome, in which climate change is entangled in centuries of related and unrelated regional disasters, elevated risks and unprecedented opportunities, will resemble neither 'apocalypse' nor 'hoax', the tropes favoured by warmists and American sceptics. Responding constructively to that ambiguous future will require, and reward, the kind of depolarization we have modelled here.

While we recognize the discomfort ecocritics might feel in inviting such writers to the literary table, scorning or ignoring 'puzzling' texts does not make them go away. Scholars who truly believe in the transformative potential, individual and social, of literary study ought to be prepared to take the risk of encountering a new, all too familiar, kind of alterity. Greeting 'the other as other', as Derek Attridge suggests, necessarily alters the 'rules and schemata' (loc. 796) by which these others are occluded. Perhaps they are shifting now.

Notes

Chapter 1

1 'Does Demonizing the Other Side Promote Constructive Debate Over Climate Change?' Watts Up With That? 21 April 2016, https://wattsupwiththat.com/2016/04/21/does-demonizing-the-other-side-promote-constructive-debate-over-climate-change/. The supposed author of the blog post, Professor G. Cornelis van Kooten, later admitted that he had only drafted the post, and 'left it to another person to rewrite in a journalistic fashion' (personal communication).

2 The notion of a 'national literature' is problematic in several respects. One of our aims, discussed below, is in fact to overcome the methodological nationalism of ecocriticism. Nevertheless, we use this phrase throughout the book for the sake of economy.

3 See this article for a visualization of party sorting, and a reasoned defence of polarization: Thomas's https://www.nytimes.com/192017/10/12/opinion/democrats-are-playing-checkers-while-trump-is-playing-chess.html (accessed on 29 June 2018).

4 Over the period during which we were writing this book, moral psychologist Jonathan Haidt set up the 'Heterodox Academy', whose members pledge: 'I believe that university life requires that people with diverse viewpoints and perspectives encounter each other in an environment where they feel free to speak up and challenge each other. I am concerned that many academic fields and universities currently lack sufficient viewpoint diversity – particularly political diversity. I will support viewpoint diversity in my academic field, my university, my department, and my classroom.' Taken from:

'FAQs'. Heterodox Academy, 26 June 2018, heterodoxacademy.org/aboutus/faqs/. https://heterodoxacademy.org/frequently-asked-questions/

5 According to Stéphane Foucart, journalist for *Le Monde*, the expression 'Flat Earth' alludes to the reliance of the solar radiance theory of global warming (a popular challenger to the greenhouse gas hypothesis, defended by Courtillot and Allègre among others) on a flat earth model. If so, what appears to be a mere slur is actually an erudite criticism.

6 http://scienceblogs.com/pharyngula/files/2014/03/fpsyg-04-00073.pdf.

For a pro-Lewandowsky account of the controversy: Tania Lombrozo, 'What Do Aliens, Climate Change and Princess Di Have in Common?' *NPR*, 10 December

2012, http://www.npr.org/sections/13.7/2012/12/10/166733644/what-do-aliens-climate-change-and-princess-di-have-in-common; for a critical perspective: 'Stephan Lewandowsky's Slow Motion Psychological Science Train Wreck', https://wattsupwiththat.com/2012/09/05/stephan-lewandowskys-slow-motion-social-science-train-wreck/. Lewandowsky co-authored an account of the 'War on Science' to which he has allegedly been subjected: Stephan Lewandowsky et al., 'The Subterranean War on Science', Association for Psychological Science, www.psychologicalscience.org/index.php/publications/observer/2013/november-13/the-subterranean-war-on-science.html. For discussion of the third paper in the sequence: https://www.theguardian.com/environment/climate-consensus-97-per-cent/2015/jul/08/climate-denial-linked-to-conspiratorial-thinking-in-new-study

7 It is helpful to remind the reader of linguistic and cultural differences here. The term 'réchauffiste' does not appear in any official dictionary in France (*Le Petit Robert, Le Larousse* etc.). Nor is it used by Claude Allègre in his book *L'Imposture climatique* [The Climate Imposture] or by French climate sceptics on their main website Climato-réalistes. When the word 'réchauffiste' is used online, it most often appears in quotation marks as if to maintain a certain distance with respect to the English term. The extent to which French climate scepticism has or has not taken up strains of Anglophone climate scepticism will be discussed in the fifth chapter.

Chapter 2

1 Jesse Oak Taylor states that 'Wilde's quip has become a byline for an entire way of thinking about aesthetic experience, and yet those discussions rarely attend to the fact that the fog in question was itself the product of human handiwork, and was acknowledged as such'. Jesse O. Taylor, *The Sky of Our Manufacture: The London Fog in British Fiction from Dickens to Woolf, Under the Sign of Nature: Explorations in Ecocriticism* (Charlottesville; London: University of Virginia Press, 2016), 2.

2 Later notable meetings included COP 3 (Kyoto 1997), COP 15 (Copenhagen 2009) and COP 21 (Paris 2015).

3 The nickname given to the lower middle-class ex-Labour voter targeted by Blair's New Labour. The Mondeo is a 1990s model of Ford car (Stone-Lee, Ollie. 'UK | UK Politics | Who's the New Mondeo Man?') http://news.bbc.co.uk/2/hi/4119695.stm

4 A TV talent show.

5 A popular British term for the 2000s. 'Nought' is zero in the UK.

6 Cited at http://publicinterest.org.uk/no-pressure-an-ill-advised-piece-of-climate-communication/ (accessed on 29 June 2018).

7 Roger Bate acknowledges support from 'the Charles G. Koch Charitable Foundation' enabled him to work as 'an Environmental Research Associate at the Competitive Enterprise Institute' (8), a prominent American CTT.

8 North acknowledges financial support from the chemical company ICI, and access to their archives, but emphasizes that his conclusions are unaffected by the relationship. *Life on a Modern Planet* defends the chlorine industry against the Greenpeace campaign, but is also critical of ICI's efforts to discredit scientific evidence showing that CFCs degrade stratospheric ozone.

9 A longer open-access version is here: http://www.jri.org.uk/resource/CritiqueOf_AppealToReason.pdf (accessed on 29 June 2018).

10 'Elf and safety' is 'health and safety' pronounced with a comic 'working class' accent.

11 There have been some *ad hominem* criticisms of Peter Taylor, which draw attention to his presentations and writings on astral travelling and shamanism. For example, his 'Shamanic view of climate change' presented to the Avalon Rising festival can be seen here: https://www.youtube.com/watch?v=xzzwtLwIF3k (accessed on 29 June 2018). Unlike Foster, however, Taylor's questionable views impinge very little on the position articulated in *Chill*.

Chapter 3

1 In the only detailed comparative study about media coverage of climate change and the formation of policy in Germany and France, (Aykut) Stefan Aykut notes that articles in the German press have tended to adopt a uniformly alarmist tone, contrasting with debate in France, where the debate has been more open to scepticism, but less emotionally loaded.

2 See Sloterdijk. The entire 90-minute programme can be viewed on YouTube at https://www.youtube.com/watch?v=GBG6YCLtGvM.

3 Götz Warnke had already presented a psychoanalytic study in 1998 diagnosing a depressive-hysterical basis of green ideology in Germany.

4 Gärtner went on to publish *Öko-Nihilismus. Eine Kritik der politischen Ökologie* (Eco-Nihilism: A Critique of Political Ecology, 2007) and *Öko-Nihilismus 2012: Selbstmord in Grün* (Eco-Nihilism 2012: Suicide in Green, 2012).

5 The books which Hans von Storch has published with Nico Stehr (*Climate and Society: Climate as Resource, Climate as Risk*, 2009) and Werner Krauß (*Die Klimafalle. Die gefährliche Nähe von Klimapolitik und Klimaforschung*) are further helpful sources of information. See also Bilandzic and Soentgen on a critical study of the German discourse of climate scepticism which is being conducted at the University of Augsburg's Wissenschaftszentrum Umwelt (Centre for Environmental Science).

6 See http://www.sueddeutsche.de/wissen/alternative-fuer-deutschland-die-anti-wissenschafts-partei-1.2930329.
7 The same applies to German film, if *The Day After Tomorrow* (2004) can be counted as German – while it was made in Hollywood, the director (Roland Emmerich) was German, and the story has been described as typically German in critiquing consumer society, and especially energy profligacy.
8 The radical '-gethüm' only exists in ordinary German in the negative form, as 'Ungethüm', meaning 'monster', 'beast' or 'behemoth'. However, 'Gethüm' is occasionally found, used humorously as a term for an attractive or benevolent monster. Here it implies positive enormity.

Chapter 4

1 Oreskes and Conway and Riley E. Dunlap, 'Climate Change Skepticism and Denial: An Introduction'. *American Behavioral Scientist* 57 (6) 2013: 691–698 and Riley E. Dunlap and Aaron M. McCright, 'Organized Climate Change Denial', in *The Oxford Handbook of Climate Change and Society*, ed. John S. Dryzek, Richard B. Norgaard, and David Schlosberg (Oxford: Oxford University Press, 2011), 144–160.
2 As Conway and Oreskes note, 'In 1989 – the very year the Berlin Wall fell – the Marshall Institute [previously dedicated to fighting the Cold War] issued its first report attacking climate science. Within a few years, they would be attacking climate scientists as well' (186).
3 See http://www.creationcare.org/ and http://www.republicen.org/ (accessed on 29 June 2018).
4 See also Katherine Hayhoe's dissection of this research and its implications for strategies of communication about climate change (2015).
5 For background on the Alliance, see http://cornwallalliance.org/2017/02/the-making-of-the-cornwall-alliance/ (accessed on 29 June 2018).
6 See my essay 'Anthropocentrism and the Postsecularity of the Environmental Humanities: Aronofksy's *Noah*', forthcoming in *Modern Fiction Studies*.
7 This quote is taken verbatim from the YouTube clip, which is an edited adaptation of a passage from *Jurassic Park*, pp. 411–413.

Chapter 5

1 All translations are my own unless otherwise stated.
2 Skipping over one hundred years of French history does not mean that no ecological thinking occurred during this time. More complete histories of

French *éco-pensée* [eco-thought] can be found in Roger Cans's *Petite Histoire du mouvement écolo* (2006) [Short History of the Eco-Movement], Kerry Whiteside's *Divided Natures: French Contributions to Political Ecology* (2002), and Jean-Paul Deléage's *Une histoire de l'écologie* (1994) [A History of Ecology].

3 For an excellent analysis of early conservation policies in France, see Caroline Ford's work that explains: (1) the emphasis on *patrimoine culturel* [cultural heritage] in France rather than wilderness and (2) the use of the American model to create national parks in French colonies, for example, the establishment and management of *réserves naturelles* [nature reserves] in Algeria.

4 The rise of anti-ecological attitudes in the early 1990s in France coincides with the increasing attention given to environmentalism both nationally and internationally. It was clear that ecology was becoming a subject to be taken seriously: environmental journalism was taking up more and more space in newspapers like *Le Monde*, nature shows like Nicholas Hulot's *Ushaïa* were regularly aired on television, and intellectuals were focusing on environmentalist discourse as a serious, scholarly topic, with Pierre Lascoumes's *L'Éco-pouvoir. Environnements et politiques* (1994) [Eco-power. Environments and Politics] being one of the most notable such studies at the time.

5 See, for example, Denis Chartier and Estienne Rodary's assessment of Ferry's book as playing into 'a fear of globalization and cultural upheaval' and shoring up 'a certain pride in *French* ideas' (553–54; italics in the original).

6 In addition to the work of Catherine Larrère, see the recent publications of philosophers Hicham-Stéphane Afeissa (*La Fin du monde et de l'humanité. Essai de généalogie du discours écologique* (2014) [The End of the World and Humanity. Essay on the Genealogy of Ecological Discourse], *Éthique de l'environnement - Nature, valeur, respect* (2007) [The Environmental Ethic - Nature, Value, Respect], *Portraits de philosophes en écologistes* (2012) [Portraits of Philosophers as Ecologists]) and Émilie Hache (*Écologie politique, Cosmos, communautés, milieux* (2012) [Political Ecology, Cosmos, Communities, Places], *Ce à quoi nous tenons. Propositions pour une écologie pragmatique* (2011) [That to Which We Hold Dear. Proposals for a Pragmatic Ecology]).

7 One of the main themes of Allègre's book is his proposal to replace a 'false ecology', that only argues about climate change and CO_2 emissions, with a 'true ecology', that is concerned with 'real' environmental problems such as water and air quality in developing countries.

8 I prefer Aykut et al.'s carefully contextualized sociological analysis to general surveys of public attitudes towards climate change in France. But for those interested in statistics, Toussaint Nothias and James Painter's 'Country Result: France' in *Climate Change in the Media: Reporting Risk and Uncertainty* (2013) is a good place to start. They note that in 2009, 81 per cent of the French public agreed that climate change was a serious threat, and in 2012, 69 per cent agreed that climate change had been proven by science (93).

9 It might be more accurate to say that the National Front has no consistent position on environmental issues. Its leader, Marie le Pen, has strongly opposed fracking while also describing those who resist this kind of economic development as having "une vision d'âge de pierre" ['a view from the Stone Ages'] (Chapelle, "Municipales"). French climatologist Valérie Masson-Delmotte maintains that the National Front is simply "climatosceptique non-revendiqué" ['covertly climate sceptic'] (Chapelle, "Les Nouvelles Figures").

10 In their study of climate scepticism in Sweden, Jonas Anshelm and Martin Hultman speculate on the prevalence of male voices in this debate: 'Understanding Climate Sceptics in terms of a threat to their masculinity may therefore broaden the debate regarding environmental politics and gender policies' (116). Whether older French scientists defend climate scepticism as a way of bolstering their masculinity is beyond the scope of my study. It can however be noted that climate scepticism in general is dominated by male voices.

11 Although Ewald's climate scepticism is an interesting case, I will not discuss it elsewhere in the chapter. As Michel Foucault's former assistant in the 1970s and currently the overseer of his literary estate, Ewald is deeply immersed in post-structuralist thought and extremely critical of science as an apparatus of power. He defends Allègre on these grounds: climate change has been raised 'au rang d'un dogme incontestable, plaçant tout sceptique en situation d'excommunication' ('Apologie de Claude Allègre' n.p.) ['to the level of uncontestable dogma, placing sceptics under the ban of excommunication'].

12 Painter and Ashe (2012) show peaks in the French media's coverage of climate scepticism first in 2007 and then again in 2010.

13 Foucart's analysis of climate scepticism in France has been the more popular of the two rebuttals. It has since been republished in Folio version as *L'Avenir du climat. Enquête sur les climato-sceptiques* (2015) [The Future of Climate. An Inquiry into Climate Scepticism].

14 According to Foucart, the internet has served as both 'importateur'['importer'] and 'incubateur' ['incubator'] for climate scepticism in France ('La Blogosphère').

15 See Emily Eakin's article, 'The Gallic Gadfly', that includes an excellent critique of the English translation of Bruckner's book, *The Fanaticism of the Apocalypse*. Eakin nicely highlights Bruckner's 'aphoristic eloquence and affinity for paradox' and clearly explains his position as a 'conservative liberal' (n.p.).

16 In *Au temps des catastrophes. Résister à la barbarie qui vient* (2009) [translated into English as *In Catastrophic Times: Resisting the Coming Barbarism*], Isabelle Stengers predicts exactly the kind of traditional humanist politics that Bruckner embraces in his 2011 book: 'Those who have set up camp in the position of the guardians of reason and progress will certainly scream about irrationality. They will denounce a panicky regression that would make us forget the "heritage of the Enlightenment," the grand narrative of human emancipation shaking off the yoke of transcendences.

Their role has already been assigned. After having contributed to skepticism with regard to climate change (think of Claude Allègre), they will devote all their energy to reminding an always credulous public opinion that it must not be diverted, that it must believe in the destiny of Man and in his capacity to triumph in the face of every challenge. Concretely, this signifies the duty to believe in science, the brains of humanity, and in technology, in the service of progress' (48; qtd. from the 2015 English translation).

17 Research director at the CNRS and professor at Paris's *École Polytechnique*, Godard has been particularly harsh in his critique of climate scepticism in France.

18 Hulot founded the Ushaia Foundation in 1990, convinced five of twelve presidential candidates to sign his *Pacte écologique* [Ecological pact] in 2007, and was appointed minister of Ecological and Solidary Transition in 2017. But his detractors call him the *éco-Tartuffe*, a derogatory term I will explain later in the chapter.

19 See my earlier point about *faucheurs volontaires d'OGM* [volunteer GMO reapers] who destroy swaths of GMO plants and are often fined and even imprisoned for their actions. I had the pleasure of meeting Jean-Pierre Lebrun, a *faucheur volontaire* and member of *Semences paysannes*, at *La Haute herberie*, an activist theater-farm, in Pouancé, France in May 2015. He spoke at length about successful local resistance to multinationals like Monsanto.

20 See *Génération Cobaye*'s collection of humorous YouTube videos such as 'Comment le pétrole a niqué notre libido' ('How oil screwed up our libido') that aim to raise awareness about environmental issues without playing on fears of future apocalypse. In comparison, websites like climate sceptic Duran's *La Pensée unique* are content heavy with unreadably long chunks of text broken up by dated gif animations.

21 This tactic is also used by writers whose main objective is to denounce the falsified science behind climate scepticism. Environmental journalist Stéphane Foucart begins his book *Le Populisme climatique* [Climate Populism]: 'Cette histoire est celle d'intérêts industriels et contrariés et des efforts faits par plusieurs entreprises pour discréditer la science [...] C'est aussi une histoire qui s'écrit principalement sur les nouveaux médias, et Internet joue un rôle crucial' (Kindle, loc. 4 per cent) ['This is a story about frustrated industrial interests and efforts made by such companies to discredit science [...] It's also a story written largely by new media and in which the Internet plays a key role.']

22 An obvious counter-example is Allègre's book that reads like the transcript of an interview and feels at times quite hastily put together.

23 This trope is overused by climate sceptics and environmentalists alike. For a sample of titles, see Claude Allègre's *L'Imposture climatique* (2010), Jean-Louis Butré's *L'Imposture. Pourquoi l'éolien est un danger pour la France* (2008) [The Imposture. Why Wind Turbines Are a Danger for France], Pierre Kohler's *L'Imposture verte* (2002) [The Green Imposture], Christian Laurut's *L'Imposture écologiste* (2011) [The Imposture of Ecologists], Gil Rivière-Wekstein's *Abeilles: l'imposture écologique*

(2006) [Bees: The Ecological Imposture]; on the environmentalist side, see Sylvestre Huet's *L'Imposteur, c'est lui* (2010) [The Imposter, It's Him] and Corinne Lepage's *De l'écologie. Hors de l'imposture et de l'opportunisme* (2003) [Ecology. Away From Imposture and Opportunism].

24 Unsurprisingly, Galileo's name often comes up in climate sceptic texts (see Chapter 7). Allègre refers to him on multiple occasions, but denies the interviewer's direct comparison, while Rittaud concludes his book by describing the 'sceptics pantheon' in which scientists like Galileo can be found, then adding that he will probably never rise to such heights.

25 I'm following a different line of argumentation here than the one adopted by environmental journalist Sylvestre Huet, who counters Allègre's attack by calling him out as the duper in *L'Imposteur, c'est lui* (2010) [The Imposter, It's Him]. Even though Huet corrects many of Allègre's false affirmations, he does not address the pitfalls of this recursive practice of calling out the duper; there is always someone else to assert that his truth claims are more accurate, more authoritative, more true.

26 There have been a handful of popular *romans d'anticipation* [speculative novels] in which climate change serves as a background to the main action of the plot: Michel Houellebecq's *La Possibiilité d'une île* (2005) [translated into English as *The Possibility of an Island*], Éric Chevillard's *Sans l'orang-outan* (2007) [Without the Orangutan], and Jean-Christophe Rufin's *Globalia* (2004). Less widely read novels that tackle the problem of climate change directly include Julien Blanc-Gras's *Paradis (avant liquidation)* (2014) [Paradise (Before Liquidation)]and Jean-Marc Ligny's eco-thriller *Aqua*™ (2004).

27 These short pieces have been published in the collection *Du souffle dans les mots: Trente écrivains s'engagent pour le climat* (Paris, Éditions Arthaud, 2015) [Breath/Inspiration in Words: Thirty Writers Commit to Climate].

28 Even if global warming has not given rise to a new literary genre in France, examples of pro-ecological sentiment can be found in French literature dating back to Rousseau and Montaigne. For an overview, see my co-edited collection with Daniel Finch-Race, *French Ecocriticism: From the Early Modern Period to the Twenty-First Century* (2017).

29 See for example Dominique Noguez's book L'Arc-en-ciel des humours (2000) [The Humour Rainbow] that describes black humour as scandalous, macabre, and unfettered by social convention. According to Walter Redfern, "black humour can house both arrogance and a strong sense of the futility of your endeavours" (119); it is meant to provoke and retaliate.

30 In a 2011 interview about the Fukushima disaster, *Le Monde*'s journalist Raphaëlle Rérolle asks Gran how literature can respond to catastrophe. Gran answers: 'Si elle peut donner du goût à la vie, ce serait déjà pas mal. Il ne faut pas lui demander davantage' (n.p.) ['If it adds flavour to life, that already would be not too bad. One shouldn't ask for more.']

31 Some of the short pieces in the collection *Du souffle dans les mots* experiment with non-human perspectives such as Éric Chevillard's 'Rapport parlementaire' [Parliamentary Report] that is spoken by a group of imaginary *animot* to a committee of humans *(à la Kafka)* and Frédéric Boyer's verse poem that adopts the voice of planet earth to say goodbye to the human species. But no book-length fictional work in French about climate change has adopted a non-human perspective (that I know of).

32 Painter, Kristiansen, and Schäfer explain that *Huffington Post* was the one exception. Its sites in English, French, German and Spanish reported on multiple environmentally related issues during the Paris climate change summit.

Chapter 6

1 In France, climate scepticism emerged within the halls of the *Académie des sciences*, ushered in by esteemed geologist and politician Claude Allègre and volcanologist Vincent Courtillot.

2 STS scholars typically distinguish between the *practice* of the sciences (or 'science in-the-making'), which they study with great interest and respect, and the *use* of an idealized version of 'Science' (Latour capitalizes it in this form) to circumvent debate. The latter has also been called 'scientism' (Brian Wynne, 'When Doubt Becomes a Weapon', *Nature* 466.7305 (2010)) and 'scientization' (Myanna Lahsen, 'Climategate: The Role of the Social Sciences', *Climatic Change* 119.3–4 (2013)). We use Steven Yearley's term 'scientification' (Steven Yearley, *Sociology, Environmentalism, Globalization: Reinventing the Globe* (Thousand Oaks, CA; London: SAGE Publications, 1996)).

Chapter 7

1 See 'Genetic Engineering'. *GREENPEACE New Zealand*, https://www.greenpeace.org/archive-international/en/campaigns/agriculture/problem/genetic-engineering/; and National Academies of Sciences. 'Genetically Engineered Crops: Experiences and Prospects'. *National Academies Press: OpenBook*, 17 May 2016, https://www.nap.edu/resourceresourcecatalogresource/23395/GEGEgenetically-engineeredGE-crops-experiences-and-prospects.report-brief.pdf

2 https://www.theguardian.com/environment/climate-consensus-97-per-cent

3 Fans of comic science fiction writer Douglas Adams will enjoy John Adams's dismissal of IAMs as 'Vogon economics' (173).

Bibliography

Abram, David. *The Spell of the Sensuous: Perception and Language in the More-Than-Human World*. New York: Vintage, 1996.

Abu-Lughod, Lila. 'Writing Against Culture', in *Recapturing Anthropology*, ed. Richard Fox. Santa Fe, NM: School of American Research Press, 1991, 137–62.

Adams, John. *Risk*. London; Bristol, PA: UCL Press, 1995.

Afeissa, Hicham-Stéphane, editor. *Éthique de l'environnement – Nature, valeur, respect*. Paris: Vrin, 2007.

Afeissa, Hicham-Stéphane. *La Fin du monde et de l'humanité. Essai de généalogie du discours écologique*. Paris: PUF, 2014.

Afeissa, Hicham-Stéphane. *Portraits de philosophes en écologistes*. Paris: Éditions Dehors, 2012.

Allègre, Claude. *L'Imposture climatique ou la fausse écologie*. Paris: Plon, 2010.

Anderegg, William R. L., James W. Prall, and Jacob Harold. 'Reply to O'Neill and Boykoff: Objective Classification of Climate Experts'. *Proceedings of the National Academy of Sciences* 107.39 (2010): E152–E52.

Anderegg, William R. L., et al. 'Expert Credibility in Climate Change'. *Proceedings of the National Academy of Sciences* 107.27 (2010): 12107–09.

Andermatt Conley, Verena. *Ecopolitics. The Environment in Poststructuralist Thought*. London; New York: Routledge, 1997.

Andrew. 'Skeptics Smeared as Holocaust Deniers, ADL Silent'. *Carbon Dioxide (CO2) Is Not Pollution*. Available online at www.populartechnology.net/2014/02/skeptics-smeared-as-holocaust-deniers.html

Anshelm, Jonas and Martin Hultman. *Discourses of Global Climate Change: Apocalyptic Framing and Political Antagonisms*. London; New York: Routledge, 2014.

Åsberg, Cecilia, Astrida Neimanis, and Johan Hedrén. 'Four Problems, Four Directions for Environmental Humanities: Toward a Critical Posthumanities for the Anthropocene'. *Ethics and the Environment* 20.2 (2015): 230–71.

Ashby, Lord and Mary Anderson. 'Studies in the Politics of Environmental Protection: The Historical Roots of the British Clean Air Act, 1956: III. The Ripening of Public Opinion, 1898–1952'. *Interdisciplinary Science Reviews* 2.3 (1977): 190–206.

Attridge, Derek. *The Singularity of Literature*. London: Routledge, 2004. Kindle.

Aykut, Stefan. 'La construction du changement climatique comme problème public – débat médiatique et expertise climatique en France et en Allemagne', in *Savoirs experts et profanes dans la construction des problèmes publics*, ed. Ludivine Damay, Benjamin Denis, and Denis Duez. Brussels: Publications des Facultés universitaires Saint-Louis, 2011, 77–114.

Aykut, Stefan, Jean-Baptiste Comby, and Hélène Guillemot. 'Climate Change Controversies in French Mass Media 1990–2010', *Journalism Studies* 13.2 (2012): 157–74.

Aykut, Stefan, Christophe Bonneuil, Jean Jouzel, Maxime Combes, Nicolas Haeringer, Valérie Cabanes, and Geneviève Azam. 'Climat: Nicolas Sarkozy, dangereux marchand de doute'. *La Libération,* 16 September 2016 Available online at http://www.liberation.fr/politiques/2016/09/16/climat-nicolas-sarkozy-dangereux-marchand-de-doute_1499625 (accessed 2 October 2017).

Bachmann, Hartmut. *Die Lüge der Klimakatastrophe. ... und wie der Staat uns damit ausbeutet. Manipulierte Angst als Mittel zur Macht*, 6th ed. Berlin: Frieling 2010.

Baqué, Joël. *La Fonte des glaces.* Paris: P.O.L., 2017.

Bartsch, Christian. 'Wider die Klimahysterie. Mehr Licht im Dunkel des Klimawandels'. *Frankfurter Allgemeine Zeitung*, 3 April 2007.

Bartsch, Christian, Günter Ederer, Matthias Horx, Wolf Lotter, Dirk Maxeiner, Josef Reichholf, and Wolfram Weimer. 'Die "Klimaskeptiker" antworten. Wir müssen Urängste relativieren'. *Frankfurter Allgemeine Zeitung*, 5 September 2007, p. 35. Available online at http://www.faz.net/aktuell/wissen/klima/die-klimaskeptiker-antworten-wir-muessen-uraengste-relativieren-1462827.html

Bate, Jonathan. *Romantic Ecology: Wordsworth and the Environmental Tradition.* London: Routledge, 1991.

Bate, Jonathan. *The Song of the Earth.* London: Picador, 2000.

Bate, Roger and Julian Morris. *Global Warming: Apocalypse or Hot Air?* London: Institute of Economic Affairs, 1994.

Bean, Richard. *The Heretic.* London: Oberon, 2011.

Beck, Glenn with Harriet Parke. *Agenda 21.* New York: Threshold Editions, 2012.

Beckerman, Wilfred. *Small Is Stupid: Blowing the Whistle on the Greens.* London: Duckworth, 1995.

Beder, Sharon. 'Neoliberal Think Tanks and Free Market Environmentalism'. *Environmental Politics* 10.2 (2001): 128–28.

Behringer, Wolfgang. *Kulturgeschichte des Klimas. Von der Eiszeit bis zur globalen Erwärmung*, 5th ed. Munich: C.H. Beck, 2010.

Beinart, Peter. 'Glenn Beck's Regrets'. *The Atlantic*, Atlantic Media Company, 13 December 2016. Available online at www.theatlantic.com/magazine/archive/2017/01/glenn-becks-regrets/508763/

Bellamy, Edward and Cecelia Tichi. *Looking Backward 2000–1887.* New York: Penguin, 1982.

Bennett, Elena. *Seeds of Good Anthropocenes.* 2016. Available online at https://goodanthropocenes.net (accessed 5 December2017).

Bennett, Oliver. *Cultural Pessimism. Narratives of Decline in the Postmodern World*, Edinburgh: Edinburgh University Press, 2001.

Bergthaller, Hannes. 'Fossil Freedoms: The Politics of Emancipation and the End of Oil', in *The Routledge Companion to the Environmental Humanities*, ed. John Christensen, Ursula K. Heise, and Michelle Niemann. London: Routledge, 2017, 424–32.

Berland, Lucie. 'Les nouveaux écolos ont tué l'écologie anxiogène', *Slate.fr.*, 2 May 2015. Available online at http://www.slate.fr/story/116652/nouveaux-ecolos-politique-sourire (accessed 17 May 2017).

Bess, Michael. *The Light-Green Society: Ecology and Technological Modernity in France, 1960–2000*. Chicago: Chicago University Press, 2002.

'Beyond Debate?' *Times Higher Education (THE)*, THEunijobs, 22 May 2015. Available online at www.timeshighereducation.com/features/beyond-debate/409454.article

Bilandzic, Helena and Jens Soentgen. 'Die Struktur klimaskeptischer Argumente', *Gaia* 23.1 (March 2014): 40–47.

Bild. 'Globale Erwärmung: Die CO2-Lüge. Renommiertes Forscher-Team behauptet: Die Klima-Katastrophe ist Panik-Mache der Politik', 6 February 2012.

Bild. 'Seit 12 Jahren ist die Erd-Erwärmung gestoppt!', 7 February 2012.

Bloor, David. *Knowledge and Social Imagery*, 2nd ed. Chicago; London: University of Chicago Press, 1991.

Blow, Charles M. 'About the "Basket of Deplorables"'. *The New York Times*, 12 September 2016. Available online at www.nytimes.com/2016/09/12/opinion/about-the-basket-of-deplorables.html

Blüchel, Kurt G. *Der Klimaschwindel. Erderwärmung, Treibhauseffekt, Klimawandel – Die Fakten*. Munich: Bertelsmann, 2007.

Blühdorn, Ingolfur. 'The Governance of Unsustainability: Ecology and Democracy after the Post-democratic Turn', *Environmental Politics* 22.1 (2013): 16–36. Available online at http://dx.doi.org/10.1080/09644016.2013.755005

Boehmer-Christiansen, Sonja. 'Science, Equity, and the War against Carbon'. *Science, Technology, & Human Values* 28.1 (2003): 69–92.

Boehmer-Christiansen, Sonja. 'A Scientific Agenda for Climate Policy?' *Nature* 372 (1994): 400–402.

Bonner, Frances. 'Top Gear: Why Does the World's Most Popular Programme Not Deserve Scrutiny?' *Critical Studies in Television* 5.1 (2010): 32–45.

Böttcher, Sven. *Prophezeiung*. Cologne: Kiepenheuer and Witsch, 2011.

Boussalis, Constantine and Travis G. Coan. 'Text-Mining the Signals of Climate Change Doubt'. *Global Environmental Change* 36 (2016): 89–100.

Boyd, David R. *The Optimistic Environmentalist: Progressing Towards a Greener Future*. Toronto, ON: ECW Press, 2015.

Boyer, Frédéric. 'De son extinction. Discours d'adieu', in *Du souffle dans les mots: Trente écrivains s'engagent pour le climat*, ed. Sylvie Gouttebaron. Paris: Éditions Arthaud, 2015, 44–60.

Boykoff, Maxwell T. 'The Cultural Politics of Climate Change Discourse in UK Tabloids'. *Political Geography* 27.5 (2008): 549–69.

Boykoff, Maxwell T. and Maria Mansfield. '"Ye Olde Hot Aire": Reporting on Human Contributions to Climate Change in the Uk Tabloid Press'. *Environmental research letters* 3.2 (2008): 024002.

Bramoullé, Gérard. *La Peste verte*. Paris: Belles Lettres, 1991.

Branch, Michael P. 'Are You Serious? A Modest Proposal for Environmental Humor', in *The Oxford Handbook of Ecocriticism*, ed. Greg Garrard. Oxford: Oxford University Press, 2013.

Brick, Phil. 'Determined Opposition: The Wise Use Movement Challenges Environmentalism'. *Environment: Science and Policy for Sustainable Development* 37.8 (1995): 17–42.

Brimblecombe, Peter. 'The Clean Air Act after 50 Years'. *Weather* 61.11 (2006): 311–14.

Brown, William. *Seven Pillars of Creation: The Bible, Science, and the Ecology of Wonder*. Oxford: Oxford University Press, 2010.

Bruckner, Pascal. *Le Fanatisme de l'Apocalypse*. Paris: Grasset & Fasquelle, 2011. Kindle edition.

Brunnengräber, Achim. *Klimaskeptiker in Deutschland und ihr Kampf gegen die Energiewende*, University of Vienna, Institut für Politikwissenschaft Working Paper 1/2013. Available online at http://politikwissenschaft.univie.ac.at/fileadmin/user_upload/inst_politikwiss/IPW_Working_Papers/IPW-WP-1_2013-Achim-Brunnengraeber.pdf

Bruni, Frank. 'I'm O.K. – You're Pure Evil'. *The New York Times*, 17 June 2017. Available online at www.nytimes.com/2017/06/17/opinion/sunday/im-ok-youre-pure-evil.html

Bryson, Bill. *A Short History of Nearly Everything*. Toronto, ON: Doubleday Canada, 2012.

Buell, Frederick. *From Apocalypse to Way of Life: Environmental Crisis in the American Century*, Kindle edition. New York; London: Routledge, 2003.

Buell, Lawrence. 'Environmental Apocalypticism', in *The Environmental Imagination. Thoreau, Nature Writing, and the Formation of American Culture*. Cambridge, MA: Harvard University Press, 1995, 283–308.

Burck, Jan, Franziska Marten, and Christoph Bals. *Results 2017. Germanwatch/Climate Action Network Europe: Climate Change Performance Index*. Available online at https://germanwatch.org/en/download/16482.pdf

Butré, Jean-Louis. *L'Imposture: Pourquoi l'éolien est un danger pour la France*. Paris: Éditions du Toucan, 2008.

Cans, Roger. *Petite Histoire du mouvement écolo en France*. Paris: Delachaux et Niestlé, 2006.

Capstick, Stuart Bryce and Nicholas Frank Pidgeon. 'What Is Climate Change Scepticism? Examination of the Concept Using a Mixed Methods Study of the UK Public'. *Global Environmental Change* 24 (2014): 389–401.

Capstick, Stuart Bryce, Nicholas Frank Pidgeon, and Karen Henwood. 'Stability and Change in British Public Discourses About Climate Change between 1997 and 2010'. *Environmental Values* 24.6 (2015): 725–53.

Capstick, Stuart, et al. 'International Trends in Public Perceptions of Climate Change over the Past Quarter Century'. *Wiley Interdisciplinary Reviews: Climate Change* 6.1 (2015): 35–61.

Carolan, Michael. 'Sociological Ambivalence and Climate Change'. *Local environment* 15.4 (2010): 309–21.

Carter, Neil. 'Party Politicization of the Environment in Britain'. *Party Politics* 12.6(2006): 747–67.

Carter, Neil. 'The Politics of Climate Change in the UK'. *Wiley Interdisciplinary Reviews: Climate Change* 5.3 (2014): 423–33.

Chapelle, Sophie. 'Les Nouvelles Figures du climatoscepticisme'. *Ritimo. Informations, outils pour un monde solidaire*, 23 November 2016. Available online at https://www.ritimo.org/Les-nouvelles-figures-du-climatoscepticisme-6269 (accessed 5 September 2017).

Chapelle, Sophie. 'Municipales: Le visage anti-social et anti-écolo du Front National', *Basta !* 20 March 2014. Available online at https://www.bastamag.net/Conseils-regionaux-le-visage-anti (accessed 15 September 2017).

Charbonnier, Pierre, Bruno Latour, and Baptiste Morizot. 'Redécouvrir la terre (Rediscovering Land)'. *Tracés. Revue des sciences humaines.* 33 (2017): 227–52.

Chartier, Denis and Estienne Rodary. 'Globalising French *écologie politique*: A Political Necessity', in *The International Handbook of Political Ecology*, ed. Raymond Bryant. Cambridge, MA: Edward Elgar Publishing, 2015, 547–60.

Chevillard, Éric. 'Rapport parlementaire,' in *Du souffle dans les mots: Trente écrivains s'engagent pour le climat*, ed. Sylvie Gouttebaron. Paris: Éditions Arthaud, 2015, 102–8.

Chevillard, Éric. *Sans l'orang-outan*. Paris: Minuit, 2007.

Chick, Martin. *Electricity and Energy Policy in Britain, France and the United States Since 1945*. Cheltenham and Northampton: Edward Elgar Publishing, 2007.

Clark, Timothy. *Ecocriticism on the Edge: The Anthropocene as a Threshold Concept*. London: Bloomsbury, 2015.

Clark, Timothy. 'Some Climate Change Ironies: Deconstruction, Environmental Politics and the Closure of Ecocriticism'. *Oxford Literary Review* 32.1 (2010): 131–49.

Clarke, Bruce. 'Science, Theory, and Systems: A Response to Glen A. Love and Jonathan Levin'. *Interdisciplinary Studies in Literature and Environment* 8.1 (2001): 149–65.

Clarkson, Jeremy. *Driven to Distraction*. London: Michael Joseph, 2009. Kindle.

Clarkson, Jeremy. *For Crying out Loud!: The World According to Clarkson, Vol. 3*. London: Penguin, 2009. Kindle.

Clarkson, Jeremy. *Is It Really Too Much to Ask?: The World According to Clarkson, Vol. 5*. London: Penguin, 2013. Kindle.

'Climate Change Act 2008'. *Legislation.gov.uk*, Queen's Printer of Acts of Parliament. Available online at www.legislation.gov.uk/ukpga/2008/27/section/1

'Climate Consensus – the 97% | Environment'. *The Guardian*, Guardian News and Media. Available online at www.theguardian.com/environment/climate-consensus-97-per-cent.

'Climate Science Glossary'. *Skeptical Science*. Available online at www.skepticalscience.com/

'Climate Science Glossary – Climate Models'. *Skeptical Science*. Available online at www.skepticalscience.com/climate-models-intermediate.htm

'Climate Science Glossary 'Close Encounters of the Absurd Kind''. *Skeptical Science*. Available online at www.skepticalscience.com/ben-santer-1995-ipcc-report.htm

'Climate Science Glossary – Cosmic Rays'. *Skeptical Science*. Available online at skepticalscience.com/cosmic-rays-and-global-warming-advanced.htm

'Climate Science Glossary – IPCC Consensus'. *Skeptical Science*. Available online at www.skepticalscience.com/ipcc-scientific-consensus-intermediate.htm

Cohen, M. *Paradigm Shift: How Expert Opinions Keep Changing on Life, the Universe, and Everything*. Exeter: Imprint Academic, 2015. Kindle.

Cook, John, et al. 'Consensus on Consensus: A Synthesis of Consensus Estimates on Human-Caused Global Warming'. *Environmental Research Letters* 11.4 (2016): 048002.

Cook, John, et al. 'Quantifying the Consensus on Anthropogenic Global Warming in the Scientific Literature'. *Environmental research letters* 8.2 (2013): 024024.

Cornwall Alliance for the Stewardship of the Creation. 'Open Letter to the Signers of "Climate Change: An Evangelical Call to Action" and Others Concerned with Global Warming'. Available online at http://cornwallalliance.org/2006/07/an-open-letter-to-the-signers-of-climate-change-an-evangelical-call-to-action-and-others-concerned-about-global-warming-2/ (accessed 31 January 2018).

Cornwall Alliance for the Stewardship of the Creation. 'What We Do'. Available online at http://cornwallalliance.org/about/what-we-do/ (accessed 31 January 2018).

Cox, Graham and Philp Lowe. 'A Battle Not the War: The Politics of the Wildlife and Countryside Act'. *Countryside Planning Yearbook* 4 (1983): 48–76.

Crichton, Michael. *Jurassic Park*. New York: Ballantine, 1993.

Crichton, Michael. 'Remarks to the Commonwealth Club, 2003'. Available online at http://sharpgary.org/ChrichtonCommonweal.html (accessed 31 January 2018).

Crichton, Michael. *State of Fear*, New York: Harper Collins, 2004. Kindle.

Crowley, Michael. 'Jurassic President'. *The New Republic,* 2006. Available online at https://newrepublic.com/article/65354/michael-crichtons-scariest-creation (accessed 31 January 2018).

Curry, Judith A. and Peter J. Webster. 'Climate Science and the Uncertainty Monster'. *Bulletin of the American Meteorological Society* 92.12 (2011): 1667–82.

THE DECAY OF LYING. Available online at virgil.org/dswo/courses/novel/wilde-lying.pdf

Deléage, Jean-Paul. *Une histoire de l'écologie*. Paris: Seuil, 1994.

Delingpole, James. *Watermelons: How Environmentalists Are Killing the Planet, Destroying the Economy and Stealing Your Children's Future*. London: Biteback, 2011. Kindle.

'"Democracy Is the Worst Form of Government … "'. Richard M. Langworth, 23 May 2016, richardlangworth.com/worst-form-of-government.

'Does Demonizing the Other Side Promote Constructive Debate Over Climate Change?' *Watts Up With That?* 21 April 2016. Available online at wattsupwiththat.com/2016/04/21/does-demonizing-the-other-side-promote-constructive-debate-over-climate-change/

'Drivers Kept Waiting as Shortages Ease'. *BBC News*, BBC, 17 September 2000. Available online at news.bbc.co.uk/2/hi/uk_news/928701.stm

Dubenko, Anna. 'Right and Left React to the Paris Climate Agreement News'. *The New York Times*, 4 June 2017. Available online at www.nytimes.com/2017/06/04/us/politics/paris-treaty-reactions.html

Dugan, Andrew. 'Conservative Republicans Alone on Global Warming's Timing'. Gallup News, 22 April 2015. Available online at http://news.gallup.com/poll/182807/conservative-republicans-alone-global-warming-timing.aspx (accessed 31 January 2018).

Dunlap, Riley E. and Aaron M. McCright. 'Climate Change Denial: Sources, Actors and Strategies'. *Routledge Handbook of Climate Change and Society* (2010): 240.

Dunlap, Riley E. and Peter J. Jacques. 'Climate Change Denial Books and Conservative Think Tanks: Exploring the Connection'. *American Behavioral Scientist* 57.6 (2013).

Duran, Jean. *La Pensée unique*, 2005–6. Available online at http://www.pensee-unique.fr/index.html (accessed 5 December 2017).

Edsall, Thomas. 'Democrats Are Playing Checkers While Trump Is Playing Chess'. *The New York Times*, 12 October 2017. Available online at www.nytimes.com/2017/10/12/opinion/democrats-are-playing-checkers-while-trump-is-playing-chess.html

Edwards, Paul N. *A Vast Machine: Computer Models, Climate Data, and the Politics of Global Warming*. London: MIT Press, 2013.

Ehrlich, Paul R. and Anne H. Ehrlich. *Betrayal of Science and Reason: How Anti-Environmental Rhetoric Threatens Our Future*. Washington, DC: Island Press, 1996.

EIKE. *Handbuch für Klimaskeptiker*. Available online at https://www.eike-klima-energie.eu/

Enzensberger, Hans Magnus. 'A Critique of Political Ecology', in *Dreamers of the Absolute. Essays on Politics, Crime and Culture*. London: Radius, 1988, 253–95.

European Commission. *Special Eurobarometer 459 Report Climate Change*, March 2017. Available online at https://ec.europa.eu/clima/sites/clima/files/support/docs/report_2017_en.pdf

'Evangelical Environmental Network'. Available online at http://www.creationcare.org/ (accessed 30 January 2018).

Evans, Dylan. *Risk Intelligence: How to Live with Uncertainty*. London: Atlantic, 2012.

Evers, Marco, Olaf Stampf and Gerald Traufetter. 'Die Wolkenschieber' *Der Spiegel* 13 (2010): 140–49.

Ewald, François. 'Apologie de Claude Allègre'. *Les Échos*, 2 March 2010. Available online at https://www.lesechos.fr/02/03/2010/LesEchos/20626-061-ECH_apologie-de-claude-allegre.htm (accessed 10 May 2018).

'FACT CHECK: Ronald Reagan "If You've Seen One Tree … "'. *Snopes.com*, 20 May 2008. Available online at www.snopes.com/quotes/reagan/redwoods.asp

'FAQs'. *Heterodox Academy*, 26 June 2018. Available online at heterodoxacademy.org/about-us/faqs/

Ferguson, Margaret W., Mary Jo Salter, and Jon Stallworthy. *The Norton Anthology of Poetry*, 5th ed. New York; London: W.W. Norton, 2005.

Ferry, Luc. 'Claude Allègre vu par Luc Ferry'. *Le Figaro*, 19 February 2015. Available online at http://www.lefigaro.fr/vox/societe/2015/02/19/31003-20150219ARTFIG00437-claude-allegre-vu-par-luc-ferry.php (accessed 10 September 2017).

Ferry, Luc. '"L'Imposture climatique" et l'indignation des belles âmes'. *Revue de la presse*. 132.4 (2010): 1080–1.

Ferry, Luc. *Le Nouvel Ordre écologique. L'arbre, l'animal et l'homme*. Paris: Grasset, 1992.

Ferry, Luc and Alain Renaut. *La Pensée '68. Essai sur l'anti-humanisme contemporain*. Paris: Gallimard, 1985.

Finch-Race, Daniel and Stephanie Posthumus. *French Ecocriticism: From the Early Modern Period to the Twenty-First Century*. Frankfurt: Peter Lang, 2017.

Fiorina, Morris P. and Samuel J. Abrams. 'Political Polarization in the American Public'. *Annual Review of Political Science* 11 (2008): 563–88.

Fiorina, Morris P., Samuel J. Abrams, and Jeremy Pope. *Culture War?: The Myth of a Polarized America*. Great Questions in Politics Series. New York: Pearson Longman, 2005.

Fleming, Chris. 'Flat Wrong: The Misunderstood History of Flat Earth Theories'. *The Conversation*, 28 June 2018. Available online at theconversation.com/flat-wrong-the-misunderstood-history-of-flat-earth-theories-53808

Ford, Caroline. 'Nature, Culture and Conservation in France and her Colonies 1840–1940'. *Past & Present* 183 (2004): 173–98.

Foster, Philip. *While the Earth Endures: Creation, Cosmology and Climate Change*. Hemingford Abbots: St. Matthew Publishing, 2009.

Foucart, Stéphane. 'La Blogosphère, incubateur du climatoscepticisme'. *Le Monde*, 2 February 2017. Available online at https://www.lemonde.fr/climat/article/2017/02/02/la-blogosphere-incubateur-du-climatoscepticisme_5073411_1652612.html (accessed 3 September 2017).

Foucart, Stéphane. *Le Populisme climatique. Claude Allègre et Cie, enquête sur les ennemis de la science*. Paris Éditions Denoël, 2010. Kindle.

Foucault, Michel. 'Authorship: What Is an Author?' *Screen* 20.1 (1979): 13–34.

Freudenburg, William R. and Violetta Muselli. 'Global Warming Estimates, Media Expectations, and the Asymmetry of Scientific Challenge'. *Global Environmental Change* 20.4 (2010): 483–91.

Friedrich, Johannes, Mengpin Ge and Alexander Tankou. '6 Charts to Understand U.S. State Greenhouse Gas Emissions'. Available online at https://www.wri.org/blog/2017/08/6-charts-understand-us-state-greenhouse-gas-emissions

Fröhlich, Tanja. *Klimaskepsis in Deutschland. Handlungsempfehlungen für Politik und Wissenschaft*. Frankfurt am Main: Peter Lang, 2014.

Fuhr, Eckhard. 'Der heilige Krieg der Klimaskeptiker', *Die Welt*, 5 September 2007.

Funtowicz, Silvio O. and Jerome R. Ravetz. 'Science for the Post Normal Age', in *Perspectives on Ecological Integrity*, ed. Laura Westra and John Lemons. Dordrecht and Boston: Kluwer Academic Publishers, 1995, 146–61.

Galam, Serge. *Les Scientifiques ont perdu le Nord*. Paris: Plon, 2008.

Galinsky, Adam D. and Gordon B. Moskowitz. 'Perspective-Taking: Decreasing Stereotype Expression, Stereotype Accessibility, and in-Group Favoritism'. *Journal of Personality and Social Psychology* 78.4 (2000): 708.

Ganteför, Gerd. *Klima. Der Weltuntergang findet nicht statt*. Weinheim: Wiley, 2012.

Garrard, Greg. *Ecocriticism* (New Critical Idiom). London: Routledge, 2004.

Garrard, Greg. 'The Unbearable Lightness of Green: Air Travel, Climate Change and Literature'. *Green Letters: Studies in Ecocriticism*, 17.2 (2013): 175–88.

Gärtner, Edgar. *CO_2: Un mythe planétaire*.Paris: Éditions du Toucan, 2009. Translation: *Climate: The Great Delusion*. London: Stacey International, 2010.

Gärtner, Edgar. *Écologie, la grande arnaque*. Paris: Albin Michel, 2007.

Gärtner, Edgar. *Öko-Nihilismus. Eine Kritik der politischen Ökologie*. Jena: TvR Medienverlag, 2007.

Gärtner, Edgar. *Öko-Nihilismus 2012: Selbstmord in Grün*. Jena: TvR Medienverlag, 2012.

'Genetic Engineering'. *GREENPEACE New Zealand*. Available online at www.greenpeace.org/archive-international/en/campaigns/agriculture/problem/genetic-engineering/

Gerstenberger, Katharina and Tanja Nusser, editors. *Catastrophe and Catharsis. Perspectives on Disaster and Redemption in German Culture and Beyond*. Rochester, NY: Camden House, 2015.

Ghosh, Amitav. *The Great Derangement. Climate Change and the Unthinkable*. Chicago: Chicago University Press, 2016.

Glover, Peter C. and Michael J. Economides. *Energy and Climate Wars: How Naive Politicians, Green Ideologues, and Media Elites Are Undermining the Truth About Energy and Climate*. London; New york: Bloomsbury Publishing, 2010.

Godard, Olivier. 'Le Climato-scepticisme médiatique en France: Un sophisme moderne'. *Écologie & Politique* 45.2 (2012): 47–69.

Gould, Peter C. *Early Green Politics: Back to Nature, Back to the Land, and Socialism in Britain, 1880–1900*. Brighton: Harvester, 1988.

Gouttebaron, Sylvie, editor. *Du souffle dans les mots: Trente écrivains s'engagent pour le climat*. Paris: Éditions Arthaud, 2015.

Gouttebaron, Sylvie and Yves Boudier. 'Les Écrivains s'engagent pour le climat'. *La Libération*, 25 December 2014. Available online at http://www.liberation.fr/terre/2014/12/25/les-ecrivains-s-engagent-pour-le-climat_1170083 (accessed 3 September 2017).

Graham, Jesse, Brian A. Nosek, and Jonathan Haidt. 'The Moral Stereotypes of Liberals and Conservatives: Exaggeration of Differences across the Political Spectrum'. *PLoS One* 7.12 (2012): e50092.

Gran, Iegor. *L'Écologie en bas de chez moi*. Paris: P.O.L., 2011.

Gran, Iegor. *O.N.G.!*. Paris: Gallimard, 2004.
Gray, John. *Straw Dogs: Thoughts on Humans and Other Animals*. London: Granta, 2002.
The Great Global Warming Swindle (2007). [Film] Dir. Martin Durkin, UK: Channel 4.
Groskopf, Christopher. 'European Politics Is More Polarized than Ever, and These Numbers Prove It'. *Quartz*, 30 March 2016. Available online at qz.com/645649/european-politics-is-more-polarized-than-ever-and-these-numbers-prove-it/
Grundmann, Reiner. 'Debunking Sceptical Propaganda'. *BioSocieties* 8.3 (2013): 370–74.
Grundmann, Reiner and Mike Scott. 'Disputed Climate Science in the Media: Do Countries Matter?'. *Public Understanding of Science* 23.2 (2012): 220–35.
Guest, Bertrand. 'Environmental Awareness and Geography: Reading Reclus Ecocritically?' in *Environmental Awareness and the Design of Literature*, ed. François Specq. Leiden; Boston: Brill, 2016, 69–89.
Guilbert-Billetdoux, Augustin. *Le Messie du peuple chauve*. Paris: Gallimard, 2012.
Guillemot, Hélène. 'Les désaccords sur le changement climatique en France: au - delà d'un climat bipolaire'. *Natures Sciences Sociétés* 4.22 (2014): 340–50.
Guillemot, Hélène and Stéfan Aykut. 'Trois débats sur le climat,' *La Recherche* 478 (August 2013): 73–77.
Guilyardi, Éric and Catherine Guilyardi. *Que feriez-vous si vous le saviez? Des climatologues face à la désinformation*. Paris: Le Pommier, 2015.
Guha, Anton-Andreas. *Der Planet schlägt zurück. Ein Tagebuch aus der Zukunft*. Göttingen: Steidl, 1993.
Hache, Émilie. *Ce à quoi nous tenons. Propositions pour une écologie pragmatique*. Paris: La Découverte, 2011.
Hache, Émilie, editor. *Écologie politique, Cosmos, communautés, milieux*. Paris: Éditions Amsterdam, 2012.
Hacking, Ian. *The Social Construction of What?* Cambridge, MA: Harvard University Press, 1999.
Hager, Carol and Christoph H. Stefes, editors. *Germany's Energy Transition: A Comparative Perspective*, New York: Palgrave Macmillan, 2016.
Hahnemann, Andy. 'Footnotes Are Real. Populäre Literatur als Wissensvermittlung'. *Non Fiktion* 1:2 (2006), 142–54.
Haidt, Jonathan. *The Happiness Hypothesis: Finding Modern Truth in Ancient Wisdom*. New York: Basic Books, 2006.
Haidt, Jonathan. *The Righteous Mind: Why Good People Are Divided by Religion and Politics*. New York: Vintage, 2012.
Hamilton, Clive. 'The Delusion of the "Good Anthropocene"'. *Clive Hamilton*, 17 June 2014. Available online at https://www.clivehamilton.com/?p=849 (accessed 9 September 2017).
Hamilton, Clive. *Requiem for a Species: Why We Resist the Truth About Climate Change*. London: Routledge, 2010. Kindle.

Handley, George. 'Anthropocentrism and the Postsecularity of the Environmental Humanities: Aronofksy's *Noah*'. *Modern Fiction Studies*. Forthcoming.

Harman, Greg. 'Agenda 21: A Conspiracy Theory Puts Sustainability in the Crosshairs'. *The Guardian*, 24 June 2015. Available online at https://www.theguardian.com/sustainable-business/2015/jun/24/agenda-21-conspiracy-theory-sustainability (accessed 31 January 2018).

Harper, Charles L. 'Religion and Environmentalism', in *The Legacy of Lynn White, Jr.: Religion and the Environment*, ed. Ronald A. Simkins. *The Journal of Religion and Society, Supplement* 3 (2008): 5–26.

Harrison, Bernard. *Inconvenient Fictions: Literature and the Limits of Theory*. New Haven, CT: Yale University Press, 1991.

Haslam, Nick. 'Concept Creep: Psychology's Expanding Concepts of Harm and Pathology'. *Psychological Inquiry* 27.1 (2016): 1–17.

Hayhoe, Katherine. 'The Bible Doesn't Talk About Climate Change, Right?', 4 January 2015. Available online at https://www.youtube.com/watch?v=SpjL_otLq6Y (accessed 31 January 2018).

Hayhoe, Katherine. 'Climate, Politics, Religion'. *Prairie Fire*, 5 June 2015, Available online at http://www.prairiefirenewspaper.com/2015/06/climate-politics-and-religion#4 (accessed 31 January 2018).

Hegerl, Gabriele, et al. 'Comment on "Climate Science and the Uncertainty Monster" Ja Curry and Pj Webster'. *Bulletin of the American Meteorological Society* 92.12 (2011): 1683–85.

Heise, Ursula. 'Science and Ecocriticism'. *American Book Review* 18.5 (1997): 4–6.

Helvarg, David. *The War against the Greens: The 'Wise-Use Movement', the New Right and Ant-Environmental Violence*. San Francisco, CA: Sierra Club Books, 1994.

Henson, Robert. *The Rough Guide to Climate Change*. London: Rough Guides Ltd., 2006.

Hesler, A. *Notes on the Clean Air Act, Smoke Control Areas and the Use of Oil by Local Authorities*, ed. National Union of Mineworkers. Durham Area: Blue Card Information Series, 1963. Vol. 2.

'Heston Reads from Crichton's *Jurassic Park*'. 2008. Available online at https://www.youtube.com/watch?v=R1hFKKmVcjg (accessed 31 January 2018).

Hobson, Kersty and Simon Niemeyer. '"What Sceptics Believe": The Effects of Information and Deliberation on Climate Change Scepticism'. *Public Understanding of Science* 22.4 (2013): 396–412.

Hochschild, Arlie Russell. *Strangers in Their Own Land: Anger and Mourning on the American Right*. New York: The New Press, 2016.

Hoffman, Andrew J. 'Talking Past Each Other? Cultural Framing of Skeptical and Convinced Logics in the Climate Change Debate'. *Organization & Environment* 24.1 (2011): 3–33.

Hoggan, James and Richard D. Littlemore. *Climate Cover-Up: The Crusade to Deny Global Warming*. Vancouver; Berkeley: Greystone Books, 2009.

Horn, Eva. *Zukunft als Katastrophe*. Frankfurt am Main: Fischer, 2014; *The Future as Catastrophe*, New York: Columbia University Press, 2018.

Horner, Chris. *Red Hot Lies: How Global Warming Alarmists Use Threats, Fraud, and Deception To Keep You Misinformed*. Washington, DC: Regnery Publishing, 2009.

Hornschuh, Tillmann. 'Skeptische Kommunikation in der Klimadebatte', in *Von der Hypothese zur Katastrophe. Der anthropogene Klimawandel im Diskurs zwischen Wissenschaft, Politik und Massenmedien*, ed. Peter Weingart, Anita Engels, and Petra Pansegrau, 2nd ed. Opladen; Farmington Hills, MI: Barbara Budrich, 2007, 141–53. [1st ed. 2002]

Hornsey, Matthew J., Emily A. Harris, and Kelly S. Fielding. 'Relationships among Conspiratorial Beliefs, Conservatism and Climate Scepticism Across Nations'. *Nature Climate Change* 8 (July 2018): 614–20.

Horstmann, Ulrich. *Das Untier. Konturen einer Philosophie der Menschenflucht*. Frankfurt am Main: Suhrkamp, 1985. [1st ed. 1983]

Houghton, J. T. *Climate Change 1995: The Science of Climate Change: Contribution of WG1 to the Second Assessment Report of the Intergovernmental Panel on Climate Change*. Cambridge: Cambridge University Press, 1996.

Huet, Sylvestre. *L'Imposteur, c'est lui. Réponse à Claude Allègre*. Paris: Stock, 2010.

Hulme, M. *Why We Disagree About Climate Change: Understanding Controversy, Inaction and Opportunity*. Cambridge; New York: Cambridge University Press, 2009.

Hutter, Claus-Peter and Eva Goris. *Die Erde schlägt zurück: Wie der Klimawandel unser Leben verändert*. Munich: Droemer, 2009.

An Inconvenient Truth (2006). [Film] Dir. Davis Guggenheim, USA: Paramount Classics.

Ingraham, Christopher. 'America's Most Gerrymandered Congressional Districts'. *The Washington Post*, 15 May 2014. Available online at www.washingtonpost.com/news/wonk/wp/2014/05/15/americas-most-gerrymandered-congressional-districts/?tid=a_inl

Inhofe, James. *The Greatest Hoax: How the Global Warming Conspiracy Threatens Your Future*. Washington, DC: WND Books, 2012.

Inhofe, James. 'Inhofe Speaks on the Senate Floor on Undoing Obama's Climate Legacy', 2017. Available online at https://www.inhofe.senate.gov/newsroom/press-releases/inhofe-speaks-on-senate-floor-on-undoing-obamas-climate-legacy

'IPCC, Intergovernmental Panel on Climate Change'. *IPCC Working Group I*. Available online at www.climatechange2013.org/

Iyengar, Shanto and Sean J. Westwood. 'Fear and Loathing across Party Lines: New Evidence on Group Polarization'. *American Journal of Political Science* 59.3 (2015): 690–707.

Jacobs, Michael. 'Environmental Modernization: The New Labour Agenda', ed. The Fabian Society. London: The Fabian Society, 1999.

Jacques, Peter J., Riley E. Dunlap, and Mark Freeman. 'The Organisation of Denial: Conservative Think Tanks and Environmental Scepticism'. *Environmental Politics* 17.3 (2008): 349–85.

Jamieson, Dale. *Reason in a Dark Time: Why the Struggle against Climate Change Failed – and What It Means for Our Future*. Oxford: Oxford University Press, 2014.

Jasanoff, Sheila. *Designs on Nature: Science and Democracy in Europe and the United States*. Princeton, NJ: Princeton University Press, 2005.

Jenkins, Willis. *The Future of Ethics: Sustainability, Social Justice, and Religious Creativity*. Georgetown: Georgetown University Press, 2013.

Jensen, Derrick. *Endgame. Volume 1: The Problem of Civilization*. New York: Penguin Random House, 2011.

JoetheElectrician. 'UK CO2 Ad: "Bedtime Stories" – Act On CO2'. *YouTube*, 21 October 2009. Available online at www.youtube.com/watch?v=SDthR9RH0gw

Johnson, Brad. 'Inhofe: God Says Global Warming Is a Hoax'. *ThinkProgress*, 9 March 2012. Available online at https://thinkprogress.org/inhofe-god-says-global-warming-is-a-hoax-cf1acaeb77c3/ (accessed 31 January 2018).

Johns-Putra, Adeline. 'Climate Change in Literature and Literary Studies: From Cli-fi, Climate Change Theater and Ecopoetry to Ecocriticism and Climate Change Criticism'. *WIREs Climate Change* 7 (March/April 2016): 266–82.

Jouzel, Jean and Anne Debroise. *Le Défi climatique*. Paris: Dunod, 2014.

Kahan, Dan M. 'Climate-Science Communication and the Measurement Problem'. *Political Psychology* 36.S1 (2015): 1–43.

Kahan, Dan M., et al. 'The Polarizing Impact of Science Literacy and Numeracy on Perceived Climate Change Risks'. *Nature Climate Change* 2.10 (2012): 732.

Kakutani, Michiko. 'The Plot Thins, or Are No Stories New?' *The New York Times*, 15 April 2005. Available online at www.nytimes.com/2005/04/15/books/the-plot-thins-or-are-no-stories-new.html

Keegan, Jon. 'Blue Feed, Red Feed'. *The Wall Street Journal*, Dow Jones & Company, 17 May 2016. Available online at graphics.wsj.com/blue-feed-red-feed/

Kelly, Caroline. 'Political Identity and Perceived Intragroup Homogeneity'. *British Journal of Social Psychology* 28.3 (1989): 239–50.

Kenny, Dorothy Ann. *Seeing through Smoke Sorting through the Science and Politics in the Making of the 1956 Clean Air Act*. Baltimore: University of Maryland, 2010. Print.

King, Thomas. *The Truth About Stories: A Native Narrative*. The Massey Lectures Series. Toronto, ON: House of Anansi Press, 2003.

Kingsolver, Barbara. *Flight Behavior*. New York: Harper Collins, 2012.

Klein, Naomi. *This Changes Everything: Capitalism Vs. The Climate*. First Simon & Schuster hardcover edition. New York: Simon & Schuster, 2014.

Koch, Egmont R. and Fritz Fahrenholt. *Seveso ist überall. Die tödlichen Risiken der Chemie*. Cologne: Kiepenheuer and Witsch, 1978.

Kohler, Pierre. *L'Imposture verte*. Paris: Albin Michel, 2002.

Koutsoyiannis, Demetris, et al. 'On the Credibility of Climate Predictions'. *Hydrological Sciences Journal* 53.4 (2008): 671–84.

Kracht, Christian and Ingo Niermann. *Metan*. Berlin: Rogner & Bernhard bei Zweitausendeins, 2007.

Krahmer, Holger, Benny Peiser, and Arman Nyilas. *Unbequeme Wahrheiten über die Klimapolitik und ihre wissenschaftliche Grundlagen. Anregungen für neue liberale Ansätze*. European Parliament, 2010. Available online at http://www.holger-krahmer.de/tl_files/userdata/images/publikationen/HK-%28Klimabroschur%29-2010.pdf

Krauss, Werner. 'Ausweitung der Kampfzone: Die Klima-Blogosphäre'. *Forschungsjournal Soziale Bewegungen* 25.2 (2012): 83–88.

Krauss, Werner, Mike S. Schäfer, and Hans Von Storch, editors. *Postnormal Science: The Case of Climate Research. Nature and Culture* 7.2 (June 2012).

Kristof, Nicholas. 'A 12-Step Program for Responding to President-Elect Trump'. *The New York Times*, 17 November 2016. Available online at www.nytimes.com/2016/11/17/opinion/a-12-step-program-for-responding-to-president-elect-trump.html?mtrref=undefined

Lack, Martin. *The Denial of Science: Analysing Climate Change Scepticism in the UK*. Bloomington, IN: AuthorHouse, 2013. Kindle.

Lahsen, Myanna. 'Climategate: The Role of the Social Sciences'. *Climatic Change* 119.3–4 (2013): 547–58.

Lahsen, Myanna. 'Seductive Simulations? Uncertainty Distribution around Climate Models'. *Social Studies of Science* 35.6 (2005): 895–922.

Lakoff, George. 'Why It Matters How We Frame the Environment'. *Environmental Communication* 4.1 (2010): 70–81.

Lambert, Richard. 'Review: An Appeal to Reason by Nigel Lawson'. *The Guardian*, Guardian News and Media, 19 April 2008. Available online at www.theguardian.com/books/2008/apr/19/climatechange.politics

Larrère, Catherine. 'Éthiques de l'environnement'. *Multitudes* 24.1 (2006): 75–84.

Larrère, Catherine. Interview. *Wildproject*. 2008. Available online at https://www.wildproject.org/journal/index (accessed 2 January 2009).

Lascar, Olivier. 'Climato-sceptiques français: une seule nuance de cheveux gris'. *Sciences et Avenir*, 9 December 2016. Available online at https://www.sciencesetavenir.fr/nature-environnement/climat/climato-sceptiques-francais-une-seule-nuance-de-cheveux-gris_108792 (accessed 15 August 2017).

Lascoumes, Pierre. *L'Éco-pouvoir. Environnements et politiques*. Paris: La Découverte, 1994.

Latour, Bruno. *Politics of Nature. How to Bring the Sciences into Democracy*. Trans. Catherine Porter. Cambridge, MA: Harvard University Press, 2004.

Latour, Bruno. 'Telling Friends from Foes in the Time of the Anthropocene', in *The Anthropocene and the Global Environment Crisis: Rethinking Modernity in a New Epoch*, ed. Clive Hamilton, Christophe Bonneuil and François Gemenne. London: Routledge, 145–55.

Latour, Bruno. *We Have Never Been Modern*. Cambridge, MA: Harvard University Press, 1993.

Latour, Bruno. 'Why Has Critique Run Out of Steam? From Matters of Fact to Matters of Concern'. *Critical Inquiry* 30.2 (2004): 225–48.

Laurut, Christian. *L'Imposture écologiste*. N.p. 2011.

Lawson, Nigel. *An Appeal to Reason: A Cool Look at Global Warming*. London: Duckworth Overlook, 2009.

Leane, Elizabeth. *Reading Popular Physics. Disciplinary Skirmishes and Textual Strategies*. Aldershot: Ashgate, 2007.

Lenoir, Yves. *La Vérité sur l'effet de serre. Histoire d'une manipulation planétaire*. Paris: La Découverte, 1992.

Lehmann, Harry, Klaus Müschen, Steffi Richter, and Klaus Mäder. *Und sie erwärmt sich doch. Was steckt hinter der Debatte um den Klimawandel*. Berlin: Umweltbundesamt, 2013. Available online at https://www.umweltbundesamt.de/sites/default/files/medien/378/publikationen/und_sie_erwaermt_sich_doch_131201.pdf

Leiserowitz, Anthony. 'International Public Opinion, Perception, and Understanding of Global Climate Change'. *Human Development Report* (2007).

Leiserowitz, A., Maibach, E., Roser-Renouf, C., Feinberg, G., and Rosenthal, S. *Climate Change in the American Mind*, October 2015, Yale University and George Mason University. New Haven, CT: Yale Program on Climate Change Communication, 2015. Available online at http://climatecommunication.yale.edu/wp-content/uploads/2015/11/Climate-Change-American-Mind-October-20151.pdf (accessed 31 January 2018).

Lepage, Corinne. *De l'écologie. Hors de l'imposture et de l'opportunisme*. Paris: Éditions Raphaël, 2003.

Lewandowsky, Stephan, Naomi Oreskes, James S. Risbey, Ben R. Newell and Michael Smithson 'Seepage: Climate Change Denial and Its Effect on the Scientific Community'. *Global Environmental Change* 33 (2015): 1–13.

Lilienthal, Volker. 'Irrlichter aus dem Dunkel der Zukunft. Zur neueren deutschen Katastrophenliteratur', in *Pluralismus und Postmodernismus. Zur Literatur – und Kulturgeschichte in Deutschland 1980–1995*, ed. Helmut Kreuzer. Frankfurt am Main: Peter Lang, 1996.

Limbaugh, Rush. 'An Earth Day Salute to Capitalists'. The Rush Limbaugh Show, 22 April 2009. Available online at https://www.rushlimbaugh.com/daily/2009/04/22/an_earth_day_salute_to_capitalists/ (accessed 31 January 2018).

Linville, Patricia W., Gregory W. Fischer, and Peter Salovey. 'Perceived Distributions of the Characteristics of in-Group and out-Group Members: Empirical Evidence and a Computer Simulation'. *Journal of Personality and Social Psychology* 57.2 (1989): 165.

Lomborg, Bjorn. *Cool It: The Skeptical Environmentalist's Guide to Global Warming*. New York: Knopf Doubleday Publishing Group, 2007.

MacKay, David J. C. *Sustainable Energy – without the Hot Air*. Cambridge: UIT, 2009.

Mann, Torsten. *Rote Lügen im grünen Gewand: Der kommunistische Hintergrund der Öko-Bewegung*. Rottenburg: Kopp Verlag, 2009.

Margolina, Sonja. *Die gemütliche Apokalypse: Unbotmässiges zu Klimahysterie und Einwanderungsdebatte in Deutschland*. Berlin: Siedler, 1995.

Margolina, Sonja. 'Die ideologischen Seiten des Klimawandels', *Neue Zürcher Zeitung*, 1 September 2017. Available online at https://www.nzz.ch/meinung/deutungshoheit-der-erwaermungstheoretiker-die-ideologischen-seiten-des-klimawandels-ld.1313793, 10.

Margolina, Sonja. *Kaltzeit*. Leipzig: Amazon, 2013.

Marr, Andrew. *A History of Modern Britain*. London: Macmillan, 2007.

Mars-Jones, Adam. 'Observer Review: The Seven Basic Plots by Christopher Booker'. *The Guardian*, Guardian News and Media, 21 November 2004. Available online at www.theguardian.com/books/2004/nov/21/fiction.features

Marshall, George. *Don't Even Think About It: Why Our Brains Are Wired to Ignore Climate Change*. New York: Bloomsbury USA, 2014.

Masson-Delmotte, Valérie. *Climat: le vrai et le faux*. Paris: Le Pommier, 2011.

Maxeiner, Dirk. *Alles grün und gut? Eine Bilanz des ökologischen Denkens*. Munich: Knaus, 2014.

Maxeiner, Dirk. *Hurra. Wir retten die Welt! Wie Politik und Medien mit der Klimaforschung umspringen*. Berlin: WJS, 2007.

Maxeiner, Dirk. *Lexikon der Öko-Irrtümer. Fakten statt Mythen*. Frankfurt am Main: Eichborn, 1998.

Maxeiner, Dirk. 'Wider die Ökodiktatur'. *Die Welt* 5 September 2007. Available online at https://www.welt.de/wissenschaft/article1159330/Wider-die-Oekodiktatur.html.

Maxeiner, Dirk and Michael Miersch. *Öko-Optimismus*. Düsseldorf: Metropolitan-Verlag, 1996.

Mayer, Jane. *Dark Money: The Hidden History of the Billionaires Behind the Rise of the Radical Right*, 1st ed. New York: Doubleday, 2016.

mbalax32. 'Armstrong & Miller Physics Special'. *YouTube*, 29 November 2009. Available online at www.youtube.com/watch?v=3wHKBavY_h8

McCauley, James. 'Emmanuel Macron Speaks to the World. But What about the French?' *The Washington Post*, 10 December 2018. Available online at https://www.washingtonpost.com/world/europe/emmanuel-macron-speaks-to-the-world-but-what-about-the-french/2017/12/08/c0b22612-d9e1-11e7-a241-0848315642d0_story.html?noredirect=on&utm_term=.a571e98004e2 (accessed 11 December 2018).

McCormick, John. *British Politics and the Environment*. London: Earthscan, 1991. Print.

McCright, Aaron M. 'Challenging Global Warming as a Social Problem: An Analysis of the Conservative Movement's Counter-Claims'. *Social Problems* 47.4 (2000): 499–522.

McCright, Aaron M. 'Cool Dudes: The Denial of Climate Change among Conservative White Males in the United States'. *Global Environmental Change* 21.4 (2011): 1163–72.

McCright, Aaron M. 'The Politicization of Climate Change and Polarization in the American Public's Views of Global Warming, 2001–2010'. *The Sociological Quarterly* 52.2 (2011): 155–94.

McCright, Aaron M. and Riley E. Dunlap. 'Anti-Reflexivity the American Conservative Movement's Success in Undermining Climate Science and Policy'. *Theory, Culture & Society* 27.2–3 (2010): 100–33.

McEwan, Ian. 'Ian McEwan: Only Love and Then Oblivion'. *The Guardian*, Guardian News and Media, 15 September 2001. Available online at www.theguardian.com/world/2001/sep/15/september11.politicsphilosophyandsociety2

Metzler, Birgit. *'Erst stirbt der Wald, dann Du!'. Das Waldsterben als westdeutsches Politikum (1978–1986)*. Frankfurt am Main: Campus, 2015.

Miersch, Michael. 'Oberstes Gericht hat entschieden: Bundesbehörde darf Journalisten denunzieren'. EIKE – Europäisches Institut für Klima und Energie, 5 March 2017. Available online at https://www.eike-klima-energie.eu/2017/03/05/oberstes-gericht-hat-entschieden-bundesbehoerde-darf-journalisten-denunzieren/

Miller, C. Andrew and Cynthia L. Gage. 'Potential Adverse Environmental Impacts of Greenhouse Gas Mitigation Strategies', in *Global Climate Change – The Technology Challenge*, ed. Frank Princiotta. Dordrecht: Springer Netherlands, 2011, 377–415.

Mitchell, Dr. Tommy. 'A God of Suffering?' *Answers in Genesis*, 2016, Film. Available online at https://answersingenesis.org/media/video/god/god-of-suffering/(accessed 31 January 2018).

Möller, Andreas. *Das grüne Gewissen – Wenn die Natur zur Ersatzreligion wird*. Munich: Hanser, 2013.

Monbiot, George. 'How Much Reality Can You Take?' 21 September 2006. Available online at www.monbiot.com/2006/09/21/how-much-reality-can-you-take/

Monbiot, George. 'Selling Indulgences'. 19 October 2006. Available online at www.monbiot.com/2006/10/19/selling-indulgences

Monbiot, George. 'The Semantics of Denial'. *The Guardian*, 27 February 2009. Available online at www.theguardian.com/environment/georgemonbiot/2009/feb/27/climate-change-deniers-sceptics

Monitor, Magazine. 'The World of 100% Election Victories'. *BBC News*, 11 March 2014. Available online at www.bbc.com/news/blogs-magazine-monitor-26527422

Morano, Marc. *The Politically Incorrect Guide to Climate Change*. Washington, DC: Regnery Publishing, 2018. Kindle.

Morris, William. *News from Nowhere and Other Writings*. London: Penguin, 1993.

National Academies of Sciences. 'Genetically Engineered Crops: Experiences and Prospects'. *National Academies Press: OpenBook*, 17 May 2016. Available online at www.nap.edu/catalog/23395/genetically-engineered-crops-experiences-and-prospects

Neuhaus, Nele. *Wer Wind sät. Kriminalroman*. Berlin: Ullstein, 2011.

Nisbet, Matthew C. 'Communicating Climate Change: Why Frames Matter for Public Engagement'. *Environment: Science and Policy for Sustainable Development* 51.2 (2009): 12–23.

Noguez, Dominique. *L'Arc-en-ciel des humours*. Paris: Biblio essais, 2000.

Norgaard, Kari Marie. *Living in Denial: Climate* Change, *Emotions, and Everyday Life*. Cambridge, MA; London: MIT Press, 2011. Kindle.

North, Richard. *Life on a Modern Planet: A Manifesto for Progress*. Manchester: Manchester University Press, 1995.

Nothias, Toussaint and James Painter. 'Country Result: France', in *Climate Change in the Media: Reporting Risk and* Uncertainty, ed. J. Painter. London: Tauris, 2013, 89–98.

Nottret, Patric. *H_2O*. Paris: Laffont, 2004.

Nottret, Patric. *Mort sur la forêt*. Paris: Laffont, 2007.

Nottret, Patric. *Poison vert*. Paris: Laffont, 2002.

Oard, Michael J. and Dr. Jason Lisle. 'Global Warming: A Scientific Exposé of Climate Change'. *Answers in Genesis*, 2009, Film. Available online at https://answersingenesis.org/media/video/science/global-warming/ (accessed 31 January 2018).

'Obama: No Time for a Meeting of the Flat Earth Society'. *BBC News*, 25 June 2013. Available online at www.bbc.com/news/world-us-canada-23057369

Olivier, Jos. *TRENDS IN GLOBAL CO2 EMISSIONS – Edgar.jrc.ec.europa.eu*. PBL Netherlands Environmental Assessment Agency, 2015. Available online at edgar.jrc.ec.europa.eu/news_docs/jrc-2015-trends-in-global-co2-emissions-2015-report-98184.pdf

O'Neill, Saffron J. and Max Boykoff. 'Climate Denier, Skeptic, or Contrarian?' *Proceedings of the National Academy of Sciences of the United States of America* 107.39 (2010): E151.

Openshaw, Pamela. 'Theory of Climate Change a Scare Tactic with Ulterior Motives'. *Daily Herald*, 11 August 2009. Available online at http://www.heraldextra.com/news/opinion/local-guest-opinions/theory-of-climate-change-a-scare-tactic-with-ulterior-motives/article_3f67d91b-390d-5158-b171-8624a47a8569.html (accessed 31 January 2018).

Oreskes, Naomi. Interview by Yves Sciama. 'Un discours simple et conservateur'. *La Recherche* 425 (December 2008): 44–47.

Oreskes, Naomi and Erick M. Conway. *Merchants of Doubt: How a Handful of Scientists Obscured the Truth on Issues from Tobacco Smoke to Global Warming*. 1st US ed. New York: Bloomsbury, 2010. Kindle.

Oreskes, Naomi. 'The Scientific Consensus on Climate Change'. *Science* 306.5702 (2004): 1686–86.

Oreskes, Naomi and Erik M. Conway. *The Collapse of Western Civilization: A View from the Future*. New York: Columbia University Press, 2014.

Oreskes, Naomi, David A. Stainforth, and Leonard A. Smith. 'Adaptation to Global Warming: Do Climate Models Tell Us What We Need to Know?' *Philosophy of Science* 77.5 (2010): 1012–28.

Oreskes, Naomi, Kristin Shrader-Frechette, and Kenneth Belitz. 'Verification, Validation, and Confirmation of Numerical Models in the Earth Sciences'. *Science* 263.5147 (1994): 641–46.

Painter, James. 'Communicating Uncertainties: Climate Skeptics in the International Media'. *Communication, Controversies and Uncertainty Facing the Scientific Consensus on Climate Change*, ed. José-Luis, P. R., et al. Tenerife: Cuadernos Artesanos de Latina, 2012.

Painter, James. *Poles Apart: The International Reporting of Climate Scepticism*. Oxford: Reuters Institute for the Study of Journalism, 2011.

Painter, James and Teresa Ashe. 'Cross-national Comparison of the Presence of Climate Scepticism in the Print Media in Six Countries, 2007–10'. *Environmental Research Letters*. 7 (2012). Available online at http://iopscience.iop.org/article/10.1088/1748-9326/7/4/044005 (accessed 10 September 2017).

Painter, James, Silje Kristiansen, and Mike S. Schäfer. 'How "Digital-born" Media Cover Climate Change in Comparison to Legacy Media: A Case Study of the COP 21 Summit in Paris'. *Global Environmental Change* 48 (2018): 1–10, https://www.sciencedirect.com/science/article/pii/S0959378017301437.

Palin, Sarah. 'Sarah Palin on the Politicization of the Copenhagen Climate Conference'. *The Washington Post*, 9 December 2009. Available online at http://www.washingtonpost.com/wp-dyn/content/article/2009/12/08/AR2009120803402.html (accessed 16 June 2018).

Pantle, Christian. 'Es wird wärmer – gut so!' *Focus Magazin*, 29 November 2010. Available online at www.focus.de/wissen/wissenschaft/klima/tid-20790/titel-es-wird-waermer-gut-so_aid_576648.html

Paraire, Philippe. *L'Utopie verte. Écologie des riches, écologie des pauvres*. Paris: Hachette, 1992.

Pariser, Eli. 'Transcript of "Beware Online 'Filter Bubbles'"'. *TED: Ideas Worth Spreading*. Available online at www.ted.com/talks/eli_pariser_beware_online_filter_bubbles/transcript?language=en

Park, Bernadette and Charles M. Judd. 'Rethinking the Link between Categorization and Prejudice within the Social Cognition Perspective'. *Personality and Social Psychology Review* 9.2 (2005): 108–30.

Payton, Laura. 'Justin Trudeau Takes His Fight into Enemy Territory'. *Macleans.ca*, 14 October 2015. Available online at www.macleans.ca/politics/ottawa/trudeau-takes-his-fight-into-enemy-territory/

Pearce, Fred. *The Last Generation: How Nature Will Take Her Revenge for Climate Change*. London: Eden Project Books, 2006.

Pearce, Fred. 'Part 11: "Climategate" Was PR Disaster That Could Bring Healthy Reform of Peer Review'. *The Guardian*, Guardian News and Media, 9 February 2010. Available online at www.theguardian.com/environment/2010/feb/09/climate-emails-pr-disaster-peer-review

Pearce, Warren, et al. 'Beyond Counting Climate Consensus'. *Environmental Communication* 11.6 (2017): 723–30.

Peck, Sally. 'Al Gore's "Nine Inconvenient Untruths"'. *The Telegraph*, Telegraph Media Group, 11 October 2007. Available online at www.telegraph.co.uk/news/earth/earthnews/3310137/Al-Gores-nine-Inconvenient-Untruths.html

Poortinga, Wouter, et al. 'Uncertain Climate: An Investigation into Public Scepticism About Anthropogenic Climate Change'. *Global Environmental Change* 21.3 (2011): 1015–24.

Pope Francis. *Encyclical Letter Laudato Sí of the Holy Father Francis On Care For Our Common Home*, 2015. Available online at http://w2.vatican.va/content/francesco/en/encyclicals/documents/papa-francesco_20150524_enciclica-laudato-si.html

Posthumus, Stephanie. *French* Écocritique*: Reading Contemporary French Theory and Fiction Ecologically*. Toronto, ON: University of Toronto Press 2017.

Posthumus, Stephanie. 'L'Exception écologiste française: *Globalia* de Jean-Christophe Rufin'. *Sites: Contemporary French & Francophone Studies* 12.4 (2008): 445–53.

Posthumus, Stephanie. 'Penser/parodier l'extinction à l'ère de l'Anthropocène', in *Écocritiques: Nouvelles territorialités*, ed. Anne-Rachel Hermetet and Bertrand Guest. Paris: Garniers Classiques, forthcoming.

Pottier, Antonin. 'Le Climato-scepticisme. Réflexions sur la confusion des genres'. *Futuribles*, December, 380 (2011): 27–40. Available online at https://www.futuribles.com/fr/revue/380/le-climato-scepticisme-reflexions-sur-la-confusion/ (accessed 10 September 2017).

Poujade, Robert and Stéphane Frioux. 'Le Premier Ministère de l'Environnement (1971–1974). L'Invention d'un possible'. *Vingtième Siècle. Revue d'histoire* 1.113 (2012): 51–54.

Powell, James Lawrence. *The Inquisition of Climate Science*. New York: Columbia University Press, 2011.

Prud'homme, Rémy. *L'Idéologie du réchauffement. Science molle et doctrine dure*. Paris: L'Artilleur, 2015.

Prugh, Thomas, Robert Costanza, and Herman E. Daly. *The Local Politics of Global Sustainability*. Washington, DC: Island Press, 2000.

Quero, Yann. *L'Avenir ne sera plus ce qu'il était*. Paris: Éditions Arkuiris, 2010.

Quero, Yann. *Le Procès de l'homme blanc*. Paris: Éditions Arkuiris, 2005.

Rahmstorf, Stefan. 'The Climate Sceptics'. *Potsdam Institute for Climate Impact Research* (2004).

Rahmstorf, Stefan. 'Die deutsche Lust am Untergang und der Klimawandel', 5 January 2012. Available online at https://scilogs.spektrum.de/klimalounge/die-deutsche-lust-am-untergang-und-der-klimawandel/

Rahmstorf, Stefan. 'Klimawandel: Deutsche Medien betreiben Desinformation'. *Frankfurter Allgemeine Zeitung*, 31 August 2007. Available online at http://www.pik-potsdam.de/~stefan/Publications/Other/rahmstorf_universitas_2007.pdf

Ramírez-i-Ollé, Meritxell. 'Rhetorical Strategies for Scientific Authority: A Boundary-Work Analysis of "Climategate"'. *Science as Culture* 24.4 (2015): 384–411.

Rao, Nathan. 'Uproar as BBC Muzzles Climate Change Sceptics'. *Express.co.uk*, 20 July 2011. Available online at www.express.co.uk/news/uk/260164/Uproar-as-BBC-muzzles-climate-change-sceptics

Ratter, Beate M. W., Katharina H. I. Philipp, and Hans von Storch. 'Between Hype and Decline: Recent Trends in Public Perception of Climate Change'. *Environmental Science & Policy* 18 (2012): 3–8.

Ravetz, J. R. '"Climategate" and the Maturing of Post-Normal Science'. *Futures* 43.2 (2011): 149–57.

Raw, Louise. *Striking a Light: The Bryant and May Matchwomen and Their Place in History*. Rev. ed. London: Continuum, 2011.

Redfern, Walter. *French Laughter: Literary Humour from Diderot to Tournier*. Oxford; New York: Oxford University Press, 2008.

Reichholf, Josef H. *Eine kurze Naturgeschichte des letzten Jahrtausends*. Frankfurt am Main: Fischer, 2007.

'RepublicEn: Energy Optimists – Climate Realists'. Available online at http://www.republicen.org/ (accessed 30 January 2018).

Rérolle, Raphaëlle. Interview with Iegor Gran. 'L'actualité est un morceau de papier alu qui brille'. *Le Monde*, 20 May 2011. Available online at https://www.lemonde.fr/livres/article/2011/05/19/l-actualite-est-un-morceau-de-papier-alu-qui-brille_1524227_3260.html (accessed 18 September 2017).

Rittaud, Benoît. *Le Mythe climatique*. Paris: Seuil, 2010.

Rittaud, Benoît. *La Peur exponentielle*. Paris: PUF, 2015.

Rivière-Wekstein, Gil. *Abeilles: l'imposture écologique*. Paris: Le Publieur, 2006.

Robinson, Mike. *The Greening of British Party Politics*. Manchester: Manchester University Press, 1992.

Roser-Renouf, Connie, Maibach, Edward, Leiserowitz, Anthony, Feinberg, Geoffrey, and Rosenthal, Seth. 'Faith, Morality and the Environment: Portraits of Global Warming's Six Americas'. Yale University and George Mason University. New Haven, CT: Yale Program on Climate Change Communication, 2016. Available online at http://climatecommunication.yale.edu/wp-content/uploads/2016/01/Faith-Morality-Six-Americas.pdf (accessed 31 January 2018).

Roser-Renouf, Connie, Edward Maibach, Anthony Leiserowitz, and Seth Rosenthal. 'Global Warming, God, and the "End of Times"'. Yale University and George Mason University. New Haven, CT: Yale Program on Climate Change Communication, 26 July 2016. Available online at http://climatecommunication.yale.edu/publications/global-warming-god-end-times/ (accessed 31 January 2018).

Rowell, Andrew. *Green Backlash: Global Subversion of the Environmental Movement*. London: Routledge, 1996.

Rufin, Jean-Christophe. *Globalia*. Paris: Gallimard/Folio, 2005 [2004].

Rufin, Jean-Christophe. *Le Parfum d'Adam*. Paris: Gallimard/Folio, 2008 [2007].

Ryghaug, Marianne and Tomas Moe Skjølsvold. 'The Global Warming of Climate Science: Climategate and the Construction of Scientific Facts'. *International Studies in the Philosophy of Science* 24.3 (2010): 287–307.

Safranski, Rüdiger, Peter Sloterdijk, Gerd Ganteför, and Frank Schätzing. 'Klimawandel – ein Glaubenskrieg? Wahrheitsfindung zwischen Wissenschaft und Ideologie'. ARD TV, *Philosophisches Quartett*, November 2011.

Sainteny, Guillaume. *L'Introuvable Écologisme français ?* Paris: PUF, 2000.

Sanderson, John B. 'The National Smoke Abatement Society and the Clean Air Act (1956)'. *Political Studies* 9.3 (1961): 236–53.

Scarrow, Howard A. 'The Impact of British Domestic Air Pollution Legislation'. *British Journal of Political Science* 2.3 (1972): 261–82.

Schätzing, Frank. *Der Schwarm. Roman*. Cologne: Kiepenheuer and Witsch, 2004.

Schätzing, Frank. *The Swarm. A Novel of the Deep*. Los Angeles: ReganBooks, 2006.

Scherer, Aaron M., Paul D. Windschitl, and Jesse Graham. 'An Ideological House of Mirrors Political Stereotypes as Exaggerations of Motivated Social Cognition Differences'. *Social Psychological and Personality Science* 6.2 (2015): 201–09.

Schipani, Vanessa, et al. 'FactChecking Trump's Climate Speech'. *FactCheck.org*, 27 October 2017. Available online at www.factcheck.org/2017/06/factchecking-trumps-climate-speech/

Schneider, Marcel. *Jean-Jacques Rousseau ou l'espoir écologiste*. Paris: Éditions Pygmalion, 1978.

Schneider, Michael. *Nur tote Fische schwimmen mit dem Strom. Essays, Aphorismen, Polemiken*. Cologne: Kiepenheuer and Witsch, 1984.

'Scientific Opinion on Climate Change'. *Wikipedia*, Wikimedia Foundation, 26 June 2018. Available online at en.wikipedia.org/wiki/Scientific_opinion_on_climate_change

Segnit, Nat and Gill Ereaut. 'Warm Words: The Evolution of the Climate Change Story'. *Consumer Policy Review* 18.4 (2008): 91–95.

Serres, Michel. *Le Contrat naturel*. Paris: Flammarion, 1990. *The Natural Contract*. Trans. Elizabeth MacArthur and William Paulson. Ann Arbor: University of Michigan Press, 1995.

Shackley, Simon and Brian Wynne. 'Representing Uncertainty in Global Climate Change Science and Policy: Boundary-Ordering Devices and Authority'. *Science, Technology, & Human Values* 21.3 (1996): 275–302.

Shackley, Simon and Tora Skodvin. 'IPCC Gazing and the Interpretative Social Sciences: A Comment on Sonja Boehmer-Christiansen's: "Global Climate Protection Policy: The Limits of Scientific Advice"'. *Global Environmental Change* 5.3 (1995): 175–80.

Sides, John. 'Gerrymandering Is Not What's Wrong with American Politics'. *The Washington Post*, WP Company, 3 February 2013. Available online at www.washingtonpost.com/news/wonk/wp/2013/02/03/gerrymandering-is-not-whats-wrong-with-american-politics/

Sismondo, Sergio. *An Introduction to Science and Technology Studies*. 2nd ed. Chichester: Wiley-Blackwell, 2010.

Sloterdijk, Peter. 'Klimawandel – ein Glaubenskrieg?' Available online at https://petersloterdijk.net/das-philosophische-quartett/klimawandel-ein-glaubenskrieg/

Smith, Angela. 'Top Gear as a Bastion of Heterosexual Masculinity', in *Popular Media and Communication: Essays on Publics, Practices, and Processes*, ed. Karen Ross and Stuart Price. Newcastle upon Tyne: Cambridge Scholars Press, 2009, 82–101.

'The Social Affairs Unit – Web Review: Global Warming May Not Matter as Much as Polite Opinion Claims – but It Might Matter a Lot More than Nigel Lawson Is Willing to Acknowledge, Argues Richard D. North: An Appeal to Reason: A Cool Look at Global Warming – Nigel Lawson'. *The Social Affairs Unit – Web Review: How Historically Accurate Is Valkyrie? Brendan Simms on Valkyrie – Bryan Singer.* Available online at www.socialaffairsunit.org.uk/blog/archives/001770.php

Sokal, Alan and Jean Bricmont. *Impostures intellectuelles.* Paris: Odile Jacob, 1997.

Solomon, Lawrence. *The Deniers: The World-Renowned Scientists Who Stood Up to Global Warming Hysteria, Political Persecution, and Fraud.* Minneapolis, MN: Richard Vigilante Books, 20087.

'Speech to the Royal Society'. *Margaret Thatcher Foundation.* Available online at www.margaretthatcher.org/document/107346

Spencer, Roy. *The Great Global Warming Blunder: How Mother Nature Fooled the World's Top Climate Scientists.* New York: Encounter Books, 2012.

Spiegel 'Angst vor der Endzeit: Umwelt-Hysterie und Aktionismus – Die Deutschen im Öko-Fieber'. *Der Spiegel* (25 September 1995): 40–62.

Spiegel 'Das Weltklima gerät aus den Fugen'. *Der Spiegel* (11 August 1986): 122–134.

Spiegel 'Im Chor der Gutmenschen'. *Der Spiegel* (25 September 1995): 34–38.

Spiegel. 'Wir stehen vor einem ökologischen Hiroschima'. *Der Spiegel* (14 February 1983): 72–92.

Squarzoni, Philippe. *Saison brune.* Paris: Delcourt, 2012. *Climate Changed: A Personal Journey through the Science.* Trans. Ivanka Hahneberger. New York: Abrams, 2014.

Steentjes, K., N. Pidgeon, W. Poortinga, A. Corner, A. Arnold, G. Böhm, C. Mays, M. Poumadère, M. Ruddat, D. Scheer, M. Sonnberger, and E. Tvinnereim. *European Perceptions of Climate Change: Topline Findings of a Survey Conducted in Four European Countries in 2016.* Cardiff: Cardiff University, 2017. Available online at http://orca.cf.ac.uk/98660/7/EPCC.pdf

Stehr, Nico and Hans von Storch. *Climate and Society. Climate as resource, Climate as Risk.* Singapore: World ScientificPublishing Co. Pte. Ltd., 2009.

Stengers, Isabelle. *Au temps des catastrophes. Résister à la barbarie qui vient.* Paris: La Découverte, 2009. *In Catastrophic Times. Resisting the Coming Barbarism.* Trans. Andrew Goffey. London: Open Humanities Press, 2015.

Stengers, Isabelle. *Cosmopolitics I.* Trans. Robert Bononno. Minneapolis; London: University of Minnesota Press, 2010.

Stokes, Bruce, Richard Wike, and Jill Carle. *Global Concern About Climate Change, Broad Support for Limiting Emissions.* Pew Research Center, 2015. Available online at http://assets.pewresearch.org/wp-content/uploads/sites/2/2015/11/Pew-Research-Center-Climate-Change-Report-FINAL-November-5-2015.pdf

Stoll, Mark. *Inherit the Holy Mountain: Religion and the Rise of American Environmentalism.* Oxford: Oxford University Press, 2015.

Storch, Hans von. 'Good Science, Bad Politics'. *The Wall Street Journal,* Dow Jones & Company, 22 December 2009. Available online at www.wsj.com/articles/SB10001424052748704238104574601443947078538

Stone-Lee, Ollie. 'UK | UK Politics | Who's the New Mondeo Man?'

'The Subterranean War on Science'. *Association for Psychological Science*. Available online at www.psychologicalscience.org/index.php/publications/observer/2013/november-13/the-subterranean-war-on-science.html

'Sweaters and Sweaters'. *Introduction to the Metaphysics of Morals by Immanuel Kant*. Available online at www.marxists.org/archive/morris/works/1888/commonweal/07-sweaters.htm

Switzer, Jacqueline Vaughn. *Green Backlash: The History and Politics of the Environmental Opposition in the U.S.* Boulder, CO; London: L. Rienner, 1997.

'Synthesis Report Summary for Policymakers Chapter – IPCC'. *Climate Change 2014 Synthesis Report Summary for Policymakers Chapter*. Available online at www.ipcc.ch/pdf/assessment-report/ar5/syr/AR5_SYR_FINAL_SPM.pdf

Taylor, Jesse O. *The Sky of Our Manufacture: The London Fog in British Fiction from Dickens to Woolf. Under the Sign of Nature: Explorations in Ecocriticism*. Charlottesville; London: University of Virginia Press, 2016.

Taylor, Peter. *Chill, a Reassessment of Global Warming Theory: Does Climate Change Mean the World Is Cooling, and If So What Should We Do About It?* East Sussex: Clairview Books, 2009. Kindle.

Thompson, Derek. 'The White House Exaggerated the Growth of Coal Jobs by About 5,000 Percent'. *The Atlantic*, Atlantic Media Company, 6 June 2017. Available online at www.theatlantic.com/business/archive/2017/06/pruitt-epa-coal-jobsexaggerate/529311/

Thorsheim, Peter. *Inventing Pollution: Coal, Smoke, and Culture in Britain since 1800*. Athens, OH: Ohio University Press, 2006.

Tol, Richard. 'The Claim of a 97% Consensus on Global Warming Does Not Stand up | Richard Tol'. *The Guardian*, Guardian News and Media, 6 June 2014. Available online at www.theguardian.com/environment/blog/2014/jun/06/97-consensus-global-warming

Tol, Richard S. J. 'Quantifying the Consensus on Anthropogenic Global Warming in the Literature: A Re-Analysis'. *Energy Policy* 73 (2014): 701–05.

Tranter, Bruce and Kate Booth. 'Scepticism in a Changing Climate: A Cross-National Study'. *Global Environmental Change* 33 (2015): 154–64.

Tranter, Kieran and Damien Martin. '"The Cutting Edge of Cocking About": Top Gear, Automobility and Law'. *Law and Humanities* 7.1 (2013): 1–18.

Trexler, Adam. *Anthropocene Fictions: The Novel in a Time of Climate Change*. Charlottesville: University of Virginia Press, 2015.

Trojanow, Ilija. *EisTau*. Munich: Hanser, 2011.

Trojanow, Ilija. *The Lamentations of Zeno*. New York: Verso, 2016.

Uekötter, Frank. *The Greenest Nation? A New History of German Environmentalism*. Cambridge, MA; London: MIT Press, 2014.

U.S. Department of State. Available online at www.state.gov/secretary/remarks/2015/12/250423.htm

'Uncertainty, Risk, and (in)Action'. *Climate Etc.*, 28 May 2011. Available online at judithcurry.com/2011/05/28/uncertainty-risk-and-inaction/

Vahrenholt, Fritz. 'Die Kalte Sonne'. *Die Welt* (22 December 2010).

Vahrenholt, Fritz and Sebastian Lüning. *Die kalte Sonne. Warum die Klimakatastrophe nicht stattfindet*. Hamburg: Hoffmann and Campe, 2012.

Vahrenholt, Fritz and Sebastian Lüning. *The Neglected Sun: Why the Sun Precludes Climate Catastrophe*. London: Stacey International, 2013.

Vaidyanathan, Gayathri. 'How to Determine the Scientific Consensus on Global Warming'. *Scientific American*, 24 July 2014. Available online at www.scientificamerican.com/article/how-to-determine-the-scientific-consensus-on-global-warming/

Van Der Sluijs, Jeroen. 'Uncertainty as a Monster in the Science–Policy Interface: Four Coping Strategies'. *Water science and technology* 52.6 (2005): 87–92.

Van Rensburg, Willem. 'Climate Change Scepticism: A Conceptual Re-Evaluation'. *SAGE Open* 5.2 (2015): 1–13.

Vasset, Philippe. *Le Journal intime d'une prédatrice*. Paris: Fayard, 2010.

Vercier, Bruno and Dominique Viart. *La Littérature française au present*. Paris: Bordas, 2005.

Verheggen, Bart, et al. 'Scientists' Views About Attribution of Global Warming'. *Environmental Science & Technology* 48.16 (2014): 8963–71.

Von Petersdorff, Winand. 'Grüne Revolution. Die herzliche Ökodiktatur'. *Frankfurter Allgemeine Zeitung* (16 May 2011).

Von Storch, Hans and Nico Stehr. 'Klima inszenierter Angst', *Der Spiegel* (24 January 2005): 160–61.

Von Storch, Hans and Werner Krauß. *Die Klimafalle. Die gefährliche Nähe von Politik und Klimaforschung*. Munich: Hanser, 2013.

Vondung, Klaus. *Die Apokalypse in Deutschland*. Munich: Deutscher Taschenbuch Verl, 1988.

Washington, Haydn and John Cook. *Climate Change Denial: Heads in the Sand*. London: Earthscan, 2011. Kindle.

Warnke, Götz. *Die grüne Ideologie – Heile-Welt-Mythen, Gesellschaftsutopien und Naturromantik als Ausdruck einer angstbestimmten Politik*. Frankfurt am Main: Peter Lang, 1998.

Weiner, Mark S. 'Climate Change Denial as the Historical Consciousness of Trumpism: Lessons from Carl Schmitt'. *Defending the Open Society*, 17 November 2017. Available online at https://niskanencenter.org/blog/climate-change-denial-historical-consciousness-trumpism-lessons-carl-schmitt/ (accessed 31 Jan 2018).

Westwood, Sean J., et al. 'The Tie That Divides: Cross-National Evidence of the Primacy of Partyism'. *European Journal of Political Research* 57.2 (2018): 333–354.

Whiteside, Kerry. *Divided Natures: French Contributions to Political Ecology*. Cambridge: MIT, 2002.

Whitmarsh, Lorraine. 'Scepticism and Uncertainty About Climate Change: Dimensions, Determinants and Change over Time'. *Global Environmental Change* 21.2 (2011): 690–700.

Will, George F. 'Fossil Fuels Belie Environmentalism'. *The Washington Post*, 22 November, 2009. Available online at http://www.washingtonpost.com/wp-dyn/content/article/2009/11/20/AR2009112002619.html?noredirect=on (accessed 16 June 2018).

Williams, Richard. 'The Modern Earth Narrative. Natural and Human History of the Earth', in *Earth Matters: The Earth Sciences, Philosophy, and the Claims of Community*, ed. Robert Frodemann. Upper Saddle River, NJ: Prentice Hall, 1999, 35–49.

Wilson, Alexander. *The Culture of Nature: North American Landscape from Disney to the Exxon Valdez*. Cambridge, MA: Blackwell, 1992.

Wynne, Brian. 'When Doubt Becomes a Weapon'. *Nature* 466.7305 (2010): 441–42.

Yearley, Steven. *Sociology, Environmentalism, Globalization: Reinventing the Globe*. London; Thousand Oaks, CA: SAGE Publications, 1996.

Zehr, Stephen C. 'Public Representations of Scientific Uncertainty About Global Climate Change'. *Public Understanding of Science* 9.2 (2000): 85–103.

Zhou, Min. 'Public Environmental Skepticism: A Cross-National and Multilevel Analysis'. *International Sociology* 30.1 (2015): 61–85.

Zizek, Slavov. 'Nature and Its Discontents'. *SubStance* 37.3 (2008): 37–72.

Index

Note: Locators with letter 'n' refer to notes.

Abram, David 151
Abrams, Samuel J., 11–12
acid rain 97–8. *See also Waldsterben*
ad hominem argument 32, 73, 208, 214, 247 n.11
Adams, John 34, 63, 72, 232–3, 240, 253 n.3
alarmism, 4, 6, 30, 45, 58–59, 66, 95–98, 105, 109, 116–120, 127–128, 157, 211, 223, 237–238
Anderegg, William 25
Anderson, Gillian 62
anti-environmentalism 8–9, 26–8, 36, 223, 226, 238. *See also* climate scepticism
  in Germany 97–105, 107
  in UK 36, 41–53, 61
  in USA 41–2, 135, 144, 146, 160
apocalypse 63, 81, 101–2, 121, 160, 187–8, 200, 237, 244. *See also* narrative, apocalyptic; climate catastrophe
  biblical 154
apocalypticism 81, 83, 89, 102, 128, 130, 243. *See also* catastrophism
archetype 24, 79–80, 240
Armborst, Matthias 110
Armstrong and Miller Show (BBC1, 2007–2010) 53–4, 56, 62
Armstrong, Franny 62, 229
Arndt, Ernst Moritz 92
Aronofsky, Darren 154
Attenborough, Sir David 61, 70
Attridge, Derek 19, 244
Aykut, Stéfan 37, 182–3, 195, 220, 236, 247 n.1

Bachmann, Hartmut 114, 119
Baliunas, Sallie 26
Barad, Karen 207
Bartsch, Christian 110
Bate, Jonathan 43
Bate, Roger 63–4, 247 n.7
Baudrillard, Jean 180
Bean, Richard 73, 81–3, 90, 240
Beck, Glenn 81, 133, 164–5
Beckerman, Wilfred 54, 63–7, 239
Behringer, Wolfgang 105
Beisner, Calvin 150
Bellamy, Edward 45–7
Bengtsson, Lennart 230
Berdymukhamedov, Kurbanguly 229
Bergounioux, Pierre 197
Bergthaller, Hannes 36, 149
Besant, Annie 46
Bess, Michael 178
Blair, Tony (Prime Minister) 43, 52, 55, 58, 78
Blanche, Eugene Terre 127
Bloch, Ernst 99
blogs 9, 20, 96, 134, 245 n.1
Bloor, David 7
Boehmer-Christiansen, Sonja 211–13, 220
Bonner, Frances 71–2
Booker, Christopher 45, 57, 78–81, 84–5, 125, 240
Booth, Kate 27
Botkin, Daniel 161
Boyd, David 2
Boykoff, Max 25, 57–8, 72
Branch, Michael 226
Brexit 90. *See also* Euro-scepticism
Bricmont, Jean 193
British Broadcasting Corporation (BBC) 62, 70, 72, 83, 208, 229
Brown, Gordon 56–7
Brown, William 153
Bruckner, Pascal 187, 203
Buell, Frederick 8
Buell, Lawrence 101
Bulwer, Edward 126
Byron, Lord (George Gordon) 44, 48, 82

Cameron, David 56
Capstick, Stuart 34, 60–1, 69
Carolan, Michael 241
Carson, Rachel 76, 114, 156
Carter, Neil 55
catastrophism 96, 101–2, 136, 156, 187, 236. *See also* alarmism; apocalypticism
Chamberlin, Shaun 125
Chapman, James 57
Charbonnier, Pierre 204
Chomsky, Noam 160
Christian conservatives 138, 140, 144, 155, 157, 159, 168, 170, 172
Churchill, Sir Winston (prime minister) 21, 30
civic epistemology 51, 83, 93
Clark, Timothy 36, 71
Clarke, Bruce 207
Clarkson, Jeremy 58, 69–73, 75, 84, 90, 208, 239, 243. *See also Top Gear* (BBC2, 2002-present)
Clean Air Act (CAA) (UK 1956) 43, 49
Clean Power Plan (USA 2015) 3
cli-fi 157, 166, 240. *See* ecocriticism; climate fiction
climate activism 42, 54, 69, 75, 81, 89, 96, 133, 209, 211, 214, 229, 239
climate catastrophe 108–9, 112, 118, 124. *See also* apocalypse
climate change 1–4, 6–8, 10–12, 14–18, 20–2, 24–6, 28, 30–8, 42–4, 46, 48, 50, 52–64, 66–76, 78, 80, 82, 84–90, 92, 94–102, 104–30, 133–50, 152–60, 162–4, 166, 168–72, 176, 178, 180, 182–205, 207–23, 226–32, 234–4. *See also* climate science; climatology
  adaptation 66–67, 126, 131, 232–233
  as divine providence 75–7, 137, 157, 167
  as hoax 23, 33, 114, 145, 156, 210, 239, 244. *See also* hoax
  mitigation 60, 65, 67, 73, 89–90, 107, 134–5, 138, 141, 147, 159, 171–2, 226, 232,
  politicization of 7, 37, 47, 53, 55, 61, 67, 75, 89, 135, 227, 230, 239. *See also* climate science, politicization of; IPCC, politicization of
Climate Change Act (CCA) (UK 2008) 54, 57, 59–61, 90
climate scepticism 1, 3–4, 7–8, 10, 23–4, 26–36, 39, 41–3, 45, 47, 49, 51, 53–5, 57–61, 63, 65, 67, 69, 71, 73, 75, 77–9, 81, 83, 85, 87, 89–91, 94, 97, 105–7, 109, 120–2, 124, 127–8, 130–1, 133, 135–43, 145–9, 151, 153–7, 159, 161, 163, 165–7, 169–73, 176, 178, 181–8, 190, 203, 209, 214, 218, 220, 225, 229, 231, 235–41, 243–4
  as cultural identity 15–16, 138, 229
  in France 34, 36, 175–205, 235–8
  in Germany 10, 28, 34, 36, 43, 54, 91–131, 170, 235–8, 240, 243, 247 n.1
  in UK 28, 33–4, 37, 41–90, 94–5, 238–40. *See also* comic nihilism; thin hegemony
  in USA 2–3, 6, 28–35, 37, 54, 57, 94, 107, 133–73, 184, 230, 238–40, 243
  literary study of 4–5, 7, 9–10, 19–20, 35, 242–4
  organized 37, 41, 107, 121, 130, 158, 178, 215, 238, 241
  sociological study of 7, 9, 14, 26–35, 57–61, 105, 143–4, 182–3, 236, 241–2, 249 n.8
  transnational analysis 28, 36–7, 235–40
  typology of 7, 24, 33–5, 65, 67
climate sceptics 2–5, 9, 16–18, 20, 22–4, 26–8, 32, 34–5, 39, 41, 43, 45, 56, 60, 62–3, 73, 82–3, 89, 97, 99, 105, 107–8, 110, 114, 118–19, 121–3, 129–31, 136, 150, 163, 171, 176–7, 183–5, 187–94, 211, 215, 222–3, 225, 227–9, 231, 233, 235–7, 239–41, 243–4
  as heretics 33, 43, 51, 62, 74, 89, 229
  environmentalists as 28, 78, 85, 87–9, 103–5, 130, 191, 237, 249 n.7
  heterogeneity of 24–5, 35–8, 41–2, 76, 99–105, 242–3
  humanist 84, 181, 183, 198, 200, 237, 250 n.16
  scientists as 20, 41, 63, 118, 130, 134–5, 239
climate science 2, 15–16, 20, 23, 25, 29, 31, 33, 35, 38, 63–4, 66, 74, 76–8, 83,

85, 87, 89, 94, 106–7, 113, 115, 118, 121–2, 124, 133–5, 137–8, 141, 145, 147, 149–50, 152–3, 156–7, 159–61, 165–6, 171, 193, 207, 209, 211, 213–14, 218–21, 229, 231, 234, 236, 238–9, 243. *See also* climatology
consensus 33–4, 38, 53–4, 59, 65, 82, 95, 106, 110, 134–41, 150, 159, 210, 221, 228–9, 240
models 6, 22, 61, 63–4, 81–2, 85–7, 89, 114, 121, 134, 171, 185, 188, 192, 207, 212–14, 218–20, 231–4
politicization of 214–16, 227. *See also* politicization of IPCC
Climategate 32, 58, 60, 94, 121–3, 209, 218–19, 221, 223, 229, 238
and Science and Technology Studies 209, 218–19, 221, 223, 253 n.2
in sceptical texts 63, 121–3, 219, 238
investigations 219
climatology 64, 73, 78, 96, 158, 188, 190, 192–5, 223. *See also* climate science
history of 73–4, 184–6, 190–2, 232
close reading 7, 9, 37, 86
coal 2–3, 24, 47–50, 55, 94–5, 115, 117, 214
Cohen, Martin 77–8, 85, 228
Cohen, Stanley 34
Comby, Baptiste 183
comic nihilism 59, 69, 73, 239
confirmation bias 20
Conley, Verena Andermatt 180
Conservative Think Tanks (CTTs) 9, 26, 29–32, 37, 41, 133–4, 170, 185, 209, 211, 229–30, 238
as counter-intelligentsia 30
in Europe 95, 107–8, 133, 185
in UK 29, 37, 211, 238
in USA 29–33, 37, 41, 133–4, 170, 211, 230, 238, 247 n.7
conservative white men 26, 28, 41
conspiracy 3, 22, 31, 33, 89–90, 112, 114, 116, 123–4, 126–7, 142, 145–6, 156, 162, 164, 208, 219, 221, 227, 242
of CTTs 31–3, 208, 211, 214
socialist 73–5, 89, 208, 226–7
contrarian 21, 25, 29, 58, 130, 208, 230
Conway, Erick M., 3, 30–2, 208, 219, 223
Cook, John 20
COP 15 (Copenhagen climate conference) 1, 56. *See* Copenhagen
COP 21 (Paris climate conference) 2–3, 22, 199, 203–4
Copenhagen 1, 56, 58, 60, 106, 121, 201. *See* COP 15 (Copenhagen climate conference)
Corbyn, Jeremy 10
Courtillot, Vincent 115, 184–5
Creationism 75–6, 94, 137, 148–52
Crichton, Michael 39, 68, 80, 83, 120, 136, 152, 156–72, 199, 215, 239, 243
Crosland, Anthony 64
Crowley, Michael 163
Cruise, Tom 161
cultural pessimism 101, 237
Curry, Judith 230
Curtis, Richard 62

'David and Goliath' myth 8, 208–9
Deguy, Michel 197
Deleuze, Gilles 193
Delingpole, James 21, 41, 45, 62, 73–5, 84, 89–90, 208–10, 218, 239
denial 7, 20–1, 23–5, 29–30, 34, 69, 73, 83, 106, 108, 115, 125, 130, 134–5, 141, 211, 220
pathologization of 77. *See also* stigmatization
Derrida, Jacques 102
Desbiolles, Maryline 197
Dickens, Charles 48
Diderot, Denis 176
Dimmock, Stewart 62
Dobson, James 11
Dunlap, Riley 26
Duran, Jean 187
Durkheim, Emile 114
Durkin, Martin 41

echo chamber 13, 29, 112. *See also* filter bubble
ecocriticism 2, 4, 6, 8, 10, 12, 14, 16, 18, 20, 22, 24, 26, 28, 30, 32, 34, 36, 38–9, 41–2, 44, 46, 48, 50, 52, 54, 56, 58, 60, 62, 64, 66, 68, 70, 72, 74, 76, 78, 80, 82, 84, 86, 88, 90, 92, 94,

96, 98, 100, 102, 104, 106, 108, 110, 112, 114, 116, 118, 120, 122, 124, 126, 128, 130, 134, 136, 138, 140, 142, 144–6, 148, 150, 152, 154, 156, 158, 160, 162, 164, 166, 168, 170, 172, 176, 178, 180–2, 184, 186, 188, 190, 192, 194, 196, 198, 200, 202, 204, 207–8, 210, 212, 214, 216, 218, 220, 222–3, 226, 228, 230, 232, 234, 236, 238, 240, 242
and climate fiction 39, 120, 166, 196, 240, 244
and climate scepticism 8, 41, 176, 239
as filter bubble 39
and politics 8, 16, 36, 39, 222–3
and Science and Technology Studies 207, 211, 214, 220–3
Edwards, Paul N., 87, 213, 232, 239
Eisenhut, Dirk 123
Energiewende 91–2, 105, 108, 112, 116, 119, 121
Environmental Protection Agency (EPA) 3, 114, 134, 147
environmentalism 8–9, 28, 36–7, 41–3, 47, 51–3, 55, 57, 61, 65, 70–1, 75, 80, 89, 92–3, 97–100, 105, 109, 111–12, 117, 119, 131, 136, 146, 148, 152, 156, 158–61, 166, 169, 178, 188, 198–9, 204, 216, 226, 237, 243
as politics 18, 43, 47, 50, 93, 204, 220
as religion 104, 111, 118–19, 147, 156, 159–60, 212–13, 243
history of 28–9, 36, 42, 47, 50–2, 54–7, 90–4, 179–81
Enzensberger, Hans Magnus 99–101
Ereault, Gill 34
Euro-scepticism 55, 61, 238
European Commission 51, 53, 94
European Union 2, 43, 51–2, 56–8, 70, 87, 90, 227
Evans, Dylan 38–9, 235

fascism 2, 24, 74–5, 181–2, 194
Ferry, Luc 181–2, 187, 193, 198, 203, 237
Feyerabend, Paul 78
filter bubble 13–14, 38–9. *See also* echo chamber
Fiorina, Morris 11
Flat Earth Society 22
Flat Earther 22–3
Fleming, Chris 22
fossil fuel companies 1, 3, 26, 41–2, 73, 133, 209–10, 214, 229
Foster, Philip 75–7, 90, 146, 238, 247 n.11
Foucault, Michel 9
frame analysis 5. *See* narrative framing
Frankfurter Allgemeine (German newspaper) 110–111
Franzen, Jonathan 243
Freud, Sigmund 101
Friedrich, Caspar David 92
fuel protests (UK, 2000) 56
Funtowicz, Silvio 217

Garrard, Greg 41, 102
General Circulation Models (GCMs) 231–2
gerrymandering 13
Giegengack, Robert 208
Gilpin, Thomas 43
Gingrich, Newt 135
Global Climate Coalition 74
Global Warming Potential (GWP) 212
Gore, Al 6, 11, 21, 62, 73, 81, 106, 117, 134–6, 140, 142, 147, 165, 193, 199
Goris, Eva 120
Gran, Iegor 198
Gray, John 67–9, 77, 167
Great Global Warming Swindle, The (dir. Durkin 2007) 41, 134
Great London Fog (UK, 1952) 48, 50
Green Party 55, 91, 99–100, 179–80, 182, 226
in France 178–80, 182
in Germany 91, 99–100, 105, 107, 110, 119
in UK 55
Greenpeace 65, 73, 98, 117, 208, 228, 247 n.8
Griffin, Webster 125
Grudem, Wayne 148
Guardian, The (UK newspaper) 58, 70, 228
Guha, Andreas 101
Guilyardi, Catherine 195
Gummer, John Selwyn 55

Hacking, Ian 230
Haidt, Jonathan 12, 18, 30–1, 165, 241, 245 n.4

Ham, Ken 149
Hamilton, Clive 69, 72, 88
Hannity, Sean 133
Hansen, James 32, 81
Haraway, Donna 207
Hawking, Stephen 126
Hayhoe, Katherine 142, 153–4, 248 n.4
Heartland Institute 9, 29, 33, 41, 107, 114, 134, 210
Heidegger, Martin 101
Heise, Ursula 36, 207
Heller, Mavie 124
Herder, Johann Gottlieb 92
heresy 54, 82. *See also* climate sceptics, as heretics
Herzog, Werner 167
Hess, Rudolf 99
Heston, Charlton 68, 166–8, 172
history of science 77, 191, 194
hoax 23, 33, 114, 145, 156, 191, 193, 210, 239, 244
Hobson, Kersty 34
Hochschild, Arlie Russell 14, 42, 147
Hodgkin, Dorothy 52
Hoffman, Andrew 37
Holocaust denial 21, 23, 130
homogeneity 6, 16, 41, 212, 231, 239. *See also* stereotypes
Horkheimer, Max 101
Horner, Chris 134, 136
Horstmann, Ulrich 102
Horx, Matthias 102
Houghton, Sir John 66
Howard, Michael 58
Huet, Sylvestre 186, 208
Hulme, Mike 35, 88, 217–18
Hulot, Nicholas 189, 199
Hunt, William Holman 48
Hutter, Peter 120

in France 181, 194–5
Inconvenient Truth, An (dir.Guggenheim 2006) 21, 54, 62, 134–5, 227
indulgences, medieval papal 70, 118–19, 209
Inglis, Bob 140
Inhofe, (Senator) James 32, 134, 145–7, 150–1, 156, 238
Institute for Public Policy Research (IPPR) 22, 58
Integrated Assessment Models (IAMs) 64–5, 231–3
Intergovernmental Panel on Climate Change (IPCC) 1, 4, 8, 16–17, 25, 33–5, 39, 43, 51, 54, 58, 61, 66, 73–4, 76, 79, 81, 83, 86–9, 94, 106, 118, 123, 129, 135, 158, 189–90, 193, 195, 199, 207, 209, 211–17, 220, 223, 228–9, 234, 244
  consensus 2–4, 39, 86–7, 209, 213–14, 220, 228–9
  criticisms of 4, 16, 34–5, 66, 73–5, 79, 86–90, 94, 123, 129, 158, 209, 211–20, 229, 234, 244. *See also* scientification
  interests and 32, 211–15, 220
  politicization of 4, 34–5, 73–5, 79, 89, 158–9, 190, 193, 195, 209, 211–17, 227
  reform 92, 102, 105, 110
Iyengar, Shanto 12–14, 16

Jacobs, Michael 55
Jamieson, Dale 71, 88
Jasanoff, Sheila 36, 51, 83, 215, 236. *See* civic epistemology
Jauss, Hans Robert 130
Jeffers, Robinson 167
Jenkins, Willis 139
Jensen, Derrick 152
Jesus Christ 160
Jouzel, Jean 188–9, 202

Kahan, Dan 15–16, 138, 141, 210, 229, 241
Kiefer, Anselm 92
King, David 56
King, Thomas 80
Kingsolver, Barbara 120, 144, 166, 240
Klein, Naomi 35
Koutsoyiannis, Demetris 232
Kracht, Christian 121, 125–6, 243
Krahmer, Holger 107
Krauss, Werner 112, 220
Krauthammer, Charles 134
Kristeva, Julia 193
Krugman, Paul 233
Kuhn, Thomas 217
Kunzig, Robert 125
Kyoto Protocol 2, 55, 78

Lacan, Jacques 193
Lack, Martin 7
Lafont, Robert 198
Lahsen, Myanna 208, 219–20, 231
Lakoff, George 5
Lalonde, Brice 178, 180
Lambert, Richard 67
Latif, Mojib 130
Latour, Bruno 97, 142, 193–4, 203–4, 207, 216, 222, 242
Lawson, Nigel (Lord) 34, 41, 90, 125, 214
Le Pen, Marine 10
Leiserowitz, Anthony 28
Leopold, Aldo 181
Lewandowsky, Stephan 23, 230, 245 n.6
liberal bias 6, 18, 23–4, 30–2. *See also* stigmatization
Limbaugh, Rush 8, 11, 32, 134, 166–7
Lindzen, Richard 20, 41, 63, 118
literary analysis 4–5, 9–10, 19–20. *See* close reading
Lovelock, James 125, 227

Mackay, David 88
Macron, Emmanuel (President) 10, 175, 204
Major, John (Prime Minister) 55
Mann, Michael 24, 121
Marcuse, Herbert 99
Margolina, Sonja 121
Marr, Andrew 52
Marshall, Gavin 58
Marshall, George 68, 73, 80
Martin, Damien 71
Martin, Yves 185–6
'matchgirls strike' (UK 1888) 45–6
Mattingly, Terry 11
Maxeiner, Dirk 103, 110, 117, 241
'May 1968' (French social movements) 178, 181
May, James 71–2
Merkel, Angela (Chancellor) 115, 119
Merton, Robert 158–9, 163, 215–16. *See also* Science and Technology Studies (STS), scientific ethos in; scientific idealism
methodological agnosticism 4, 214
methodological nationalism 36, 245 n.2
Metzler, Birgit 97
Michaels, Patrick 41
Miersch, Michael 103, 117
Miller, Perry 92
Mitchell, Tommy 150, 172
Moe, Tomas 221
Monbiot, George 21, 70
Monckton, Christopher 41
Morano, Marc 32, 134, 208, 227
Morizot, Baptiste 204
Morris, Julian 63
Morris, William 45, 47–8
motivated reasoning 20, 32, 208, 210
Murdoch, James 58

narrative 6, 9, 19, 29, 31, 56, 73, 80–1, 84, 100–2, 109–11, 122, 124–7, 130, 145, 151–2, 156, 168–9, 172, 188–91, 201–2, 213, 228, 238, 240
  apocalyptic 67, 81, 98, 101–3, 107, 135, 166, 202, 211. *See also* alarmism; catastrophism
  biblical 81, 124, 148, 150, 153–4, 171–2
  climate change as 5–6, 35, 59, 73, 80–1, 84–5, 101–2, 109–11, 152, 238, 240
  framing 5–7, 54, 58, 122, 135–7, 183, 190, 214, 220, 222, 230–1
  scientific 168–9, 213, 228
National Union of Mineworkers 49
Nazism 21–2, 74, 111, 126, 199
neoliberalism 51, 110
Nesbit, Matthew 6
newspapers 13, 35, 48, 57–8, 183, 203, 208
Newton, Isaac 68
Niemeyer, Simon 34
Niermann, Ingo 121, 126, 243
Nietzsche, Friedrich 68
Niven, Larry 243
Nobel Peace Prize (to IPCC and Al Gore 2007) 193, 195, 209
Nordhaus, Ted 226
Norgaard, Kari 34, 130, 242
North, Richard D., 54, 65–7
Nothias, Toussaint 184
Nottret, Patric 197
nuclear power 50, 64, 88–9, 91, 98–9, 103, 108, 115, 119, 122, 127–9, 179–80, 211

Obama, Barack (President) 3, 22
Oppenheimer, Michael 32
Oreskes, Naomi 3, 184, 223

Painter, James 34, 184
Palin, Sarah 136, 145
Paraire, Philippe 181
Pariser, Eli 13
Parke, Harriet 164
partisan politics 10. *See also* polarization
effects of 2, 10–18, 48, 54, 135–6, 185, 239
party sorting 12, 245 n.3
Patten, Chris 52
peace movement 92, 100
Pearce, Fred 125, 219
peer review 23, 30, 158, 210, 217
perspective-taking 16, 18–19, 37, 39, 225. *See also* literary analysis
philosophy of science 213
Pidgeon, Nicholas 34
polar bear 6, 35, 84, 116, 203
polarization 3–4, 6, 10–16, 18, 35, 37–8, 60, 67, 94, 111, 143, 170, 210, 220, 223, 226, 230, 236, 238, 240–1, 243, 245 n.3
affective 12, 14–16, 60, 68, 201, 240
counteracting 8–9, 14–15, 18–20, 35–9, 119–20, 210
political 3–4, 6, 10–18, 24–5, 35–9, 59–60, 94, 111–12, 128, 142–3, 210–211, 226, 230–1, 239, 242
in UK 3, 14–15, 37, 61, 65, 74, 87, 89–90, 243
in USA 10–15, 37–9, 210–211, 243
political correctness 18, 20, 69, 198–9, 214
political science 15–16
Pompidou, Georges (President) 179
Pope Francis 142, 144
Popper, Karl 213, 228
popular science 97, 100, 103, 111, 113–14, 119, 236
post-normal science (PNS) 217–18
Pottier, Antonin 184
Poujade, Robert 179
Pruitt, Scott 3
Putin, Vladimir 78

Quero, Yann 202

racism 12–13
Rahmstorf, Stefan 24, 33, 110, 115, 123, 130
rationalism 7, 34, 102, 177, 193, 237
Ravetz, Jerome 217
Raw, Louise 46
Rawles, James Wesley 125
Reagan, Ronald (President) 45, 61, 135
reflexivity 9, 23, 29, 31, 129, 230–1
Reichholf, Joseph 114
Renaut, Alain 181
renewable energy 2, 57, 92, 94, 106–7, 111, 115, 119, 121–2, 203, 211, 214, 227
Ricardou, Jean 196
Ridley, Matt 66, 104, 188
Ridley, Nicholas 52
Riefenstahl, Leni 199
Riehl, Wilhelm Heinrich 92
Rigby, Kate 36
risk 7, 17, 34, 36–9, 46, 63, 65, 71–3, 93, 149, 152, 155, 172, 210–211, 230–1, 233–5, 240, 244
cultural theory of 34, 63, 240
Robertson, Pat 133, 145
Robinson, Mike 50
Romantic 43–4, 47–8, 61, 82–3, 93, 166, 177, 236
British 43–4, 47, 82, 92–3, 236
German 92–3, 236
socialism 16, 46–7, 122
Rosenthal, Olivia 197
Rousseau, Jean-Jacques 177, 188
Rove, Karl 156
Ruskin, John 48
Ryghaug, Marianne 221

Sarkozy, Nicholas (President) 184
Sarraute, Nathalie 196
satire 41–3, 54, 62, 82, 84–5, 90, 102, 117, 166, 196, 200, 202, 236–7. *See also* comic nihilism
Schellenberger, Michael 226
Schellnhuber, Hans Joachim 130
Schneider, Michael 102
Schneider, Peter 100
Science and Technology Studies (STS) 37, 86, 89, 97, 136, 183, 194, 207–23, 231–3, 253 n.2
scientific ethos in 163, 215, 218, 221, 228. *See* Merton, Robert
Strong Programme 7
symmetrical analysis 211

scientific idealism 83–4, 136, 159, 163, 209, 215–16, 218, 220–1, 228, 238, 253 n.2
scientification 17, 31, 215, 217, 220, 222, 241
Segnit, Nat 34
Seifert, Alwin 99
Serres, Michel 139, 181, 193, 207
Shackley, Simon 212
Shellenburger, Michael 215
Singer, Fred 32, 41, 118
singularity 7, 19, 36, 243. *See* Attridge, Derek
Sinn, Werner 105
Skodvin, Tora 212
Sloterdijk, Peter 95, 128
Smith, Angela 71
smoke abatement 47–8
socialism 10, 16, 45–7, 89, 122, 156, 178, 180, 184, 227
Sokal, Alan 193
Solomon, Lawrence 134
Sontag, Susan 102
Soviet Union 101, 116
Spencer, Roy 134, 150
Spengler, Oswald 101
Der Spiegel (German newspaper) 108–9, 237
Spielberg, Steven 79
Squarzoni, Philippe 202
Stehr, Nico 109, 247 n.5
Stengers, Isabelle 189, 203, 222, 227
stereotypes 5, 7–8, 16–20, 24, 27, 36–9, 41, 48, 75, 83, 89, 135, 215, 226, 238
  of climate sceptics 3, 20, 24, 26, 83, 99, 123, 131, 150, 190, 194, 215, 239
  of environmentalists 28, 63, 67, 163, 209
stigmatization 21, 23–5, 49, 118, 129, 211, 223, 229, 231
  in academic research 23, 33, 230, 245 n.6
  language and 10, 20–6, 137, 197, 211, 229–31
Stoll, Mark 160
Storch, Hans Von 113, 131
Streisand, Barbra 11
Sun, The (UK newspaper) 21, 58, 69
Switzer, Jacqueline Vaughn 41–3, 146

tabloid newspapers 21, 57–8, 109
Tapley, Webster Griffin 125
Taylor, Jesse Oak 246 n.1
Taylor, Peter 28, 78, 85–90, 241, 247 n.11
Thatcher, Margaret (Prime Minister) 43, 47, 50–3, 89
theology 75–6, 137–8, 140, 145–6, 148–51, 154–5, 157, 160–1, 168, 170–2
thin hegemony 54, 56–8, 61–3, 239
Thoreau, Henry David 177
Thorsheim, Peter 48
Todt, Fritz 99
Tol, Richard 229
Top Gear (BBC2, 2002-present) 69–72, 243
trade unions 50, 52, 55
Tranter, Bruce 27
Tranter, Kieran 71
Trepl, Ludwig 100
Trexler, Adam 120
Trojanow, Ilija 120
Trudeau, Justin (Prime Minister) 10
Trump, Donald S. (President) 6, 20, 38, 121, 134, 153, 170, 204, 223, 238

Vahrenholt, Fritz 105, 114
van Rensburg, Willem 161, 164, 238
Vasset, Philippe 200
Vondung, Klaus 101
Voynet, Dominique 180

Waechter, Antoine 180
Waldsterben ('forest death', Germany 1980s) 97–8
warmism 8, 20, 26, 89–90, 97, 134–5, 166, 210–211, 214, 220, 229, 235, 241–2, 244
  heterogeneity of 6–7, 16, 24, 26, 35, 235, 240–2
  invisibility of 25–6, 211, 235. *See also* liberal bias
Wegener, Alfred 228
Weiner, Mark 141
Welzk, Stefan 100
Wesley, James 125
Westwood, Sean J., 12–16
Whitmarsh, Lorraine 211
Wilde, Oscar 44–5, 48, 61, 246 n.1
Wildlife and Countryside Bill and Act (WCA) (UK 1981) 51, 53
Williams, Richard 169
Wolf, Christa 100
Wordsworth, William 43–4, 70

Zhou, Min 26
Žižek, Slavoj 226